FAVORITE BRAND NAME

BEST-LOVED

LIGHT

· RECIPES ·

PUBLICATIONS INTERNATIONAL, LTD.

Front cover photography: Peter Walters Photography, Chicago

Pictured on the front cover *(clockwise from right):* Grilled Chicken Sienna *(page 162)*, Athenian Rice with Feta Cheese *(page 276)* and Luscious Chocolate Cheesecake *(page 312)*.

Pictured on the back cover *(clockwise from top right):* Black Forest Chocolate Fudge Cake *(page 288)*, Fresh Vegetable Lasagna *(page 282)*, Nacho Salad *(page 230)* and Margarita Pork Kabobs *(page 104)*.

Nutritional Analysis: In the case of multiple choices, the first ingredient, the lowest amount and the lowest serving yield are used to calculate the nutritional analysis. "Serve with" suggestions are not included unless otherwise stated.

Microwave Cooking: Microwave ovens vary in wattage. The microwave cooking times given in this publication are approximate. Use the cooking times as guidelines and check for doneness before adding more time. Consult manufacturer's instructions for suitable microwave-safe cooking dishes.

Contents

Page 57

Page 141

Page 217

Page 317

INTRODUCTION 4

APPETIZERS & BEVERAGES 6

BREAKFAST & BRUNCH 56

MEATS 100

POULTRY 140

SEAFOOD 180

SALADS 216

VEGETABLES & SIDE DISHES 252

CAKES & CHEESECAKES 288

COOKIES & BARS 316

DESSERTS 342

ACKNOWLEDGMENTS 373

INDEX 374

Page 101

Page 181

Page 343

Introduction

Light cooking is more than just a passing fad—it's the new way of life in today's health-conscious society. Quick weight loss schemes may be tempting, but they often produce little more than short-lived and ultimately disappointing results. The alternative choice—learning healthy cooking and eating habits—is an important lifestyle change with long-lasting and far-reaching benefits. Fortunately, developing these habits does *not* mean eating very small quantities of food with very little flavor. This spectacular collection of recipes contains everything from savory, party-perfect appetizers to rich chocolate desserts, most with under 300 calories and 10 grams of fat or less per serving!

Calories, fat and cholesterol are major factors in healthy eating, of course, but it is important to look at them as part of the bigger picture and not just as independent values that need changing. The U.S. Department of Agriculture and the Department of Health and Human Services have developed a Food Guide Pyramid to illustrate how easy it is to eat a healthier diet. It is not a rigid prescription, but rather a general guide that lets you choose a healthful diet that's right for you. It calls for eating a wide variety of foods to get the nutrients you need, and, at the same time, the right amount of calories to maintain a healthy weight.

Food Guide Pyramid
A Guide to Daily Food Choices

Fats, Oils & Sweets
Use Sparingly
(Also found in other groups; see text.)

KEY
•Fat (naturally occurring and added) ▾Sugar (added)
These symbols show fats, oils and added sugars in foods.

Milk, Yogurt & Cheese Group
2–3 Servings

Meat, Poultry, Fish, Dry Beans, Eggs & Nuts Group
2–3 Servings

Vegetable Group
3–5 Servings

Fruit Group
2–4 Servings

Bread, Cereal, Rice & Pasta Group
6–11 Servings

The amount of fat in our diets has become a primary concern, and with very good reason. High-fat diets have been linked with increased blood cholesterol levels (which in turn produce greater risk for heart disease) as well as increased risks for obesity and some types of cancers. Nutrition experts recommend diets that contain 30% or less of total daily calories from fat, a goal that applies to a total diet over time rather than a single food or meal. Reaching this goal simply requires making smart choices—and having the information to make these choices.

Many lower fat options are already popular choices at the supermarket, such as nonfat or low-fat dairy products, lean meats and skinless chicken. Other healthy choices include a wide range of complex carbohydrates, such as grains, beans, fruits and vegetables. These may be eaten in larger quantities than high-fat foods because a gram of fat contains nine calories while a gram of carbohydrate or protein contains only four. Thus a large, filling, low-fat salad or baked potato might have the same number of calories as a tiny portion of potato chips, which is usually consumed quickly and leaves people hungry for more.

The recipes in this book are designed to help you with these choices, while proving that the good-for-you dishes can be the good tasting ones as well. Choose from hundreds of flavorful low-calorie, low-fat recipes—from appetizers to desserts, from breakfast to dinner and everything in between. The nutritional information that follows each recipe tells you the number of calories, the grams (g) of fat, the milligrams (mg) of cholesterol and the milligrams (mg) of sodium per serving. Most recipes contain less than 300 calories and 10 grams of fat or less per serving, so preparing meals that all fit into a healthy lifestyle has never been easier!

About the Nutritional Information

The analysis of each recipe includes all the ingredients that are listed in that recipe, except ingredients labeled as "optional" or "for garnish." If a range is offered for an ingredient (¼ to ½ teaspoon, for example), the *first* amount given was used to calculate the nutritional information. If an ingredient is presented with an option ("2 tablespoons margarine or butter"), the *first* item listed was used to calculate the nutritional information. Foods shown in photographs on the same serving plate and offered as "serve with" suggestions at the end of a recipe are *not* included in the recipe analysis unless it is stated in the per serving line.

The nutritional information that appears with each recipe was submitted in part by the participating companies and associations. Every effort has been made to check the accuracy of these numbers. However, because numerous variables account for a wide range of values for certain foods, nutritive analyses in this book should be considered approximate.

This cookbook offers you a wide variety of recipes that are, on a per serving basis, low in calories, fat and cholesterol. The recipes in this book are NOT intended as a medically therapeutic program, nor as a substitute for medically approved diet plans for people on fat-, cholesterol- or sodium-restricted diets. You should consult your physician before beginning any diet plan. The recipes offered here can be part of a healthy lifestyle that meets recognized dietary guidelines. A healthy lifestyle includes not only eating a balanced diet, but engaging in proper exercise as well.

5

Appetizers & Beverages

Peppy Snack Mix

3 plain rice cakes, broken into bite-size pieces
1½ cups bite-size frosted shredded wheat biscuit cereal
¾ cup pretzel sticks, halved
3 tablespoons reduced-calorie margarine, melted
2 teaspoons low sodium Worcestershire sauce
¾ teaspoon chili powder
⅛ to ¼ teaspoon ground red pepper

Preheat oven to 300°F. Combine rice cakes, wheat biscuits and pretzels in 13×9-inch baking pan. Combine margarine, Worcestershire sauce, chili powder and pepper in small bowl. Drizzle over cereal mixture; toss to coat. Bake, uncovered, 20 minutes, stirring after 10 minutes.   *Makes 6 servings (4 cups)*

NUTRIENTS PER SERVING			
Calories	118	Fat	3 g
Cholesterol	0 mg	Sodium	156 mg

Peppy Snack Mix

Chicken Sesame with Oriental Crème

⅓ cup reduced sodium soy sauce
2 teaspoons minced garlic
1 teaspoon dark sesame oil
½ teaspoon ground ginger
1 pound boneless, skinless chicken breasts, cut into 4×½-inch
       strips
6 ounces (1 carton) ALPINE LACE® Fat Free Cream Cheese
       with Garlic & Herbs
2 tablespoons finely chopped green onions
2 tablespoons sesame seeds, toasted
1 tablespoon extra virgin olive oil

1. To marinate the chicken: In a small bowl, whisk the soy sauce, garlic, sesame oil and ginger. Reserve 2 tablespoons and pour the remaining marinade into a self-sealing plastic bag. Add the chicken pieces and seal the bag. Turn the bag to coat the chicken. Refrigerate for at least 2 hours, turning occasionally.

2. To make the Oriental Crème: In another small bowl, place the cream cheese. Whisk in the reserved 2 tablespoons of marinade and stir in the green onions. Cover with plastic wrap and refrigerate.

3. To prepare the chicken: Remove the chicken from the marinade and discard any remaining marinade. Spread the sesame seeds on a plate and roll the chicken strips in them until lightly coated.

4. In a large nonstick skillet, heat the olive oil over medium-high heat. Add the chicken and stir-fry for 6 minutes or until golden brown and the juices run clear when the chicken is pierced with a fork. Serve with the Oriental Crème.

Makes 24 appetizer servings

NUTRIENTS PER SERVING			
Calories	43	Fat	1 g
Cholesterol	13 mg	Sodium	192 mg

Chicken Sesame with Oriental Crème

Easy Bean Nachos

24 (about 1 ounce) GUILTLESS GOURMET® Baked Tortilla
    Chips (yellow, white or blue corn)
½ cup GUILTLESS GOURMET® Bean Dip (Black or Pinto, mild
    or hot)
¼ cup chopped green onions
¼ cup GUILTLESS GOURMET® Nacho Dip (mild or spicy)
    Chopped red bell pepper strips (optional)

Microwave Directions: Spread tortilla chips on flat microwave-safe plate. Dab 1 teaspoon bean dip on each chip; sprinkle with onions. Dot ½ teaspoon nacho dip on each chip. Microwave on HIGH (100% power) 30 seconds or until nacho dip starts to melt. Serve hot. Garnish with red pepper, if desired.

Makes 24 nachos

Hint: To keep chips crisp and prevent them from getting soggy, microwave each chip separately.

Conventional Directions: Preheat oven to 325°F. Spread tortilla chips on baking sheet. Prepare nachos as directed. Bake about 5 minutes or until nacho dip starts to melt. Serve hot.

NUTRIENTS PER SERVING			
(1 nacho)			
Calories	13	Fat	<1 g
Cholesterol	0 mg	Sodium	40 mg

Top to bottom: Easy Bean Nachos and Chicken Nachos (page 12)

Chicken Nachos

22 (about 1 ounce) GUILTLESS GOURMET® Baked Tortilla
      Chips (yellow, white or blue corn)
½ cup (4 ounces) cooked and shredded boneless chicken breast
¼ cup chopped green onions
¼ cup GUILTLESS GOURMET® Nacho Dip (mild or spicy)
      Sliced green and red chilies (optional)

Microwave Directions: Spread tortilla chips on flat microwave-safe plate.
Sprinkle chicken and onions over chips. Place nacho dip in small microwave-
safe bowl. Microwave on HIGH (100% power) 30 seconds; pour over chips,
chicken and onions. Microwave on HIGH 30 seconds more or until nacho dip
starts to bubble. Serve hot. Garnish with chilies, if desired.

Makes 22 nachos

Conventional Directions: Preheat oven to 325°F. Spread tortilla chips on baking
sheet. Sprinkle chicken and onions over chips. Heat nacho dip in small
saucepan over medium heat until warm; pour over chips, chicken and onions.
Bake about 5 minutes or until nacho dip starts to bubble. Serve hot.

NUTRIENTS PER SERVING			
(1 nacho)			
Calories	13	Fat	<1 g
Cholesterol	3 mg	Sodium	24 mg

Pot Stickers

1 boneless, skinless chicken breast, finely chopped
1 cup cooked rice
½ cup finely chopped fresh mushrooms
1 carrot, finely shredded
2 green onions, finely chopped
1 tablespoon white wine
1 teaspoon cornstarch
1 teaspoon dark sesame oil
¼ teaspoon salt
¼ teaspoon ground white pepper
50 wonton skins
5 tablespoons vegetable oil, divided
2½ cups water, divided
    Soy sauce, Chinese hot mustard or sweet and sour sauce

Combine chicken, rice, mushrooms, carrot, onions, wine, cornstarch, sesame oil, salt and pepper in medium bowl. Cut corners from wonton skins with knife or round cookie cutter to make circles. Place 1 teaspoon chicken mixture on center of each circle. Fold circles in half, pressing edges together with fork. Heat 1 tablespoon vegetable oil in large skillet until very hot. Place 10 pot stickers in single layer in skillet; fry 2 minutes or until bottoms are golden brown. Add ½ cup water to skillet. Cover and cook 6 to 7 minutes or until water is absorbed. Repeat with remaining pot stickers, adding 1 tablespoon vegetable oil and ½ cup water per batch. Serve warm with your choice of sauce for dipping.

Makes 50 appetizers

NUTRIENTS PER SERVING			
Calories	49	Fat	2 g
Cholesterol	4 mg	Sodium	86 mg

Favorite recipe from **USA Rice Council**

Party Chicken Tarts

2   tablespoons butter or margarine
1   cup chopped fresh mushrooms
¼   cup finely chopped celery
¼   cup finely chopped onion
2   tablespoons all-purpose flour
1½ cups chopped cooked chicken
6   tablespoons sour cream
½   teaspoon garlic salt
1   package (10 ounces) flaky refrigerator biscuits
      (10 to 12 count)
    Vegetable cooking spray
1   tablespoon butter or margarine, melted
    Grated Parmesan cheese

Melt 2 tablespoons butter in large skillet. Add mushrooms, celery and onion; cook and stir 4 to 5 minutes. Sprinkle with flour; stir in chicken and sour cream. Cook until thoroughly heated. Stir in garlic salt; set aside. Cut each biscuit into quarters; press each piece into miniature muffin tins coated with cooking spray to form tart shell. Brush each piece with melted butter. Bake at 400°F 6 minutes. Remove from oven; *reduce oven temperature to 350°F.* Fill each tart with 1 teaspoon chicken mixture; sprinkle with cheese. Bake 14 to 15 minutes more. Serve immediately.   *Makes 40 to 48 appetizers*

Note: For ease in serving at party time, prepare filling ahead and cook tarts 5 minutes. Fill and bake just before serving for best flavor.

NUTRIENTS PER SERVING			
Calories	49	Fat	3 g
Cholesterol	8 mg	Sodium	131 mg

Favorite recipe from **National Broiler Council**

Party Chicken Tarts

Cheesy Potato Skins with Black Beans & Salsa

6 medium potatoes (6 ounces each), baked
¾ cup GUILTLESS GOURMET® Black Bean Dip (mild or spicy)
¾ cup GUILTLESS GOURMET® Nacho Dip (mild or spicy)
¾ cup GUILTLESS GOURMET® Salsa (mild, medium or hot)
¾ cup low fat sour cream
Fresh cilantro sprigs (optional)

Preheat oven to 400°F. Cut baked potatoes in half lengthwise and scoop out potato pulp, leaving ¼-inch pulp attached to skin (avoid breaking skin). (Save potato pulp for another use, such as mashed potatoes.) Place potato skins on large baking sheet, skin sides down; bake 5 minutes.

Fill each potato skin with 1 tablespoon bean dip and 1 tablespoon nacho dip. Return to oven; bake 10 minutes. Remove from oven; let cool 5 minutes. Dollop 1 tablespoon salsa and 1 tablespoon sour cream onto each potato. Garnish with cilantro, if desired. Serve hot.

Makes 12 servings

NUTRIENTS PER SERVING			
(1 potato skin)			
Calories	133	Fat	1 g
Cholesterol	5 mg	Sodium	216 mg

Cheesy Potato Skins with Black Beans & Salsa

Ground Turkey Chinese Spring Rolls

    1   pound Ground Turkey
    1   large clove garlic, minced
 1½   teaspoons fresh ginger, minced
    2   cups bok choy, sliced paper thin
  ½   cup thinly sliced green onions
    2   tablespoons reduced-sodium soy sauce
    1   teaspoon dry sherry or rice wine
    1   teaspoon sesame oil
    8   sheets phyllo pastry
        Nonstick cooking spray

Preheat oven to 400°F. In medium nonstick skillet, over medium-high heat, cook and stir turkey, garlic and ginger 4 to 5 minutes or until turkey is no longer pink. Drain thoroughly.

In medium-size bowl combine turkey mixture, bok choy, onions, soy sauce, sherry and oil.

On clean, dry counter, layer phyllo sheets into a stack and cut into 2 (18×7-inch) rectangles. Work with one rectangle of phyllo at a time. (Keep remaining phyllo covered with a damp cloth following package instructions.)

Coat half sheet of phyllo with nonstick cooking spray. On counter arrange phyllo sheet so 7-inch side is parallel to counter edge. Place ¼ cup of turkey mixture in 5-inch strip, 1-inch away from bottom and side edges of phyllo. Fold 1-inch bottom edge of phyllo over filling and fold longer edges of phyllo toward center; roll-up, jelly-roll style. Phyllo may break during rolling, but will hold filling once roll is completed.

Repeat process with remaining rectangles of phyllo and filling to make remaining spring rolls. Place rolls, seam-side-down, on 2 (15×10-inch) cookie

continued on page 20

Ground Turkey Chinese Spring Rolls

Ground Turkey Chinese Spring Rolls, continued

sheets coated with nonstick cooking spray. Coat tops of rolls with nonstick cooking spray. Bake 14 to 16 minutes or until rolls are golden brown.

Serve immediately with Chinese mustard, hoisin sauce and additional soy sauce, if desired. *Makes 16 servings*

NUTRIENTS PER SERVING			
Calories	86	Fat	3 g
Cholesterol	14 mg	Sodium	140 mg

Favorite recipe from **National Turkey Federation**

Herbed Stuffed Tomatoes

15	cherry tomatoes
½	cup 1% low-fat cottage cheese
1	tablespoon thinly sliced green onion
1	teaspoon chopped fresh chervil *or* ¼ teaspoon dried chervil leaves
½	teaspoon chopped fresh dill *or* ⅛ teaspoon dried dill weed
⅛	teaspoon lemon pepper

Cut thin slice off bottom of each tomato. Scoop out pulp with small spoon; discard pulp. Invert tomatoes on paper towels to drain. Combine cottage cheese, green onion, chervil, dill and lemon pepper in small bowl. Spoon into tomatoes. Serve at once or cover and refrigerate up to 8 hours.

Makes 5 servings

NUTRIENTS PER SERVING			
(3 stuffed tomatoes)			
Calories	27	Fat	<1 g
Cholesterol	1 mg	Sodium	96 mg

Herbed Stuffed Tomatoes

Savory Corn Cakes

2 cups all-purpose flour
1 teaspoon baking powder
½ teaspoon salt
2 cups frozen whole kernel corn, thawed
1 cup skim milk
1 cup (4 ounces) shredded smoked Cheddar cheese
2 egg whites, beaten
1 whole egg, beaten
4 green onions, finely chopped
2 cloves garlic, minced
1 tablespoon chili powder
Prepared salsa (optional)

1. Combine flour, baking powder and salt in large bowl with wire whisk. Stir in corn, milk, cheese, egg whites, egg, green onions, garlic and chili powder until well blended.

2. Spray large nonstick skillet with nonstick cooking spray; heat over medium-high heat.

3. Drop batter by ¼ cupfuls into skillet. Cook 3 minutes per side or until golden brown. Serve with prepared salsa.   *Makes 12 cakes*

NUTRIENTS PER SERVING			
(1 cake)			
Calories	152	Fat	3 g
Cholesterol	25 mg	Sodium	227 mg

Savory Corn Cakes

Fiesta Quesadillas with Fruit Salsa

1 can (11 ounces) DOLE® Mandarin Oranges, drained and
    finely chopped
1 tablespoon chopped fresh cilantro or fresh parsley
1 tablespoon lime juice
4 (8-inch) whole wheat or flour tortillas
¾ cup shredded low fat Monterey Jack, mozzarella or Cheddar
    cheese
⅔ cup finely chopped DOLE® Pitted Dates or Chopped Dates or
    finely chopped Pitted Prunes
⅓ cup crumbled feta cheese
2 tablespoons chopped DOLE® Green Onion

• **Combine** mandarin oranges, cilantro and lime juice in small bowl for salsa;
set aside.

• **Place** two tortillas on large baking sheet. Sprinkle half of shredded cheese,
dates, feta and green onion over each tortilla to within ½ inch of edge.

• **Brush** outer ½-inch edge of each tortilla with water. Top with remaining
tortillas; press down edges gently to seal.

• **Bake** at 375°F 5 to 8 minutes or until hot. Cut each quesadilla into 6 wedges.

• **Drain** salsa just before serving, if desired; serve over warm quesadillas.

Makes 6 servings

Prep time: 15 minutes
Bake time: 8 minutes

NUTRIENTS PER SERVING			
Calories	225	Fat	8 g
Cholesterol	22 mg	Sodium	317 mg

Top to bottom: Fresh Garden Dip (page 26)
and Fiesta Quesadillas with Fruit Salsa

Fresh Garden Dip

1½ cups fat free or reduced fat mayonnaise
1½ cups shredded DOLE® Carrots
1 cup finely chopped DOLE® Broccoli Florets
⅓ cup finely chopped DOLE® Green Onions
2 teaspoons dried dill weed
¼ teaspoon garlic powder
    DOLE® Broccoli Florets, Cauliflower Florets or Peeled Mini
    Carrots

• **Stir** together mayonnaise, shredded carrots, chopped broccoli, green onions, dill and garlic powder in medium bowl until blended.

• **Spoon** into serving bowl. Cover and chill 1 hour or overnight. Serve with assorted fresh vegetables. Refrigerate any leftovers in airtight container.

Makes 3½ cups

Prep time: 15 minutes
Chill time: 1 hour

NUTRIENTS PER SERVING			
(1 tablespoon)			
Calories	8	Fat	0 g
Cholesterol	0 mg	Sodium	97 mg

Chili con Queso con Surimi

1 cup chopped onion

2 tablespoons olive or vegetable oil

1 can (16 ounces) tomatoes, coarsely chopped

1 can (4 ounces) diced green chilies

8 ounces (2 cups) shredded low-fat or regular Monterey Jack
    cheese

8 ounces (2 cups) shredded low-fat Cheddar cheese

1 tablespoon cornstarch

8 ounces surimi seafood, flake-style or chunk-style, coarsely
    chopped

Cook onion in oil in large saucepan over medium heat until tender but not brown, stirring occasionally. Add tomatoes and chilies; bring to a simmer and cook 5 minutes. Meanwhile, toss cheeses with cornstarch; gradually add to tomato mixture and stir until melted. Stir in surimi seafood. Transfer to top of chafing dish or fondue pot (over hot water, alcohol or candle burner) to keep warm. Serve with corn chips, crackers and raw vegetables for dipping.

Makes 4½ cups

NUTRIENTS PER SERVING			
(1 tablespoon)			
Calories	27	Fat	1 g
Cholesterol	3 mg	Sodium	91 mg

Favorite recipe from **National Fisheries Institute**

Fresh Tomato Eggplant Spread

1 medium eggplant
2 large ripe tomatoes, seeded and chopped
1 cup minced zucchini
¼ cup chopped green onions with tops
2 tablespoons red wine vinegar
1 tablespoon olive oil
1 teaspoon honey
1 clove garlic, minced
1 tablespoon minced fresh basil
2 teaspoons minced fresh oregano
1 teaspoon minced fresh thyme
⅛ teaspoon ground black pepper
¼ cup pine nuts or slivered almonds
32 melba toast rounds

1. Preheat oven to 375°F. Poke holes in surface of eggplant with fork. Bake 20 to 25 minutes or until tender. Cool completely; peel and mince. Place in colander; press to release excess water.

2. Combine eggplant with tomatoes, zucchini, green onions, vinegar, oil, honey, garlic, basil, oregano, thyme and black pepper in large bowl. Mix well. Refrigerate 2 hours to allow flavors to blend.

3. Stir in pine nuts just before serving. Serve with melba toast rounds.

Makes 8 servings

NUTRIENTS PER SERVING			
Calories	117	Fat	4 g
Cholesterol	0 mg	Sodium	65 mg

Fresh Tomato Eggplant Spread

Festive Chicken Dip

1½ pounds boneless, skinless chicken breasts, finely chopped
    (about 3 cups)
¼ cup lime juice, divided
2 garlic cloves, minced
1 teaspoon salt
½ teaspoon ground black pepper
1 can (16 ounces) refried beans
1½ cups sour cream, divided
1 package (1¼ ounces) dry taco seasoning mix, divided
1 tablespoon picante sauce
1 avocado, chopped
1 tablespoon olive oil
1 cup (4 ounces) shredded sharp Cheddar cheese
1 small onion, finely chopped
2 tomatoes, finely chopped
1 can (2¼ ounces) sliced black olives, drained and chopped
1 bag (10 ounces) tortilla chips
   Fresh cilantro for garnish

Place chicken in small bowl. Sprinkle with 3 tablespoons lime juice, garlic, salt and pepper; mix well. Set aside. Combine beans, ½ cup sour cream, 2½ tablespoons taco seasoning mix and picante sauce in medium bowl. Spread bean mixture in bottom of shallow 2-quart casserole dish. Combine avocado and remaining 1 tablespoon lime juice in small bowl; sprinkle over bean mixture. Combine remaining 1 cup sour cream and 2½ tablespoons taco seasoning mix in small bowl; set aside. Heat oil in large skillet over high heat until hot; add chicken in single layer. *Do not stir.* Cook about 2 minutes or until chicken is brown on bottom. Turn chicken and cook until other side is brown and no liquid remains. Break chicken into separate pieces with fork.

continued on page 32

Festive Chicken Dip

Festive Chicken Dip, continued

Layer chicken, sour cream mixture, cheese, onion and tomatoes over avocado mixture. Top with olives. Refrigerate until completely chilled. Serve with chips. Garnish with cilantro.   *Makes 2 quarts dip (about 30 appetizers)*

NUTRIENTS PER SERVING			
Calories	158	Fat	9 g
Cholesterol	20 mg	Sodium	331 mg

Favorite recipe from **National Broiler Council**

PHILLY® FREE® Salsa Dip

1   package (8 ounces) PHILADELPHIA BRAND® FREE® Fat
      Free Cream Cheese, softened
½ cup salsa

BEAT cream cheese with electric mixer on medium speed until well blended.

ADD salsa, mixing until blended. Refrigerate.

SERVE with assorted cut-up vegetables or lowfat tortilla chips.
                                   Makes 12 servings (1½ cups)

Prep time: 5 minutes

NUTRIENTS PER SERVING			
(2 tablespoons)			
Calories	20	Fat	0 g
Cholesterol	5 mg	Sodium	140 mg

Chunky Hawaiian Spread

1   package (3 ounces) light cream cheese, softened
½   cup fat free or light sour cream
1   can (8 ounces) DOLE® Crushed Pineapple, well-drained
¼   cup mango chutney*
    Low fat crackers

• **Beat** cream cheese, sour cream, pineapple and chutney in bowl until blended. Cover and chill 1 hour or overnight. Serve with crackers. Refrigerate any leftover spread in airtight container for up to one week.   *Makes 2½ cups*

*If there are large pieces of fruit in chutney, cut into small pieces.

NUTRIENTS PER SERVING			
(1 tablespoon)			
Calories	21	Fat	1 g
Cholesterol	1 mg	Sodium	23 mg

Lemon Dill Seafood Spread

2   packages (8 ounces each) light cream cheese, at room
    temperature
½   cup bottled lemon butter-dill cooking sauce
½   cup thinly sliced green onions
½   teaspoon lemon pepper seasoning
16   ounces surimi seafood, crab- or lobster-flavored, flake- or
    coarsely chopped chunk-style, drained

Blend cream cheese, cooking sauce, green onions and lemon pepper seasoning in electric mixer or by hand. Stir in surimi seafood; press mixture into a 4-cup mold lined with plastic wrap. Cover and refrigerate several hours or overnight. Unmold on serving platter and garnish, if desired, with fresh dill or other fresh herbs. Serve with crackers or melba toast.   *Makes 4 cups*

NUTRIENTS PER SERVING			
(1 tablespoon)			
Calories	32	Fat	2 g
Cholesterol	7 mg	Sodium	100 mg

Favorite recipe from **National Fisheries Institute**

Light and Zippy Dip

1   cup low fat cottage cheese
⅓   cup HEINZ® Chili Sauce
2   green onions, thinly sliced, including tops
1   teaspoon prepared horseradish
⅛   teaspoon ground red pepper*
    Crisp raw vegetables

Combine cottage cheese and chili sauce in food processor or blender. Process until smooth, scraping sides. Stir in onions, horseradish and red pepper. Cover; chill to blend flavors. Serve with vegetables.   *Makes about 1½ cups*

*Substitute 1/4 teaspoon black pepper for ground red pepper.

NUTRIENTS PER SERVING			
(2 tablespoons)			
Calories	22	Fat	<1 g
Cholesterol	1 mg	Sodium	176 mg

35

Five-Layered Mexican Dip

½ cup low fat sour cream
½ cup GUILTLESS GOURMET® Salsa (mild, medium or hot)
1 jar (12.5 ounces) GUILTLESS GOURMET® Bean Dip (Black or
    Pinto, mild or spicy)
2 cups shredded lettuce
½ cup chopped tomato
¼ cup (1 ounce) shredded sharp Cheddar cheese
    Chopped fresh cilantro and cilantro sprigs (optional)
1 large bag (7 ounces) GUILTLESS GOURMET® Baked Tortilla
    Chips (yellow, white or blue corn)

Mix together sour cream and salsa in small bowl. Spread bean dip in shallow glass bowl. Top with sour cream-salsa mixture, spreading to cover bean dip.* Just before serving, top with lettuce, tomato and cheese. Garnish with cilantro, if desired. Serve with tortilla chips.   *Makes 8 servings*

*Dip may be prepared to this point; cover and refrigerate up to 24 hours.

NUTRIENTS PER SERVING			
(⅔ cup dip and 20 chips)			
Calories	199	Fat	3 g
Cholesterol	8 mg	Sodium	425 mg

Fresh Tomato Pasta Soup

1   tablespoon olive oil
½   cup chopped onion
1   clove garlic, minced
3   pounds fresh tomatoes, coarsely chopped
3   cups fat-free reduced-sodium chicken broth
1   tablespoon minced fresh basil
1   tablespoon minced fresh marjoram
1   tablespoon minced fresh oregano
1   teaspoon fennel seed
½   teaspoon ground black pepper
¾   cup uncooked rosamarina or other small pasta
½   cup (2 ounces) shredded part-skim mozzarella cheese

1. Heat oil in large saucepan over medium heat. Add onion and garlic; cook and stir until onion is tender. Add tomatoes, broth, basil, marjoram, oregano, fennel seed and black pepper.

2. Bring to a boil; reduce heat. Cover; simmer 25 minutes. Remove from heat; cool slightly.

3. Puree tomato mixture in food processor or blender in batches. Return to saucepan; bring to a boil. Add pasta; cook 7 to 9 minutes or until tender. Transfer to serving bowls. Sprinkle with mozzarella. Garnish with marjoram sprigs, if desired.

Makes 8 (¾-cup) servings

NUTRIENTS PER SERVING			
Calories	116	Fat	4 g
Cholesterol	4 mg	Sodium	62 mg

Fresh Tomato Pasta Soup

Onion Soup with Crouton Crust

ONION SOUP

1	tablespoon vegetable oil
3	pounds large yellow onions, halved and thinly sliced (about 9 cups)
3	tablespoons all-purpose flour
⅔	cup apple brandy or water
5	cups low sodium beef stock or broth
2⅓	cups low sodium chicken stock or broth
1	tablespoon snipped fresh thyme leaves or 1 teaspoon dried thyme
1	teaspoon freshly ground black pepper
¼	teaspoon salt

CROUTON CRUST

8	slices (½ inch thick) whole wheat or white French bread
¾	cup (3 ounces) shredded ALPINE LACE® Reduced Fat Swiss Cheese

1. To make the Onion Soup: Spray a 6-quart Dutch oven or stockpot with nonstick cooking spray. Add the oil and heat over medium-high heat.

2. Add the onions and cook, stirring occasionally, for about 10 minutes or until browned and caramelized. Stir in the flour, then the brandy. Bring to a boil.

3. Add both of the stocks, the thyme, pepper and salt. Return to a boil, then reduce the heat to low and simmer, uncovered, for 30 minutes.

4. While the soup simmers, make the Crouton Crust: Preheat the broiler. Place the bread slices on a baking sheet and broil until nicely browned on both sides. Remove the bread slices from the baking sheet and set aside.

continued on page 42

Onion Soup with Crouton Crust

Onion Soup with Crouton Crust, continued

5. Place 8 ovenproof soup bowls on the baking sheet. Ladle the soup into the bowls and top each with a crouton. Sprinkle crouton and soup with the cheese. Broil 6 inches from the heat for 1 to 2 minutes or until cheese is melted and bubbly.

Makes 8 first-course servings (1 cup each)

NUTRIENTS PER SERVING			
Calories	273	Fat	5 g
Cholesterol	10 mg	Sodium	366 mg

Dilled Vichyssoise

1 cup chopped leeks
1 large potato, peeled and cubed
¼ cup finely chopped green onions
2 cloves garlic, minced
2 teaspoons sugar
3 cups chicken broth
1 cup water
¾ cup 2% milk
2 tablespoons fresh dill, chopped finely

Place leeks, potato, green onions, garlic and sugar in large saucepan. Add chicken broth and water; simmer over medium heat 15 to 20 minutes or until potatoes are very tender. Remove from heat; puree soup in food processor or blender in batches. Stir in milk. Cover and refrigerate at least 3 hours before serving.

Makes 6 servings

NUTRIENTS PER SERVING			
Calories	75	Fat	1 g
Cholesterol	3 mg	Sodium	154 mg

Favorite recipe from **The Sugar Association, Inc.**

Country Cream of Chicken Chowder

¼ cup CRISCO® Savory Seasonings Roasted Garlic Flavor oil
¼ cup finely chopped onion
¼ cup all-purpose flour
4 cups chicken broth
2 cups skim milk
1 bay leaf
3 cups frozen hash brown potatoes
1 package (10 ounces) frozen whole kernel corn
1 package (10 ounces) frozen cut green beans
1 package (10 ounces) frozen peas
1 package (10 ounces) frozen sliced carrots
1½ cups finely chopped cooked chicken
⅛ teaspoon pepper
2 tablespoons chopped fresh parsley or chives

1. Heat oil in large saucepan on medium heat. Add onion. Cook and stir until tender. Stir in flour. Cook until bubbly. Gradually stir in broth and milk. Cook and stir until mixture is bubbly and slightly thickened. Add bay leaf.

2. Add potatoes, corn, beans, peas and carrots. Increase heat to medium-high. Bring mixture back to a boil. Reduce heat to low. Simmer 5 minutes or until beans are tender. Stir in chicken and pepper. Heat thoroughly. Remove bay leaf. Serve sprinkled with parsley. *Makes 10 servings*

NUTRIENTS PER SERVING			
Calories	220	Fat	7 g
Cholesterol	20 mg	Sodium	685 mg

SMUCKER'S® Chilled Berry Soup

½ cup SMUCKER'S® Strawberry Jelly
3 cups fresh blueberries
2 cups fresh raspberries
  Juice of 1 lemon
1½ cups water, divided
1 teaspoon cornstarch dissolved in 2 tablespoons cold water
1 quart fresh strawberries, cleaned and sliced
1 cup plain nonfat yogurt or sour cream

In a large saucepan, combine the Smucker's® Strawberry Jelly with the blueberries, raspberries, lemon juice and 1 cup of the water. Bring to a boil; simmer about 5 minutes until the blueberries begin to lose some of their juice. Stir in the cornstarch dissolved in cold water; cook until slightly thickened, about 3 more minutes. Add the remaining ½ cup of water. Cool, then refrigerate the berry mixture until thoroughly chilled.

Place the chilled berry mixture in a blender or food processor. Blend on low speed for 5 minutes. Combine the puréed berry soup with the sliced strawberries. Spoon into serving bowls; stir a few tablespoons of yogurt or sour cream into each serving. *Makes 6 (1-cup) servings*

Prep time: 20 minutes
Chill time: 2 hours or longer

NUTRIENTS PER SERVING			
Calories	183	Fat	1 g
Cholesterol	1 mg	Sodium	38 mg

SMUCKER'S® Chilled Berry Soup

Hearty Tortilla Chip Soup

1 cup chopped onion
¾ cup finely chopped carrots
1 clove garlic, minced
6 ounces GUILTLESS GOURMET® Unsalted or Blue Corn Baked
    Tortilla Chips, divided
3 cans (14½ ounces each) low sodium chicken broth, defatted
2 cups water
½ cup *each* GUILTLESS GOURMET® Roasted Red Pepper and
    Green Tomatillo Salsas
1 can (6 ounces) low sodium tomato paste
1 cup (4 ounces) shredded low fat Monterey Jack cheese

Microwave Directions: Combine onion, carrots and garlic in 3-quart microwave-safe casserole. Cover with vented plastic wrap or lid; microwave on HIGH (100% power) 7 minutes or until vegetables are tender. Finely crush half the tortilla chips. Add crushed chips, broth, water, salsas and tomato paste; stir well. Cover; microwave on HIGH 6 minutes or until soup bubbles. Microwave on MEDIUM (50% power) 5 minutes. To serve, divide remaining tortilla chips and half the cheese among 6 individual soup bowls. Ladle soup over cheese and chips, dividing evenly. Sprinkle with remaining cheese.   *Makes 8 servings*

Stove Top Directions: Bring 2 tablespoons broth to a boil in 3-quart saucepan over medium-high heat. Add onion, carrots and garlic; cook and stir about 5 minutes until vegetables are tender. Finely crush half the tortilla chips. Add crushed chips, remaining broth, water, salsas and tomato paste; stir well. Cook over medium heat until soup comes to a boil. Reduce heat to low; simmer 5 minutes. Serve as directed above.

NUTRIENTS PER SERVING			
Calories	180	Fat	4 g
Cholesterol	10 mg	Sodium	337 mg

Hearty Tortilla Chip Soup

Slimming Chocoberry Splash

Crushed ice
¾ cup cold skim milk
¼ cup sliced fresh strawberries
2 tablespoons HERSHEY®S Syrup
2 tablespoons vanilla ice milk
2 tablespoons club soda

Fill two tall glasses with crushed ice. In blender container, place all remaining ingredients except club soda. Cover; blend until smooth. Pour into glasses over crushed ice; add club soda. Serve immediately. Garnish as desired.

Makes 2 (6-ounce) servings

Variations: Substitute any of the following for strawberries: ⅓ cup drained canned peach slices; 3 tablespoons frozen raspberries; 2 pineapple slices *or* ¼ cup drained crushed canned pineapple.

NUTRIENTS PER SERVING			
Calories	100	Fat	1 g
Cholesterol	5 mg	Sodium	70 mg

Slimming Chocoberry Splash

Pineapple-Mint Lemonade

1 cup sugar
⅔ cup water*
1 can (46 ounces) DOLE® Pineapple Juice
1 cup lemon juice
⅓ cup chopped fresh mint
   Fresh mint sprigs (optional)

• **Combine** sugar and water in large saucepan; bring to boil. Boil 1 minute; remove from heat.

• **Stir** in pineapple juice, lemon juice and chopped mint; let stand 15 minutes.

• **Strain** lemonade into large pitcher; discard chopped mint. Serve over ice cubes in tall glasses. Garnish with mint sprigs.   *Makes 8 servings*

Prep time: 15 minutes
Cook/Stand time: 20 minutes

*For less tart lemonade, use 1 cup water instead of ⅔ cup.

Summer Spritzer: Combine 2 cups Pineapple-Mint Lemonade with 2 cups mineral or sparkling water. Serve over ice. Makes 4 servings.

NUTRIENTS PER SERVING			
Calories	204	Fat	0 g
Cholesterol	0 mg	Sodium	9 mg

Clockwise from top right: Peach-Melon Cooler (page 52), Pineapple-Mint Lemonade and DOLE® Juice Spritzer (page 52)

Peach-Melon Cooler

3 cups cubed DOLE® Cantaloupe
5 cups DOLE® Orchard Peach Juice or Pineapple Orange Juice,
    divided

• **Place** melon and 1 cup juice in blender or food processor container; blend until smooth.

• **Combine** melon mixture and remaining juice in large pitcher. Chill 1 hour before serving.

Makes 7 servings

Prep time: 10 minutes
Chill time: 1 hour

NUTRIENTS PER SERVING			
Calories	124	Fat	0 g
Cholesterol	0 mg	Sodium	28 mg

DOLE® Juice Spritzer

½ cup DOLE® Pine-Passion-Banana Juice or other DOLE® Juice
½ cup mineral or sparkling water or club soda
    Strawberry or sliced fresh fruit (optional)

• **Pour** juice and mineral water over ice cubes in large glass. Garnish with fruit.

Makes 1 serving

Prep time: 5 minutes

NUTRIENTS PER SERVING			
Calories	70	Fat	0 g
Cholesterol	0 mg	Sodium	3 mg

Easy Chocolate Pudding Milk Shake

3 cups cold skim milk
1 package (4-serving size) JELL-O® Chocolate Flavor Fat Free
     Sugar Free Instant Reduced Calorie Pudding & Pie Filling
3 scoops (about 1½ cups) vanilla frozen lowfat yogurt

Pour cold milk into blender container. Add pudding mix and frozen yogurt; cover. Blend on high speed 15 seconds or until smooth.

Serve at once or refrigerate and stir before serving. (Mixture thickens as it stands. Thin with additional milk, if desired.)

Makes about 5 (1-cup) servings

NUTRIENTS PER SERVING			
Calories	160	Fat	2 g
Cholesterol	20 mg	Sodium	330 mg

Pineberry Smoothie

1 ripe DOLE® Banana, quartered
1 cup DOLE® Pineapple Juice
½ cup nonfat vanilla or plain yogurt
½ cup fresh or frozen strawberries, raspberries or blueberries

• **Combine** all ingredients in blender or food processor container. Blend until thick and smooth. Serve immediately.

Makes 2 servings

Prep time: 5 minutes

NUTRIENTS PER SERVING			
Calories	174	Fat	0 g
Cholesterol	1 mg	Sodium	37 mg

53

Hot Cocoa with Cinnamon

3 tablespoons sugar
3 tablespoons HERSHEY'S Cocoa
½ cup hot water
1 (3-inch) stick cinnamon
3 cups skim milk
½ teaspoon vanilla extract

In medium saucepan, stir together sugar and cocoa; gradually stir in water. Add cinnamon. Cook over medium heat, stirring constantly, until mixture boils; boil and stir 1 minute. Immediately stir in milk; continue cooking and stirring until mixture is hot. *Do not boil.* Remove from heat; discard cinnamon stick. Stir in vanilla. Beat with rotary beater or whisk until foamy. Serve immediately.

Makes 4 (7-ounce) servings

NUTRIENTS PER SERVING			
Calories	120	Fat	1 g
Cholesterol	5 mg	Sodium	95 mg

Hot Cocoa with Cinnamon

Breakfast & Brunch

· · · · · · · · · ·

Black Bean Pancakes & Salsa

1 cup GUILTLESS GOURMET® Black Bean Dip (mild or spicy)
2 egg whites
½ cup unbleached all-purpose flour
½ cup skim milk
1 tablespoon canola oil
Nonstick cooking spray
4 ounces fat free sour cream
½ cup GUILTLESS GOURMET® Salsa (mild, medium or hot)
Yellow tomatoes and fresh mint leaves (optional)

For pancake batter, place bean dip, egg whites, flour, milk and oil in blender or food processor; blend until smooth. Refrigerate 2 hours or overnight.

Preheat oven to 350°F. Coat large nonstick skillet with cooking spray; heat over medium heat until hot. For each pancake, spoon 2 tablespoons batter into skillet; cook until bubbles form and break on pancake surface. Turn pancakes over; cook until lightly browned on other side. Place on baking sheet; keep warm in oven. Repeat to make 16 small pancakes. (If batter becomes too thick, thin with more milk.) Serve hot with sour cream and salsa. Garnish with tomatoes and mint, if desired.

Makes 4 servings

NUTRIENTS PER SERVING			
(4 pancakes, 1 ounce sour cream and 2 tablespoons salsa)			
Calories	192	Fat	4 g
Cholesterol	0 mg	Sodium	403 mg

Black Bean Pancakes & Salsa

PB & J French Toast

¼ cup blueberry preserves, or any flavor
6 slices whole wheat bread, divided
¼ cup creamy peanut butter
½ cup EGG BEATERS® Healthy Real Egg Product
¼ cup skim milk
2 tablespoons FLEISCHMANN'S® Margarine
1 large banana, sliced
1 tablespoon honey
1 tablespoon orange juice
1 tablespoon PLANTER'S® Dry Roasted Unsalted Peanuts, chopped
Low fat vanilla yogurt (optional)

Spread preserves evenly over 3 bread slices. Spread peanut butter evenly over remaining bread slices. Press preserves and peanut butter slices together to form 3 sandwiches; cut each diagonally in half. In shallow bowl, combine Egg Beaters® and milk. In large nonstick griddle or skillet, over medium-high heat, melt margarine. Dip each sandwich in egg mixture to coat; transfer to griddle. Cook sandwiches for 2 minutes on each side or until golden. Keep warm.

In small bowl, combine banana slices, honey, orange juice and peanuts. Arrange sandwiches on platter; top with banana mixture. Serve warm with a dollop of yogurt, if desired.

Makes 6 servings

Prep time: 25 minutes
Cook time: 10 minutes

NUTRIENTS PER SERVING			
Calories	242	Fat	11 g
Cholesterol	1 mg	Sodium	262 mg

PB & J French Toast

Silver Dollar Pancakes with Mixed Berry Topping

1¼ cups all-purpose flour
2 tablespoons sugar
2 teaspoons baking soda
1½ cups buttermilk
½ cup EGG BEATERS® Healthy Real Egg Product
3 tablespoons FLEISCHMANN'S® Margarine, melted, divided
Mixed Berry Topping (recipe follows)

In large bowl, combine flour, sugar and baking soda. Stir in buttermilk, Egg Beaters® and 2 tablespoons margarine just until blended.

Brush large nonstick griddle or skillet with some of remaining margarine; heat over medium-high heat. Using 1 heaping tablespoon batter for each pancake, spoon batter onto griddle. Cook until bubbly; turn and cook until lightly browned. Repeat with remaining batter, using remaining margarine as needed to make 28 pancakes. Serve hot with Mixed Berry Topping.

Makes 28 (2-inch) pancakes

Prep time: 20 minutes
Cook time: 20 minutes

Mixed Berry Topping: In medium saucepan, over medium-low heat, combine 1 (12-ounce) package frozen mixed berries,* thawed, ¼ cup honey and ½ teaspoon grated gingerroot (*or* ⅛ teaspoon ground ginger). Cook and stir just until hot and well blended. Serve over pancakes.

*3 cups mixed fresh berries may be substituted.

NUTRIENTS PER SERVING			
(4 pancakes, ¼ cup topping)			
Calories	228	Fat	6 g
Cholesterol	2 mg	Sodium	491 mg

Silver Dollar Pancakes with Mixed Berry Topping

Sunrise Pizza

2 small DOLE® Bananas, peeled
4 frozen waffles
¼ cup lowfat whipped cream cheese
1 can (11 ounces) DOLE® Mandarin Orange Segments, drained
2 teaspoons honey
   Dash ground cinnamon
   Fresh berry garnish

• **Thinly** slice bananas on diagonal.

• **Prepare** waffles according to package directions.

• **Spread** waffle with cream cheese. Arrange banana slices on top, overlapping.

• **Arrange** orange segments in center of each pizza. Drizzle with honey. Sprinkle with cinnamon. Top each pizza with berries.   *Makes 4 servings*

Prep time: 15 minutes

NUTRIENTS PER SERVING			
Calories	230	Fat	6 g
Sodium	281 mg	Cholesterol	53 mg

Golden Apple French Toast

1 Golden Delicious apple, cored and sliced
½ cup apple juice
1 large egg, beaten
¼ teaspoon vanilla extract
2 slices bread
1 teaspoon cornstarch
⅛ teaspoon salt
⅛ teaspoon ground cardamom
1 tablespoon cold water

1. In small saucepan, combine apple slices and apple juice; heat to a simmer. Cook until apple slices are tender but still retain their shape, about 8 minutes. Remove from heat and set aside while preparing French toast.

2. For French toast, in wide, shallow bowl, combine egg and vanilla. Dip bread slices in egg mixture to coat both sides. In nonstick skillet, cook bread slices until lightly browned on both sides. Remove French toast to serving plates. With slotted spoon, remove apple slices from saucepan and arrange on top of French toast. For syrup, combine cornstarch, salt, cardamom, and water; stir into reserved apple juice in saucepan. Bring mixture to a boil, stirring constantly; cook until thickened and clear. Spoon syrup over apple slices and French toast and serve.

Makes 2 servings

NUTRIENTS PER SERVING			
Calories	198	Fat	4 g
Cholesterol	131 mg	Sodium	243 mg

Favorite recipe from **Washington Apple Commission**

Spicy Mexican Frittata

1 jalapeño pepper
1 clove garlic
1 medium tomato, peeled, halved, seeded and quartered
½ teaspoon ground coriander
½ teaspoon chili powder
½ cup chopped onion
1 cup frozen corn
6 egg whites
2 eggs
¼ cup skim milk
¼ teaspoon salt
¼ teaspoon black pepper
¼ cup (1 ounce) shredded part-skim farmer or mozzarella cheese

Add jalapeño pepper and garlic to food processor or blender. Process until finely chopped. Add tomato, coriander and chili powder. Cover; process until tomato is almost smooth.

Spray large skillet with nonstick cooking spray; heat skillet over medium heat. Cook and stir onion in hot skillet until tender. Stir in tomato mixture and corn. Cook 3 to 4 minutes or until liquid is almost evaporated, stirring occasionally.

Combine egg whites, eggs, milk, salt and black pepper in medium bowl. Add egg mixture all at once to skillet. Cook, without stirring, 2 minutes until eggs begin to set. Run large spoon around edge of skillet, lifting eggs for even cooking. Remove skillet from heat when eggs are almost set but surface is still moist. Sprinkle with cheese. Cover; let stand 3 to 4 minutes or until surface is set and cheese melts. Cut into wedges.

Makes 4 servings

NUTRIENTS PER SERVING			
Calories	129	Fat	3 g
Cholesterol	108 mg	Sodium	371 mg

Spicy Mexican Frittata

Western Omelet

½ cup finely chopped red or green bell pepper
⅓ cup cubed cooked potato
2 slices turkey bacon, diced
¼ teaspoon dried oregano leaves
2 teaspoons FLEISCHMANN'S® Margarine, divided
1 cup EGG BEATERS® Healthy Real Egg Product
   Fresh oregano sprig, for garnish

In 8-inch nonstick skillet, over medium heat, sauté bell pepper, potato, turkey bacon and dried oregano in 1 teaspoon margarine until tender.* Remove from skillet; keep warm.

In same skillet, over medium heat, melt remaining margarine. Pour Egg Beaters® into skillet. Cook, lifting edges to allow uncooked portion to flow underneath. When almost set, spoon vegetable mixture over half of omelet. Fold other half over vegetable mixture; slide onto serving plate. Garnish with fresh oregano.

Makes 2 servings

Prep time: 15 minutes
Cook time: 10 minutes

*For frittata, sauté vegetables and turkey bacon in 2 teaspoons margarine. Pour Egg Beaters® evenly into skillet over prepared vegetables. Cook without stirring for 4 to 5 minutes or until cooked on bottom and almost set on top. Carefully turn frittata; cook for 1 to 2 minutes more or until done. Slide onto serving platter; cut into wedges to serve.

NUTRIENTS PER SERVING			
Calories	147	Fat	6 g
Cholesterol	10 mg	Sodium	384 mg

Western Omelet

Eggs Santa Fe

2 eggs
½ cup GUILTLESS GOURMET® Black Bean Dip (mild or spicy)
¼ cup GUILTLESS GOURMET® Salsa (mild, medium or hot)
1 ounce (about 20) GUILTLESS GOURMET® Unsalted Baked
    Tortilla Chips
2 tablespoons low fat sour cream
1 teaspoon chopped fresh cilantro
    Fresh cilantro sprigs (optional)

To poach eggs, bring water to a boil in small skillet over high heat; reduce heat to medium-low and maintain a simmer. Gently break eggs into water, being careful not to break yolks. Cover and simmer 5 minutes or until desired firmness.

Meanwhile, place bean dip in small microwave-safe bowl or small saucepan. Microwave bean dip on HIGH (100% power) 2 to 3 minutes or heat over medium heat until warm. To serve, spread ¼ cup warm bean dip in center of serving plate; top with 1 poached egg and 2 tablespoons salsa. Arrange 10 tortilla chips around egg. Dollop with 1 tablespoon sour cream and sprinkle with ½ teaspoon chopped cilantro. Repeat with remaining ingredients. Garnish with cilantro sprigs, if desired.

Makes 2 servings

NUTRIENTS PER SERVING			
Calories	217	Fat	6 g
Cholesterol	218 mg	Sodium	430 mg

Eggs Santa Fe

Asparagus-Swiss Soufflé

¼ cup unsalted butter substitute
½ cup chopped yellow onion
¼ cup all-purpose flour
½ teaspoon salt
¼ teaspoon cayenne pepper
1 cup 2% low fat milk
1 cup (4 ounces) shredded ALPINE LACE® Reduced Fat
    Swiss Cheese
1 cup egg substitute or 4 large eggs
1 cup coarsely chopped fresh asparagus pieces, cooked or
    frozen asparagus pieces, thawed and drained
3 large egg whites

1. Preheat the oven to 325°F. Spray a 1½-quart soufflé dish with nonstick cooking spray. In a large saucepan, melt the butter over medium heat, add the onion and sauté for 5 minutes or until soft. Stir in the flour, salt and pepper and cook for 2 minutes or until bubbly. Add the milk and cook, stirring constantly, for 5 minutes or until the sauce thickens. Add the cheese and stir until melted.

2. In a small bowl, whisk the egg substitute (or the whole eggs). Whisk in a little of the hot cheese sauce, then return this egg mixture to the saucepan and whisk until well blended. Remove from the heat and fold in the asparagus.

3. In a medium-size bowl, using an electric mixer set on high, beat the egg whites until stiff peaks form. Fold the hot cheese sauce into the whites, then spoon into the soufflé dish.

4. Place the soufflé on a baking sheet and bake for 50 minutes or until golden brown and puffy. *Makes 8 servings*

NUTRIENTS PER SERVING			
Calories	164	Fat	9 g
Cholesterol	13 mg	Sodium	247 mg

Asparagus-Swiss Soufflé

Breakfast Burritos

4 slices LOUIS RICH® Turkey Bacon
2 flour tortillas (7 inches in diameter)
2 tablespoons shredded sharp Cheddar cheese
2 large egg whites
1 tablespoon chopped mild chilies
   Salsa or taco sauce (optional)
   Additional shredded sharp Cheddar cheese (optional)

Cook and stir turkey bacon in nonstick skillet over medium-high heat 8 to 10 minutes or until lightly browned.

Place 2 turkey bacon slices on each tortilla; sprinkle each tortilla with 1 tablespoon cheese.

Beat egg whites and chilies; add to hot skillet. Cook and stir about 2 minutes or until set.

Divide egg mixture between tortillas. Fold tortillas over filling. Top with salsa and additional cheese, if desired.   *Makes 2 burritos*

To keep burritos warm: Wrap filled burritos in foil and place in warm oven up to 30 minutes.

NUTRIENTS PER SERVING			
(1 burrito)			
Calories	220	Fat	9 g
Cholesterol	25 mg	Sodium	470 mg

Black Pepper Patties

1 package (about 1 pound) LOUIS RICH® Ground Turkey
1 teaspoon instant chicken bouillon
¼ teaspoon dried thyme leaves, crushed
1 teaspoon coarsely ground black pepper

SAUCE

1 large tomato, chopped
½ cup plain nonfat yogurt
1 tablespoon chopped fresh parsley

Mix turkey, bouillon and thyme in large bowl. Shape into four 4-inch patties. Sprinkle pepper on patties (about ⅛ teaspoon per side), lightly pressing pepper into turkey. Cook patties in nonstick skillet over medium heat about 12 minutes or until no longer pink, turning occasionally.

Meanwhile, mix sauce ingredients in small bowl. Serve cold sauce over turkey patties.

Makes 4 servings

73

NUTRIENTS PER SERVING			
(1 patty)			
Calories	190	Fat	8 g
Cholesterol	75 mg	Sodium	315 mg

Brunch Rice

1 teaspoon margarine
¾ cup shredded carrots
¾ cup diced green bell pepper
¾ cup (about 3 ounces) sliced fresh mushrooms
6 egg whites, beaten
2 eggs, beaten
½ cup skim milk
½ teaspoon salt
¼ teaspoon ground black pepper
3 cups cooked brown rice
½ cup (2 ounces) shredded Cheddar cheese
6 corn tortillas, warmed (optional)

Heat margarine in large skillet over medium-high heat until hot. Add carrots, green pepper and mushrooms; cook and stir 2 minutes. Combine egg whites, eggs, milk, salt and black pepper in small bowl. Reduce heat to medium and pour egg mixture over vegetables. Continue stirring 1½ to 2 minutes. Add rice and cheese; stir to gently separate grains. Cook 2 minutes. Serve immediately or spoon mixture into warmed corn tortillas. *Makes 6 servings*

To Microwave: Heat margarine in 2- to 3-quart microproof baking dish. Add carrots, green pepper and mushrooms; cover and cook on HIGH (100% power) 4 minutes. Combine egg whites, eggs, milk, salt and black pepper in small bowl; pour over vegetables. Cook on HIGH 4 minutes, stirring with fork after each minute to cut cooked eggs into small pieces. Stir in rice and cheese; cook on HIGH about 1 minute or until thoroughly heated. Serve immediately or spoon mixture into warmed corn tortillas.

NUTRIENTS PER SERVING			
Calories	212	Fat	7 g
Cholesterol	79 mg	Sodium	353 mg

Favorite recipe from **USA Rice Council**

Brunch Quesadillas with Fruit Salsa

1   pint fresh strawberries, hulled and diced
1   fresh ripe Anjou pear, cored and diced
1   tablespoon chopped fresh cilantro
1   tablespoon honey
1   cup (4 ounces) SARGENTO® Preferred Light Fancy Supreme
       Shredded Mozzarella Cheese
4   flour tortillas (8 inches in diameter)
2   teaspoons light margarine, melted
2   tablespoons light sour cream

To make Fruit Salsa, combine strawberries, pear, cilantro and honey in medium bowl; set aside.

Sprinkle 2 tablespoons cheese on one half of each tortilla. Top with ⅓ cup Fruit Salsa (drain and discard any liquid from fruit) and another 2 tablespoons cheese. Fold tortillas in half. Brush top of each folded tortilla with some of the melted margarine.

Grill folded tortillas, greased sides down, in dry preheated skillet until light golden brown and crisp, about 2 minutes. Brush tops with remaining melted margarine; turn and brown other sides. Remove to serving plate or platter. Cut each tortilla in half. Serve with remaining Fruit Salsa. Garnish with sour cream. Serve immediately.   *Makes 4 servings*

NUTRIENTS PER SERVING			
Calories	278	Fat	9 g
Cholesterol	14 mg	Sodium	264 mg

Brunch Quesadillas with Fruit Salsa

Breakfast Risotto

4   cups cooked brown rice
2   cups (8 ounces) shredded GJETOST cheese
1   cup 1% low-fat milk
½   cup chopped walnuts or pecans (optional)
½   cup raisins
     Scant teaspoon cinnamon

In saucepan over medium heat, gently stir all ingredients together until hot and cheese is melted. Or, stir ingredients in microwave-safe pie plate and microwave on HIGH (100% power) 2½ minutes. Stir, then cook 1 additional minute if necessary.

Serve with green and red apple slices, strawberries or other fruit.

Makes 6 to 8 servings

NUTRIENTS PER SERVING			
Calories	279	Fat	9 g
Cholesterol	21 mg	Sodium	106 mg

Golden Apple Oatmeal

½   cup diced Golden Delicious apple
⅓   cup apple juice
⅓   cup water
¼   teaspoon salt (optional)
⅛   teaspoon ground cinnamon
⅛   teaspoon ground nutmeg
⅓   cup uncooked quick-cooking rolled oats

In small saucepan, combine apple, juice, water, salt (if desired), cinnamon, and nutmeg; heat to a boil. Stir in oats and cook 1 minute. Cover and let stand 2 minutes before serving.

Makes 2 (½-cup) servings

NUTRIENTS PER SERVING			
Calories	122	Fat	1 g
Cholesterol	0 mg	Sodium	661 mg

Favorite recipe from Washington Apple Commission

Breakfast S'mores

½ package KAVLI® Muesli crispbreads, cut in half crosswise
   while still wrapped
1 apple, thinly sliced
1 nectarine, thinly sliced
1 banana, thinly sliced
¼ cup natural-style peanut butter, with oil poured off
1 tablespoon honey
1 cup mini marshmallows

Arrange 9 crispbread pieces on baking sheet. (Reserve remaining 9 pieces for tops.)

Place sliced fruit on crispbreads in thin layers* (about ½ inch high).

Mix peanut butter with honey and place ¼ teaspoon on center of each fruit layer, circling it with 2 to 3 mini marshmallows.

Bake in 350°F oven 4 to 8 minutes or until marshmallows are melted. Place Kavli® lids on top and serve.　*Makes 9 s'mores*

*Keep fruits separate for kids' s'mores; mix fruits for teens and adults.

NUTRIENTS PER SERVING			
Calories	109	Fat	4 g
Cholesterol	0 mg	Sodium	44 mg

Peach Gingerbread Muffins

2   cups all-purpose flour
2   teaspoons baking powder
1   teaspoon ground ginger
½   teaspoon salt
½   teaspoon ground cinnamon
¼   teaspoon ground cloves
½   cup sugar
½   cup MOTT'S® Chunky Apple Sauce
¼   cup MOTT'S® Apple Juice
¼   cup GRANDMA'S® Molasses
1   egg
2   tablespoons vegetable oil
1   (16-ounce) can peaches in juice, drained and chopped

1. Preheat oven to 400°F. Line 12 (2½-inch) muffin cups with paper liners or spray with nonstick cooking spray.

2. In large bowl, combine flour, baking powder, ginger, salt and spices.

3. In small bowl, combine sugar, apple sauce, apple juice, molasses, egg and oil.

4. Stir apple sauce mixture into flour mixture just until moistened. Fold in peaches.

5. Spoon evenly into prepared muffin cups.

6. Bake 20 minutes or until toothpick inserted in centers comes out clean. Immediately remove from pan; cool on wire rack 10 minutes. Serve warm or cool completely.

Makes 12 servings

NUTRIENTS PER SERVING			
Calories	190	Fat	3 g
Sodium	150 mg	Cholesterol	20 mg

Cranberry Poppy Seed Loaf

2½   cups all-purpose flour
¾   cup granulated sugar
2   tablespoons poppy seed
1   tablespoon DAVIS® Baking Powder
1   cup skim milk
⅓   cup FLEISCHMANN'S® Margarine, melted
¼   cup EGG BEATERS® Healthy Real Egg Product
1   teaspoon vanilla extract
2   teaspoons grated lemon peel
1   cup fresh or frozen cranberries, chopped
    Powdered Sugar Glaze (recipe follows, optional)

In large bowl, combine flour, granulated sugar, poppy seed and baking powder; set aside.

In small bowl, combine milk, margarine, Egg Beaters®, vanilla and lemon peel. Stir milk mixture into flour mixture just until moistened. Stir in cranberries. Spread batter into greased 8½×4½×2¼-inch loaf pan. Bake at 350°F for 60 to 70 minutes or until toothpick inserted in center comes out clean. Cool in pan on wire rack. Drizzle with Powdered Sugar Glaze if desired.

Makes 12 servings

Powdered Sugar Glaze: In small bowl, combine 1 cup powdered sugar and 5 to 6 teaspoons water until smooth.

Prep time: 20 minutes
Cook time: 70 minutes

NUTRIENTS PER SERVING			
Calories	216	Fat	6 g
Cholesterol	0 mg	Sodium	172 mg

Cranberry Poppy Seed Loaf

Apple Sauce Cinnamon Rolls

ROLLS

4 cups all-purpose flour, divided
1 package active dry yeast
1 cup MOTT'S® Natural Apple Sauce, divided
½ cup skim milk
⅓ cup plus 2 tablespoons granulated sugar, divided
2 tablespoons margarine
½ teaspoon salt
1 egg, beaten lightly
2 teaspoons ground cinnamon

ICING

1 cup sifted powdered sugar
1 tablespoon skim milk
½ teaspoon vanilla extract

1. **To prepare Rolls,** in large bowl, combine 1½ cups flour and yeast. In small saucepan, combine ¾ cup apple sauce, ½ cup milk, 2 tablespoons granulated sugar, margarine and salt. Cook over medium heat, stirring frequently, until mixture reaches 120°F to 130°F and margarine is almost melted (milk will appear curdled). Add to flour mixture along with egg. Beat with electric mixer on low speed 30 seconds, scraping bowl frequently. Beat on high speed 3 minutes. Stir in 2¼ cups flour until soft dough forms.

2. Turn out dough onto lightly floured surface; flatten slightly. Knead 3 to 5 minutes or until smooth and elastic, adding remaining ¼ cup flour to prevent sticking if necessary. Shape dough into ball; place in large bowl sprayed with nonstick cooking spray. Turn dough over so that top is greased. Cover with towel; let rise in warm place about 1 hour or until doubled in bulk.

continued on page 86

Apple Sauce Cinnamon Rolls

Apple Sauce Cinnamon Rolls, continued

3. Spray two 8- or 9-inch round baking pans with nonstick cooking spray.

4. Punch down dough; turn out onto lightly floured surface. Cover with towel; let rest 10 minutes. Roll out dough into 12-inch square. Spread remaining ¼ cup apple sauce over dough to within ½ inch of edges. In small bowl, combine remaining ⅓ cup granulated sugar and cinnamon; sprinkle over apple sauce. Roll up dough jelly-roll style. Moisten edge with water; pinch to seal seam. Cut roll into 12 (1-inch) slices with sharp floured knife. Arrange 6 rolls ½ inch apart in each prepared pan. Cover with towel; let rise in warm place about 30 minutes or until nearly doubled in bulk.

5. Preheat oven to 375°F. Bake 20 to 25 minutes or until lightly browned. Cool on wire rack 5 minutes. Invert each pan onto serving plate.

6. To prepare Icing, in small bowl, combine powdered sugar, 1 tablespoon milk and vanilla until smooth. Drizzle over tops of rolls. Serve warm.

Makes 12 servings

NUTRIENTS PER SERVING			
Calories	260	Fat	3 g
Sodium	100 mg	Cholesterol	25 mg

Choco-Lowfat Muffins

1½ cups all-purpose flour
¾ cup granulated sugar
¼ cup HERSHEY₂S Cocoa or HERSHEY₂S European Style Cocoa
2 teaspoons baking powder
1 teaspoon baking soda
½ teaspoon salt
⅔ cup vanilla lowfat yogurt
⅔ cup skim milk
½ teaspoon vanilla extract
    Powdered sugar (optional)

Heat oven to 400°F. Line 14 muffin cups (2½ inches in diameter) with paper bake cups. In medium bowl, stir together flour, granulated sugar, cocoa, baking powder, baking soda and salt; stir in yogurt, milk and vanilla just until combined. *(Do not beat.)* Fill muffin cups ⅔ full with batter.

Bake 15 to 20 minutes or until wooden pick inserted in centers comes out clean. Cool slightly in pans on wire racks. Remove from pans. Sprinkle powdered sugar over tops of muffins, if desired. Serve warm. Store, covered, at room temperature or freeze in airtight container for longer storage.

Makes 14 muffins

NUTRIENTS PER SERVING			
(1 muffin)			
Calories	100	Fat	1 g
Cholesterol	0 mg	Sodium	200 mg

Apricot Carrot Bread

1¾ cups all-purpose flour
1 teaspoon baking powder
¼ teaspoon baking soda
¼ teaspoon salt
½ cup granulated sugar
½ cup finely shredded carrots
½ cup MOTT'S® Natural Apple Sauce
1 egg, beaten lightly
2 tablespoons vegetable oil
⅓ cup dried apricots, snipped into small bits
½ cup powdered sugar
2 teaspoons MOTT'S® Apple Juice

1. Preheat oven to 350°F. Spray 8×4-inch loaf pan with nonstick cooking spray.

2. In large bowl, combine flour, baking powder, baking soda and salt.

3. In small bowl, combine granulated sugar, carrots, apple sauce, egg and oil.

4. Stir apple sauce mixture into flour mixture just until moistened. (Batter will be thick.) Fold in apricots. Spread batter into prepared pan.

5. Bake 45 to 50 minutes or until toothpick inserted in center comes out clean. Cool in pan 10 minutes. Invert onto wire rack; turn right side up. Cool completely. For best flavor, wrap loaf in plastic wrap or foil; store at room temperature overnight.

6. Just before serving, in small bowl, combine powdered sugar and apple juice until smooth. Drizzle over top of loaf. Cut into 12 slices.   *Makes 12 servings*

NUTRIENTS PER SERVING			
Calories	160	Fat	3 g
Cholesterol	20 mg	Sodium	95 mg

Apricot Carrot Bread

Jelly Donut Muffins

1¼ cups nonfat milk
¼ cup Prune Purée (recipe follows) or prepared prune butter
1 egg
2 tablespoons vegetable oil
1 teaspoon vanilla
2 cups all-purpose flour
⅓ cup sugar
1 tablespoon baking powder
1 teaspoon ground cardamom or cinnamon
½ teaspoon salt
¼ cup strawberry jam

Preheat oven to 425°F. Coat twelve 2¾-inch (⅓-cup capacity) muffin cups with vegetable cooking spray. In large bowl, beat first five ingredients until well blended. In medium bowl, combine flour, sugar, baking powder, cardamom and salt. Add to milk mixture; mix just until blended. Spoon about half of batter into prepared muffin cups. Top each with 1 teaspoon jam and remaining batter, covering jam completely. Bake 15 to 20 minutes or until springy to the touch. Cool in pans 10 minutes. Remove to wire rack to cool slightly. Serve warm.

Makes 12 muffins

Prune Purée: Combine 1⅓ cups (8 ounces) pitted prunes and 6 tablespoons hot water in container of food processor or blender. Pulse on and off until prunes are finely chopped and smooth. Store leftovers in a covered container in the refrigerator for up to two months. Makes 1 cup.

NUTRIENTS PER SERVING			
(1 muffin)			
Calories	160	Fat	3 g
Cholesterol	20 mg	Sodium	280 mg

Favorite recipe from **California Prune Board**

Jelly Donut Muffins

Apple Sauce Coffee Ring

BREAD

1	package active dry yeast
⅓	cup plus 1 teaspoon granulated sugar, divided
¼	cup warm water (105° to 115°F)
½	cup skim milk
½	cup MOTT'S® Natural Apple Sauce
1	egg
2	tablespoons margarine, melted and cooled
1	teaspoon salt
1	teaspoon grated lemon peel
5	cups all-purpose flour
1	teaspoon skim milk

FILLING

1½	cups MOTT'S® Chunky Apple Sauce
½	cup raisins
⅓	cup firmly packed light brown sugar
1	teaspoon ground cinnamon

GLAZE

1	cup powdered sugar
2	tablespoons skim milk
1	teaspoon vanilla extract

1. To **prepare Bread**, in large bowl, sprinkle yeast and 1 teaspoon granulated sugar over warm water; stir until yeast dissolves. Let stand 5 minutes or until mixture is bubbly. Stir in ½ cup milk, ½ cup apple sauce, remaining ⅓ cup granulated sugar, egg, margarine, salt and lemon peel.

continued on page 94

Apple Sauce Coffee Ring

Apple Sauce Coffee Ring, continued

2. Stir in flour, 1 cup at a time, until soft dough forms. Turn out dough onto floured surface; flatten slightly. Knead 5 minutes or until smooth and elastic, adding any remaining flour to prevent sticking if necessary. Shape dough into ball; place in large bowl sprayed with nonstick cooking spray. Turn dough over so that top is greased. Cover with damp towel; let rise in warm place 1 hour or until doubled in bulk.

3. Punch down dough. Roll out dough on floured surface into 15-inch square. Spray baking sheet with nonstick cooking spray.

4. **To prepare Filling,** in small bowl, combine 1½ cups chunky apple sauce, raisins, brown sugar and cinnamon. Spread filling over dough to within ½ inch of edges. Roll up dough jelly-roll style. Moisten edge with water; pinch to seal seam. Moisten ends of dough with water; bring together to form ring. Pinch to seal seam. Place on prepared baking sheet. Make ⅛-inch-deep cuts across width of dough at 2-inch intervals around ring.

5. Let dough rise in warm place, uncovered, 30 minutes.

6. Preheat oven to 350°F. Brush top lightly with 1 teaspoon milk.

7. Bake 45 to 50 minutes or until lightly browned and ring sounds hollow when tapped. Remove from baking sheet; cool completely on wire rack.

8. **To prepare Glaze,** in small bowl, combine powdered sugar, 2 tablespoons milk and vanilla until smooth. Drizzle over top of ring. Cut into 24 slices.

Makes 24 servings

NUTRIENTS PER SERVING			
Calories	170	Fat	2 g
Sodium	110 mg	Cholesterol	10 mg

Chili-Cheese Cornbread

1   cup yellow cornmeal
⅔   cup all-purpose flour
2   teaspoons baking powder
½   teaspoon salt
¾   cup nonfat sour cream alternative
2   egg whites
1   egg
¼   cup CRISCO® Oil
1½ cups finely chopped fat free process cheese product slices
         (¾ ounce each)
1   can (8¾ ounces) whole kernel corn, drained
1   can (4 ounces) chopped green chilies, drained

1. Heat oven to 400°F. Grease 9-inch square pan.

2. Combine cornmeal, flour, baking powder and salt in small bowl.

3. Combine "sour cream," egg whites, egg and oil in medium bowl. Stir well. Add cornmeal mixture, cheese, corn and chilies. Mix well. Pour into pan.

4. Bake at 400°F for 30 to 35 minutes or until toothpick inserted in center comes out clean. Cool 10 to 15 minutes. Cut into squares. Serve warm.

Makes 8 servings

NUTRIENTS PER SERVING			
Calories	255	Fat	8 g
Cholesterol	30 mg	Sodium	860 mg

Blueberry Muffins

1 cup fresh or thawed frozen blueberries
1¾ cups plus 1 tablespoon all-purpose flour, divided
2 teaspoons baking powder
1 teaspoon grated lemon peel
½ teaspoon salt
½ cup MOTT'S® Apple Sauce
½ cup sugar
1 whole egg
1 egg white
2 tablespoons vegetable oil
¼ cup skim milk

1. Preheat oven to 375°F. Line 12 (2½-inch) muffin cups with paper liners or spray with nonstick cooking spray.

2. In small bowl, toss blueberries with 1 tablespoon flour.

3. In large bowl, combine remaining 1¾ cups flour, baking powder, lemon peel and salt.

4. In another small bowl, combine apple sauce, sugar, whole egg, egg white and oil.

5. Stir apple sauce mixture into flour mixture alternately with milk. Mix just until moistened. Fold in blueberry mixture.

6. Spoon evenly into prepared muffin cups.

7. Bake 20 minutes or until toothpick inserted in centers comes out clean. Immediately remove from pan; cool on wire rack 10 minutes. Serve warm or cool completely. *Makes 12 servings*

NUTRIENTS PER SERVING			
Calories	150	Fat	3 g
Sodium	150 mg	Cholesterol	20 mg

Blueberry Muffins

Oatmeal Apple Cranberry Scones

2 cups all-purpose flour
1 cup uncooked rolled oats
⅓ cup sugar
2 teaspoons baking powder
½ teaspoon salt
½ teaspoon baking soda
½ teaspoon ground cinnamon
¾ cup MOTT'S® Natural Apple Sauce, divided
2 tablespoons margarine
½ cup coarsely chopped cranberries
½ cup peeled, chopped apple
¼ cup skim milk
¼ cup plus 2 tablespoons honey, divided

1. Preheat oven to 425°F. Spray baking sheet with nonstick cooking spray. In large bowl, combine flour, oats, sugar, baking powder, salt, baking soda and cinnamon. Add ½ cup apple sauce and margarine; cut in with pastry blender or fork until mixture resembles coarse crumbs. Stir in cranberries and apple.

2. In small bowl, combine milk and ¼ cup honey. Add milk mixture to flour mixture; stir together until dough forms a ball. Turn out dough onto well-floured surface; knead 10 to 12 times. Pat into 8-inch circle. Place on baking sheet. Use tip of knife to score dough into 12 wedges.

3. In another small bowl, combine remaining ¼ cup apple sauce and 2 tablespoons honey. Brush mixture over top of dough.

4. Bake 12 to 15 minutes or until lightly browned. Immediately remove from baking sheet; cool on wire rack 10 minutes. Serve warm or cool completely. Cut into 12 wedges.

Makes 12 servings

NUTRIENTS PER SERVING			
Calories	170	Fat	2 g
Sodium	200 mg	Cholesterol	0 mg

Oatmeal Apple Cranberry Scones

Meats

● ● ● ● ● ● ● ● ●

Sweet and Spicy Pork Tenderloin

- 2 teaspoons dried tarragon leaves
- ½ teaspoon dried thyme leaves
- ⅛ to ½ teaspoon black pepper
- ¼ teaspoon ground red pepper
  Dash salt
- 1 pound pork tenderloin, trimmed and cut crosswise into ½-inch pieces
- 2 tablespoons margarine, melted
- 1½ tablespoons honey

In small bowl, combine tarragon, thyme, peppers and salt; blend well. Brush both sides of each pork tenderloin piece with margarine; sprinkle both sides with seasoning mixture. Arrange tenderloin pieces on broiler pan. Broil, 5 to 6 inches from heat source, for 2 minutes per side. Remove from broiler. Brush top side of each piece with honey. Broil for an additional minute. Place pork pieces on serving plate.

Makes 4 servings

NUTRIENTS PER SERVING			
Calories	219	Fat	10 g
Cholesterol	79 mg	Sodium	158 mg

Favorite recipe from **National Pork Producers Council**

Sweet and Spicy Pork Tenderloin

Mandarin Pork Stir-Fry

1½ cups DOLE® Mandarin Tangerine, Pineapple Orange or
Pineapple Juice, divided
Vegetable cooking spray
12 ounces lean pork tenderloin, chicken breast or turkey
tenderloin, cut into thin strips
1 tablespoon finely chopped fresh ginger *or* ½ teaspoon ground
ginger
2 cups DOLE® Shredded Carrots
½ cup chopped DOLE® Pitted Prunes or Chopped Dates
4 DOLE® Green Onions, cut into 1-inch pieces
2 tablespoons low-sodium soy sauce
1 teaspoon cornstarch

• **Heat** 2 tablespoons juice over medium-high heat in large nonstick skillet sprayed with vegetable cooking spray until juice bubbles.

• **Add** pork; cook and stir 3 minutes or until pork is no longer pink. Remove pork from skillet.

• **Heat** 3 more tablespoons juice in skillet; add carrots, prunes and green onions. Cook and stir 3 minutes.

• **Stir** soy sauce and cornstarch into remaining juice; add to carrot mixture. Stir in pork; cover and cook 2 minutes until heated through.   *Makes 4 servings*

Prep time: 15 minutes
Cook time: 15 minutes

NUTRIENTS PER SERVING			
Calories	225	Fat	4 g
Cholesterol	71 mg	Sodium	312 mg

Mandarin Pork Stir-Fry

Margarita Pork Kabobs

1 cup margarita drink mix *or* 1 cup lime juice, 4 teaspoons
   sugar and ½ teaspoon salt
1 teaspoon ground coriander
1 clove garlic, minced
1 pound pork tenderloin, cut into 1-inch cubes
2 tablespoons margarine, softened
2 teaspoons lime juice
1 tablespoon minced fresh parsley
⅛ teaspoon sugar
1 large green or red bell pepper, cut into 1-inch cubes
2 ears corn, cut into 8 pieces

Combine margarita mix, coriander and garlic in small bowl. Place pork cubes in large resealable plastic food storage bag; pour marinade over pork. Close bag securely; turn to coat. Marinate for at least 30 minutes. Combine margarine, lime juice, parsley and sugar in small bowl; set aside. Thread pork cubes onto four skewers, alternating with pieces of bell pepper and corn. (If using bamboo skewers, soak in water 20 to 30 minutes before using to prevent them from burning). Grill over hot coals for 15 to 20 minutes, basting with margarine mixture and turning frequently.

Makes 4 servings

NUTRIENTS PER SERVING			
Calories	298	Fat	9 g
Cholesterol	64 mg	Sodium	309 mg

Favorite recipe from **National Pork Producers Council**

Margarita Pork Kabobs

Stuffed Pork Tenderloin

2   teaspoons minced garlic
2   teaspoons snipped fresh rosemary leaves or ½ teaspoon dried
      rosemary
2   teaspoons snipped fresh thyme leaves or ½ teaspoon dried
      thyme
1   teaspoon salt
½   teaspoon freshly ground black pepper
1   boneless end-cut rolled pork loin with tenderloin attached
      (4 pounds), tied
1   tablespoon unsalted butter substitute
1   cup thin strips yellow onion
2   large tart apples, peeled, cored and thinly sliced (2 cups)
10 thin slices (½ ounce each) ALPINE LACE® Reduced Fat
      Swiss Cheese
1   cup apple cider or apple juice

1. Preheat the oven to 325°F. Fit a 13×9×3-inch baking pan with a rack. In a small bowl, combine the garlic, rosemary, thyme, salt and pepper. Untie and unroll the pork loin, laying it flat. Rub half of the spice mixture onto the pork.

2. In a medium-size skillet, melt the butter over medium-high heat. Add the onion and apples and sauté for 5 minutes or until soft. Spread this mixture evenly on the pork and cover with the cheese slices.

3. Starting from one of the widest ends, re-roll the pork, jelly-roll style. Tie the roast with cotton string at 1-inch intervals and rub the outside with the remaining spice mixture. Place the roast on the rack in the pan and pour the apple cider over it.

continued on page 108

Stuffed Pork Tenderloin

Stuffed Pork Tenderloin, continued

4. Roast, uncovered, basting frequently with the pan drippings, for 2 to 2½ hours or until an instant-read thermometer inserted in the thickest part registers 160°F. Let the roast stand for 15 minutes before slicing.

Makes 16 servings

NUTRIENTS PER SERVING				
(½-inch slice)				
Calories	190	Fat		10 g
Cholesterol	57 mg	Sodium		184 mg

Pork Tenderloin with Raisin Sauce

1 pound pork tenderloin, trimmed of visible fat
1 jar (12 ounces) HEINZ® Fat Free Beef Gravy
⅓ cup golden raisins
3 tablespoons apple jelly
   Dash pepper
1 tablespoon Dijon-style mustard

Cut pork crosswise into 8 pieces; pound each piece to ½-inch thickness. Spray skillet with nonstick cooking spray. Quickly brown pork in skillet, about 1 minute per side. Stir in gravy, raisins, jelly and pepper. Simmer 10 minutes or until pork is no longer pink, stirring sauce and turning pork occasionally. Remove pork. Add mustard to sauce, stirring until blended. Serve sauce over pork.

Makes 4 servings (about 1⅓ cups sauce)

NUTRIENTS PER SERVING				
Calories	232	Fat		3 g
Cholesterol	72 mg	Sodium		110 mg

Caribbean Jerk-Style Pork

¾ cup DOLE® Pineapple Juice, Pineapple Orange Juice or
   Mandarin Tangerine Juice, divided
1 tablespoon prepared yellow mustard
1 teaspoon dried thyme leaves, crushed
¼ teaspoon crushed red pepper
12 ounces boneless pork loin chops or chicken breasts, cut into
   strips
½ cup DOLE® Golden or Seedless Raisins
½ cup sliced DOLE® Green Onions
2 medium firm DOLE® Bananas, cut diagonally into
   ¼-inch slices
   Hot cooked rice or noodles (optional)

• **Stir** together ½ cup juice, mustard, thyme and red pepper in small bowl; set aside.

• **Place** pork in large, nonstick skillet sprayed with vegetable cooking spray. Cook and stir pork over medium-high heat 3 to 5 minutes or until pork is no longer pink. Remove pork from skillet.

• **Add** remaining ¼ cup juice to skillet; stir in raisins and green onions. Cook and stir 1 minute.

• **Stir** in pork and reserved mustard mixture; cover and cook 2 minutes or until heated through. Stir in bananas. Serve over hot rice.   *Makes 4 servings*

Prep time: 10 minutes
Cook time: 10 minutes

NUTRIENTS PER SERVING			
Calories	282	Fat	5 g
Cholesterol	79 mg	Sodium	111 mg

109

Pork with Sweet Hungarian Paprika

1   teaspoon olive oil, divided
1   onion, sliced
2   cloves garlic, minced
1   tomato, chopped
1   red bell pepper, chopped
1   large Anaheim *or* 1 medium green bell pepper, chopped
1   can (10½ ounces) fat-free reduced-sodium chicken broth,
      divided
2   tablespoons sweet Hungarian paprika
12 ounces pork tenderloin
3   tablespoons all-purpose flour
⅓   cup low-fat sour cream
6   cups cooked enriched egg noodles (6 ounces uncooked)
¼   cup minced parsley (optional)

1. Heat ½ teaspoon oil in medium saucepan over medium heat until hot. Add onion and garlic. Cook and stir 2 minutes. Add tomato, peppers, ½ cup chicken broth and paprika. Reduce heat to low; cover and simmer 5 minutes.

2. Cut pork crosswise into 8 slices. Pound pork to ¼-inch thickness using flat side of meat mallet or rolling pin. Heat remaining ½ teaspoon oil in nonstick skillet over medium heat until hot. Cook pork 1 minute on each side or until browned. Add onion mixture. Reduce heat to low; simmer 5 minutes. Whisk remaining chicken broth and flour in small bowl.

3. Remove pork from skillet. Stir flour mixture into liquid in skillet. Bring to a boil; remove from heat. Stir in sour cream. Serve over pork and noodles. Garnish with additional paprika and parsley, if desired.   *Makes 4 servings*

NUTRIENTS PER SERVING			
Calories	380	Fat	9 g
Cholesterol	110 mg	Sodium	96 mg

Pork with Sweet Hungarian Paprika

New Orleans Pork Gumbo

1   pound pork loin roast
    Nonstick cooking spray
1   tablespoon margarine
2   tablespoons all-purpose flour
1   cup water
1   can (16 ounces) stewed tomatoes, undrained
1   package (10 ounces) frozen cut okra
1   package (10 ounces) frozen succotash
1   beef bouillon cube
1   teaspoon hot pepper sauce
1   teaspoon coarsely ground black pepper
1   bay leaf

1. Cut pork into ½-inch cubes. Spray large Dutch oven with cooking spray. Heat over medium heat until hot. Add pork; cook and stir 4 minutes or until pork is browned. Remove pork from Dutch oven.

2. Add margarine to Dutch oven. Stir in flour. Cook and stir until roux is browned. Whisk in water. Add pork and remaining ingredients. Bring to a boil. Reduce heat to low and simmer 15 minutes. Remove bay leaf and discard.

Makes 4 servings

NUTRIENTS PER SERVING			
Calories	295	Fat	10 g
Cholesterol	45 mg	Sodium	602 mg

Tandoori Pork Sauté

Nutty Rice (recipe follows)
8 ounces lean pork, cut into 2×½-inch strips
½ cup sliced onion
1 clove garlic, minced
4 fresh California plums, halved, pitted and cut into thick wedges
1 cup plain low-fat yogurt
1 tablespoon all-purpose flour
1½ teaspoons grated fresh ginger
½ teaspoon ground turmeric
⅛ teaspoon ground black pepper
Additional plum wedges, orange sections and sliced green onions

Prepare Nutty Rice. Cook pork in nonstick skillet 2 minutes or until browned, turning occasionally. Transfer to platter. Add onion and garlic to skillet; cook 1 minute. Add plums; cook and stir 1 minute. Remove from heat and return pork to pan. Combine yogurt and flour; add to skillet. Stir in ginger, turmeric and pepper. Bring to a boil; reduce heat and simmer 10 minutes, stirring occasionally. Serve over Nutty Rice and surround with plum wedges, orange sections and green onions.
Makes 4 servings

Nutty Rice: Bring 2 cups water to a boil in medium saucepan. Add ¾ cup brown rice and ¼ cup wheat berries. (Or, omit wheat berries and use 1 cup brown rice.) Return to a boil. Reduce heat to low; cover and simmer 40 to 45 minutes or until rice is tender and liquid is absorbed. Makes about 2 cups.

NUTRIENTS PER SERVING			
Calories	287	Fat	4 g
Cholesterol	44 mg	Sodium	73 mg

Favorite recipe from **California Tree Fruit Agreement**

Tandoori Pork Sauté

Potato and Pork Frittata

12 ounces (about 3 cups) frozen hash brown potatoes
1 teaspoon Cajun seasoning
4 egg whites
2 whole eggs
¼ cup 1% low fat milk
1 teaspoon dry mustard
¼ teaspoon coarsely ground black pepper
10 ounces (about 3 cups) frozen stir-fry vegetables
¾ cup chopped cooked lean pork
½ cup (2 ounces) shredded Cheddar cheese

1. Preheat oven to 400°F. Spray baking sheet with nonstick cooking spray. Spread potatoes on baking sheet; sprinkle with Cajun seasoning. Bake 15 minutes or until hot. Remove from oven. Reduce oven temperature to 350°F.

2. Beat egg whites, eggs, milk, mustard and pepper in small bowl. Place vegetables and ⅓ cup water in medium nonstick skillet. Cook over medium heat 5 minutes or until vegetables are crisp-tender; drain.

3. Add pork and potatoes to vegetables in skillet; stir lightly. Add egg mixture. Sprinkle with cheese. Cook over medium-low heat 5 minutes. Place skillet in 350°F oven and bake 5 minutes or until egg mixture is set and cheese is melted.

Makes 4 servings

NUTRIENTS PER SERVING			
Calories	251	Fat	7 g
Cholesterol	135 mg	Sodium	394 mg

Potato and Pork Frittata

Beef & Bean Burritos

Nonstick cooking spray
½ pound beef round steak, cut into ½-inch pieces
3 cloves garlic, minced
1 can (about 15 ounces) pinto beans, rinsed and drained
1 can (4 ounces) diced mild green chilies, drained
¼ cup finely chopped fresh cilantro
6 (6-inch) flour tortillas
½ cup (2 ounces) shredded reduced fat Cheddar cheese

1. Spray nonstick skillet with cooking spray; heat over medium heat until hot. Add steak and garlic; cook and stir 5 minutes or until steak is cooked to desired doneness.

2. Stir beans, chilies and cilantro into skillet; cook and stir 5 minutes or until heated through.

3. Spoon steak mixture evenly down center of each tortilla; sprinkle cheese evenly over each tortilla. Fold bottom end of tortilla over filling; roll to enclose. Garnish with salsa and nonfat sour cream, if desired.   *Makes 6 servings*

NUTRIENTS PER SERVING			
Calories	278	Fat	7 g
Cholesterol	31 mg	Sodium	956 mg

Beef & Bean Burrito

Old-Fashioned Beef Stew

1   tablespoon CRISCO® Savory Seasonings Roasted Garlic Flavor oil
1¼ pounds boneless beef round steak, trimmed and cut into
      1-inch cubes
2¾ cups water, divided
1   teaspoon Worcestershire sauce
2   bay leaves
1   clove garlic, minced
½   teaspoon paprika
¼   teaspoon pepper
8   medium carrots, quartered
8   small potatoes, peeled and quartered
4   small onions, quartered
1   package (9 ounces) frozen cut green beans
1   tablespoon cornstarch
    Salt (optional)

1. Heat oil in Dutch oven on medium-high heat. Add beef. Cook and stir until browned. Add 1½ cups water, Worcestershire sauce, bay leaves, garlic, paprika and pepper. Bring to a boil. Reduce heat to low. Cover and simmer 1 hour 15 minutes, stirring occasionally. Remove bay leaves.

2. Add carrots, potatoes and onions. Cover and simmer 30 to 45 minutes or until vegetables are almost tender. Add beans. Simmer 5 minutes or until tender. Remove from heat. Add 1 cup water to Dutch oven.

3. Combine remaining ¼ cup water and cornstarch in small bowl. Stir well. Stir into ingredients in Dutch oven. Return to low heat. Cook and stir until thickened. Season with salt, if desired.   *Makes 8 servings*

NUTRIENTS PER SERVING			
Calories	290	Fat	8 g
Cholesterol	60 mg	Sodium	95 mg

Mighty Hero Sandwich

1 (16 ounce) round loaf sourdough bread
¼ cup balsamic vinegar
1 tablespoon olive oil
2 cloves garlic, minced
1 teaspoon dried oregano leaves
1 teaspoon dried parsley flakes
¼ teaspoon pepper
1 cup sliced fresh mushrooms
6 (¼-inch-thick) tomato slices
2 (¼-inch-thick) red onion slices, separated into rings
2 cups shredded zucchini
1 cup (4 ounces) HEALTHY CHOICE® Fat Free Mozzarella
Shreds
4 ounces HEALTHY CHOICE® Deli Thin Sliced Bologna
4 ounces HEALTHY CHOICE® Deli Thin Oven Roasted
Turkey Breast

Slice bread in half horizontally. Remove soft bread from inside each half, leaving ½-inch-thick shells; set shells aside. Reserve soft inside bread for another use.

Combine vinegar and next 5 ingredients in shallow dish; add mushrooms, tomato and onion. Let stand 15 minutes.

Drain vegetables, reserving marinade. Brush marinade inside bread shells. Layer half each of zucchini, mushroom mixture and cheese in bottom half of loaf; top with bologna. Repeat layers; top with turkey and top half of loaf. Wrap in plastic wrap; chill. To serve, unwrap loaf and cut into wedges.

Makes 8 servings

NUTRIENTS PER SERVING			
Calories	192	Fat	4 g
Cholesterol	16 mg	Sodium	591 mg

121

Beef Cubed Steaks Provençale

2 cloves garlic, minced
½ teaspoon dried basil leaves
¼ teaspoon black pepper
4 lean beef cubed steaks (about 4 ounces each)
1½ teaspoons olive oil
2 small zucchini, thinly sliced
6 cherry tomatoes, cut in half
1½ teaspoons grated Parmesan cheese
Salt (optional)

Combine garlic, basil and pepper; divide mixture in half. Press half of seasoning mixture evenly into both sides of beef cubed steaks; set aside. Heat oil and remaining seasoning mixture in large nonstick skillet over medium heat. Add zucchini; cook and stir 3 minutes. Add tomatoes; continue cooking 1 minute, stirring frequently. Remove zucchini mixture to platter; sprinkle with cheese and keep warm. Increase heat to medium-high. Add 2 steaks to same skillet; cook to desired doneness, 3 to 4 minutes, turning once. Repeat with remaining 2 steaks. Season steaks with salt, if desired. Serve with zucchini mixture; garnish as desired. *Makes 4 servings*

NUTRIENTS PER SERVING			
Calories	223	Fat	10 g
Cholesterol	81 mg	Sodium	60 mg

Favorite recipe from **National Cattlemen's Beef Association**

Beef Cubed Steak Provençale

Grilled Flank Steak with Horseradish Sauce

1 pound beef flank steak
2 tablespoons reduced-sodium soy sauce
1 tablespoon red wine vinegar
2 cloves garlic, minced
½ teaspoon pepper
1 cup nonfat sour cream
1 tablespoon prepared horseradish
1 tablespoon Dijon mustard
¼ cup finely chopped fresh parsley
½ teaspoon salt
6 sourdough rolls, split
6 romaine lettuce leaves

1. Place flank steak in large resealable plastic food storage bag. Add soy sauce, vinegar, garlic and pepper. Close bag securely; turn to coat. Marinate in refrigerator at least 1 hour.

2. Prepare grill or preheat broiler. Drain steak; discard marinade. Grill or broil over medium-high heat 5 minutes. Turn beef; grill 6 minutes for medium-rare or until desired doneness. Cover with foil; let stand 15 minutes. Thinly slice steak across grain.

3. Combine sour cream, horseradish, mustard, parsley and salt in small bowl until well blended. Spread rolls with horseradish sauce; layer with sliced steak and lettuce. Garnish with small pickles, if desired. *Makes 6 servings*

NUTRIENTS PER SERVING			
Calories	220	Fat	6 g
Cholesterol	35 mg	Sodium	542 mg

Grilled Flank Steak with Horseradish Sauce

GUEST CHECK

CHECK NUMBER
4948

SERVER
3

TABLE

Lasagna

1 cup chopped onion
3 cloves garlic, minced
1 tablespoon CRISCO® Savory Seasonings Roasted Garlic Flavor oil
1 pound extra lean ground beef
2 cans (14½ ounces each) no-salt-added stewed tomatoes
1 can (6 ounces) no-salt-added tomato paste
2 teaspoons dried basil leaves, crushed
1 teaspoon dried oregano leaves, crushed
½ teaspoon sugar
¼ teaspoon black pepper
2 cups low-fat cottage cheese
½ cup grated Parmesan cheese, divided
¼ cup chopped fresh parsley
8 ounces wide lasagna noodles
1 cup (4 ounces) shredded low-moisture part-skim mozzarella
 cheese, divided

Cook and stir onion and garlic in oil in large skillet over medium heat until soft. Push to side of skillet. Add ground beef. Cook, stirring well to crumble beef. Drain, if necessary. Add tomatoes with juice, breaking up tomatoes. Add tomato paste, basil, oregano, sugar and pepper. Stir until well blended. Simmer 30 minutes. Combine cottage cheese, ¼ cup Parmesan cheese and parsley.

Cook noodles 7 minutes in unsalted boiling water. Drain well. Heat oven to 350°F. Place thin layer of meat sauce in 13×9×2-inch pan. Add, in layers, half the noodles, half the cottage cheese mixture, 2 tablespoons Parmesan, ⅓ cup mozzarella and thin layer of sauce. Repeat noodle and cheese layers. Top with remaining sauce and ⅓ cup mozzarella. Bake at 350°F for 45 minutes. Let stand 15 minutes. Cut into 12 rectangles. *Makes 12 servings*

NUTRIENTS PER SERVING			
Calories	270	Fat	10 g
Cholesterol	55 mg	Sodium	300 mg

Chili con Carne

1 tablespoon CRISCO® Oil
1 cup chopped onion
1 cup chopped green bell pepper
1 pound ground beef round
1 can (28 ounces) whole tomatoes, undrained and chopped
1 can (8 ounces) tomato sauce
1 tablespoon chili powder
1 teaspoon salt
¼ teaspoon black pepper
  Dash of hot pepper sauce (optional)
1 can (30 ounces) kidney beans, undrained

1. Heat oil in large saucepan or Dutch oven on medium heat. Add onion and green pepper. Cook and stir until tender. Add meat. Cook until browned, stirring occasionally. Stir in tomatoes, tomato sauce, chili powder, salt, black pepper and hot pepper sauce (if used). Bring to a boil. Reduce heat to low. Simmer 45 minutes, stirring occasionally.

2. Add beans. Heat thoroughly, stirring occasionally. *Makes 8 servings*

NUTRIENTS PER SERVING			
Calories	185	Fat	5 g
Cholesterol	35 mg	Sodium	505 mg

Mediterranean Meatballs and Couscous

1 can (about 14 ounces) fat-free reduced-sodium chicken broth
2½ cups water
1½ cups couscous
¾ cup golden raisins
¼ cup chopped parsley
3 tablespoons lemon juice, divided
3 teaspoons grated lemon peel, divided
2 teaspoons ground cinnamon, divided
1 teaspoon turmeric
½ teaspoon ground cumin
1 pound ground round beef
½ cup crushed saltine crackers
¼ cup evaporated skimmed milk
½ teaspoon dried oregano leaves

1. Pour chicken broth and water into 2-quart saucepan. Bring to a boil over high heat. Remove from heat. Add couscous, raisins, parsley, 2 tablespoons lemon juice, 2 teaspoons lemon peel, 1½ teaspoons cinnamon, turmeric and cumin. Cover and let stand 5 minutes.

2. Combine beef, crackers, milk, remaining 1 tablespoon lemon juice, 1 teaspoon lemon peel, ½ teaspoon cinnamon and oregano in large bowl. Mix until well blended. Shape into 24 meatballs. Place in large microwavable baking dish. Cover loosely with waxed paper. Microwave at HIGH 4 minutes or until meatballs are cooked through. Stir couscous mixture and spoon onto platter. Top with meatballs. Garnish with lemon and fresh oregano, if desired.

Makes 6 servings

NUTRIENTS PER SERVING			
Calories	434	Fat	11 g
Cholesterol	50 mg	Sodium	180 mg

Mediterranean Meatballs and Couscous

Beef Burgers with Corn Salsa

½ cup frozen corn
½ cup peeled, seeded and chopped tomato
1 can (4 ounces) diced green chilies, divided
1 tablespoon chopped fresh cilantro *or* 1 teaspoon dried
   cilantro leaves
1 tablespoon vinegar
1 teaspoon olive oil
¼ cup fine dry bread crumbs
3 tablespoons skim milk
¼ teaspoon garlic powder
12 ounces 95% lean ground beef

Prepare corn according to package directions, omitting salt; drain. Combine corn, tomato, 2 tablespoons green chilies, cilantro, vinegar and oil in small bowl. Cover and refrigerate.

Preheat broiler. Combine bread crumbs, remaining green chilies, skim milk and garlic powder in medium bowl. Add beef; blend well to combine. Shape to form four ¾-inch-thick patties. Place on broiler pan. Broil 4 inches from heat 6 minutes. Turn and broil 6 to 8 minutes or until beef is no longer pink in center. Spoon salsa over patties.

Makes 4 servings

NUTRIENTS PER SERVING			
Calories	180	Fat	6 g
Cholesterol	33 mg	Sodium	101 mg

Beef Burgers with Corn Salsa

Apple-icious Lamb Kabobs

1 cup apple juice or cider
2 tablespoons Worcestershire sauce
½ teaspoon lemon pepper
2 cloves garlic, peeled and sliced
1½ pounds fresh American lamb (leg or shoulder), cut into
     1¼-inch cubes
     Apple Barbecue Sauce (page 134)
1 large apple, cut into 12 wedges
     Assorted vegetables, such as green or red bell pepper, onion
     or summer squash, cut into wedges

Combine apple juice, Worcestershire sauce, lemon pepper and garlic in large resealable plastic food storage bag or nonmetal container. Add lamb cubes and coat well. To marinate, refrigerate 2 to 24 hours.

Prepare Apple Barbecue Sauce. Preheat grill or broiler. Remove meat from marinade and thread onto skewers, alternating meat, apple and vegetables. (If using bamboo skewers, soak in water for 20 to 30 minutes before using to prevent them from burning.)

To grill, place kabobs 4 inches from medium coals. Cook about 10 to 12 minutes, turning occasionally and brushing with Apple Barbecue Sauce. To broil, place kabobs on broiler pan sprayed with nonstick cooking spray. Broil 4 inches from heat about 10 to 12 minutes for medium-rare, turning occasionally and brushing with Apple Barbecue Sauce.   *Makes 6 servings*

NUTRIENTS PER SERVING			
(not including sauce)			
Calories	165	Fat	5 g
Cholesterol	57 mg	Sodium	62 mg

continued on page 134

Apple-icious Lamb Kabob

Apple-icious Lamb Kabobs, continued

APPLE BARBECUE SAUCE

½ cup apple juice or cider
½ cup finely chopped onion
1 cup chili sauce
½ cup unsweetened applesauce
2 tablespoons packed brown sugar
1 tablespoon Worcestershire sauce
1 teaspoon dry mustard
5 drops hot pepper sauce

Combine apple juice and onion in small saucepan; simmer 2 minutes. Stir in chili sauce, applesauce, brown sugar, Worcestershire sauce, dry mustard and hot pepper sauce. Simmer 10 minutes, stirring occasionally. Remove from heat.

Makes about 2 cups

NUTRIENTS PER SERVING			
Calories	90	Fat	1 g
Cholesterol	0 mg	Sodium	36 mg

Favorite recipe from **American Lamb Council**

Spring Lamb Skillet

2 teaspoons olive oil
1 pound boneless lamb, cut into 1-inch cubes
2 cups thinly sliced yellow squash
2 cups (about 8 ounces) sliced fresh mushrooms
2 medium tomatoes, seeded and chopped
½ cup sliced green onions
3 cups cooked brown rice
½ teaspoon dried rosemary
½ teaspoon salt
½ teaspoon cracked black pepper

Heat oil in large skillet over medium heat until hot. Add lamb and cook 3 to 5 minutes or until lamb is browned. Remove from skillet; reserve. Add squash, mushrooms, tomatoes and onions to skillet; cook 2 to 3 minutes or until vegetables are tender. Stir in rice, rosemary, salt, pepper and reserved lamb. Cook until heated through.

Makes 6 servings

NUTRIENTS PER SERVING			
Calories	258	Fat	8 g
Cholesterol	50 mg	Sodium	313 mg

Favorite recipe from **USA Rice Council**

135

Pronto Pizza

6 ounces lean fresh ground American lamb
½ teaspoon onion salt
½ teaspoon fennel seeds
¼ teaspoon dried oregano leaves
¼ teaspoon dried basil leaves
⅛ teaspoon red pepper flakes
½ cup chopped bell pepper
½ cup chopped Italian plum tomatoes
1 (10- to 12-inch) prebaked pizza shell
½ cup pizza sauce
1 tablespoon grated Parmesan cheese
¼ cup thinly sliced fresh basil leaves (optional)
½ cup (2 ounces) shredded part-skim mozzarella cheese

Preheat oven to 450°F. Combine lamb, onion salt, fennel seeds, oregano, dried basil and red pepper flakes in small bowl; knead until well blended. Spray nonstick skillet with nonstick cooking spray. Cook and stir lamb over medium-high heat until lightly browned, stirring to separate lamb. Drain on paper towel. In same skillet, cook and stir bell pepper 3 to 4 minutes, stirring occasionally. Add tomatoes; cook and stir 1 minute. Place pizza shell on cookie sheet or pizza pan; top with pizza sauce and vegetables. Sprinkle with Parmesan cheese, fresh basil, cooked lamb and mozzarella cheese. Bake 8 to 10 minutes. Cool 5 minutes and slice into wedges.

Makes 6 to 8 servings

Microwave Directions: Cook lamb mixture in 2-quart microwavable dish on HIGH (100% power) 3 minutes, stirring several times to crumble lamb. Add bell pepper and tomatoes; microwave on HIGH 2 minutes, stirring once. Drain well. Assemble pizza as directed above.

NUTRIENTS PER SERVING			
Calories	218	Fat	5 g
Cholesterol	20 mg	Sodium	360 mg

Favorite recipe from **American Lamb Council**

136

Veal in Gingered Sweet Bell Pepper Sauce

1 teaspoon olive oil
¾ pound veal cutlets, thinly sliced
½ cup skim milk
1 tablespoon finely chopped fresh tarragon
2 teaspoons crushed capers
1 jar (7 ounces) roasted red peppers, drained
1 tablespoon lemon juice
½ teaspoon freshly grated ginger
½ teaspoon ground black pepper

1. Heat oil in medium saucepan over high heat. Add veal; lightly brown both sides. Reduce heat to medium. Add milk, chopped tarragon and capers. Cook, uncovered, 5 minutes or until veal is fork-tender and milk evaporates.

2. Place roasted peppers, lemon juice, ginger and black pepper in food processor or blender; process until smooth. Set aside.

3. Remove veal from pan with slotted spoon; place in serving dish. Spoon roasted pepper sauce over veal. Sprinkle with cooked capers and fresh tarragon, if desired.

Makes 4 servings

NUTRIENTS PER SERVING			
Calories	120	Fat	4 g
Cholesterol	54 mg	Sodium	89 mg

Veal in Gingered Sweet Bell Pepper Sauce

Poultry

• • • • • • • • • • •

Crunchy Apple Salsa with Grilled Chicken

2 cups Washington Gala apples, halved, cored and chopped
¾ cup (1 large) Anaheim chili pepper, seeded and chopped
½ cup chopped onion
¼ cup lime juice
   Salt and pepper to taste
   Grilled Chicken (recipe follows)

Combine all ingredients except chicken and mix well; set aside to allow flavors to blend about 45 minutes. Prepare Grilled Chicken. Serve salsa over or alongside Grilled Chicken.

Makes 3 cups salsa

Grilled Chicken: Marinate 2 whole boneless, skinless chicken breasts in mixture of ¼ cup dry white wine, ¼ cup apple juice, ½ teaspoon grated lime peel, ½ teaspoon salt and dash pepper for 20 to 30 minutes. Drain and grill over medium-hot coals, turning once, until chicken is no longer pink in center. Makes 4 servings.

NUTRIENTS PER SERVING			
Calories	211	Fat	3 g
Cholesterol	73 mg	Sodium	155 mg

Favorite recipe from **Washington Apple Commission**

Crunchy Apple Salsa with Grilled Chicken

Spicy Marinated Chicken Kababs over Rice

½ cup white wine
¼ cup lime juice
¼ cup vegetable oil
2 cloves garlic, minced
1 jalapeño pepper, seeded and finely chopped
2 tablespoons chopped fresh cilantro
½ teaspoon salt
½ teaspoon ground black pepper
1½ pounds boneless, skinless chicken breast, cut into 1-inch cubes
1 medium-size red onion, cut into 1-inch pieces
2 medium-size red or green bell peppers, cut into 1-inch pieces
2 medium-size yellow squash, cut into 1-inch pieces
12 wooden or metal skewers*
Vegetable cooking spray
3 cups hot cooked rice

Combine wine, lime juice, oil, garlic, jalapeño, cilantro, salt and black pepper in gallon size resealable plastic food storage bag. Add chicken, onion, bell peppers and squash. Seal; turn to coat. Marinate in refrigerator 30 to 45 minutes. Remove chicken and vegetables. Place marinade in small saucepan. Bring to a boil over medium-high heat; keep warm. Alternate chicken and vegetables on skewers. Place on broiler rack coated with cooking spray; brush with marinade. Broil 4 to 6 inches from heat 8 to 10 minutes, turning and basting frequently with marinade. Serve over hot rice. *Makes 6 servings*

*Soak wooden skewers in water before using to prevent burning.

NUTRIENTS PER SERVING			
Calories	280	Fat	5 g
Cholesterol	73 mg	Sodium	262 mg

Favorite recipe from **USA Rice Council**

Spicy Marinated Chicken Kababs over Rice

Spinach-Stuffed Chicken Breasts

2   boneless skinless chicken breasts (8 ounces each), halved
5   ounces frozen chopped spinach, thawed, well drained
2   tablespoons freshly grated Parmesan cheese
1   teaspoon grated lemon peel
¼   teaspoon ground black pepper
    Olive oil-flavored nonstick cooking spray
1   cup thinly sliced mushrooms
6   slices (2 ounces) thinly sliced low-fat turkey-ham
1   cup white grape juice

1. Trim fat from chicken; discard. Place each chicken breast between 2 sheets of plastic wrap. Pound with meat mallet until chicken is about ¼ inch thick.

2. Preheat oven to 350°F. Pat spinach dry with paper towels. Combine spinach, Parmesan, lemon peel and black pepper in large bowl. Spray small nonstick skillet with cooking spray; add mushrooms. Cook and stir over medium heat 3 to 4 minutes or until tender.

3. Arrange 1½ slices turkey-ham over each chicken breast. Spread each with one-fourth of spinach mixture. Top each with mushrooms. Beginning with longer side, roll chicken tightly. Tie with kitchen string.

4. Place stuffed chicken breasts in 9-inch square baking pan, seam side down. Lightly spray chicken with cooking spray. Pour white grape juice over top. Bake 30 minutes or until chicken is no longer pink.

5. Remove string; cut chicken rolls into ½-inch diagonal slices. Arrange on plate. Pour pan juices over chicken. Garnish as desired.   *Makes 4 servings*

NUTRIENTS PER SERVING			
Calories	187	Fat	4 g
Cholesterol	71 mg	Sodium	302 mg

Spinach-Stuffed Chicken Breasts

Chicken with Zucchini and Tomatoes

8   broiler-fryer chicken thighs, boned, skinned
1   tablespoon olive oil
2   small zucchini, cut in ¼-inch slices
1   can (14½ ounces) stewed tomatoes
½   teaspoon Italian seasoning
¼   teaspoon salt
⅛   teaspoon pepper

In large skillet, heat oil over medium-high heat. Add chicken and cook, turning, 10 minutes or until browned. Drain off excess fat. Add zucchini, tomatoes, Italian seasoning, salt and pepper. Reduce heat to medium-low; cover and cook about 10 minutes more or until chicken and zucchini are fork-tender.

Makes 4 servings

NUTRIENTS PER SERVING			
Calories	232	Fat	9 g
Cholesterol	114 mg	Sodium	373 mg

Favorite recipe from **Delmarva Poultry Industry, Inc.**

Broiled Lemon Chicken

4   skinless boneless chicken breast halves (about 1 pound)
¼   cup HEINZ® Worcestershire Sauce
2   tablespoons lemon juice
1   teaspoon minced garlic
½   teaspoon pepper
½   teaspoon grated lemon peel
    Vegetable oil

Lightly flatten chicken breasts to uniform thickness; place in shallow pan or bowl. For marinade, combine Worcestershire sauce and next 4 ingredients; pour over chicken. Cover; marinate 30 minutes, turning once. Place chicken on broiler pan; brush lightly with oil. Broil, 4 to 5 inches from heat source, 3 to 4 minutes; turn. Brush with marinade, then with oil; broil an additional 3 to 4 minutes.
Makes 4 servings

NUTRIENTS PER SERVING			
Calories	142	Fat	3 g
Cholesterol	66 mg	Sodium	239 mg

Lemon-Dilly Chicken Sauté

4   broiler-fryer chicken breast halves, boned, skinned
½   cup dry bread crumbs
1   teaspoon lemon pepper
¼   teaspoon dried dill weed
3   tablespoons lemon juice
2   tablespoons olive oil

With meat mallet or similar flattening utensil, pound chicken breasts to ¼-inch thickness. In shallow dish, mix together bread crumbs, lemon pepper and dill. In second dish, place lemon juice. Add chicken, one piece at a time, first to lemon juice, then to crumb mixture, turning to coat all sides. In large nonstick skillet, heat oil over medium-high heat. Add chicken and cook, turning, about 10 minutes or until chicken is brown and fork-tender.
Makes 4 servings

NUTRIENTS PER SERVING			
Calories	243	Fat	9 g
Cholesterol	68 mg	Sodium	187 mg

Favorite recipe from **Delmarva Poultry Industry, Inc.**

147

Chicken & Tortilla Casserole

¼ cup low sodium chicken broth, defatted and divided
½ cup finely chopped red bell pepper
½ cup finely chopped green bell pepper
½ cup finely chopped red onion
1 can (28 ounces) low sodium tomatoes, undrained
¼ cup GUILTLESS GOURMET® Spicy Nacho Dip
3 ounces (about 60) GUILTLESS GOURMET® Unsalted Baked
    Tortilla Chips, divided
1 cup cooked and shredded boneless chicken breast
    Fresh herb sprig (optional)

NACHO SAUCE
¾ cup GUILTLESS GOURMET® Spicy Nacho Dip
¼ cup low fat sour cream
¼ cup skim milk

Preheat oven to 350°F. Heat 2 tablespoons broth in medium nonstick skillet until hot. Add peppers and onion; cook about 5 minutes, stirring often. Add remaining 2 tablespoons broth and cook until peppers are soft. Remove from heat; set aside. Drain off about ¾ juice from tomatoes; discard. Coarsely chop tomatoes. To assemble casserole, spread ¼ cup nacho dip on bottom of 1½- to 2-quart casserole dish. Top with layer of tortilla chips (about 30). Cover with pepper mixture, followed by another layer of tortilla chips (about 30). Evenly spread chicken over chips; top with tomatoes and remaining juice. Combine Nacho Sauce ingredients in small saucepan; heat over medium heat 2 to 3 minutes or until warm. Drizzle half the mixture evenly over tomato layer.

Cover and bake 25 to 35 minutes or until mixture bubbles. Drizzle with remaining nacho sauce. Garnish, if desired.   *Makes 4 servings*

NUTRIENTS PER SERVING			
Calories	247	Fat	3 g
Cholesterol	22 mg	Sodium	400 mg

Chicken & Tortilla Casserole

Maui Chicken Sandwich

1   can (8 ounces) DOLE® Pineapple Slices
½   teaspoon dried oregano leaves, crushed
¼   teaspoon garlic powder
4   skinless, boneless small chicken breast halves
½   cup light prepared Thousand Island salad dressing
½   cup finely chopped jicama or water chestnuts
¼   teaspoon ground red pepper (optional)
4   whole grain or whole wheat sandwich rolls
    DOLE® Red or Green Bell Pepper, sliced into rings or
      shredded DOLE® Iceberg Lettuce

• **Combine** undrained pineapple, oregano and garlic powder in shallow, non-metallic dish. Add chicken; turn to coat all sides. Cover and marinate 15 minutes in refrigerator.

• **Grill** or broil chicken and pineapple, brushing occasionally with marinade, 5 to 8 minutes on each side or until chicken is no longer pink in center and pineapple is golden brown. Discard any remaining marinade.

• **Combine** dressing, jicama and red pepper. Spread on rolls. Top with chicken, pineapple and bell pepper rings. Serve open-face, if desired.

Makes 4 servings

Prep time: 10 minutes
Marinate time: 15 minutes
Cook time: 15 minutes

NUTRIENTS PER SERVING			
Calories	284	Fat	8 g
Cholesterol	82 mg	Sodium	452 mg

Maui Chicken Sandwich

Rosemary Chicken with Asparagus Lemon Rice

¼ cup dry white wine
3 cloves garlic, minced
1 tablespoon finely chopped fresh rosemary
1 tablespoon vegetable oil
1 tablespoon reduced-sodium soy sauce
1 teaspoon sugar
½ teaspoon ground black pepper
6 boneless, skinless chicken breast halves (about 2¼ pounds)
Vegetable cooking spray
3 cups cooked rice (cooked in low-sodium chicken broth)
10 spears asparagus, blanched and cut into 1-inch pieces
(¼ pound)
1 teaspoon grated lemon peel
1 teaspoon lemon pepper
½ teaspoon salt
Lemon slices for garnish
Fresh rosemary sprigs for garnish

Combine wine, garlic, rosemary, oil, soy sauce, sugar and pepper in large shallow glass dish. Add chicken, turning to coat; cover and marinate in refrigerator at least 1 hour. Heat large skillet coated with cooking spray over medium-high heat until hot. Add chicken and marinade; cook 7 minutes on each side or until brown and no longer pink in center. Combine rice, asparagus, lemon peel, lemon pepper and salt in large bowl. To serve, spoon rice on individual serving plates. Cut chicken into strips; fan over rice. Garnish with lemon and rosemary.

Makes 6 servings

NUTRIENTS PER SERVING			
Calories	294	Fat	6 g
Cholesterol	73 mg	Sodium	437 mg

Favorite recipe from **USA Rice Council**

Rosemary Chicken with Asparagus Lemon Rice

Balsamic Chicken

6 boneless skinless chicken breast halves
1½ teaspoons fresh rosemary, minced *or* ½ teaspoon dried
rosemary
2 cloves garlic, minced
¾ teaspoon pepper
½ teaspoon salt
1 tablespoon olive oil
¼ cup good-quality balsamic vinegar

1. Rinse chicken and pat dry. Combine rosemary, garlic, pepper and salt in small bowl; mix well. Place chicken in large bowl; drizzle chicken with oil and rub with spice mixture. Cover and refrigerate overnight.

2. Preheat oven to 450°F. Spray heavy roasting pan or iron skillet with nonstick cooking spray. Place chicken in pan; bake 10 minutes. Turn chicken over, stirring in 3 to 4 tablespoons water if drippings are beginning to stick to pan.

3. Bake about 10 minutes or until chicken is golden brown and no longer pink in center. If pan is dry, stir in another 1 to 2 tablespoons water to loosen drippings.

4. Drizzle balsamic vinegar over chicken in pan. Transfer chicken to plates. Stir liquid in pan; drizzle over chicken. Garnish, if desired. *Makes 6 servings*

NUTRIENTS PER SERVING			
Calories	174	Fat	5 g
Cholesterol	73 mg	Sodium	242 mg

Chicken with Mandarin Orange and Water Chestnut Sauce

1 can (11 ounces) mandarin oranges, drained
1 can (8 ounces) sliced water chestnuts, drained
4 teaspoons packed brown sugar
2 tablespoons white vinegar
1 tablespoon reduced-sodium soy sauce
2 teaspoons cornstarch
¼ cup water
1½ cups chicken broth or stock
4 split chicken breast halves, skinned and boned

In small saucepan, combine mandarin oranges, water chestnuts, brown sugar, vinegar, soy sauce and cornstarch dissolved in ¼ cup water. Cook until mixture becomes clear and thickens, about 4 to 5 minutes, stirring occasionally. Remove from heat. In large skillet, bring broth to a simmer. Pound chicken breasts with meat mallet to ½-inch thickness. Place chicken in skillet; cover and simmer over medium-low heat about 8 to 10 minutes or until chicken is no longer pink in center. Remove chicken from poaching liquid. Place on serving platter. Heat sauce if needed; spoon sauce over chicken.

Makes 4 servings

NUTRIENTS PER SERVING			
Calories	253	Fat	5 g
Cholesterol	73 mg	Sodium	755 mg

Skillet Chicken Pot Pie

1   can (10¾ ounces) fat-free reduced-sodium cream of chicken
     soup
1¼ cups skim milk, divided
1   package (10 ounces) frozen mixed vegetables
2   cups diced cooked chicken
½   teaspoon ground black pepper
1   cup buttermilk biscuit baking mix
¼   teaspoon summer savory or parsley

1. Heat soup, 1 cup milk, vegetables, chicken and pepper in medium skillet over medium heat until mixture comes to a boil.

2. Combine biscuit mix and summer savory in small bowl. Stir in 3 to 4 tablespoons milk just until soft batter is formed. Drop batter by tablespoonfuls onto chicken mixture to make 6 dumplings. Partially cover and simmer 12 minutes or until dumplings are cooked through, spooning liquid from pot pie over dumplings once or twice during cooking. Garnish with additional summer savory, if desired.

Makes 6 servings

NUTRIENTS PER SERVING			
Calories	241	Fat	5 g
Cholesterol	33 mg	Sodium	422 mg

Skillet Chicken Pot Pie

Tomato Chutney Chicken

4 broiler-fryer chicken breast halves, boned, skinned
1 can (16 ounces) tomatoes with juice, cut up
1 cup peeled and chopped cooking apple
¼ cup chopped onion
¼ cup chopped green bell pepper
¼ cup golden raisins
2 tablespoons brown sugar
2 tablespoons lemon juice
1 teaspoon grated lemon peel
1 clove garlic, minced
¼ teaspoon red pepper flakes
½ teaspoon ground cinnamon
¼ teaspoon salt

In large skillet, place tomatoes, apple, onion, green bell pepper, raisins, brown sugar, lemon juice, lemon peel, garlic, red pepper flakes and cinnamon; stir to mix. Cook, stirring, over medium-high heat until mixture boils. Sprinkle salt over chicken breasts. Place chicken over tomato mixture. Reduce heat to medium-low; cover and cook, stirring and turning frequently, about 15 minutes or until chicken is fork-tender. Arrange chicken on serving platter; spoon sauce over chicken.

Makes 4 servings

NUTRIENTS PER SERVING			
Calories	230	Fat	4 g
Cholesterol	68 mg	Sodium	364 mg

Favorite recipe from **Delmarva Poultry Industry, Inc.**

Tomato Chutney Chicken

Chicken Chop Suey

1 package (1 ounce) dried black Chinese mushrooms
3 tablespoons reduced-sodium soy sauce
1 tablespoon cornstarch
1 pound boneless skinless chicken breasts or thighs
2 cloves garlic, minced
1 tablespoon peanut or vegetable oil
½ cup thinly sliced celery
½ cup sliced water chestnuts
½ cup bamboo shoots
1 cup chicken broth
   Hot cooked white rice or chow mein noodles
   Thinly sliced green onions (optional)

Place mushrooms in small bowl; cover with warm water. Soak 20 minutes to soften. Drain; squeeze out excess water. Discard stems; quarter caps.

Blend soy sauce with cornstarch in cup until smooth.

Cut chicken into 1-inch pieces; toss with garlic in small bowl. Heat wok or large skillet over medium-high heat; add oil. Add chicken mixture and celery; stir-fry 2 minutes. Add water chestnuts and bamboo shoots; stir-fry 1 minute. Add broth and mushrooms; cook and stir 3 minutes or until chicken is no longer pink.

Stir soy sauce mixture and add to wok. Cook and stir 1 to 2 minutes until sauce boils and thickens. Serve over rice. Garnish with green onions, if desired.

Makes 4 servings

NUTRIENTS PER SERVING			
Calories	208	Fat	6 g
Cholesterol	58 mg	Sodium	657 mg

Chicken Chop Suey

Grilled Chicken Sienna

1   package (about 1¼ pounds) PERDUE® Fit 'n Easy® fresh
      skinless & boneless chicken breasts & thighs
2   tablespoons lemon juice
1   tablespoon olive oil
1   teaspoon dried Italian herb seasoning
      Salt and ground pepper to taste
      Pinch sugar
1   cup seeded and finely diced tomato
3   cups arugula leaves, well washed

Trim off and discard visible fat from chicken. In shallow baking dish, combine lemon juice, olive oil and Italian seasoning. Add chicken; cover and marinate in refrigerator 1 to 2 hours. Add pinch of salt, pepper and sugar to tomato; set aside.

Prepare outdoor grill or preheat broiler. Drain chicken, reserving marinade. Grill or broil chicken 6 to 8 inches from heat source 15 to 25 minutes until cooked through. Meanwhile, in small saucepan, bring marinade to a boil. Turn chicken 2 to 3 times during cooking and brush with boiled marinade. Slice chicken and arrange on bed of arugula; top with tomato mixture.

Makes 6 servings

NUTRIENTS PER SERVING			
Calories	139	Fat	5 g
Cholesterol	67 mg	Sodium	85 mg

Grilled Chicken Sienna

Busy Day Oven-Fried Chicken Breasts

¾ cup plain dry bread crumbs
¼ cup all-purpose flour
1 teaspoon paprika
1 teaspoon poultry seasoning
1 teaspoon onion salt
½ teaspoon garlic powder
½ teaspoon dried thyme leaves
¼ teaspoon pepper
1 tablespoon plus 1½ teaspoons CRISCO® Oil
4 whole chicken breasts, skinned and split (about 4 pounds)

1. Heat oven to 400°F.

2. Combine bread crumbs, flour, paprika, poultry seasoning, onion salt, garlic powder, thyme and pepper in shallow dish. Stir with fork until well blended. Add oil gradually. Toss with fork to blend.

3. Moisten chicken with water. Roll in coating mixture. Place in single layer in 15½×10½×¾-inch jelly roll pan or other large shallow pan. Sprinkle any remaining crumb mixture over chicken.

4. Bake at 400°F for 30 minutes or until chicken is no longer pink in center.

Makes 8 servings

NUTRIENTS PER SERVING			
Calories	200	Fat	5 g
Cholesterol	65 mg	Sodium	145 mg

Carefree Golden Oven Stew

4   small chicken breast halves, skinned
1   lemon, halved
½   teaspoon salt
1/16 teaspoon pepper
1   Golden Delicious apple, sliced
1   small onion, sliced lengthwise
1   cup mushrooms, halved
½   cup sliced carrots
⅔   cup chicken broth
¼   cup white wine
1   teaspoon dried tarragon leaves, crushed
1   teaspoon fresh chopped parsley

Rub chicken with lemon and let stand 15 minutes. Sprinkle with salt and pepper. Place chicken breasts in 2-quart baking dish. Add apple, onion, mushrooms and carrots. In separate bowl combine chicken broth, wine and tarragon; pour over chicken mixture. Sprinkle with parsley. Bake, covered, at 350°F about 1 hour or until chicken is tender.   *Makes 4 servings*

NUTRIENTS PER SERVING			
Calories	255	Fat	8 g
Cholesterol	83 mg	Sodium	517 mg

Favorite recipe from **Washington Apple Commission**

Chicken Florentine with Lemon Mustard Sauce

2   whole boneless skinless chicken breasts, halved (1 pound)
¼   cup EGG BEATERS® Healthy Real Egg Product
½   cup plain dry bread crumbs
1   teaspoon dried basil leaves
1   teaspoon garlic powder
2   tablespoons FLEISCHMANN'S® Sweet Unsalted Margarine,
      divided
⅓   cup water
2   tablespoons GREY POUPON® Dijon Mustard
2   tablespoons lemon juice
1   tablespoon sugar
1   (10-ounce) package frozen chopped spinach, cooked, well
      drained and kept warm

Pound chicken breasts to ¼-inch thickness. Pour Egg Beaters® into shallow bowl. Combine bread crumbs, basil and garlic. Dip chicken breasts into Egg Beaters®, then coat with bread crumb mixture.

In large nonstick skillet, over medium-high heat, melt 1 tablespoon margarine. Add chicken; cook for 5 to 7 minutes on each side or until browned and no longer pink in center. Remove chicken from skillet; keep warm. In same skillet, melt remaining margarine; stir in water, mustard, lemon juice and sugar. Simmer 1 minute or until thickened. To serve, arrange chicken on serving platter. Top with spinach; drizzle with lemon-mustard sauce. Garnish as desired.   *Makes 4 servings*

Prep time: 25 minutes
Cook time: 15 minutes

NUTRIENTS PER SERVING			
Calories	278	Fat	8 g
Cholesterol	69 mg	Sodium	468 mg

Chicken Florentine with Lemon Mustard Sauce

SMUCKER'S® Orange Chili Barbecue Sauce

1 cup SMUCKER'S® Sweet Orange Marmalade
1 cup tomato sauce or crushed tomatoes packed in
    tomato purée
2 tablespoons red wine vinegar
2 tablespoons chili powder
1 teaspoon ground cumin
1 teaspoon chopped garlic
½ teaspoon salt
¼ teaspoon ground red pepper or hot pepper sauce (for a
    spicier sauce)

Combine all ingredients in a small saucepan and mix well. Heat the sauce until it comes to a boil, stirring constantly. Simmer for 1 minute.

Use the sauce immediately as a marinade and baste for grilled chicken, ribs, beef or pork. Or, cool and store in the refrigerator for future use.

Makes 6 servings

Microwave Directions: Combine all ingredients in a microwave-safe bowl. Cover with plastic wrap and heat on HIGH (100% power) for 2 minutes. Stir; cover and heat for 1 minute.

Prep time: 5 minutes
Cook time: 1 to 2 minutes

NUTRIENTS PER SERVING			
Calories	160	Fat	1 g
Cholesterol	0 mg	Sodium	459 mg

Honey-Orange Chicken Legs

4   whole broiler-fryer chicken legs (thigh and drumstick
    attached), skinned, fat trimmed
½   teaspoon salt
¼   teaspoon pepper
6   tablespoons orange juice
4   teaspoons honey
1½   teaspoons Worcestershire sauce
½   teaspoon dry mustard

In baking pan, place chicken in single layer. Sprinkle salt and pepper over chicken. Bake in 350°F oven 25 minutes. In small dish, mix together orange juice, honey, Worcestershire sauce and mustard. Spoon sauce over chicken. Bake, basting frequently, 30 minutes more or until chicken is brown and fork-tender.

Makes 4 servings

NUTRIENTS PER SERVING			
Calories	193	Fat	5 g
Cholesterol	104 mg	Sodium	398 mg

Favorite recipe from **Delmarva Poultry Industry, Inc.**

Oven Chicken & Rice

1   package (4.3 ounces) RICE-A-RONI® Long Grain & Wild Rice
    Pilaf
4   bone-in chicken breast halves
½   teaspoon dried thyme leaves or dried basil leaves
¼   teaspoon garlic powder
1   tablespoon margarine or butter, melted
½   teaspoon paprika
1   cup chopped tomato or red bell pepper

1. Heat oven to 375°F. In 11×7-inch glass baking dish or 1½-quart casserole, combine 1¼ cups water, rice and contents of seasoning packet; mix well.

2. Place chicken over rice. Sprinkle evenly with thyme and garlic powder. Brush with margarine; sprinkle with paprika. Cover with foil; bake 45 minutes. Stir in tomato. Bake, uncovered, 15 minutes or until liquid is absorbed and chicken is no longer pink in center. *Makes 4 servings*

NUTRIENTS PER SERVING			
Calories	280	Fat	5 g
Cholesterol	70 mg	Sodium	1,000 mg

Chicken Breasts with Orange Basil Pesto

½ cup fresh basil leaves
2 tablespoons grated orange peel
2 cloves garlic
3 tablespoons Florida orange juice
1 tablespoon Dijon mustard
2 teaspoons olive oil
6 chicken breast halves

Preheat broiler. Place basil, orange peel and garlic in food processor; process until finely chopped. Add orange juice, mustard, oil, and salt and pepper to taste; process several seconds or until paste forms. Spread equal amounts of basil mixture under skin and on bone side of each chicken breast. Place chicken, skin-side down, on broiler pan; place pan 4 inches from heat source. Broil 10 minutes. Turn chicken over and broil 10 to 12 minutes or until chicken is no longer pink in center. If chicken browns too quickly, cover with foil. Remove skin from chicken before serving. *Makes 6 servings*

NUTRIENTS PER SERVING			
Calories	206	Fat	6 g
Cholesterol	91 mg	Sodium	113 mg

Favorite recipe from **Florida Department of Citrus**

Mexican Lasagna

½ pound lean ground turkey
½ cup chopped onion
½ cup chopped bell pepper
½ teaspoon black pepper
½ teaspoon dried basil leaves, crushed
1 can (8 ounces) low sodium tomato sauce
1 cup GUILTLESS GOURMET® Salsa (mild, medium or hot),
      divided
1 cup low fat cottage cheese
½ cup GUILTLESS GOURMET® Nacho Dip (mild or spicy)
      Nonstick cooking spray
1 bag (7 ounces) GUILTLESS GOURMET® Unsalted Baked
      Tortilla Chips, crushed*
      Carrot strip and fresh parsley sprig (optional)

Preheat oven to 350°F. Cook turkey, onion, bell pepper, black pepper and basil in nonstick skillet over medium heat until turkey is no longer pink, breaking up meat and stirring occasionally. Stir in tomato sauce and ½ cup salsa; remove from heat. Combine cottage cheese and nacho dip in small bowl. Coat 8×8-inch baking dish with cooking spray. Set aside.

To assemble lasagna, place ⅓ of crushed chips in bottom of prepared dish, spreading to cover. Top with half the turkey mixture. Spread half the cheese mixture over turkey mixture. Repeat layers once. Top with remaining crushed chips; pour remaining salsa evenly over chips. Bake 30 minutes or until heated through. Let stand 10 minutes before serving. Garnish with carrot and parsley.

Makes 4 servings

*Crush tortilla chips in the original bag or crush between two pieces of waxed paper with a rolling pin.

NUTRIENTS PER SERVING			
Calories	257	Fat	2 g
Cholesterol	20 mg	Sodium	495 mg

Mexican Lasagna

Turkey Gyros

1 turkey tenderloin (8 ounces)
1½ teaspoons Greek seasoning
1 cucumber
⅔ cup plain nonfat yogurt
¼ cup finely chopped onion
2 teaspoons dried dill weed
2 teaspoons fresh lemon juice
1 teaspoon olive oil
4 pita breads
1½ cups washed and shredded romaine lettuce
1 tomato, thinly sliced
2 tablespoons crumbled feta cheese

1. Cut turkey tenderloin across the grain into ¼-inch slices. Place turkey slices on plate; lightly sprinkle both sides with Greek seasoning. Let stand 5 minutes.

2. Cut two-thirds of cucumber into thin slices. Finely chop remaining cucumber. Combine chopped cucumber, yogurt, onion, dill weed and lemon juice in small bowl.

3. Heat olive oil in large skillet over medium heat until hot. Add turkey. Cook 2 minutes on each side or until cooked through. Wrap 2 pita breads in paper toweling. Microwave at HIGH (100% power) 30 seconds or just until warmed. Repeat with remaining pita breads. Divide lettuce, tomato, cucumber slices, turkey, cheese and yogurt-cucumber sauce evenly among pita breads. Fold edges over and secure with wooden picks. *Makes 4 servings*

NUTRIENTS PER SERVING			
Calories	319	Fat	4 g
Cholesterol	55 mg	Sodium	477 mg

Turkey Gyro

Barbecue Bacon Meatloaf

  2 packages (1 pound each) LOUIS RICH® Ground Turkey
 12 slices LOUIS RICH® Turkey Bacon, diced
  1 cup quick-cooking oats, uncooked
  1 medium onion, finely chopped
 ½ cup barbecue sauce
  2 large egg whites
  1 tablespoon Worcestershire sauce

Mix all ingredients in large bowl. Press mixture into ungreased 9×5-inch loaf pan. Top with additional barbecue sauce, if desired. Bake at 375°F for 1 hour 15 minutes. Allow to stand 10 minutes before slicing.   *Makes 10 servings*

Note: Meatloaf ingredients may be combined 1 day ahead and refrigerated. Bake at 375°F for 1½ hours.

NUTRIENTS PER SERVING			
Calories	215	Fat	9 g
Cholesterol	70 mg	Sodium	525 mg

Spiced Turkey, Squash and Apple Medley

 1½ pounds Turkey Thighs, skin removed
  1 pound acorn squash, cut crosswise into 1-inch rings
  1 pound cooking apples, cored and cut crosswise into ½-inch rings
 ¼ cup apple juice
  3 tablespoons packed brown sugar
 ½ teaspoon ground cinnamon
 ¼ teaspoon ground nutmeg

1. Place turkey thighs to one side of 13×9×2-inch baking dish. Alternately layer squash and apple rings in other side of dish.

2. Combine apple juice, brown sugar and spices; pour over turkey, squash and apples. Cover with foil and bake 1 hour in 350°F oven; uncover and baste with juices. Bake, uncovered, 15 minutes or until internal temperature of thighs registers 180°F on meat thermometer. *Makes 4 servings*

NUTRIENTS PER SERVING			
Calories	283	Fat	5 g
Cholesterol	85 mg	Sodium	97 mg

Favorite recipe from **National Turkey Federation**

Barbecued Turkey Tenderloins

1½ cups (12-ounce can) lemon-lime soda
¼ cup soy sauce
¼ cup vegetable oil
1 teaspoon horseradish powder
1 teaspoon garlic powder
1 pound Turkey Tenderloins, cut in half lengthwise
 Nonstick cooking spray

1. Combine soda, soy sauce, oil, horseradish powder and garlic powder in resealable plastic freezer bag. Add turkey tenderloins; seal bag and turn to coat. Refrigerate at least 2 hours. Remove grill rack from charcoal grill and lightly coat with cooking spray; set aside. Preheat grill for direct-heat cooking.

2. Position grill rack over hot coals. Remove turkey from bag and discard marinade. Place turkey tenderloins on grill rack and cook 5 to 6 minutes per side or until turkey is no longer pink in center. *Makes 4 servings*

NUTRIENTS PER SERVING			
Calories	157	Fat	4 g
Cholesterol	70 mg	Sodium	242 mg

Favorite recipe from **National Turkey Federation**

Fusilli Pizzaiola with Turkey Meatballs

1   pound ground turkey breast
1   egg, lightly beaten
1   tablespoon skim milk
¼   cup Italian-seasoned dry bread crumbs
2   tablespoons chopped fresh parsley
¼   teaspoon ground black pepper, divided
½   cup *each* chopped onion and grated carrots
1   clove garlic, minced
2   teaspoons olive oil
2   cans (14½ ounces each) no-salt-added tomatoes, undrained
2   tablespoons chopped fresh basil
1   tablespoon no-salt-added tomato paste
½   teaspoon dried thyme leaves
1   bay leaf
8   ounces uncooked fusilli or other spiral-shaped pasta

1. Preheat oven to 350°F. Combine turkey, egg and milk; blend in bread crumbs, parsley and ⅛ teaspoon black pepper. With wet hands, shape mixture into small balls. Spray baking sheet with nonstick cooking spray. Arrange meatballs on baking sheet. Bake 25 minutes or until no longer pink in center.

2. Place onion, carrots, garlic and oil in saucepan. Cook and stir over high heat 5 minutes. Add tomatoes, basil, tomato paste, thyme, bay leaf and remaining ⅛ teaspoon black pepper; bring to a boil. Simmer 25 minutes over low heat; add meatballs. Cover; simmer until sauce thickens slightly. Discard bay leaf.

3. Cook pasta according to package directions, omitting salt. Drain. Place in serving bowl; top with meatballs and sauce.   *Makes 4 servings*

NUTRIENTS PER SERVING			
Calories	330	Fat	10 g
Cholesterol	116 mg	Sodium	111 mg

Fusilli Pizzaiola with Turkey Meatballs

Seafood

• • • • • • • • •

Shrimp in Tomatillo Sauce over Rice

 1 teaspoon olive oil
 ¼ cup chopped onion
 1 cup GUILTLESS GOURMET® Green Tomatillo Salsa
 ¾ cup white wine
    Juice of ½ lemon
12 ounces medium-size raw shrimp, peeled and deveined
 4 cups hot cooked white rice
    Lemon peel strip (optional)

Heat oil in large nonstick skillet over medium-high heat until hot. Add onion; cook and stir until onion is translucent. Add salsa, wine and juice, stirring just until mixture begins to boil. Reduce heat to medium-low; simmer 10 minutes. Add shrimp; cook about 2 minutes or until shrimp turn pink and opaque, stirring occasionally. To serve, place 1 cup rice in each of 4 individual serving bowls. Pour shrimp mixture evenly over rice. Garnish with lemon peel, if desired.

Makes 4 servings

NUTRIENTS PER SERVING			
Calories	274	Fat	2 g
Cholesterol	130 mg	Sodium	479 mg

Shrimp in Tomatillo Sauce over Rice

Broccoli, Scallop and Linguine Toss

12   ounces fresh or frozen scallops
2   medium onions, cut in half lengthwise and sliced
1   cup apple juice
2   tablespoons dry white wine
2   cloves garlic, minced
2   teaspoons dried marjoram leaves
1   teaspoon dried basil leaves
¼   teaspoon pepper
3   cups broccoli flowerets
¼   cup water
4   teaspoons cornstarch
1½   cups chopped seeded tomatoes
¼   cup grated Parmesan cheese
4   cups cooked linguine

Cut large scallops into 1-inch pieces. Combine onions, apple juice, wine, garlic, marjoram, basil and pepper in large skillet. Bring to a boil over high heat. Add broccoli; return to a boil. Reduce heat to medium-low. Cover and simmer 7 minutes; add scallops. Return to a boil; reduce heat. Cover and simmer 1 to 2 minutes or until scallops are opaque. Remove scallops and vegetables.

Combine water and cornstarch in small bowl. Stir into mixture in skillet. Cook and stir over medium heat until mixture boils and thickens. Cook and stir 2 minutes more. Stir in tomatoes and cheese; heat through. Return scallops and vegetables to skillet; heat through. Toss mixture with linguine.

Makes 4 servings

NUTRIENTS PER SERVING			
Calories	248	Fat	4 g
Cholesterol	33 mg	Sodium	309 mg

Broccoli, Scallop and Linguine Toss

Shrimp Pita

¾ cup olive oil
½ cup red wine vinegar
2 medium onions, chopped, divided
2 cloves garlic, minced, divided
2 teaspoons Italian seasoning, divided
1 pound medium shrimp, peeled and deveined
2 medium red or green bell peppers, julienned
4 cups fresh spinach leaves, stems removed and torn
3 cups cooked brown rice
1 teaspoon salt
½ teaspoon ground black pepper
3 pieces pita bread (about 6 inches), each cut in half

Combine olive oil, vinegar, ½ cup chopped onion, 1 clove garlic and 1 teaspoon Italian seasoning in large bowl. Add shrimp; stir until well coated. Cover and marinate in refrigerator 4 hours or overnight.

Thoroughly drain shrimp; discard marinade. Heat large skillet over medium-high heat until hot. Add shrimp, remaining onion, bell peppers, spinach and remaining 1 clove garlic; sauté 3 to 5 minutes or until shrimp are no longer pink and spinach is wilted. Add rice, remaining 1 teaspoon Italian seasoning, salt and black pepper. Cook and stir 2 to 3 minutes or until flavors are well blended. To serve, fill each pita with ½ to ¾ cup rice mixture.

Makes 6 servings

NUTRIENTS PER SERVING			
Calories	296	Fat	6 g
Cholesterol	61 mg	Sodium	677 mg

Favorite recipe from USA Rice Council

Shrimp Pita

Barbecued Shrimp with Spicy Rice

1 pound large shrimp, peeled and deveined
4 wooden* or metal skewers
  Vegetable cooking spray
⅓ cup prepared barbecue sauce
  Spicy Rice (recipe follows)

Thread shrimp on skewers. To broil in oven, place on broiler rack coated with cooking spray. Broil 4 to 5 inches from heat 4 minutes. Brush with barbecue sauce. Turn and brush with remaining barbecue sauce. Broil 2 to 4 minutes longer or until shrimp are done. To cook on outdoor grill, cook skewered shrimp over hot coals 4 minutes. Brush with barbecue sauce. Turn and brush with remaining barbecue sauce. Grill 4 to 5 minutes longer or until shrimp are done. Serve with Spicy Rice. *Makes 4 servings*

*Soak wooden skewers in water before using to prevent burning.

SPICY RICE

½ cup sliced green onions
½ cup minced carrots
½ cup minced red bell pepper
1 jalapeño or serrano pepper, minced
1 tablespoon vegetable oil
2 cups cooked rice (cooked in chicken broth)
2 tablespoons snipped cilantro
1 tablespoon lime juice
1 teaspoon soy sauce
  Hot pepper sauce to taste

Cook onions, carrots, bell pepper and jalapeño pepper in oil in large skillet over medium-high heat until tender crisp. Stir in rice, cilantro, lime juice, soy sauce and pepper sauce; cook until thoroughly heated.

continued on page 188

Barbecued Shrimp with Spicy Rice

Barbecued Shrimp with Spicy Rice, continued

Microwave Directions: Combine onions, carrots, bell pepper, jalapeño pepper and oil in 2-quart microproof baking dish. Cook on HIGH (100% power) 2 to 3 minutes or until vegetables are tender crisp. Add rice, cilantro, lime juice, soy sauce and pepper sauce. Cook on HIGH 3 to 4 minutes, stirring after 2 minutes, or until thoroughly heated.

NUTRIENTS PER SERVING			
Calories	285	Fat	5 g
Cholesterol	175 mg	Sodium	839 mg

Favorite recipe from **USA Rice Council**

Spicy Pasta Del Mar

1	medium onion, diced
1	teaspoon olive oil
1	(10-ounce) can baby clams, drained
2	teaspoons minced garlic
1	(26-ounce) jar HEALTHY CHOICE® Traditional Pasta Sauce
1	teaspoon dried basil leaves
½	teaspoon dried thyme leaves
⅛	teaspoon black pepper
⅛	teaspoon cayenne pepper
½	pound raw medium shrimp, peeled and deveined
½	pound linguini, cooked and drained

In large saucepan, sauté onion in hot oil until tender. Add clams and garlic; cook and stir 1 minute longer. Stir in pasta sauce, basil, thyme, black pepper and cayenne pepper. Heat, stirring occasionally, until mixture comes to a boil. Add shrimp; reduce heat to medium. Cook until shrimp are pink and cooked through. Serve sauce over linguini. *Makes 6 servings*

NUTRIENTS PER SERVING			
Calories	278	Fat	3 g
Cholesterol	105 mg	Sodium	520 mg

Shrimp Classico

⅔ cup milk

2 tablespoons margarine or butter

1 package (4.8 ounces) PASTA RONI® Herb Sauce with Angel Hair Pasta

1 clove garlic, minced

1 package (10 ounces) frozen chopped spinach, thawed, well drained

1 package (10 ounces) frozen precooked shrimp, thawed, well drained

1 jar (2 ounces) chopped pimiento, drained

1. In 3-quart round microwavable glass casserole, combine 1⅔ cups water, milk and margarine. Microwave, uncovered, on HIGH 4 to 5 minutes or until boiling.

2. Gradually add pasta while stirring. Separate pasta with a fork, if needed. Stir in contents of seasoning packet and garlic.

3. Microwave, uncovered, on HIGH 4 minutes, stirring gently after 2 minutes. Separate pasta with a fork, if needed. Stir in spinach, shrimp and pimiento. Microwave on HIGH 1 to 2 minutes. Sauce will be very thin, but will thicken upon standing.

4. Let stand, uncovered, 2 minutes or until desired consistency. Stir before serving.

Makes 4 servings

NUTRIENTS PER SERVING			
Calories	290	Fat	10 g
Cholesterol	140 mg	Sodium	725 mg

Butterflied Shrimp Parmesan

1½ pounds large shrimp
1 cup (4 ounces) shredded ALPINE LACE® Fat Free
    Pasteurized Process Skim Milk Cheese Product—For
    Parmesan Lovers
¼ cup Italian seasoned dry bread crumbs
2 tablespoons unsalted butter substitute
¾ cup chopped red bell pepper
½ cup thinly sliced green onions
1 tablespoon minced garlic
⅛ teaspoon crushed red pepper flakes or to taste
⅓ cup minced fresh parsley
6 tablespoons 2% low fat milk

1. Peel the shrimp, leaving the tails on. Then butterfly each shrimp by cutting it along the outer curved edge almost all the way through. Open the shrimp up like a book and remove the dark vein. In a small bowl, toss the cheese with the bread crumbs and set aside.

2. In a large nonstick skillet, melt the butter over medium-high heat. Add the bell pepper, green onions, garlic and red pepper flakes and cook for 5 minutes or until soft. Add the shrimp and sauté for 5 minutes or just until the shrimp turn pink and opaque. Stir in the parsley.

3. In a small saucepan, bring the milk just to a boil, then stir into the shrimp mixture. Stir in the cheese mixture and cook until the cheese is melted. Serve immediately.

Makes 4 servings

NUTRIENTS PER SERVING			
Calories	312	Fat	9 g
Cholesterol	281 mg	Sodium	504 mg

Butterflied Shrimp Parmesan

Seafood Paella

Nonstick cooking spray
1   cup finely chopped red bell pepper
⅔   cup finely chopped onion
1   tablespoon minced garlic
½   teaspoon ground turmeric
½   teaspoon paprika
2   teaspoons vegetable flavor bouillon granules
1½ cups uncooked medium grain white rice
1   cup frozen artichoke hearts, thawed, halved
1   pound medium shrimp, peeled and deveined, cut lengthwise
      in half
½   pound sea scallops, cut into quarters
¾   cup frozen baby lima beans, thawed
½   cup frozen sweet peas, thawed

1. Spray large heavy saucepan or deep skillet with cooking spray; heat over medium-high heat until hot. Add bell pepper, onion and garlic; cook and stir 3 minutes or until vegetables are crisp-tender. Stir in turmeric and paprika.

2. Stir 3¼ cups water and bouillon granules into saucepan; bring to a boil over high heat. Stir in rice and artichoke hearts. Cover; reduce heat to medium-low. Simmer 18 minutes, stirring occasionally.

3. Stir shrimp, scallops, beans and peas into saucepan; cover. Simmer 5 minutes or until seafood is opaque and liquid is absorbed. Remove saucepan from heat. Let stand 5 minutes before serving.   *Makes 6 servings*

NUTRIENTS PER SERVING			
Calories	340	Fat	2 g
Cholesterol	132 mg	Sodium	570 mg

Seafood Paella

Shrimp Curry

1¼ pounds raw large shrimp
1 large onion, chopped
½ cup canned light coconut milk
3 cloves garlic, minced
2 tablespoons finely chopped fresh ginger
2 to 3 teaspoons hot curry powder
¼ teaspoon salt
1 can (14½ ounces) diced tomatoes
1 teaspoon cornstarch
2 tablespoons chopped fresh cilantro
3 cups hot cooked rice

1. Peel shrimp, leaving tails attached and reserving shells. Place shells in large saucepan; cover with water. Bring to a boil over high heat. Reduce heat to low; simmer 15 to 20 minutes. Strain shrimp stock and set aside. Discard shells.

2. Spray large skillet with nonstick cooking spray; heat over medium heat. Add onion; cover and cook 5 minutes. Add coconut milk, garlic, ginger, curry powder, salt and ½ cup shrimp stock; bring to a boil. Reduce heat to low and simmer 10 to 15 minutes or until onion is tender.

3. Add shrimp and tomatoes to skillet; return mixture to a simmer. Cook 3 minutes.

4. Stir cornstarch into 1 tablespoon cooled shrimp stock until dissolved. Add mixture to skillet with cilantro; simmer 1 to 2 minutes or just until slightly thickened, stirring occasionally. Serve over rice. Garnish with carrot and lime slices, if desired.

Makes 6 servings

NUTRIENTS PER SERVING			
Calories	219	Fat	2 g
Cholesterol	145 mg	Sodium	369 mg

Angel Hair Pasta with Seafood Sauce

½ pound firm whitefish, such as sea bass, monkfish or grouper
2 teaspoons olive oil
½ cup chopped onion
2 cloves garlic, minced
3 pounds fresh plum tomatoes, seeded and chopped
¼ cup chopped fresh basil
2 tablespoons chopped fresh oregano
1 teaspoon red pepper flakes
½ teaspoon sugar
2 bay leaves
½ pound fresh bay scallops or shucked oysters
8 ounces uncooked angel hair pasta
2 tablespoons chopped fresh parsley

1. Cut whitefish into ¾-inch pieces. Set aside.

2. Heat oil in large nonstick skillet over medium heat; add onion and garlic. Cook and stir 3 minutes or until onion is tender. Reduce heat to low; add tomatoes, basil, oregano, crushed red pepper flakes, sugar and bay leaves. Cook, uncovered, 15 minutes, stirring occasionally.

3. Add whitefish and scallops. Cook, uncovered, 3 to 4 minutes or until fish flakes easily when tested with fork and scallops are opaque. Remove bay leaves; discard. Set seafood sauce aside.

4. Cook pasta according to package directions, omitting salt. Drain well.

5. Combine pasta with seafood sauce in large serving bowl. Mix well. Sprinkle with parsley. Serve immediately. *Makes 6 servings*

NUTRIENTS PER SERVING			
Calories	272	Fat	5 g
Cholesterol	31 mg	Sodium	134 mg

Angel Hair Pasta with Seafood Sauce

SMUCKER'S® Mandarin Shrimp and Vegetable Stir Fry

1 cup SMUCKER'S® Orange Marmalade
3 tablespoons soy sauce
2 tablespoons white vinegar
2 teaspoons hot pepper sauce
4½ teaspoons cornstarch
2 tablespoons vegetable oil
1 tablespoon fresh ginger, chopped
1 tablespoon garlic, chopped
24 fresh jumbo shrimp, peeled and deveined
1 red bell pepper, chopped
1 yellow or green bell pepper, chopped
3 cups broccoli florets (about 1 bunch)
½ cup water
1 cup scallions, chopped (about 1 bunch)

Combine the Smucker's® Orange Marmalade, soy sauce, vinegar, hot pepper sauce and cornstarch in a small bowl. Stir to dissolve the cornstarch and set aside.

Place a large skillet or wok over high heat. Heat the pan for 1 minute, then add the vegetable oil. Heat the oil for 30 seconds, then add the ginger, garlic and shrimp. Stir-fry for 2 to 3 minutes until the shrimp begin to turn rosy pink in color. Remove the shrimp from the pan and set aside.

Add the peppers and broccoli florets to the pan and cook on high heat for 1 minute. Add the water; cover and reduce heat to medium. Cook the vegetables 4 to 5 minutes or until tender.

Uncover pan and increase the heat to high. Add shrimp and Smucker's® Orange Marmalade mixture. Cook shrimp for another 2 minutes until sauce is thickened and the shrimp are completely cooked. Correct seasoning with salt and fresh ground black pepper as needed.

Stir in the scallions and serve with boiled rice. *Makes 4 to 6 servings*

NUTRIENTS PER SERVING			
Calories	278	Fat	6 g
Cholesterol	62 mg	Sodium	633 mg

Linguine with White Clam Sauce

2   tablespoons CRISCO® Savory Seasonings
      Roasted Garlic Flavor oil
2   cloves garlic, minced
2   cans (6½ ounces each) chopped clams, undrained
½   cup chopped fresh parsley
¼   cup dry white wine
1   teaspoon dried basil leaves
1   pound linguine, cooked (without salt or fat) and well drained

1. Heat oil and garlic in medium skillet on medium heat.

2. Drain clams, reserving liquid. Add reserved liquid and parsley to skillet. Reduce heat to low. Simmer 3 minutes, stirring occasionally.

3. Add clams, wine and basil. Simmer 5 minutes, stirring occasionally. Add to hot linguine. Toss lightly to coat. *Makes 8 servings*

NUTRIENTS PER SERVING			
Calories	185	Fat	5 g
Cholesterol	30 mg	Sodium	55 mg

Chilled Poached Salmon with Cucumber Sauce

1   cup water
½   teaspoon chicken or fish bouillon granules
⅛   teaspoon pepper
4   fresh or thawed frozen pink salmon fillets (about 6 ounces each)
½   cup chopped seeded peeled cucumber
⅓   cup plain low-fat yogurt
2   tablespoons sliced green onion
2   tablespoons nonfat salad dressing or mayonnaise
1   tablespoon chopped fresh cilantro
1   teaspoon Dijon mustard
2   cups shredded lettuce

Combine water, bouillon granules and pepper in large skillet. Bring to a boil over high heat. Carefully place salmon in skillet; return just to a boil. Reduce heat to medium-low. Cover and simmer 8 to 10 minutes or until salmon flakes easily when tested with fork. Remove salmon. Cover and refrigerate.

Meanwhile, combine cucumber, yogurt, onion, salad dressing, cilantro and mustard in small bowl. Cover and refrigerate. Place chilled salmon fillets on lettuce-lined plates. Spoon sauce over salmon.

Makes 4 servings

NUTRIENTS PER SERVING			
Calories	223	Fat	6 g
Cholesterol	89 mg	Sodium	322 mg

Chilled Poached Salmon with Cucumber Sauce

No-Fuss Tuna Quiche

    1   unbaked 9-inch deep-dish pastry shell
 1½   cups low-fat milk
    3   extra large eggs
  ⅓   cup chopped green onions
    1   tablespoon chopped drained pimiento
    1   teaspoon dried basil leaves
  ½   teaspoon salt
    1   can (6 ounces) STARKIST® Tuna, drained and flaked
  ½   cup (2 ounces) shredded low-fat Cheddar cheese
    8   spears (4 inches each) broccoli

Preheat oven to 450°F. Bake pastry shell for 5 minutes; remove to rack to cool. *Reduce oven temperature to 325°F.* For filling, in large bowl whisk together milk and eggs. Stir in onions, pimiento, basil and salt. Fold in tuna and cheese. Pour into prebaked pastry shell. Bake at 325°F for 30 minutes.

Meanwhile, in a saucepan steam broccoli spears over simmering water for 5 minutes. Drain; set aside. After 30 minutes baking time, arrange broccoli spears, spoke-fashion, over quiche. Bake 25 to 35 minutes more or until a knife inserted 2 inches from center comes out clean. Let stand for 5 minutes. Cut into 8 wedges, centering a broccoli spear in each wedge.   *Makes 8 servings*

Note: If desired, 1 cup chopped broccoli may be added to the filling before baking.

NUTRIENTS PER SERVING			
Calories	226	Fat	10 g
Cholesterol	95 mg	Sodium	461 mg

No-Fuss Tuna Quiche

Southern Breaded Catfish

⅓ cup pecan halves
¼ cup cornmeal
2 tablespoons all-purpose flour
1 teaspoon paprika
¼ teaspoon ground red pepper
2 egg whites
4 catfish fillets (about 1 pound)
4 cups cooked rice

1. Place pecans in food processor or blender; process until finely chopped. Combine pecans, cornmeal, flour, paprika and ground red pepper in shallow bowl.

2. Beat egg whites in small bowl with wire whisk until foamy. Dip catfish fillets in pecan mixture, then in egg whites, then again in pecan mixture. Place fillets on plate; cover and refrigerate at least 15 minutes.

3. Spray large nonstick skillet with nonstick cooking spray; heat over medium-high heat. Place catfish fillets in single layer in skillet.

4. Cook fillets 2 minutes per side or until golden brown. Serve over rice. Serve with vegetables and garnish, if desired.

Makes 4 servings

NUTRIENTS PER SERVING			
Calories	297	Fat	8 g
Cholesterol	65 mg	Sodium	76 mg

Southern Breaded Catfish

Snapper Veracruz

Nonstick cooking spray
1 teaspoon olive oil
¼ large onion, thinly sliced
⅓ cup low sodium fish or vegetable broth, defatted*
2 cloves garlic, minced
1 cup GUILTLESS GOURMET® Salsa (mild, medium or hot)
20 ounces fresh red snapper, tilapia, sea bass or halibut fillets

Preheat oven to 400°F. Coat baking dish with cooking spray. (Dish needs to be large enough for fish to fit snugly together.) Heat oil in large nonstick skillet over medium heat until hot. Add onion; cook and stir until onion is translucent. When skillet becomes dry, stir in 3 tablespoons broth. Add garlic; cook and stir 1 minute more. Stir in remaining broth and salsa. Bring mixture to a boil. Reduce heat to low; simmer about 2 minutes or until heated through.

Wash fish thoroughly; pat dry with paper towels. Place in prepared baking dish, overlapping thin edges to obtain an overall equal thickness. Pour and spread salsa mixture over fish.

Bake 15 minutes or until fish turns opaque and flakes easily when tested with fork. Serve hot.

Makes 4 servings

*To defat broth, simply chill the canned broth thoroughly. Open the can and use a spoon to lift out any solid fat floating on the surface of the broth.

NUTRIENTS PER SERVING			
Calories	184	Fat	3 g
Cholesterol	52 mg	Sodium	353 mg

Snapper Veracruz

Golden Apple Stuffed Fillets

1 cup grated, peeled Golden Delicious apple
½ cup grated carrot
½ cup minced green onions
2 tablespoons fresh lemon juice
¼ teaspoon ground ginger
¼ teaspoon ground mustard
¼ teaspoon salt
¼ teaspoon ground black pepper
⅛ teaspoon dried thyme
4 sole, cod or other white fish fillets (4 to 5 ounces each)
¼ cup chicken broth or water

1. Heat oven to 400°F; lightly oil small roasting pan. In medium bowl, combine apple, carrot, green onions, lemon juice, ginger, mustard, salt, pepper and thyme; mix well.

2. Spread apple mixture evenly over length of fillets; carefully roll up from shorter ends. Place stuffed fillets, seam side down, in oiled pan. Pour broth over rolled fillets; cover with aluminum foil and bake 10 to 15 minutes or until fish is opaque and barely flakes. *Makes 4 servings*

Microwave Directions: Prepare apple stuffing mixture and roll up fillets as above. Place stuffed fillets, seam side down, in oiled microwave-safe dish. Pour broth over rolled fillets; cover with waxed paper and microwave on HIGH (100% power) 5 to 7 minutes or until fish is opaque and barely flakes. (If microwave does not have carousel, rotate dish halfway through cooking.)

NUTRIENTS PER SERVING			
Calories	176	Fat	2 g
Cholesterol	75 mg	Sodium	314 mg

Favorite recipe from **Washington Apple Commission**

Ragoût of Tuna

2 cloves garlic, minced, divided
1 or 2 sprigs fresh mint, chopped *or* 1 teaspoon dried mint
      leaves
½ to 1 teaspoon salt, divided
      Pepper to taste
2 to 2½ pounds fresh tuna or swordfish
2 teaspoons olive oil
½ cup dry white wine
2 medium onions, thinly sliced
1 teaspoon sugar
1 pound ripe tomatoes, coarsely chopped
1 cup hot water
4 cups hot cooked noodles or rice (optional)

Combine half of garlic, mint, half of salt and pepper in small bowl. Make about 12 cuts into sides of fish. Insert garlic mixture into each cut. Heat oil over medium-high heat in large nonstick skillet; add fish and brown on both sides. Pour wine over fish; continue cooking, basting with liquid, until wine has completely evaporated, about 5 minutes. Transfer fish to warm casserole.

Add remaining garlic and onions to skillet. Sprinkle with sugar and remaining salt; cook over low heat, about 5 minutes. Return fish to skillet. Add tomatoes and hot water; simmer until fish is cooked through and sauce thickens. To serve, pour sauce over fish and serve remaining sauce with noodles or rice, if desired.

Makes 6 servings

NUTRIENTS PER SERVING			
Calories	224	Fat	3 g
Cholesterol	69 mg	Sodium	243 mg

Favorite recipe from **The Sugar Association, Inc.**

Ragoût of Tuna

Microwave Flounder with Carrots

1 pound carrots, julienned (about 4 large)
2 tablespoons minced parsley
1 teaspoon olive oil
⅛ teaspoon salt
⅛ teaspoon pepper
4 flounder fillets* (4 to 5 ounces each)
2 teaspoons coarse-grain Dijon mustard
1 teaspoon honey

Combine carrots, parsley, oil, salt and pepper in 11×7×2-inch microwave-safe baking dish. Cover with waxed paper. Microwave at HIGH (100% power) 5 minutes, stirring once.

Fold thin fillets in half to give all fillets even thickness. Place fillets over carrots in corners of dish with thick parts toward outside and thin parts toward center. Combine mustard and honey; spread over fillets.

Cover with waxed paper. Microwave at HIGH 2 minutes. Rotate fillets, placing cooked parts toward the center; continue to cook 1 to 3 minutes longer or just until fish flakes easily when tested with a fork. Let stand, covered, 2 minutes. Arrange fish and carrots on 4 warm plates. *Makes 4 servings*

*Or, substitute other fish fillets, such as tilapia, sole, cod, catfish, halibut, ocean perch, trout, orange roughy or pollock.

NUTRIENTS PER SERVING			
(4 ounces)			
Calories	170	Fat	3 g
Cholesterol	54 mg	Sodium	229 mg

Favorite recipe from **National Fisheries Institute**

Microwave Flounder with Carrots

Salmon Steaks with Lemon Dill Sauce

½ cup finely chopped red onion
2 teaspoons FLEISCHMANN'S® Margarine
2 tablespoons all-purpose flour
1⅓ cups skim milk
½ cup EGG BEATERS® Healthy Real Egg Product
2 teaspoons grated lemon peel
¼ cup lemon juice
2 teaspoons dried dill weed
8 (½-inch-thick) salmon steaks (2 pounds)
Fresh dill sprigs, for garnish

In small saucepan, over low heat, sauté onion in margarine until tender-crisp. Stir in flour; cook for 1 minute. Over medium heat, gradually stir in milk; cook, stirring until mixture thickens and boils. Boil, stirring constantly, for 1 minute; remove from heat. Whisk in Egg Beaters®, lemon peel, lemon juice and dried dill; return to heat. Cook, stirring constantly until thickened. *Do not boil.*

Meanwhile, grill or broil salmon steaks for 3 to 5 minutes on each side or until fish flakes easily when tested with fork. Top with sauce. Garnish with dill sprigs. *Makes 8 servings*

Prep time: 15 minutes
Cook time: 15 minutes

NUTRIENTS PER SERVING			
Calories	255	Fat	11 g
Cholesterol	83 mg	Sodium	118 mg

Salmon Steak with Lemon Dill Sauce

Wisconsin Tuna Cakes with Lemon-Dill Sauce

1 can (12 ounces) STARKIST® Tuna, drained and finely flaked
¾ cup seasoned bread crumbs
¼ cup minced green onions
2 tablespoons chopped drained pimientos
1 egg
½ cup low-fat milk
½ teaspoon grated lemon peel
2 tablespoons margarine or butter

LEMON–DILL SAUCE
¼ cup chicken broth
1 tablespoon lemon juice
¼ teaspoon dried dill weed
Hot steamed shredded zucchini and carrots
Lemon slices

In large bowl, toss together tuna, bread crumbs, onions and pimientos. In small bowl, beat together egg and milk; stir in lemon peel. Stir into tuna mixture; toss until moistened. With lightly floured hands, shape into eight 4-inch patties.

In large nonstick skillet, melt margarine. Fry patties, a few at a time, until golden brown on both sides, about 3 minutes per side. Place on ovenproof platter in 300°F oven until ready to serve.

For Lemon-Dill Sauce, in small saucepan, heat broth, lemon juice and dill. Serve tuna cakes with zucchini and carrots; spoon sauce over cakes. Garnish with lemon slices.   *Makes 4 servings*

NUTRIENTS PER SERVING			
(2 patties plus 1 tablespoon sauce)			
Calories	278	Fat	10 g
Cholesterol	85 mg	Sodium	576 mg

Wisconsin Tuna Cakes with Lemon-Dill Sauce

Salads

• • • • • • • • •

Mediterranean Pasta Salad

1 package (8 ounces) refrigerated or frozen cheese tortellini
1 package (9 ounces) DOLE® Italian Style Vegetables
1 can (8 ounces) DOLE® Pineapple Chunks
2 tablespoons balsamic or red wine vinegar
1 tablespoon olive or vegetable oil
¼ pound fresh link turkey sausage, cooked, drained and sliced
1 medium DOLE® Red, Yellow or Green Bell Pepper, cubed

• **Prepare** tortellini according to package directions, adding Italian Style Vegetables (reserve seasoning packet) during last 2 minutes of cooking. Meanwhile, prepare dressing.

• **Drain** pineapple; reserve ¼ cup juice.

• **Combine** reserved juice, vinegar, oil and tomato basil seasoning packet from vegetable package in large serving bowl.

• **Drain** tortellini and vegetables. Add tortellini, vegetables, sausage, bell pepper and pineapple to dressing; toss well to evenly coat. Serve at room temperature or chilled. Toss before serving. *Makes 6 servings*

Prep time: 10 minutes
Cook time: 20 minutes

NUTRIENTS PER SERVING			
Calories	184	Fat	5 g
Cholesterol	19 mg	Sodium	290 mg

Mediterranean Pasta Salad

Hot to Go Thai Salad

¾ pound sirloin steak
⅓ cup vegetable oil, divided
⅓ cup rice vinegar*
¼ cup reduced-sodium soy sauce
1 fresh jalapeño or serrano pepper, finely chopped, divided
2 cloves garlic, minced
1 tablespoon minced fresh gingerroot
½ teaspoon red pepper flakes
1 (9-ounce) package French-style green beans, thawed and drained
2 carrots, halved and thinly sliced
1 cucumber, peeled, seeded and sliced
4 cups cooked brown rice
Chopped fresh mint leaves (optional)

Partially freeze steak; slice across grain into ¼-inch strips. Place in large bowl. Combine all but 1 tablespoon oil, vinegar, soy sauce, ½ of the jalapeño, garlic, gingerroot and red pepper flakes in small bowl. Pour mixture over beef; marinate 1 hour. Drain beef; discard marinade. Heat remaining 1 tablespoon oil in large skillet over medium-high heat until hot. Add beef and remaining jalapeño; cook 3 to 5 minutes or until no longer pink. Combine beef, liquid from skillet, beans, carrots, cucumber and rice in large bowl. Toss to coat. Sprinkle with mint, if desired. *Makes 6 servings*

*White wine vinegar may be substituted.

NUTRIENTS PER SERVING			
Calories	296	Fat	8 g
Cholesterol	38 mg	Sodium	565 mg

Favorite recipe from **USA Rice Council**

218

Three-Pepper Tuna Salad

2 cups thinly sliced zucchini
½ cup red bell pepper strips
½ cup green bell pepper strips
½ cup yellow bell pepper strips
1 cup cherry tomatoes, halved
1 can (6 ounces) solid albacore tuna packed in water, drained
¼ cup chopped green onions with tops
¼ cup chopped fresh basil
2½ tablespoons red wine vinegar
1 tablespoon olive oil
½ teaspoon minced fresh garlic
½ teaspoon fresh marjoram
⅛ teaspoon ground black pepper

1. Pour ¾ cup water into medium saucepan. Add zucchini and bell pepper strips. Steam vegetables about 10 minutes or until crisp-tender. Remove from heat; drain any excess water. Transfer to serving bowl. Add tomatoes, tuna, green onions and basil.

2. Combine vinegar, oil, garlic, marjoram and black pepper in jar or bottle with tight-fitting lid; shake well. Pour dressing over vegetable mixture; mix well. Garnish as desired.

Makes 4 servings

NUTRIENTS PER SERVING			
Calories	134	Fat	5 g
Cholesterol	18 mg	Sodium	175 mg

Three-Pepper Tuna Salad

Healthy Chef's Salad

PEPPER CRÈME DRESSING

⅔ cup reduced caloric mayonnaise
⅔ cup fat free sour cream
⅓ cup bottled chili sauce
⅓ cup chopped red bell pepper
¼ cup minced chives or green onions
2 tablespoons fresh lemon juice
½ teaspoon freshly ground black pepper

CHEF'S SALAD

12 cups washed and coarsely torn mixed salad greens
  (leaf lettuce, romaine and endive)
1 small cucumber, halved lengthwise and thinly sliced
⅓ cup finely chopped green onions, divided
1 cup cooked corn kernels
1 cup cooked green peas
3 cups peeled and grated carrots
4 medium-size ripe tomatoes, cut into wedges
12 ounces skinless roasted turkey breast, cut into thin strips
6 ounces ALPINE LACE® Boneless Cooked Ham, cut into thin
  strips
6 ounces ALPINE LACE® Reduced Fat Swiss Cheese, cut into
  thin strips
6 ounces roast beef, cut into thin strips (optional)
2 large eggs, hard-cooked, peeled and thinly sliced (optional)

1. To make the Pepper Crème Dressing: In a medium-size bowl, whisk all of the dressing ingredients together until well blended.

2. To make the Chef's Salad: In a large, shallow salad bowl, toss the greens, cucumber, half of the green onions, the corn and peas. Mound the carrots in

continued on page 224

Healthy Chef's Salad

Healthy Chef's Salad, continued

the center and arrange the tomatoes around the edge. In a spoke design, alternately arrange on the greens the turkey, ham and cheese, plus the beef and eggs, if you wish. Sprinkle with the remaining green onions and serve with the dressing.   *Makes 10 luncheon servings or 6 supper servings*

NUTRIENTS PER SERVING			
Calories	262	Fat	10 g
Cholesterol	49 mg	Sodium	515 mg

Smoked Turkey & Fruit Salad

1   package (16 ounces) DOLE® Classic Blend Salad
1   can (11 ounces) DOLE® Mandarin Oranges, drained
4   ounces deli-sliced smoked turkey or chicken, cut into ½-inch slices
½   cup DOLE® Golden or Seedless Raisins
½   cup fat free or light ranch salad dressing
1   can (20 ounces) DOLE® Pineapple Slices, drained and cut in half

• **Toss** together salad, mandarin oranges, turkey and raisins in large bowl. Pour in dressing; toss well to evenly coat.

• **Spoon** salad onto large serving platter. Arrange halved pineapple slices around salad.   *Makes 4 servings*

Prep time: 15 minutes

NUTRIENTS PER SERVING			
Calories	160	Fat	1 g
Cholesterol	8 mg	Sodium	413 mg

Nacho Salad

3 ounces (about 60) GUILTLESS GOURMET® Unsalted Baked
   Tortilla Chips
2 teaspoons water
½ cup GUILTLESS GOURMET® Black Bean Dip (mild or spicy)
½ cup GUILTLESS GOURMET® Nacho Dip (mild or spicy)
4 cups shredded romaine lettuce
2 medium tomatoes (red or yellow), chopped
½ cup GUILTLESS GOURMET® Green Tomatillo Salsa

Divide and spread tortilla chips among 4 plates. Stir water into bean dip in
small microwave-safe bowl or small saucepan. Microwave bean dip on HIGH
(100% power) 2 to 3 minutes or heat over medium heat until warm. Heat nacho
dip in separate small microwave-safe bowl or small saucepan as directed above.
Evenly drizzle heated dips over tortilla chips. Sprinkle lettuce and tomatoes
evenly over tortilla chips. To serve, spoon 2 tablespoons tomatillo salsa over
each salad.

Makes 4 servings

NUTRIENTS PER SERVING			
Calories	171	Fat	<1 g
Cholesterol	0 mg	Sodium	445 mg

Nacho Salad

Spicy Orzo and Black Bean Salad

2 tablespoons olive oil
2 tablespoons minced jalapeño pepper, divided*
1 teaspoon chili powder
¾ cup uncooked orzo pasta
1 cup frozen mixed vegetables
1 can (16 ounces) black beans, rinsed and drained
2 thin slices red onion
¼ cup chopped cilantro
¼ cup fresh lime juice
¼ cup fresh lemon juice
4 cups washed and torn spinach leaves
2 tablespoons crumbled blue cheese (optional)

1. Combine oil, 1 tablespoon jalapeño and chili powder in medium bowl.

2. Bring 6 cups water and remaining 1 tablespoon jalapeño to a boil in large saucepan. Add orzo. Cook 10 to 12 minutes or until tender; drain. Rinse in cold water; drain.

3. Place frozen vegetables in small microwavable container. Cover and microwave at HIGH 3 minutes or until hot. Cover and let stand 5 minutes.

4. Add orzo, vegetables, black beans, onion, cilantro, lime juice and lemon juice to oil mixture in bowl. Divide spinach evenly among serving plates. Top with orzo and bean mixture. Sprinkle with blue cheese and garnish with fresh cilantro, if desired.

Makes 4 servings

*Jalapeño peppers can sting and irritate the skin; wear rubber gloves when handling peppers and do not touch eyes. Wash hands after handling jalapeño peppers.

NUTRIENTS PER SERVING			
Calories	356	Fat	9 g
Cholesterol	0 mg	Sodium	467 mg

Spicy Orzo and Black Bean Salad

Spinach-Tomato Salad

1 package (8 ounces) DOLE® Complete Spinach Salad
2 medium tomatoes, halved and cut into thin wedges
½ medium cucumber, thinly sliced
½ small onion, thinly sliced
1 can (14 to 16 ounces) low-sodium kidney or garbanzo beans, drained

• **Toss** spinach, croutons and bacon from salad bag with tomatoes, cucumber, onion and beans in medium serving bowl.

• **Pour** dressing from packet over salad; toss to coat evenly.

Makes 4 servings

Prep time: 10 minutes

NUTRIENTS PER SERVING			
Calories	210	Fat	6 g
Cholesterol	0 mg	Sodium	423 mg

Spinach-Tomato Salad

Salad Primavera

6 cups romaine lettuce, washed, torn into bite-sized pieces
1 package (9 ounces) frozen artichoke hearts, thawed, drained,
    cut into bite-sized pieces
1 cup chopped watercress
1 orange, peeled, separated into segments, cut into halves
½ cup chopped red bell pepper
¼ cup chopped green onions with tops
    Citrus-Caper Dressing (recipe follows)
2 tablespoons freshly grated Parmesan cheese

1. Combine lettuce, artichoke hearts, watercress, orange segments, bell pepper and green onions in large bowl. Prepare Citrus-Caper Dressing. Add dressing to lettuce mixture. Mix well. Sprinkle with Parmesan before serving.

Makes 8 servings

CITRUS–CAPER DRESSING

⅓ cup orange juice
¼ cup white wine vinegar
2 tablespoons chopped fresh parsley
2 teaspoons Dijon mustard
¼ teaspoon olive oil
1 tablespoon minced capers
1 teaspoon sugar
1 teaspoon minced fresh garlic
¼ teaspoon ground black pepper

1. Combine all ingredients in jar or bottle with tight-fitting lid; shake well. Refrigerate until ready to serve. Shake well before using.

Makes ½ cup dressing

NUTRIENTS PER SERVING			
Calories	55	Fat	1 g
Cholesterol	1 mg	Sodium	102 mg

Salad Primavera

Vegetable Potato Salad

½ cup cider vinegar
¼ cup CRISCO® Oil
½ teaspoon prepared mustard
½ teaspoon salt
¼ teaspoon pepper
2¾ pounds unpeeled medium red potatoes
3 medium carrots, cut into thin 2-inch sticks
3 ribs celery, sliced
3 green onions with tops, chopped
6 radishes, sliced
4 tomatoes, quartered

1. Combine vinegar, oil, mustard, salt and pepper in container with tight-fitting lid. Shake well.

2. Cook potatoes just until tender. Cool 5 minutes. Cut into bite-size pieces. Combine in large salad bowl with carrots, celery, onions and radishes. Shake dressing. Pour over salad. Toss to mix well. Serve immediately or refrigerate. Top with tomato wedges.   *Makes 8 servings*

NUTRIENTS PER SERVING			
Calories	225	Fat	7 g
Cholesterol	0 mg	Sodium	175 mg

238

Marinated Vegetable Spinach Salad

Mustard-Tarragon Marinade (recipe follows)
8 ounces fresh mushrooms, quartered
2 slices purple onion, separated into rings
16 cherry tomatoes, halved
4 cups fresh spinach leaves, washed and stems removed
3 slices (3 ounces) SARGENTO® Preferred Light Sliced
   Mozzarella Cheese, cut into julienne strips
Freshly ground black pepper

Prepare Mustard-Tarragon Marinade; set aside. Place mushrooms, onion and tomatoes in bowl. Toss with marinade and let stand 15 minutes. Arrange spinach on 4 individual plates. Divide marinated vegetables among plates and top each salad with ¼ of cheese. Serve with freshly ground black pepper, if desired.
Makes 4 servings

MUSTARD–TARRAGON MARINADE

3 tablespoons red wine vinegar
1 tablespoon Dijon-style mustard
½ tablespoon dried tarragon
2 tablespoons olive oil

Combine first 3 ingredients in small bowl. Slowly whisk oil into mixture until slightly thickened.

NUTRIENTS PER SERVING			
Calories	147	Fat	10 g
Cholesterol	7 mg	Sodium	252 mg

239

Roasted Red Pepper, Corn & Garbanzo Bean Salad

2 cans (15 ounces each) garbanzo beans
1 jar (11.5 ounces) GUILTLESS GOURMET® Roasted Red
    Pepper Salsa
1 cup frozen whole kernel corn, thawed and drained
½ cup GUILTLESS GOURMET® Green Tomatillo Salsa
2 green onions, thinly sliced
8 lettuce leaves
    Fresh tomato wedges and sunflower sprouts (optional)

Rinse and drain beans well; place in 2-quart casserole dish. Add roasted red pepper salsa, corn, tomatillo salsa and onions; stir to combine. Cover and refrigerate 1 hour or up to 24 hours.

To serve, line serving platter with lettuce. Spoon bean mixture over top. Garnish with tomatoes and sprouts, if desired. *Makes 8 servings*

NUTRIENTS PER SERVING			
Calories	174	Fat	2 g
Cholesterol	0 mg	Sodium	268 mg

Roasted Red Pepper, Corn & Garbanzo Bean Salad

Minted Fruit Rice Salad

⅔ cup DOLE® Pineapple Orange Juice, Mandarin Tangerine
     Juice or Pineapple Juice
⅓ cup water
 1 cup uncooked instant rice
 1 can (11 ounces) DOLE® Mandarin Oranges, drained
 1 can (8 ounces) DOLE® Crushed Pineapple
½ cup chopped cucumber
⅓ cup chopped DOLE® Red Onion
 3 tablespoons chopped fresh mint

• **Combine** juice and water in medium saucepan. Bring to boil. Stir in rice. Remove from heat; cover. Let stand 10 minutes.

• **Stir** together rice, drained mandarin oranges, undrained pineapple, cucumber, onion and mint in medium serving bowl. Serve at room temperature or chilled.   *Makes 4 servings*

Prep time: 5 minutes
Cook time: 15 minutes

NUTRIENTS PER SERVING			
Calories	106	Fat	0 g
Cholesterol	0 mg	Sodium	4 mg

242

Minted Fruit Rice Salad

Cool Summer Gazpacho Salad

1 large DOLE® Fresh Pineapple
2 cups chopped tomatoes, drained
1 large cucumber, halved lengthwise and thinly sliced
¼ cup chopped DOLE® Green Onions
¼ cup red wine vinegar
4 teaspoons olive or vegetable oil
½ teaspoon dried basil leaves, crushed

• **Twist** off crown from pineapple. Cut pineapple in quarters lengthwise. Remove fruit. Core and dice fruit. Drain fruit.

• **Stir** together pineapple and remaining ingredients in large bowl. Cover; chill 1 hour or overnight to blend flavors. Stir before serving.   *Makes 10 servings*

Prep time: 20 minutes
Chill time: 1 hour

NUTRIENTS PER SERVING			
Calories	68	Fat	2 g
Cholesterol	0 mg	Sodium	5 mg

Cool Summer Gazpacho Salad

Summer Fruit Salad

2 cups cooked rice, cooled to room temperature
½ cup quartered strawberries
½ cup grape halves
½ cup pineapple tidbits
2 kiwifruit, sliced into quarters
½ cup banana slices
¼ cup pineapple juice
2 tablespoons plain nonfat yogurt
1 tablespoon honey
Lettuce leaves

Combine rice and fruit in large bowl. Blend pineapple juice, yogurt, and honey in small bowl. Pour over rice mixture; toss lightly. Serve on lettuce leaves.

Makes 4 servings

NUTRIENTS PER SERVING			
Calories	239	Fat	1 g
Cholesterol	1 mg	Sodium	396 mg

Favorite recipe from **USA Rice Council**

Summer Fruit Salad

Southwest Salsa Dressing

⅔ cup mild salsa*
2 tablespoons plain nonfat yogurt
4 teaspoons sugar
2 teaspoons chopped fresh cilantro (optional)

In a small bowl stir all ingredients together. Or, blend ingredients in a food processor for a smoother dressing. Chill or serve immediately over green salad, chicken or turkey salad, taco salad or seafood salad. *Makes 4 servings*

*For a hotter and spicier dressing, use medium or hot salsa.

NUTRIENTS PER SERVING			
(approximately 2 tablespoons)			
Calories	30	Fat	<1 g
Cholesterol	226 mg	Sodium	226 mg

Favorite recipe from **The Sugar Association, Inc.**

Mock Blue Cheese Dressing

¾ cup buttermilk
¼ cup low-fat cottage cheese
2 tablespoons blue cheese, crumbled
2 teaspoons sugar
1 teaspoon lemon juice
¼ teaspoon celery seed
⅛ teaspoon pepper
⅛ teaspoon salt
4 drops hot sauce

In a blender or food processor blend all ingredients. Chill and serve over green salad.

Makes 6 servings

NUTRIENTS PER SERVING			
(approximately 2 tablespoons)			
Calories	22	Fat	1 g
Cholesterol	3 mg	Sodium	148 mg

Favorite recipe from **The Sugar Association, Inc.**

Microwave or Roasted Bell Pepper Dressing

  1 green or red bell pepper
 ½ cup buttermilk
  2 teaspoons sugar
  1 teaspoon fresh parsley (optional)
 ¾ teaspoon lemon juice
 ¼ teaspoon paprika
 ⅛ teaspoon salt
 ⅛ teaspoon pepper
 ⅛ teaspoon onion powder

Microwave bell pepper for 5 minutes on HIGH (100% power) until tender (cooking time may vary depending on microwave). Or, roast pepper at 375°F for 20 to 25 minutes until tender. Cut pepper in half and remove seeds. Pat dry with paper towel. In a blender or food processor blend all ingredients thoroughly. Chill and serve over green salad.

Makes 6 servings

NUTRIENTS PER SERVING			
(approximately 2 tablespoons)			
Calories	21	Fat	<1 g
Cholesterol	1 mg	Sodium	67 mg

Favorite recipe from **The Sugar Association, Inc.**

Creamy Garlic Dressing

12 ounces (2 cartons) ALPINE LACE® Fat Free Cream Cheese
      with Garlic & Herbs
½ cup 2% low fat milk
¼ cup fat free sour cream
2 tablespoons fresh lemon juice
1 tablespoon prepared horseradish
½ teaspoon freshly ground black pepper
      Radish slices (optional)

1. In a food processor or blender, process all of the ingredients for 30 seconds or until well blended. Refrigerate until ready to serve. Garnish with the radish slices, if you wish.

2. Serve this dressing over vegetable or meat salads. It's also a great sauce for grilled meat, chicken and fish.

Makes 2 cups

NUTRIENTS PER SERVING			
Calories	34	Fat	0 g
Cholesterol	4 mg	Sodium	123 mg

Vegetables & Side Dishes

●●●●●●●●●●

Country Green Beans with Ham

2 teaspoons olive oil
¼ cup minced onion
1 clove garlic, minced
1 pound fresh green beans, rinsed and drained
1 cup chopped fresh tomatoes
6 slices (2 ounces) thinly sliced low-fat smoked turkey-ham
1 tablespoon chopped fresh marjoram
2 teaspoons chopped fresh basil
⅛ teaspoon ground black pepper
¼ cup herbed croutons

1. Heat oil in medium saucepan over medium heat. Add onion and garlic; cook and stir about 3 minutes or until onion is tender. Reduce heat to low.

2. Add green beans, tomatoes, turkey-ham, marjoram, basil and black pepper. Cook about 10 minutes, stirring occasionally, until liquid from tomatoes is absorbed. Top with croutons.

Makes 4 servings

NUTRIENTS PER SERVING			
Calories	100	Fat	3 g
Cholesterol	12 mg	Sodium	194 mg

Country Green Beans with Ham

Mini Vegetable Quiches

2 cups cut-up vegetables (bell peppers, broccoli, zucchini and/or carrots)
2 tablespoons chopped green onions
2 tablespoons FLEISCHMANN'S® Margarine
4 (8-inch) flour tortillas, each cut into 8 triangles
1 cup EGG BEATERS® Healthy Real Egg Product
1 cup skim milk
½ teaspoon dried basil leaves

In medium nonstick skillet, over medium-high heat, sauté vegetables and green onions in margarine until tender.

Arrange 4 tortilla pieces in each of 8 (6-ounce) greased custard cups or ramekins, placing points of tortilla pieces at center of bottom of cup and pressing lightly to form shape of cup. Divide vegetable mixture evenly among cups. In small bowl, combine Egg Beaters®, milk and basil. Pour evenly over vegetable mixture. Place cups on baking sheet. Bake at 375°F for 20 to 25 minutes or until puffed and knife inserted into centers comes out clean. Let stand 5 minutes before serving.

Makes 8 servings

254

NUTRIENTS PER SERVING			
Calories	122	Fat	4 g
Cholesterol	1 mg	Sodium	198 mg

Mini Vegetable Quiches

Stacked Burrito Pie

½ cup GUILTLESS GOURMET® Mild Black Bean Dip
2 teaspoons water
5 low fat flour tortillas (6 inches each)
½ cup nonfat sour cream or plain yogurt
½ cup GUILTLESS GOURMET® Roasted Red Pepper Salsa
1¼ cups (5 ounces) shredded low fat Monterey Jack cheese
4 cups shredded iceberg or romaine lettuce
½ cup GUILTLESS GOURMET® Salsa (mild, medium or hot)
Lime slices and chili pepper (optional)

Preheat oven to 350°F. Combine bean dip and 2 teaspoons water in small bowl; mix well. Line 7½-inch springform pan with 1 tortilla. Spread 2 tablespoons bean dip mixture over tortilla, then spread with 2 tablespoons sour cream and 2 tablespoons red pepper salsa. Sprinkle with ¼ cup cheese. Repeat layers 3 more times. Place remaining tortilla on top and sprinkle with remaining ¼ cup cheese.

Bake 40 minutes or until heated through. (Place sheet of foil under springform pan to catch any juices that may seep through the bottom.) Cool slightly before unmolding. To serve, cut into 4 quarters. Place 1 cup lettuce on 4 serving plates. Top each serving with 1 quarter burrito pie and 2 tablespoons salsa. Garnish with lime slices and pepper, if desired. *Makes 4 servings*

NUTRIENTS PER SERVING			
(1 quarter)			
Calories	302	Fat	7 g
Cholesterol	12 mg	Sodium	650 mg

Stacked Burrito Pie

Polenta with Black Bean Salsa

Olive oil-flavored nonstick cooking spray
2 teaspoons chicken flavor bouillon granules
¾ cup uncooked polenta or stone ground cornmeal
1 cup rinsed, drained canned black beans
¾ cup chunky salsa
⅔ cup frozen whole kernel corn, thawed
⅓ cup minced fresh cilantro
4 teaspoons olive oil
6 tablespoons nonfat sour cream (optional)

1. Spray 9-inch-square pan with cooking spray; set aside.

2. Combine 3 cups water and bouillon granules in large saucepan; bring to a boil over high heat. Gradually add polenta, stirring constantly with wire whisk. Reduce heat to medium-low. Simmer 10 to 15 minutes or until polenta is thickened and pulls away from side of pan, stirring constantly with wooden spoon. Spread polenta evenly into prepared pan. Cover with plastic wrap; refrigerate 1 to 2 hours or until polenta is firm.

3. Combine beans, salsa, corn and cilantro in medium bowl. Cover with plastic wrap; refrigerate 1 hour. Bring to room temperature before serving.

4. Cut polenta into 6 rectangles; cut each rectangle diagonally to form 2 triangles. Brush both sides of triangles with oil. Spray large nonstick skillet with cooking spray; heat over medium-high heat until hot. Cook triangles, 4 at a time, 6 to 8 minutes or until browned, turning once. Place 2 polenta triangles on each serving plate; top each serving evenly with black bean salsa and sour cream if desired. Garnish as desired. *Makes 6 servings*

NUTRIENTS PER SERVING			
Calories	136	Fat	4 g
Cholesterol	1 mg	Sodium	639 mg

Polenta with Black Bean Salsa

Vegetables in Garlic-Cream Sauce

1   cup water
4   cups cut-up vegetables such as DOLE® Asparagus, Bell
       Peppers, Broccoli, Carrots, Cauliflower or Sugar Peas
1   teaspoon olive or vegetable oil
4   garlic cloves, finely chopped
⅓   cup fat free or reduced fat mayonnaise
⅓   cup nonfat or low fat milk
2   tablespoons chopped fresh parsley

• **Place** water in large saucepan; bring to boil. Add vegetables; reduce heat to low. Cook, uncovered, 9 to 12 minutes or until vegetables are tender-crisp; meanwhile, prepare sauce.

• **Heat** oil in small saucepan over medium heat. Add garlic; cook and stir garlic until golden brown. Remove from heat; stir in mayonnaise and milk.

• **Drain** vegetables; place in serving bowl. Pour in garlic sauce; toss to evenly coat. Sprinkle with parsley.   *Makes 4 servings*

Prep time: 10 minutes
Cook time: 15 minutes

NUTRIENTS PER SERVING			
Calories	89	Fat	2 g
Cholesterol	1 mg	Sodium	293 mg

New England Style Vegetables with Garlic-Cream Sauce: Substitute 2 packages (9 ounces each) DOLE® New England Style Vegetables for 4 cups cut-up vegetables. Cut potatoes in half. Cook vegetables according to package directions; drain. Place vegetables in serving bowl. Prepare sauce as directed above. Pour sauce over vegetables in serving bowl; toss to evenly coat. Sprinkle with parsley.

Indian-Style Vegetable Stir-Fry

1 teaspoon canola oil
1 teaspoon curry powder
1 teaspoon ground cumin
⅛ teaspoon red pepper flakes
1½ teaspoons finely chopped, seeded jalapeño pepper
2 cloves garlic, minced
¾ cup chopped red bell pepper
¾ cup thinly sliced carrots
3 cups cauliflower florets
½ cup water, divided
½ teaspoon salt
2 teaspoons finely chopped cilantro (optional)

1. Heat oil in large nonstick skillet over medium-high heat. Add curry powder, cumin and red pepper flakes; cook and stir about 30 seconds.

2. Stir in jalapeño and garlic. Add bell pepper and carrots; mix well to coat with spices. Add cauliflower; reduce heat to medium.

3. Stir in ¼ cup water; cook and stir until water evaporates. Add remaining ¼ cup water; cover and cook about 8 to 10 minutes or until vegetables are crisp-tender, stirring occasionally.

4. Add salt; mix well. Sprinkle with cilantro and garnish with mizuna and additional red bell pepper, if desired. Serve immediately. *Makes 6 servings*

NUTRIENTS PER SERVING			
Calories	40	Fat	1 g
Cholesterol	0 mg	Sodium	198 mg

Vegetable Strata

2 slices white bread, cubed
¼ cup shredded reduced-fat Swiss cheese
½ cup sliced carrots
½ cup sliced mushrooms
¼ cup chopped onion
1 clove garlic, crushed
1 teaspoon FLEISCHMANN'S® Margarine
½ cup chopped tomato
½ cup snow peas
1 cup EGG BEATERS® Healthy Real Egg Product
¾ cup skim milk

Place bread cubes evenly into bottom of greased 1½-quart casserole dish. Sprinkle with cheese; set aside.

In medium nonstick skillet, over medium heat, sauté carrots, mushrooms, onion and garlic in margarine until tender. Stir in tomato and snow peas; cook 1 to 2 minutes more. Spoon over cheese. In small bowl, combine Egg Beaters® and milk; pour over vegetable mixture. Bake at 375°F for 45 to 50 minutes or until knife inserted in center comes out clean. Let stand 10 minutes before serving.   *Makes 6 servings*

Prep time: 15 minutes
Cook time: 55 minutes

NUTRIENTS PER SERVING			
Calories	94	Fat	2 g
Cholesterol	3 mg	Sodium	161 mg

Vegetable Strata

Southwestern Twice-Baked Spuds

2   baking potatoes with skins (about 6 ounces each)
½   cup GUILTLESS GOURMET® Nacho Dip (mild or spicy)
¼   cup finely chopped green onions
¼   teaspoon coarsely ground black pepper
2   tablespoons GUILTLESS GOURMET® Salsa (mild, medium
     or hot)
2   tablespoons chopped fresh cilantro
     Nasturtium flowers (optional)

Preheat oven to 400°F. Scrub potatoes with vegetable brush; pierce in several places with fork. Bake potatoes 45 to 50 minutes or until fork-tender. Remove from oven; cool potatoes until safe enough to handle.

Reduce oven temperature to 300°F. Slice potatoes in half lengthwise. Form 4 shells by scooping out most of potato pulp, being careful not to pierce skin. Place pulp in large bowl; mash with potato masher or whip with electric mixer. Add nacho dip, onions and pepper. Blend until smooth. Add salsa and cilantro; mix until blended. Fill potato shells with equal amount of potato mixture, heaping to form mounds. Wrap skins in foil, leaving tops open. Place on baking sheet.

Bake 25 minutes or until heated through. Serve hot. Garnish with edible flowers, if desired.   *Makes 4 servings*

NUTRIENTS PER SERVING			
Calories	112	Fat	<1 g
Cholesterol	0 mg	Sodium	193 mg

Southwestern Twice-Baked Spud

South-of-the-Border Pizza

1   prepared pizza shell or crust (about 12 inches)
1   cup cooked low-sodium kidney beans, rinsed and drained
1   cup frozen whole kernel corn, thawed
1   tomato, chopped
¼   cup finely chopped fresh cilantro
1   jalapeño pepper, finely chopped
¼   cup (4 ounces) shredded reduced-fat Monterey Jack cheese

1. Preheat oven to 450°F. Place pizza shell on ungreased pizza pan or baking sheet.

2. Arrange beans, corn, tomato, cilantro and jalapeño over pizza shell. Sprinkle evenly with cheese.

3. Bake pizza 8 to 10 minutes or until cheese is melted and lightly browned. Garnish with green bell pepper, if desired.   *Makes 4 servings*

NUTRIENTS PER SERVING			
Calories	361	Fat	7 g
Cholesterol	20 mg	Sodium	569 mg

Iowa Corn Pudding

½ cup egg substitute or 2 large eggs
2 large egg whites
3 tablespoons all-purpose flour
1 tablespoon sugar
½ teaspoon freshly ground black pepper
1 can (16½ ounces) cream-style corn
2 cups fresh corn kernels or frozen corn, thawed and drained
1 cup (4 ounces) shredded ALPINE LACE® American Flavor
   Pasteurized Process Cheese Product
½ cup finely chopped red bell pepper
⅓ cup 2% low fat milk
1 tablespoon unsalted butter substitute
¼ teaspoon paprika
   Sprigs of fresh parsley

1. Preheat the oven to 350°F. Spray an 8-inch round baking dish with nonstick cooking spray. (A deep-dish pie plate works well.) Place in the oven to heat.

2. Meanwhile, in a large bowl, using an electric mixer set on high, beat the egg substitute (or the whole eggs) and egg whites with the flour, sugar and black pepper until smooth. Stir in the creamed corn, corn kernels, cheese, bell pepper and milk. Pour into the hot baking dish.

3. Dot with the butter and sprinkle with the paprika. Bake, uncovered, for 55 minutes or until set. Let stand for 15 minutes before serving. Garnish with the parsley.   *Makes 6 servings*

NUTRIENTS PER SERVING			
Calories	226	Fat	6 g
Cholesterol	17 mg	Sodium	556 mg

Iowa Corn Pudding

Apple-Potato Pancakes

1¼ cups unpeeled, finely chopped apples
1 cup peeled, grated potatoes
½ cup MOTT'S® Natural Apple Sauce
½ cup all-purpose flour
2 egg whites
1 teaspoon salt
   Additional MOTT'S® Natural Apple Sauce or apple slices
   (optional)

1. Preheat oven to 475°F. Spray cookie sheet with nonstick cooking spray.

2. In medium bowl, combine apples, potatoes, ½ cup apple sauce, flour, egg whites and salt.

3. Spray large nonstick skillet with nonstick cooking spray; heat over medium heat until hot. Drop rounded tablespoonfuls of batter 2 inches apart into skillet. Cook 2 to 3 minutes on each side or until lightly browned. Place pancakes on prepared cookie sheet.

4. Bake 10 to 15 minutes or until crisp. Serve with additional apple sauce or apple slices, if desired. Refrigerate leftovers.   *Makes 12 servings*

NUTRIENTS PER SERVING			
(1 pancake)			
Calories	60	Fat	0 g
Cholesterol	0 mg	Sodium	190 mg

270

Garden-Style Risotto

1 can (14½ ounces) low-sodium chicken broth
1¾ cups water
2 garlic cloves, finely chopped
1 teaspoon dried basil leaves, crushed
½ teaspoon dried thyme leaves, crushed
1 cup arborio rice
2 cups packed DOLE® Fresh Spinach, torn
1 cup DOLE® Shredded Carrots
3 tablespoons grated Parmesan cheese

• **Combine** broth, water, garlic, basil and thyme in large saucepan. Bring to boil; meanwhile, prepare rice.

• **Place** rice in large, nonstick saucepan sprayed with vegetable cooking spray. Cook and stir rice over medium heat about 2 minutes or until rice is browned.

• **Pour** 1 cup boiling broth into saucepan with rice; cook, stirring constantly, until broth is almost absorbed (there should be some broth left).

• **Add** enough broth to barely cover rice; continue to cook, stirring constantly, until broth is almost absorbed. Repeat adding broth and cooking, stirring constantly, until broth is almost absorbed, about 15 minutes; add spinach and carrots with the last addition of broth.

• **Cook** 3 to 5 minutes more, stirring constantly, or until broth is almost absorbed and rice and vegetables are tender. *Do not overcook.* (Risotto will be saucy and have a creamy texture.) Stir in Parmesan cheese. Serve warm.

Makes 6 servings

Prep time: 5 minutes
Cook time: 25 minutes

continued on page 274

Garden-Style Risotto

Couscous with Chick-peas and Vegetables

1 cup dried chick-peas (garbanzo beans)
2 cans (14 ounces each) fat-free reduced-sodium chicken broth
1 large onion, quartered and sliced
2 large cloves garlic, minced
1 teaspoon ground cinnamon
1 teaspoon red pepper flakes
½ teaspoon paprika
½ teaspoon saffron or turmeric (optional)
½ teaspoon salt
½ pound eggplant, cut into ¾-inch cubes
1 large sweet potato, peeled and cut into ¾-inch cubes
¾ pound zucchini, cut into ¾-inch cubes
1 can (14½ ounces) chopped tomatoes
2 tablespoons finely chopped fresh parsley
2 tablespoons finely chopped fresh cilantro
4 cups hot cooked couscous, cooked without salt

1. Sort and rinse chick-peas. Cover with water and let soak overnight; drain. Place in Dutch oven with chicken broth; bring to a boil over high heat.

2. Add onion, garlic, cinnamon, red pepper flakes, paprika and saffron; reduce heat to low. Cover and simmer 1 hour or until beans are tender. Stir in salt.

3. Add eggplant and sweet potato; cook 10 minutes. Add zucchini and tomatoes; cook 10 minutes or just until all vegetables are tender. Stir in parsley and cilantro; spoon mixture over hot couscous. Garnish with sweet potato slices and chives, if desired.

Makes 6 servings

NUTRIENTS PER SERVING			
Calories	324	Fat	2 g
Cholesterol	0 mg	Sodium	330 mg

Couscous with Chick-peas and Vegetables

Alpine Fettuccine

½ pound white fettuccine, preferably fresh
½ pound green fettuccine, preferably fresh
1½ teaspoons extra virgin olive oil
1 cup sliced fresh mushrooms
1 cup chopped red bell pepper
½ cup skim milk
6 ounces (1 carton) ALPINE LACE® Fat Free Cream Cheese
with Garlic & Herbs

1. Cook the fettuccine according to package directions until al dente. Drain well and place in a large shallow pasta bowl. Toss with the oil and keep warm.

2. Meanwhile, spray a medium-size nonstick skillet with nonstick cooking spray. Add the mushrooms and bell pepper and sauté until soft. Toss with the fettuccine.

3. In a small saucepan, bring the milk to a boil over medium heat. Add the cream cheese and stir until melted. Toss with pasta and serve immediately.

Makes 9 side-dish servings (1 cup each) or
6 main-dish servings (1½ cups each)

NUTRIENTS PER SERVING			
Calories	228	Fat	3 g
Cholesterol	51 mg	Sodium	138 mg

Alpine Fettuccine

Fresh Vegetable Lasagna

  8 ounces uncooked lasagna noodles
  1 package (10 ounces) frozen chopped spinach, thawed and
       well drained
  1 cup shredded carrots
$\frac{1}{2}$ cup sliced green onions
$\frac{1}{2}$ cup sliced red bell pepper
$\frac{1}{4}$ cup chopped fresh parsley
$\frac{1}{2}$ teaspoon ground black pepper
$1\frac{1}{2}$ cups low-fat cottage cheese
  1 cup buttermilk
$\frac{1}{2}$ cup plain nonfat yogurt
  2 egg whites
  1 cup sliced mushrooms
  1 can (14 ounces) artichoke hearts, drained and chopped
  2 cups (8 ounces) shredded part-skim mozzarella cheese
$\frac{1}{4}$ cup freshly grated Parmesan cheese

1. Cook pasta according to package directions, omitting salt. Drain. Rinse under cold water; drain well. Set aside.

2. Preheat oven to 375°F. Pat spinach with paper towels to remove excess moisture. Combine spinach, carrots, green onions, bell pepper, parsley and black pepper in large bowl. Set aside.

3. Combine cottage cheese, buttermilk, yogurt and egg whites in food processor or blender; process until smooth.

4. Spray 13×9-inch baking pan with nonstick cooking spray. Arrange half of lasagna noodles in bottom of pan. Spread with half each of cottage cheese mixture, vegetable mixture, mushrooms, artichokes and mozzarella. Repeat layers, ending with noodles. Sprinkle with Parmesan.

continued on page 284

Fresh Vegetable Lasagna

Fresh Vegetable Lasagna, continued

5. Cover and bake 30 minutes. Remove cover; continue baking 20 minutes or until bubbly and heated through. Let stand 10 minutes before serving.

Makes 8 servings

NUTRIENTS PER SERVING			
Calories	250	Fat	8 g
Cholesterol	22 mg	Sodium	508 mg

Pineapple Noodle Pudding

1¼   cups cooked macaroni
1   cup unsweetened canned pineapple chunks, juice reserved
¾   cup low-fat cottage cheese
¼   cup imitation sour cream
1   egg white
3   tablespoons dark brown sugar
¼   cup wheat flakes
1   tablespoon granulated sugar
¼   teaspoon cinnamon

Preheat oven to 350°F. Spray 1-quart casserole dish with nonstick cooking spray. Measure ¼ cup juice from pineapple; discard any remaining juice. In large bowl combine macaroni, pineapple, ¼ cup reserved juice, cottage cheese, sour cream, egg white and brown sugar. Pour into casserole dish. In small bowl mix wheat flakes, granulated sugar and cinnamon. Sprinkle flake topping over noodle mixture. Bake uncovered 25 minutes or until bubbly.   *Makes 6 servings*

NUTRIENTS PER SERVING			
Calories	138	Fat	2 g
Cholesterol	1 mg	Sodium	149 mg

Favorite recipe from **The Sugar Association, Inc.**

Creamy Macaroni and Cheese

2 tablespoons CRISCO® Oil
½ cup chopped green onions with tops
1 clove garlic, minced
2 tablespoons all-purpose flour
¼ teaspoon dried basil leaves
¼ teaspoon dry mustard
⅛ teaspoon pepper
2 cups skim milk
1 cup (4 ounces) shredded (⅓ less fat) sharp Cheddar cheese
½ cup nonfat sour cream alternative
1 teaspoon Worcestershire sauce
Dash of hot pepper sauce
1½ cups uncooked small elbow macaroni, cooked (without salt or fat) and well drained
1 tablespoon plain dry bread crumbs

1. Heat oven to 350°F. Oil 2-quart casserole lightly. Set aside.

2. Heat 2 tablespoons oil in large skillet on medium heat. Add onions and garlic. Cook and stir until tender.

3. Stir in flour, basil, dry mustard and pepper. Stir until well blended. Stir in milk. Cook and stir until mixture thickens and just comes to a boil. Stir in cheese, "sour cream," Worcestershire sauce and hot pepper sauce.

4. Combine macaroni and sauce in large bowl. Toss to coat. Spoon into casserole. Sprinkle with bread crumbs.

5. Bake at 350°F for 25 minutes.   *Makes 6 servings*

NUTRIENTS PER SERVING			
Calories	260	Fat	9 g
Cholesterol	15 mg	Sodium	215 mg

Stuffed Shells Florentine

1 cup (about 4 ounces) coarsely chopped mushrooms
½ cup chopped onion
1 clove garlic, minced
1 teaspoon Italian seasoning
¼ teaspoon ground black pepper
1 tablespoon FLEISCHMANN'S® Margarine
1 (16-ounce) container fat-free cottage cheese
1 (10-ounce) package frozen chopped spinach, thawed and well
   drained
½ cup EGG BEATERS® Healthy Real Egg Product
24 jumbo pasta shells, cooked in unsalted water and drained
1 (15¼-ounce) jar reduced-sodium spaghetti sauce

In large skillet, over medium-high heat, sauté mushrooms, onion, garlic, Italian seasoning and pepper in margarine until tender. Remove from heat; stir in cottage cheese, spinach and Egg Beaters®. Spoon mixture into shells.

Spread ½ cup spaghetti sauce in bottom of 13×9×2-inch baking dish; arrange shells over sauce. Top with remaining sauce; cover. Bake at 350°F for 35 minutes or until hot.

Makes 7 servings

Prep time: 30 minutes
Cook time: 40 minutes

NUTRIENTS PER SERVING			
Calories	255	Fat	2 g
Cholesterol	6 mg	Sodium	515 mg

286

Stuffed Shells Florentine

Cakes & Cheesecakes

• • • • • • • • • • •

Black Forest Chocolate Fudge Cake

      2   cups cake flour
      1   cup unsweetened cocoa powder
      1   teaspoon baking powder
    ½   teaspoon salt
  1½   cups packed brown sugar
      2   eggs
      1   egg white
      1   cup Prune Purée (page 90) or prepared prune butter
    ¾   cup nonfat milk
      4   teaspoons vanilla
      1   cup boiling water
      2   tablespoons instant espresso coffee powder
      2   teaspoons baking soda
      2   cups frozen pitted unsweetened dark sweet cherries, coarsely
            chopped, thawed and well drained
    ½   cup chopped toasted walnuts
          Mocha Glaze (page 290)
          Chocolate Drizzle (optional, page 290)
          Fresh cherries or frozen cherries, thawed
          Mint sprigs, for garnish

continued on page 290

Black Forest Chocolate Fudge Cake

Black Forest Chocolate Fudge Cake, continued

Preheat oven to 350°F. Coat 12- to 16-cup Bundt or other tube pan with vegetable cooking spray. In large bowl, combine flour, cocoa, baking powder and salt; mix in brown sugar. In medium bowl, whisk eggs, egg white, Prune Purée, milk and vanilla. In 2-cup measure, combine boiling water, espresso powder and baking soda. Stir prune and water mixtures into flour mixture; mix just until blended. Pour half the batter into prepared pan; sprinkle cherries and walnuts evenly over batter. Top with remaining batter. Bake in center of oven about 45 minutes until pick inserted into center comes out clean. Cool in pan on wire rack 15 minutes; remove from pan. Cool completely on wire rack. Prepare Mocha Glaze. Spoon over cake, allowing glaze to run down sides. Prepare Chocolate Drizzle, if desired. Drizzle over glaze. Fill cake center with additional cherries and garnish with mint.   *Makes 16 servings*

Mocha Glaze: Place 1 cup powdered sugar in small bowl. Dissolve ⅛ teaspoon instant espresso coffee powder in 4 teaspoons water. Stir into sugar until smooth, adding 1 teaspoon water, if needed, for desired consistency.

Chocolate Drizzle: In top of double boiler or bowl set over simmering water, melt 2 tablespoons semisweet chocolate chips. Stir in 2 teaspoons hot water until blended. Cool until desired consistency.

NUTRIENTS PER SERVING			
Calories	221	Fat	4 g
Cholesterol	27 mg	Sodium	201 mg

Favorite recipe from **California Prune Board**

Trimtime Chocolate Cake Roll

½ cup all-purpose flour
¼ cup HERSHEY®S European Style Cocoa or HERSHEY®S Cocoa
1 teaspoon baking powder
4 eggs
⅓ cup sugar
1 teaspoon vanilla extract
2 cups (1 pint) vanilla nonfat frozen yogurt, slightly softened
    Powdered sugar (optional)

1. Heat oven to 400°F. Spray 15½×10½×1-inch jelly-roll pan with vegetable cooking spray. Line with waxed paper; spray again.

2. Sift together flour, cocoa and baking powder. In small mixer bowl, beat eggs, sugar and vanilla until pale in color, about 5 minutes. Fold in cocoa mixture; spread batter into prepared pan.

3. Bake 5 to 7 minutes or until top springs back when touched lightly in center. Invert cake onto clean towel; remove waxed paper. Roll up cake with towel from short side. Cool completely on wire rack.

4. Unroll cake; spread with frozen yogurt. Reroll cake without towel; press seam side down. Cover; freeze until firm. Sprinkle top lightly with powdered sugar, if desired. Cover; freeze leftover cake roll. *Makes 12 servings*

NUTRIENTS PER SERVING			
Calories	130	Fat	2 g
Cholesterol	70 mg	Sodium	95 mg

Mocha Marble Pound Cake

2   cups all-purpose flour
2   teaspoons DAVIS® Baking Powder
1   teaspoon baking soda
½   teaspoon salt
1   cup sugar
¼   cup FLEISCHMANN'S® Margarine, softened
1   teaspoon vanilla extract
½   cup EGG BEATERS® Healthy Real Egg Product
1   (8-ounce) container low fat coffee yogurt
¼   cup unsweetened cocoa
    Mocha Yogurt Glaze (recipe follows)

In small bowl, combine flour, baking powder, baking soda and salt; set aside. In large bowl, with electric mixer at medium speed, beat sugar, margarine and vanilla until creamy. Add Egg Beaters®; beat until smooth. With mixer at low speed, add yogurt alternately with flour mixture, beating well after each addition. Remove half of batter to medium bowl. Beat cocoa into batter remaining in large bowl. Alternately spoon coffee and chocolate batters into greased 9×5×3-inch loaf pan. Cut through batters for marbled effect. Bake at 325°F for 60 to 65 minutes or until toothpick inserted in center comes out clean. Cool in pan on wire rack 10 minutes. Remove from pan; cool completely on wire rack. Frost with Mocha Yogurt Glaze.   *Makes 16 servings*

Mocha Yogurt Glaze: In small bowl, combine ½ cup powdered sugar, 1 tablespoon unsweetened cocoa and 1 tablespoon low fat coffee yogurt until smooth; add more yogurt if necessary to make spreading consistency.

Prep time: 20 minutes
Cook time: 65 minutes

NUTRIENTS PER SERVING			
Calories	159	Fat	3 g
Sodium	215 mg	Cholesterol	1 mg

Mocha Marble Pound Cake

A Lighter Chocolate Decadence

1¼ cups sugar, divided
⅔ cup unsweetened cocoa powder
2 tablespoons all-purpose flour
¾ cup nonfat milk
5 ounces semisweet chocolate chips (about ¾ cup)
¼ cup Prune Purée (page 90) or prepared prune butter
1 egg
1 egg yolk
1 teaspoon vanilla
2 egg whites
⅛ teaspoon cream of tartar
   Raspberry Sauce (page 296)
1½ cups low fat nondairy whipped topping
   Fresh raspberries and mint leaves, for garnish

Preheat oven to 350°F. Line 9-inch round layer cake pan with parchment paper or waxed paper; coat with vegetable cooking spray. In medium saucepan, combine 1 cup sugar, cocoa and flour. Slowly whisk in milk until blended. Bring to a simmer over low heat, stirring constantly. Place chocolate chips in large bowl; pour in hot mixture, stirring until chocolate melts. Whisk in Prune Purée, egg, egg yolk and vanilla until blended. Set aside to cool. In mixer bowl, beat egg whites with cream of tartar until foamy. Gradually beat in remaining ¼ cup sugar until stiff peaks form. Fold half the egg white mixture into cooled chocolate mixture; fold in remaining egg white mixture. Pour into prepared pan. Bake in center of oven 30 to 35 minutes until puffy and center is set but still moist. (Do not overbake.) Cool completely in pan on wire rack. (Cake will sink as it cools.) Remove from pan. Wrap securely; chill 24 hours before serving. Prepare Raspberry Sauce. Cut dessert into wedges; serve with Raspberry Sauce and whipped topping. Garnish with raspberries and mint leaves.

Makes 12 servings

continued on page 296

A Lighter Chocolate Decadence

A Lighter Chocolate Decadence, continued

Raspberry Sauce: Puree 1 package (12 ounces) thawed frozen raspberries in blender; strain. Sweeten to taste with sugar. Makes 1 cup.

NUTRIENTS PER SERVING			
Calories	200	Fat	10 g
Cholesterol	35 mg	Sodium	30 mg

Favorite recipe from **California Prune Board**

Sensibly Delicious Chocolate Chip Snacking Cake

2   cups all-purpose flour
¾   cup granulated sugar
1   teaspoon baking soda
½   teaspoon ground cinnamon
¼   teaspoon salt
¾   cup unsweetened applesauce
¼   cup nonfat milk
¼   cup margarine, melted
1   egg white
2   teaspoons vanilla extract
2   cups (12-ounce package) NESTLÉ® TOLL HOUSE®
      Semi-Sweet Chocolate Morsels, divided

COMBINE flour, sugar, baking soda, cinnamon and salt in large bowl. Stir in applesauce, milk, margarine, egg white and vanilla just until blended. Stir in *1 cup* morsels. Spoon into greased 9×9-inch baking pan. Sprinkle with *remaining* morsels.

BAKE in preheated 350°F oven for 25 to 35 minutes or until wooden pick inserted in center comes out clean. Cool in pan. Cut into 2¼-inch squares.

Makes 16 servings

NUTRIENTS PER SERVING

Calories	240	Fat	10 g
Cholesterol	0 mg	Sodium	150 mg

Sensibly Delicious Chocolate Pound Cake

- 3 cups all-purpose flour
- ⅓ cup NESTLÉ® TOLL HOUSE® Baking Cocoa
- 1 tablespoon baking powder
- ½ teaspoon salt
- 2 cups packed light brown sugar
- ½ cup LIBBY'S® Solid Pack Pumpkin
- 6 tablespoons margarine
- 4 teaspoons vanilla extract
- 5 egg whites, at room temperature
- 2 cups (12-ounce package) NESTLÉ® TOLL HOUSE® Semi-Sweet Chocolate Morsels
- 1⅔ cups nonfat milk
  Powdered sugar and fresh berries (optional)

COMBINE flour, cocoa, baking powder and salt in medium bowl. Beat brown sugar, pumpkin, margarine and vanilla in large mixer bowl. Add egg whites; beat on medium speed for 2 minutes.

MELT morsels in small, heavy saucepan over low heat, stirring until smooth; beat into creamed mixture. Gradually beat in flour mixture, alternating with milk. Spoon into 10-inch Bundt pan sprayed with no-stick cooking spray.

BAKE in preheated 350°F oven for 50 to 60 minutes or until wooden pick inserted near center comes out clean. Cool in pan for 30 minutes. Invert onto wire rack to cool completely. Sprinkle with powdered sugar; serve with berries.

Makes 24 servings

NUTRIENTS PER SERVING

Calories	245	Fat	8 g
Cholesterol	0 mg	Sodium	165 mg

HERSHEY'S Slimmed Down Chocolate Cake

6   tablespoons (40% corn oil) lower-fat margarine
1   cup sugar
1   cup skim milk
1   tablespoon white vinegar
½   teaspoon vanilla extract
1¼   cups all-purpose flour
⅓   cup HERSHEY'S Cocoa
1   teaspoon baking soda
     Slimmed Down Cocoa Frosting (recipe follows)

Heat oven to 350°F. Spray two 8-inch round baking pans with vegetable cooking spray. In medium saucepan over low heat, melt margarine; stir in sugar. Remove from heat. Add milk, vinegar and vanilla; stir until blended. Stir together flour, cocoa and baking soda. Add to sugar mixture; stir until well blended. Pour batter evenly into prepared pans. Bake 20 minutes or until wooden pick inserted in centers comes out clean. Cool 10 minutes; remove from pans to wire racks. Cool completely. Prepare Slimmed Down Cocoa Frosting. Spread one cake layer with half of prepared frosting. Place second cake layer on top; spread remaining frosting over top of cake. Refrigerate 2 to 3 hours or until chilled. Garnish as desired. Cover; refrigerate leftover cake.

Makes 12 servings

SLIMMED DOWN COCOA FROSTING

1   envelope (1.3 ounces) dry whipped topping mix
1   tablespoon HERSHEY'S Cocoa
½   cup cold skim milk
½   teaspoon vanilla extract

In small, deep narrow-bottom mixer bowl, stir together topping mix and 1 tablespoon cocoa. Add ½ cup milk and ½ teaspoon vanilla. Beat on high speed of electric mixer about 4 minutes until soft peaks form.

continued on page 300

HERSHEY'S Slimmed Down Chocolate Cake

298

HERSHEY₂S Slimmed Down Chocolate Cake, continued

NUTRIENTS PER SERVING			
Calories	160	Fat	4 g
Cholesterol	0 mg	Sodium	120 mg

Chocolate Roulade with Creamy Yogurt Filling

Creamy Yogurt Filling (page 302)
3 egg whites
½ cup granulated sugar, divided
1 container (8 ounces) liquid egg substitute
½ cup cake flour
¼ cup HERSHEY₂S Cocoa
1 teaspoon baking powder
⅛ teaspoon salt
2 tablespoons water
1 teaspoon vanilla extract
2 teaspoons powdered sugar
Peach Sauce (page 302)

Prepare Creamy Yogurt Filling. Heat oven to 375°F. Line 15½×10½×1-inch jelly-roll pan with foil; spray with vegetable cooking spray. In large mixer bowl, beat egg whites on high speed of electric mixer until foamy. Gradually add ¼ cup granulated sugar, beating well after each addition until stiff peaks hold their shape, sugar is dissolved and mixture is glossy. In small mixer bowl, beat egg substitute on medium speed until foamy; gradually add remaining ¼ cup granulated sugar, beating until mixture is thick. Fold egg substitute mixture into egg white mixture. In another small bowl, stir together flour, cocoa, baking powder and salt; gently fold into egg mixture alternately with water and vanilla. Spread batter evenly into prepared pan.

continued on page 302

Chocolate Roulade with Creamy Yogurt Filling

Chocolate Roulade with Creamy Yogurt Filling, continued

Bake 10 to 12 minutes or until top springs back when touched lightly in center. Immediately invert onto clean dishtowel sprinkled with powdered sugar; peel off foil. Roll up cake with towel from short side. Cool completely on wire rack. Unroll cake; remove towel. Spread with Creamy Yogurt Filling to within ½ inch of edges of cake. Reroll cake; place, seam-side down, on serving plate. Cover; refrigerate 2 to 3 hours or until chilled before serving. (Cake should be eaten same day as prepared.) Serve with Peach Sauce. Garnish as desired.

Makes 10 servings

CREAMY YOGURT FILLING

Yogurt Cheese (recipe follows)
1   envelope (1.3 ounces) dry whipped topping mix
⅓   cup cold skim milk
1   teaspoon vanilla extract
⅛ to ¼ teaspoon almond extract

Prepare Yogurt Cheese. Prepare topping mix as directed on package, using ⅓ cup milk, 1 teaspoon vanilla and almond extract. Gently fold Yogurt Cheese into whipped topping.

Yogurt Cheese: Use one 8-ounce container plain nonfat yogurt, no gelatin added. Line non-rusting colander or sieve with large piece of double thickness cheesecloth or large coffee filter; place colander over deep bowl. Spoon yogurt into prepared colander; cover with plastic wrap. Refrigerate until liquid no longer drains from yogurt, about 24 hours. Remove yogurt from cheesecloth and place in separate bowl; discard liquid.

Peach Sauce: In blender container, place 1½ cups fresh peach slices and 1 tablespoon sugar. Cover; blend until smooth. In medium microwave-safe bowl, stir together ¼ cup water and 1½ teaspoons cornstarch until dissolved. Add peach mixture; stir. Microwave at HIGH (100%) 2½ to 3 minutes or until mixture boils and thickens, stirring after each minute. Cool completely.

NUTRIENTS PER SERVING			
Calories	140	Fat	1 g
Cholesterol	0 mg	Sodium	130 mg

Four Way Fudgey Chocolate Cake

1¼ cups all-purpose flour
 1 cup sugar
 1 cup skim milk
 ⅓ cup HERSHEY®S Cocoa or HERSHEY®S European Style Cocoa
 ⅓ cup unsweetened applesauce
 1 tablespoon white vinegar
 1 teaspoon baking soda
 ½ teaspoon vanilla extract
    Toppings (optional): Frozen light non-dairy whipped topping,
       thawed, REESE®S Peanut Butter Chips, sliced strawberries,
       chopped almonds, raspberries

Heat oven to 350°F. Spray 9-inch square baking pan or 11×7×2-inch baking
pan with vegetable cooking spray. In large mixer bowl, stir together flour, sugar,
milk, cocoa, applesauce, vinegar, baking soda and vanilla; beat on low speed of
electric mixer until blended. Pour batter into prepared pan. Bake 30 to
35 minutes or until wooden pick inserted in center comes out clean. Cool
completely in pan on wire rack. If desired, spoon whipped topping into pastry
bag fitted with star tip; pipe stars in two lines to divide cake into four squares
or rectangles. Using plain tip, pipe lattice design into one square; place peanut
butter chips onto lattice. Place strawberries into another square. Sprinkle
almonds into third square. Place raspberries into remaining square. Serve
immediately. Cover; refrigerate leftover cake. Store ungarnished cake, covered,
at room temperature.   *Makes 12 servings*

NUTRIENTS PER SERVING			
(no toppings)			
Calories	130	Fat	0 g
Cholesterol	0 mg	Sodium	80 mg

Pineapple Upside-Down Cake

1 (8-ounce) can crushed pineapple in juice, undrained
2 tablespoons margarine, melted, divided
½ cup firmly packed light brown sugar
6 whole maraschino cherries
1½ cups all-purpose flour
2 tablespoons baking powder
¼ teaspoon salt
1 cup granulated sugar
½ cup MOTT'S® Natural Apple Sauce
1 whole egg
3 egg whites, beaten until stiff

1. Preheat oven to 375°F. Drain pineapple; reserve juice. Spray sides of 8-inch square baking pan with nonstick cooking spray.

2. Spread 1 tablespoon melted margarine evenly in bottom of prepared pan. Sprinkle with brown sugar; top with pineapple. Slice cherries in half. Arrange cherries, cut side up, so that when cake is cut, each piece will have cherry half in center.

3. In small bowl, combine flour, baking powder and salt. In large bowl, combine granulated sugar, apple sauce, whole egg, remaining 1 tablespoon melted margarine and reserved pineapple juice.

4. Add flour mixture to apple sauce mixture; stir until well blended. Fold in beaten egg whites. Gently pour batter over fruit, spreading evenly.

5. Bake 35 to 40 minutes or until lightly browned. Cool on wire rack 10 minutes. Invert cake onto serving plate. Serve warm or cool completely. Cut into 12 pieces.

Makes 12 servings

NUTRIENTS PER SERVING			
Calories	200	Fat	3 g
Cholesterol	20 mg	Sodium	240 mg

Pineapple Upside-Down Cake

Polenta Apricot Pudding Cake

¼ cup chopped dried apricots
2 cups orange juice
1 cup part-skim ricotta cheese
3 tablespoons honey
¾ cup sugar
½ cup cornmeal
½ cup all-purpose flour
¼ teaspoon grated nutmeg
¼ cup slivered almonds

1. Preheat oven to 300°F. Soak apricots in ¼ cup water in small bowl 15 minutes. Drain and discard water. Pat apricots dry with paper towels; set aside.

2. Combine orange juice, ricotta cheese and honey in medium bowl. Mix on medium speed of electric mixer 5 minutes or until smooth. Combine sugar, cornmeal, flour and nutmeg in small bowl. Gradually add sugar mixture to orange juice mixture; blend well. Slowly stir in apricots.

3. Spray 10-inch nonstick springform pan with nonstick cooking spray. Pour batter into prepared pan. Sprinkle with almonds. Bake 60 to 70 minutes or until center is firm and cake is golden brown. Garnish with powdered sugar, if desired. Serve warm.

Makes 8 servings

NUTRIENTS PER SERVING			
Calories	245	Fat	5 g
Cholesterol	10 mg	Sodium	43 mg

Polenta Apricot Pudding Cake

Angel Food Cake with Pineapple Sauce

1 can (20 ounces) DOLE® Crushed Pineapple
1 tablespoon orange marmalade, peach or apricot fruit spread
2 tablespoons sugar
1 tablespoon cornstarch
1 prepared angel food cake

• **Combine** undrained pineapple, orange marmalade, sugar and cornstarch in small saucepan. Bring to boil. Reduce heat to low; cook 2 minutes, stirring constantly, or until sauce thickens. Cool slightly. Sauce can be served warm or chilled. Cut angel food cake into 12 slices. To serve, spoon sauce over each slice.

Makes 12 servings

NUTRIENTS PER SERVING			
Calories	116	Fat	0 g
Cholesterol	0 mg	Sodium	213 mg

Chocolate Swirled Cheesecake

Yogurt Cheese (page 310)
2 tablespoons graham cracker crumbs
1 package (8 ounces) Neufchâtel cheese (light cream cheese), softened
1½ teaspoons vanilla extract
¾ cup sugar
1 tablespoon cornstarch
1 container (8 ounces) liquid egg substitute
¼ cup HERSHEY®S Cocoa
¼ teaspoon almond extract

continued on page 310

Chocolate Swirled Cheesecake

308

Chocolate Swirled Cheesecake, continued

Prepare Yogurt Cheese. Heat oven to 325°F. Spray bottom of 8- or 9-inch springform pan with vegetable cooking spray. Sprinkle graham cracker crumbs on bottom of pan. In large mixer bowl, beat Yogurt Cheese, Neufchâtel cheese and vanilla on medium speed of electric mixer until smooth. Add sugar and cornstarch; beat just until well blended. Gradually add egg substitute, beating on low speed until blended. Transfer 1½ cups batter to medium bowl; add cocoa. Beat until well blended. Stir almond extract into vanilla batter. Alternately spoon vanilla and chocolate batters into prepared pan. With knife or metal spatula, cut through batters for marble effect.

Bake 35 minutes for 8-inch pan, 40 minutes for 9-inch pan or until edge is set. With knife, loosen cheesecake from side of pan. Cool completely in pan on wire rack. Cover; refrigerate at least 6 hours before serving. Just before serving, remove side of pan. Garnish as desired. Cover; refrigerate leftover cheesecake.

Makes 16 servings

Yogurt Cheese: Use one 16-ounce container plain lowfat yogurt, no gelatin added. Line colander with large piece of double thickness cheesecloth; place over deep bowl. Spoon yogurt into colander; cover with plastic wrap. Refrigerate until liquid no longer drains from yogurt, about 24 hours. Remove yogurt from cheesecloth; discard liquid.

NUTRIENTS PER SERVING			
Calories	100	Fat	4 g
Cholesterol	10 mg	Sodium	90 mg

Trimmed Down Chocoberry Cheesecake

Graham Crust (recipe follows)
1 cup (8 ounces) nonfat cottage cheese
1 package (8 ounces) Neufchâtel cheese (light cream cheese), softened
1 cup sugar
⅓ cup HERSHEY₃S Cocoa or HERSHEY₃S European Style Cocoa
1 package (10 ounces) frozen strawberries in syrup, thawed and drained
⅓ cup liquid egg substitute
Frozen light non-dairy whipped topping, thawed (optional)
Additional strawberries (optional)

Prepare Graham Crust. Heat oven to 325°F. In food processor, place cottage cheese; process until smooth. Add Neufchâtel cheese, sugar, cocoa and 1 package strawberries; process until smooth. Stir in egg substitute. Pour gently over prepared Graham Crust.

Bake 55 to 60 minutes or just until almost set in center. With knife, loosen cheesecake from side of pan. Cool completely in pan on wire rack. Cover; refrigerate until chilled. Just before serving, remove side of pan. Serve with whipped topping and additional strawberries, if desired. Cover; refrigerate leftover cheesecake. *Makes 14 servings*

Graham Crust: In small bowl, stir together ½ cup graham cracker crumbs and 1 tablespoon melted margarine; press onto bottom of 8-inch springform pan.

NUTRIENTS PER SERVING			
Calories	160	Fat	5 g
Cholesterol	15 mg	Sodium	150 mg

311

Luscious Chocolate Cheesecake

2   cups (1 pound) nonfat cottage cheese
¾   cup liquid egg substitute
⅔   cup sugar
4   ounces (½ of 8-ounce package) Neufchâtel cheese, softened
⅓   cup HERSHEY.S Cocoa or HERSHEY.S European Style Cocoa
½   teaspoon vanilla extract
    Yogurt Topping (recipe follows)
    Sliced strawberries, raspberries or mandarin orange
       segments (optional)

Heat oven to 300°F. Spray 9-inch springform pan with vegetable cooking spray. In food processor, place cottage cheese, egg substitute, sugar, Neufchâtel cheese, cocoa and vanilla; process until smooth. Pour into prepared pan. Bake 35 minutes or until edges are set. Meanwhile, prepare Yogurt Topping. Carefully spread topping over cheesecake. Continue baking 5 minutes. Remove from oven to wire rack. With knife, loosen cheesecake from side of pan. Cool completely. Cover; refrigerate until chilled. Remove side of pan. Serve with strawberries or mandarin orange segments, if desired. Refrigerate leftover cheesecake.

Makes 12 servings

YOGURT TOPPING

⅔   cup plain nonfat yogurt
2   tablespoons sugar

In small bowl, stir together yogurt and sugar until well blended.

NUTRIENTS PER SERVING			
Calories	120	Fat	3 g
Cholesterol	10 mg	Sodium	210 mg

Luscious Chocolate Cheesecake

Key Lime Cheesecake

CRUST
¾ cup crunchy nutlike cereal nuggets
¾ cup graham cracker crumbs
¼ cup Prune Purée (page 90) or prepared prune butter
3 tablespoons sugar

FILLING
1 package (8 ounces) fat free cream cheese, softened
1 can (14 ounces) low fat sweetened condensed milk
½ cup fresh lime juice
½ cup egg substitute
1 teaspoon grated lime peel
2 egg whites
⅛ teaspoon cream of tartar

TOPPING
⅔ cup low fat nondairy whipped topping
Lime slices and lime peel, for garnish

Preheat oven to 375°F. To prepare Crust, in food processor, process cereal, graham cracker crumbs, Prune Purée and sugar until well blended. Press onto bottom and part way up side of ungreased 8½- or 9-inch springform pan. To prepare Filling, in mixer bowl, beat cream cheese on medium speed until smooth. Gradually beat in condensed milk, lime juice, egg substitute and lime peel until blended. In small mixer bowl, with clean beaters, beat egg whites with cream of tartar until soft peaks form. Fold into cream cheese mixture. Pour into prepared crust. Bake in center of oven 20 to 25 minutes or until filling is set. Cool; refrigerate until cold. Cut into wedges. Top each serving with dollop of whipped topping. Garnish with lime slice and peel.

Makes 10 servings

Favorite recipe from **California Prune Board**

Key Lime Cheesecake

Cookies & Bars

Low Fat Molasses Jumbles

½ cup Prune Purée (page 90) or prepared prune butter
½ cup sugar
½ cup molasses
1 egg
2 cups all-purpose flour
2 teaspoons ground cinnamon
1 teaspoon ground ginger
½ teaspoon baking soda
½ teaspoon salt

Preheat oven to 350°F. Coat baking sheets with vegetable cooking spray. In large bowl, mix Prune Purée, sugar and molasses until well blended. Add egg; mix well. Combine remaining ingredients; stir into prune mixture just until blended. Roll heaping tablespoonfuls of dough in additional sugar. Place on baking sheets, spacing 2 inches apart. With fork, flatten dough in crisscross fashion until ½ inch thick. Bake in center of oven about 12 to 13 minutes or until set and bottoms are lightly browned. Remove from baking sheets to wire racks to cool completely. *Makes 30 (2½-inch) cookies*

NUTRIENTS PER SERVING			
(1 cookie)			
Calories	68	Fat	1 g
Cholesterol	7 mg	Sodium	57 mg

Favorite recipe from **California Prune Board**

Chocolate Almond Biscotti

3 cups all-purpose flour
½ cup unsweetened cocoa
2 teaspoons DAVIS® Baking Powder
½ teaspoon salt
1 cup granulated sugar
⅔ cup FLEISCHMANN'S® Margarine, softened
¾ cup EGG BEATERS® Healthy Real Egg Product
1 teaspoon almond extract
½ cup whole blanced almonds, toasted and coarsely chopped
  Powdered Sugar Glaze (recipe follows)

In medium bowl, combine flour, cocoa, baking powder and salt. In large bowl, with electric mixer at medium speed, beat granulated sugar and margarine or until creamy. Add Egg Beaters® and almond extract; beat well. With mixer at low speed, gradually beat in flour mixture, just until blended; stir in almonds. On lightly greased baking sheet, form dough into two (12×2½-inch) logs. Bake at 350°F for 25 to 30 minutes or until toothpick inserted in centers comes out clean. Cool logs on wire racks 15 minutes.

Using serrated knife, slice each log diagonally into 12 (1-inch-thick) slices; place, cut sides up, on same baking sheet. Bake at 350°F for 12 to 15 minutes on each side or until crisp and browned. Cool completely on wire rack. Drizzle with Powdered Sugar Glaze. *Makes 2 dozen cookies*

Powdered Sugar Glaze: In small bowl, combine 1 cup powdered sugar and 5 to 6 teaspoons water until smooth.

Prep time: 25 minutes
Cook time: 45 minutes

NUTRIENTS PER SERVING			
	(1 cookie)		
Calories	160	Fat	7 g
Cholesterol	0 mg	Sodium	125 mg

Chocolate Almond Biscotti

Gingersnaps

2½ cups all-purpose flour
1½ teaspoons ground ginger
1 teaspoon baking soda
1 teaspoon ground allspice
½ teaspoon salt
1½ cups sugar
2 tablespoons margarine, softened
½ cup MOTT'S® Apple Sauce
¼ cup GRANDMA'S® Molasses

1. Preheat oven to 375°F. Spray cookie sheets with nonstick cooking spray.

2. In medium bowl, sift together flour, ginger, baking soda, allspice and salt.

3. In large bowl, beat sugar and margarine with electric mixer at medium speed until blended. Whisk in apple sauce and molasses.

4. Add flour mixture to apple sauce mixture; stir until well blended.

5. Drop rounded tablespoonfuls of dough 1 inch apart onto prepared cookie sheets. Flatten each cookie slightly with moistened fingertips.

6. Bake 12 to 15 minutes or until firm. Cool completely on wire rack.

Makes 3 dozen cookies

NUTRIENTS PER SERVING			
(1 cookie)			
Calories	80	Fat	1 g
Cholesterol	0 mg	Sodium	60 mg

Top to bottom: Oatmeal Cookies (page 322),
Gingersnaps

Oatmeal Cookies

1 cup all-purpose flour
1 teaspoon baking powder
½ teaspoon baking soda
½ teaspoon salt
¼ cup MOTT'S® Cinnamon Apple Sauce
2 tablespoons margarine
½ cup granulated sugar
½ cup firmly packed light brown sugar
1 egg
1 teaspoon vanilla extract
1⅓ cups uncooked rolled oats
½ cup raisins (optional)

1. Preheat oven to 375°F. Spray cookie sheets with nonstick cooking spray.

2. In small bowl, combine flour, baking powder, baking soda and salt.

3. In large bowl, place apple sauce. Cut in margarine with pastry blender or fork until margarine breaks into pea-sized pieces. Add granulated sugar, brown sugar, egg and vanilla; stir until well blended.

4. Add flour mixture to apple sauce mixture; stir until well blended. Fold in oats and raisins, if desired.

5. Drop rounded teaspoonfuls of dough 2 inches apart onto prepared cookie sheets.

6. Bake 10 to 12 minutes or until lightly browned. Cool 5 minutes on cookie sheets. Remove to wire racks; cool completely.   *Makes 3 dozen cookies*

NUTRIENTS PER SERVING			
(1 cookie)			
Calories	60	Fat	1 g
Cholesterol	5 mg	Sodium	60 mg

Mocha Cookies

   2   tablespoons plus 1½ teaspoons instant coffee granules
1½   tablespoons skim milk
   ⅓   cup packed light brown sugar
   ¼   cup granulated sugar
   ¼   cup margarine
   1   egg
   ½   teaspoon almond extract
   2   cups all-purpose flour, sifted
   ¼   cup wheat flakes
   ½   teaspoon ground cinnamon
   ¼   teaspoon baking powder

Preheat oven to 350°F. Spray cookie sheets with nonstick cooking spray.
Dissolve coffee granules in milk. In large bowl, beat brown sugar, granulated
sugar and margarine until smooth and creamy. Beat in egg, almond extract and
coffee mixture. Combine flour, wheat flakes, cinnamon and baking powder;
gradually beat flour mixture into sugar mixture. Drop by teaspoonfuls onto
prepared cookie sheets; flatten with back of fork. Bake 8 to 10 minutes.

Makes about 40 cookies

NUTRIENTS PER SERVING			
(1 cookie)			
Calories	48	Fat	1 g
Cholesterol	5 mg	Sodium	20 mg

Favorite recipe from **The Sugar Association, Inc.**

Cherry Chocolate Chip Walnut Cookies

1 cup sugar
¼ cup Prune Purée (page 90) or prepared prune butter *or* 1 jar
     (2½ ounces) first-stage baby food prunes
¼ cup water
2 tablespoons nonfat milk
1 teaspoon vanilla
½ teaspoon instant espresso coffee powder *or* 1 teaspoon
     instant coffee granules
1 cup all-purpose flour
½ cup unsweetened cocoa powder
¾ teaspoon baking soda
½ teaspoon salt
½ cup dried sour cherries
¼ cup chopped walnuts
¼ cup semisweet chocolate chips

Preheat oven to 350°F. Coat baking sheets with vegetable cooking spray. In large bowl, whisk together sugar, Prune Purée, water, milk, vanilla and espresso powder until mixture is well blended, about 1 minute. Combine flour, cocoa, baking soda and salt; mix into prune mixture until well blended. Stir in cherries, walnuts and chocolate chips. Spoon twelve equal mounds of dough onto prepared baking sheets, spacing at least 2 inches apart. Bake in center of oven 18 to 20 minutes or until set and tops of cookies feel dry to the touch. Cool on baking sheets 2 minutes; remove to wire rack to cool completely.

Makes 12 large cookies

NUTRIENTS PER SERVING			
	(1 cookie)		
Calories	215	Fat	4 g
Cholesterol	0 mg	Sodium	180 mg

Favorite recipe from **California Prune Board**

Cherry Chocolate Chip Walnut Cookies

Soft Apple Cider Cookies

1 cup firmly packed light brown sugar
½ cup FLEISCHMANN'S® Margarine, softened
½ cup apple cider
½ cup EGG BEATERS® Healthy Real Egg Product
2¼ cups all-purpose flour
1½ teaspoons ground cinnamon
1 teaspoon baking soda
¼ teaspoon salt
2 medium apples, peeled and diced (about 1½ cups)
¾ cup PLANTER'S® Almonds, chopped
Cider Glaze (recipe follows)

In large bowl, with electric mixer at medium speed, beat sugar and margarine until creamy. Add cider and Egg Beaters®; beat until smooth. With electric mixer at low speed, gradually blend in flour, cinnamon, baking soda and salt. Stir in apples and almonds.

Drop dough by tablespoonfuls, 2 inches apart, onto greased baking sheets. Bake at 375°F for 10 to 12 minutes or until golden brown. Remove from sheets; cool on wire racks. Drizzle with Cider Glaze.   *Makes 4 dozen cookies*

Cider Glaze: In small bowl, combine 1 cup powdered sugar and 2 tablespoons apple cider until smooth.

Prep time: 30 minutes
Cook time: 12 minutes

NUTRIENTS PER SERVING			
(1 cookie)			
Calories	80	Fat	3 g
Cholesterol	0 mg	Sodium	80 mg

Soft Apple Cider Cookies

Choco-Lowfat Strawberry Shortbread Bars

¼ cup (½ stick) (56 to 60% corn oil) spread
½ cup sugar
1 egg white
1¼ cups all-purpose flour
¼ cup HERSHEY'S Cocoa or HERSHEY'S European Style Cocoa
¾ teaspoon cream of tartar
½ teaspoon baking soda
    Dash salt
½ cup strawberry all-fruit spread
    Vanilla Chip Drizzle (recipe follows)

Heat oven to 375°F. Lightly spray 13×9×2-inch baking pan with vegetable cooking spray. Combine corn oil spread and sugar; beat on medium speed of electric mixer until well blended. Add egg white; beat until well blended. Mix flour, cocoa, cream of tartar, baking soda and salt; gradually add to sugar mixture. Gently press onto bottom of prepared pan. Bake 10 to 12 minutes or just until set. Cool in pan on wire rack. Spread fruit spread evenly over crust. Cut into bars or other shapes with cookie cutters. Prepare Vanilla Chip Drizzle; drizzle over tops of bars. Let stand until set. *Makes 36 bars*

VANILLA CHIP DRIZZLE

⅓ cup HERSHEY'S Vanilla Milk Chips
½ teaspoon shortening (do not use butter, margarine or oil)

In small microwave-safe bowl, place vanilla milk chips and shortening. Microwave at HIGH (100% power) 30 seconds; stir. If necessary, microwave at HIGH an additional 15 seconds at a time, stirring after each heating, just until chips are melted when stirred. Use immediately.

NUTRIENTS PER SERVING			
(1 bar with drizzle)			
Calories	50	Fat	1 g
Cholesterol	0 mg	Sodium	45 mg

Choco-Lowfat Strawberry Shortbread Bars

Tri-Layer Chocolate Oatmeal Bars

CRUST

1	cup uncooked rolled oats
½	cup all-purpose flour
½	cup firmly packed light brown sugar
¼	cup MOTT'S® Natural Apple Sauce
1	tablespoon margarine, melted
¼	teaspoon baking soda

FILLING

⅔	cup all-purpose flour
½	teaspoon baking powder
¼	teaspoon salt
¾	cup granulated sugar
¼	cup MOTT'S® Natural Apple Sauce
1	whole egg
1	egg white
2	tablespoons unsweetened cocoa powder
1	tablespoon margarine, melted
½	teaspoon vanilla extract
¼	cup low fat buttermilk

ICING

1	cup powdered sugar
1	tablespoon unsweetened cocoa powder
1	tablespoon skim milk
1	teaspoon instant coffee powder

1. Preheat oven to 350°F. Spray 8-inch square baking pan with nonstick cooking spray.

continued on page 332

Tri-Layer Chocolate Oatmeal Bars

Tri-Layer Chocolate Oatmeal Bars, continued

2. **To prepare Crust,** in medium bowl, combine oats, ½ cup flour, brown sugar, ¼ cup apple sauce, 1 tablespoon margarine and baking soda. Stir with fork until mixture resembles coarse crumbs. Press evenly into bottom of prepared pan. Bake 10 minutes.

3. **To prepare Filling,** in small bowl, combine ⅔ cup flour, baking powder and salt.

4. In large bowl, combine granulated sugar, ¼ cup apple sauce, whole egg, egg white, 2 tablespoons cocoa, 1 tablespoon margarine and vanilla.

5. Add flour mixture to apple sauce mixture alternately with buttermilk; stir until well blended. Spread filling over baked crust.

6. Bake 25 minutes or until toothpick inserted in center comes out clean. Cool completely on wire rack.

7. **To prepare Icing,** in small bowl, combine powdered sugar, 1 tablespoon cocoa, milk and coffee powder until smooth. Spread evenly over bars. Let stand until set. Run tip of knife through icing to score. Cut into 14 bars.

Makes 14 servings

NUTRIENTS PER SERVING			
Calories	190	Fat	3 g
Cholesterol	15 mg	Sodium	100 mg

332

PHILLY® FREE® Marble Brownies

1 package (20½ ounces) reduced calorie brownie mix
1 package (8 ounces) PHILADELPHIA BRAND® FREE® Fat
  Free Cream Cheese, softened
⅓ cup sugar
1 egg
½ teaspoon vanilla
1 cup BAKER'S® Semi-Sweet Real Chocolate Chips

PREPARE brownie mix as directed on package. Pour into 13×9-inch baking pan that has been sprayed with nonstick cooking spray.

BEAT cream cheese with electric mixer on medium speed until smooth. Add sugar, mixing until blended. Add egg and vanilla; mix just until blended.

POUR cream cheese mixture over brownie mixture; cut through batter with knife several times for marble effect. Sprinkle with chips.

BAKE at 350°F for 35 to 40 minutes or until cream cheese mixture is lightly browned. Cool; cut into squares.   *Makes 24 servings*

Prep time: 20 minutes
Baking time: 40 minutes

Cappuccino Brownies: Dissolve 1 tablespoon MAXWELL HOUSE® Instant Coffee in 1 tablespoon water. Stir coffee mixture into cream cheese mixture. Continue as directed.

NUTRIENTS PER SERVING			
Calories	130	Fat	3 g
Cholesterol	20 mg	Sodium	80 mg

333

Fruit and Nut Bars

  1 cup unsifted all-purpose flour
  1 cup quick oats
  ⅔ cup brown sugar
  2 teaspoons baking soda
  ½ teaspoon salt
  ½ teaspoon cinnamon
  ⅔ cup buttermilk
  3 tablespoons vegetable oil
  2 large egg whites, lightly beaten
  1 Golden Delicious apple, cored and chopped
  ½ cup dried cranberries or raisins, chopped
  ¼ cup chopped nuts
  2 tablespoons flaked coconut (optional)

1. Heat oven to 375°F. Lightly grease 9-inch square baking pan. In large mixing bowl, combine flour, oats, brown sugar, baking soda, salt and cinnamon; stir to blend.

2. Add buttermilk, oil and egg whites; beat with electric mixer just until mixed. Stir in apple, dried fruit and nuts; spread evenly in pan and top with coconut, if desired. Bake 20 to 25 minutes or until cake tester inserted in center comes out clean. Cool and cut into 10 bars.

Makes 10 bars

NUTRIENTS PER SERVING			
Calories	232	Fat	7 g
Cholesterol	1 mg	Sodium	298 mg

Favorite recipe from **Washington Apple Commission**

Fruit and Nut Bars

Bamboozlers

1 cup all-purpose flour
¾ cup packed light brown sugar
¼ cup unsweetened cocoa powder
1 egg
2 egg whites
5 tablespoons margarine, melted
¼ cup skim milk
¼ cup honey
1 teaspoon vanilla
2 tablespoons semisweet chocolate chips
2 tablespoons coarsely chopped walnuts
  Powdered sugar (optional)

1. Preheat oven to 350°F. Grease and flour 8-inch square baking pan; set aside. Combine flour, brown sugar and cocoa in medium bowl. Blend together egg, egg whites, margarine, milk, honey and vanilla in medium bowl. Add to flour mixture; mix well. Pour into prepared baking pan; sprinkle with chocolate chips and walnuts.

2. Bake brownies until they spring back when lightly touched in center, about 30 minutes. Cool completely in pan on wire rack. Sprinkle with powdered sugar just before serving.   *Makes 12 servings*

Peanutters: Substitute peanut butter chips for chocolate chips and peanuts for walnuts.

Brownie Sundaes: Top each brownie with a scoop of vanilla nonfat frozen yogurt and 2 tablespoons nonfat chocolate or caramel sauce.

NUTRIENTS PER SERVING			
Calories	188	Fat	7 g
Cholesterol	18 mg	Sodium	79 mg

336

Pumpkin Harvest Bars

1¾ cups all-purpose flour
2 teaspoons baking powder
1 teaspoon grated orange peel
1 teaspoon ground cinnamon
½ teaspoon salt
½ teaspoon ground nutmeg
¼ teaspoon ground ginger
¼ teaspoon ground cloves
¾ cup sugar
½ cup MOTT'S® Natural Apple Sauce
½ cup solid-pack pumpkin
1 whole egg
1 egg white
2 tablespoons vegetable oil
½ cup raisins

1. Preheat oven to 350°F. Spray 13×9-inch baking pan with nonstick cooking spray.

2. In small bowl, combine flour, baking powder, orange peel, cinnamon, salt, nutmeg, ginger and cloves.

3. In large bowl, combine sugar, apple sauce, pumpkin, whole egg, egg white and oil.

4. Add flour mixture to apple sauce mixture; stir until well blended. Stir in raisins. Spread batter into prepared pan.

5. Bake 25 to 30 minutes or until toothpick inserted in center comes out clean. Cool on wire rack 15 minutes; cut into 16 bars.   *Makes 16 servings*

NUTRIENTS PER SERVING			
Calories	130	Fat	2 g
Cholesterol	15 mg	Sodium	110 mg

Fruit and Oat Squares

1 cup all-purpose flour
1 cup uncooked quick oats
¾ cup packed light brown sugar
½ teaspoon baking soda
¼ teaspoon salt
¼ teaspoon ground cinnamon
⅓ cup margarine or butter, melted
¾ cup apricot, cherry or other fruit flavor preserves

1. Preheat oven to 350°F. Spray 9-inch square baking pan with nonstick cooking spray; set aside.

2. Combine flour, oats, brown sugar, baking soda, salt and cinnamon in medium bowl; mix well. Add margarine; stir with fork until mixture is crumbly.

3. Reserve ¾ cup crumb mixture for topping. Press remaining crumb mixture evenly onto bottom of prepared pan. Bake 5 to 7 minutes or until lightly browned.

4. Spread preserves onto crust; sprinkle with reserved crumb mixture.

5. Bake 20 to 25 minutes or until golden brown. Cool completely in pan on wire rack. Cut into 16 squares. *Makes 16 servings*

NUTRIENTS PER SERVING			
Calories	161	Fat	4 g
Cholesterol	0 mg	Sodium	123 mg

Fruit and Oat Squares

Desserts

• • • • • • • • • •

Apple Strudel

1   sheet (½ of a 17¼-ounce package) frozen puff pastry
1   cup (4 ounces) shredded ALPINE LACE® Reduced Fat
     Cheddar Cheese
2   large Granny Smith apples, peeled, cored and sliced ⅛ inch
     thick (12 ounces)
⅓   cup golden raisins
2   tablespoons apple brandy (optional)
¼   cup granulated sugar
¼   cup packed light brown sugar
½   teaspoon ground cinnamon
2   tablespoons unsalted butter substitute, melted

1. To shape the pastry: Thaw the pastry for 20 minutes. Preheat the oven to 350°F. On a floured board, roll the pastry into a 15×12-inch rectangle.

2. To make the filling: Sprinkle the cheese on the dough, leaving a 1-inch border. Arrange the apples on top. Sprinkle with the raisins, then the brandy, if you wish. In a small cup, mix both of the sugars with the cinnamon, then sprinkle over the apple filling.

3. Starting from one of the wide ends, roll up jelly-roll style. Place on a baking sheet, seam side down, tucking the ends under. Using a sharp knife, make 7 diagonal slits on the top, then brush with the butter. Bake for 35 minutes or until golden brown.

Makes 18 servings

NUTRIENTS PER SERVING			
Calories	151	Fat	8 g
Cholesterol	6 mg	Sodium	123 mg

Easy Fruit Tarts

12   wonton skins
      Vegetable cooking spray
 2   tablespoons apple jelly or apricot fruit spread
1½   cups sliced or cut-up fruit such as DOLE® Bananas,
      Strawberries, Raspberries or Red or Green Seedless Grapes
 1   cup nonfat or low fat yogurt, any flavor

• **Press** wonton skins into 12 muffin cups sprayed with vegetable cooking spray, allowing corners to stand over edges of muffin cups.

• **Bake** at 375°F 5 minutes or until lightly browned. Carefully remove wonton cups to wire rack; cool.

• **Cook** and stir jelly in small saucepan over low heat until jelly melts.

• **Brush** bottoms of cooled wonton cups with melted jelly. Place two fruit slices in each cup; spoon rounded tablespoon of yogurt on top of fruit. Garnish with fruit slice and mint leaves. Serve immediately.   *Makes 12 servings*

Prep time: 20 minutes
Bake time: 5 minutes

NUTRIENTS PER SERVING			
Calories	55	Fat	0 g
Cholesterol	1 mg	Sodium	60 mg

Chocolate-Filled Meringue Shells
with Strawberry Sauce

2 egg whites
¼ teaspoon cream of tartar
Dash salt
¾ cup sugar
¼ teaspoon vanilla extract
Chocolate Filling (recipe follows)
1 package (10 ounces) frozen strawberries in syrup, thawed

Heat oven to 275°F. Line 10 muffin cups (2½ inches in diameter) with paper bake cups. In small bowl, beat egg whites with cream of tartar and salt until soft peaks form. Beat in sugar, 1 tablespoon at a time, beating well after each addition until stiff peaks hold their shape and mixture is glossy. Fold in vanilla. Spoon about 3 tablespoons mixture in each muffin cup. Using back of spoon, push mixture up sides of muffin cups to form well in center.

Bake 1 hour or until meringues turn delicate cream color and feel dry to the touch. Cool in pan on wire rack. Before serving, carefully remove paper from shells. For each serving, spoon 1 heaping tablespoonful Chocolate Filling into meringue shell. In blender container, place strawberries with syrup. Blend until smooth. Spoon over filled shells. Store leftover shells loosely covered at room temperature. *Makes 10 servings*

Chocolate Filling: In small bowl, beat 4 ounces softened Neufchâtel cheese (light cream cheese) and ¼ cup HERSHEY®S Cocoa on medium speed of electric mixer until blended. Gradually add ¾ cup powdered sugar. Fold in 1 cup frozen light non-dairy whipped topping, thawed.

NUTRIENTS PER SERVING			
Calories	170	Fat	4 g
Cholesterol	10 mg	Sodium	95 mg

Chocolate-Filled Meringue Shells
with Strawberry Sauce

Pumpkin Apple Tart

CRUST

      1 cup plain dry bread crumbs
      1 cup crunchy nut-like cereal nuggets
    1/2 cup sugar
    1/2 teaspoon ground cinnamon
    1/2 teaspoon ground nutmeg
    1/4 cup MOTT'S® Natural Apple Sauce
      2 tablespoons margarine, melted
      1 egg white

FILLING

     12 ounces evaporated skim milk
   1 1/2 cups solid-pack pumpkin
    2/3 cup sugar
    1/2 cup MOTT'S® Chunky Apple Sauce
    1/3 cup GRANDMA'S® Molasses
      2 egg whites
      1 whole egg
    1/2 teaspoon ground ginger
    1/2 teaspoon ground cinnamon
    1/2 teaspoon ground nutmeg
         Frozen light nondairy whipped topping, thawed (optional)

1. Preheat oven to 375°F. Spray 9- or 10-inch springform pan with nonstick cooking spray.

2. **To prepare Crust,** in medium bowl, combine bread crumbs, cereal, 1/2 cup sugar, 1/2 teaspoon cinnamon and 1/2 teaspoon nutmeg.

3. Add 1/4 cup apple sauce, margarine and egg white; mix until moistened. Press onto bottom of prepared pan.

continued on page 350

Pumpkin Apple Tart

Pumpkin Apple Tart, continued

4. Bake 8 minutes.

5. To prepare Filling, place evaporated milk in small saucepan. Cook over medium heat until milk almost boils, stirring occasionally.

6. In large bowl, combine evaporated milk, pumpkin, ⅔ cup sugar, ½ cup chunky apple sauce, molasses, 2 egg whites, whole egg, ginger, ½ teaspoon cinnamon and ½ teaspoon nutmeg. Pour into baked crust.

7. *Increase oven temperature to 400°F.* Bake 35 to 40 minutes or until center is set.

8. Cool 20 minutes on wire rack. Remove side of pan. Spoon or pipe whipped topping onto tart, if desired. Cut into 12 slices. Refrigerate leftovers.

Makes 12 servings

NUTRIENTS PER SERVING			
Calories	210	Fat	3 g
Cholesterol	20 mg	Sodium	170 mg

SMUCKER'S® Double Apple Turnovers

½ cup SMUCKER'S® Apple Butter
½ cup apple cider or juice
½ teaspoon ground cinnamon
  Grated peel of 1 orange
¼ cup golden raisins
4 large firm apples, peeled, cored and chopped
1 package frozen phyllo dough
  Nonstick cooking spray
  Granulated sugar for garnish

Preheat oven to 375°F. Place Smucker's® Apple Butter, cider, cinnamon and orange peel in a pot and simmer for 5 minutes. Add the raisins and heat for 2 minutes more. Add the apples; cook over medium heat for about 10 minutes or until the apples begin to soften and most of the liquid evaporates. Cool in refrigerator.

Unwrap the phyllo dough. Remove one sheet of dough, keeping remaining sheets covered with damp cloth. Coat dough with cooking spray, then cover with a second sheet of dough. Spray top sheet with cooking spray.

Spoon about ⅓ cup of the apple filling on the lower right corner of the dough. Fold the dough over the filling to form a large rectangle. Then fold the turnover as if it were a flag, making a triangular packet with each turn. Repeat process with remaining dough and filling until 6 turnovers are made. Place finished turnovers on a baking sheet. Sprinkle turnovers with granulated sugar before baking. Bake approximately 25 minutes until golden.   *Makes 6 turnovers*

Prep time: 30 minutes
Cook time: 40 minutes

NUTRIENTS PER SERVING			
Calories	214	Fat	1 g
Cholesterol	0 mg	Sodium	2 mg

Tiramisu

3 cups water
3 tablespoons honey
1 cup instant nonfat dry milk
2 tablespoons cornstarch
⅛ teaspoon ground cloves
¼ teaspoon ground cinnamon
⅛ teaspoon salt
½ cup cholesterol-free egg substitute
½ cup espresso coffee
2 tablespoons orange extract
12 ladyfingers, cut in half lengthwise
¼ cup grated semisweet chocolate

1. Bring water and honey to a boil in medium saucepan over high heat. Reduce heat; simmer, uncovered, 20 minutes. Remove from heat.

2. Combine dry milk, cornstarch, cloves, cinnamon and salt in medium bowl. Slowly add milk mixture to honey mixture, stirring until smooth. Bring to a boil, stirring constantly, over medium heat. Remove from heat.

3. Pour egg substitute into small bowl. Add ½ cup hot milk mixture to egg substitute; blend well. Stir egg mixture back into remaining milk mixture in saucepan. Cook over low heat 2 minutes or until thickened. Cool 15 minutes. Combine coffee with orange extract in another small bowl. Set aside.

4. Arrange 6 ladyfingers in 1-quart serving bowl. Drizzle half the coffee mixture over ladyfingers. Spread half the custard over ladyfingers. Sprinkle with half the grated chocolate. Repeat layers; cover and refrigerate 2 hours. Spoon into individual bowls. Garnish if desired.

Makes 6 servings

NUTRIENTS PER SERVING			
Calories	223	Fat	5 g
Cholesterol	82 mg	Sodium	167 mg

Fresh Fruit with Peach Glaze

2   cups DOLE® Orchard Peach, Pine-Orange-Guava, Pineapple
    Orange, Pine-Orange-Banana, Mandarin Tangerine or
    Country Raspberry Juice
3   tablespoons sugar
1   tablespoon cornstarch
1   tablespoon lemon juice
½   teaspoon grated lemon peel
8   cups cut-up fresh fruit, such as DOLE® Fresh Pineapple,
    Bananas, Strawberries, Red or Green Seedless Grapes,
    Cantaloupe, Oranges, Peaches, Nectarines or Kiwi

• **Combine** peach juice, sugar, cornstarch, lemon juice and lemon peel in medium saucepan.

• **Cook** and stir over medium-high heat 5 minutes or until mixture comes to boil. Reduce heat to low; cook 2 minutes or until slightly thickened. Cool slightly. Sauce can be served warm or chilled.

• **Arrange** fruit in dessert dishes. Spoon glaze over fruit. Refrigerate any leftovers in air-tight container. Garnish with fresh mint leaves, if desired.

Makes 8 servings

Prep time: 5 minutes
Cook time: 5 minutes

NUTRIENTS PER SERVING			
Calories	125	Fat	0 g
Cholesterol	0 mg	Sodium	19 mg

Fresh Fruit with Peach Glaze

Baked Apple Crisp

8 cups unpeeled, thinly sliced apples (about 8 medium)
2 tablespoons granulated sugar
1½ tablespoons lemon juice
4 teaspoons ground cinnamon, divided
1½ cups MOTT'S® Natural Apple Sauce
1 cup uncooked rolled oats
½ cup firmly packed light brown sugar
⅓ cup all-purpose flour
⅓ cup evaporated skim milk
¼ cup nonfat dry milk powder
1 cup vanilla nonfat yogurt

1. Preheat oven to 350°F. Spray 2-quart casserole dish with nonstick cooking spray.

2. In large bowl, toss apple slices with granulated sugar, lemon juice and 2 teaspoons cinnamon. Spoon into prepared dish. Spread apple sauce evenly over apple mixture.

3. In medium bowl, combine oats, brown sugar, flour, evaporated milk, dry milk powder and remaining 2 teaspoons cinnamon. Spread over apple sauce.

4. Bake 35 to 40 minutes or until lightly browned and bubbly. Cool slightly; serve warm. Top each serving with dollop of yogurt. *Makes 12 servings*

NUTRIENTS PER SERVING			
Calories	185	Fat	2 g
Cholesterol	0 mg	Sodium	35 mg

Baked Apple Crisp

Sweet Holidays Pizza

Sweet Crumb Crust (recipe follows)
1½ pints (3 cups) vanilla or other desired flavor nonfat frozen
       yogurt, slightly softened
1½ pints (3 cups) chocolate or other desired flavor nonfat frozen
       yogurt, slightly softened
 1   cup canned or fresh pineapple chunks
 6   whole fresh strawberries, cut in half
 1   cup thawed frozen peach slices *or* 1 medium peach, peeled
       and sliced
 1   kiwi, peeled and sliced
12   pecan halves (optional)
 ¼   cup nonfat chocolate syrup, heated nonfat chocolate fudge
       sauce or favorite fruit flavored ice cream topping

1. Prepare Sweet Crumb Crust; freeze 15 minutes.

2. Spread yogurts onto crust to within ½ inch of edge. Cover with plastic wrap; freeze until firm, 6 hours or overnight.

3. Arrange fruits and nuts decoratively on top of pizza just before serving. Drizzle with chocolate syrup. Cut into wedges to serve.   *Makes 16 servings*

SWEET CRUMB CRUST
 2   cups graham cracker or vanilla wafer cookie crumbs
 ¼   cup sugar
 ¾   teaspoon ground cinnamon
 6   tablespoons margarine, melted

1. Line 12-inch pizza pan with aluminum foil; set aside.

2. Combine crumbs, sugar and cinnamon in medium bowl; stir in margarine. Place in prepared pizza pan; press mixture evenly onto bottom of pan.

continued on page 360

Sweet Holidays Pizza, continued

Rocky Road Pizza: Omit vanilla frozen yogurt and fruits. Increase chocolate frozen yogurt to 1½ quarts (6 cups). Substitute 3 tablespoons chopped dry roasted peanuts for pecan halves. Prepare crust as directed. Spread yogurt onto crust as directed; cover and freeze until firm. Sprinkle with ¾ cup miniature marshmallows. Drizzle with nonfat chocolate syrup.

Spumoni Pizza: Omit fruits. Reduce chocolate and vanilla frozen yogurts to 2 cups *each.* Add 2 cups slightly softened strawberry frozen nonfat yogurt. Substitute 3 tablespoons toasted slivered almonds for pecan halves. Prepare crust as directed. Spread yogurts onto crust; freeze until firm. Top with ½ cup *each* halved red and green maraschino cherries; sprinkle with almonds. Drizzle with nonfat chocolate syrup or strawberry ice cream topping.

Sweet Valentine Pizza: Omit chocolate syrup. Prepare crust as directed. Substitute 1½ quarts (6 cups) strawberry nonfat frozen yogurt for the chocolate and vanilla frozen yogurts, and ½ to ¾ cup halved fresh strawberries for assorted fresh fruits. Drizzle with nonfat chocolate syrup or strawberry ice cream topping.

NUTRIENTS PER SERVING			
Calories	302	Fat	8 g
Cholesterol	0 mg	Sodium	230 mg

Light Banana Cream Pie

1 package (1.9 ounces) sugar-free vanilla instant pudding and
   pie filling (four ½-cup servings)
2¾ cups low fat milk
4 ripe, medium DOLE® Bananas, sliced
1 (9-inch) ready-made graham cracker pie crust
1 firm, medium DOLE® Banana (optional)
  Light frozen non-dairy whipped topping, thawed (optional)

• **Prepare** pudding as directed using 2¾ cups low fat milk. Stir in 4 sliced ripe bananas.

• **Spoon** banana mixture into pie crust. Place plastic wrap over pie, lightly pressing plastic to completely cover filling. Chill 1 hour or until filling is set. Remove plastic wrap.

• **Cut** firm banana into ½-inch slices. Garnish pie with whipped topping and banana slices.   *Makes 8 servings*

Prep time: 10 minutes
Chill time: 1 hour

NUTRIENTS PER SERVING			
Calories	199	Fat	6 g
Cholesterol	3 mg	Sodium	242 mg

Rice Pudding

1¼ cups water, divided
½ cup uncooked long-grain rice
2 cups evaporated skim milk
½ cup granulated sugar
½ cup raisins
½ cup MOTT'S® Natural Apple Sauce
3 tablespoons cornstarch
1 teaspoon vanilla extract
Brown sugar or nutmeg (optional)
Fresh raspberries (optional)
Orange peel strips (optional)

1. In medium saucepan, bring 1 cup water to a boil. Add rice. Reduce heat to low and simmer, covered, 20 minutes or until rice is tender and water is absorbed.

2. Add milk, granulated sugar, raisins and apple sauce. Bring to a boil. Reduce heat to low and simmer for 3 minutes, stirring occasionally.

3. Combine cornstarch and remaining ¼ cup water in small bowl. Stir into rice mixture. Simmer about 20 minutes or until mixture thickens, stirring occasionally. Remove from heat; stir in vanilla. Cool 15 to 20 minutes before serving. Sprinkle each serving with brown sugar or nutmeg and garnish with raspberries and orange peel, if desired. Refrigerate leftovers.

Makes 8 servings

NUTRIENTS PER SERVING			
Calories	190	Fat	1 g
Cholesterol	2 mg	Sodium	75 mg

Rice Pudding

Microwave Chocolate Pudding

⅓ cup sugar
¼ cup unsweetened cocoa powder
2 tablespoons cornstarch
1½ cups 2% low-fat milk
1 teaspoon vanilla
⅛ teaspoon ground cinnamon (optional)
Assorted small candies (optional)

1. Combine sugar, cocoa powder and cornstarch in medium microwavable bowl or 1-quart glass measure. Gradually add milk, stirring with wire whisk until well blended.

2. Microwave at HIGH 2 minutes; stir. Microwave at MEDIUM-HIGH (70%) 3½ to 4½ minutes or until thickened, stirring every 1½ minutes.

3. Stir in vanilla and cinnamon. Let stand at least 5 minutes before serving, stirring occasionally to prevent skin from forming. Serve warm or chilled. Garnish with candies just before serving, if desired. *Makes 4 servings*

NUTRIENTS PER SERVING			
Calories	139	Fat	2 g
Cholesterol	7 mg	Sodium	50 mg

364

Blueberry Bread Pudding with Caramel Sauce

8 slices white bread, cubed
1 cup fresh or frozen blueberries
2 cups skim milk
1 cup EGG BEATERS® Healthy Real Egg Product
⅔ cup sugar
1 teaspoon vanilla extract
¼ teaspoon ground cinnamon
   Caramel Sauce (recipe follows)

Place bread cubes in bottom of lightly greased 8×8×2-inch baking pan. Sprinkle with blueberries; set aside.

In large bowl, combine milk, Egg Beaters®, sugar, vanilla and cinnamon; pour over bread mixture. Set pan in larger pan filled with 1-inch depth hot water. Bake at 350°F for 1 hour or until knife inserted in center comes out clean. Serve warm with Caramel Sauce. *Makes 9 servings*

Caramel Sauce: In small saucepan, over low heat, heat ¼ cup skim milk and 14 vanilla caramels until caramels are melted, stirring frequently.

Prep time: 20 minutes
Cook time: 1 hour

NUTRIENTS PER SERVING			
Calories	210	Fat	2 g
Sodium	227 mg	Cholesterol	2 mg

Blueberry Bread Pudding with Caramel Sauce

Frozen Chocolate-Covered Bananas

2 ripe medium bananas
4 wooden sticks
½ cup low-fat granola cereal without raisins
⅓ cup hot fudge sauce, at room temperature

1. Cover baking sheet or 15×10-inch jelly-roll pan with waxed paper; set aside.

2. Peel bananas; cut each in half crosswise. Insert wooden stick into center of cut end of each banana, about 1½ inches into banana half. Place on prepared baking sheet; freeze until firm, at least 2 hours.

3. Place granola in large resealable plastic food storage bag; crush slightly using rolling pin or meat mallet. Transfer granola to shallow plate. Place fudge sauce in shallow dish.

4. Working with 1 banana at a time, place frozen banana in fudge sauce; turn banana and spread fudge sauce evenly onto banana with small rubber scraper. Immediately place banana on plate with granola; turn to coat lightly. Return to baking sheet in freezer. Repeat with remaining bananas.

5. Freeze until fudge sauce is very firm, at least 2 hours. Place on small plates; let stand 5 minutes before serving.

Makes 4 servings

NUTRIENTS PER SERVING			
Calories	163	Fat	4 g
Cholesterol	0 mg	Sodium	25 mg

Frozen Chocolate-Covered Bananas

Fudge Brownie Sundaes

1   cup all-purpose flour
¾   cup granulated sugar
½   cup unsweetened cocoa powder, divided
2   teaspoons baking powder
½   teaspoon salt
½   cup skim milk
¼   cup MOTT'S® Natural Apple Sauce
1   teaspoon vanilla extract
1¾   cups hot water
¾   cup firmly packed light brown sugar
½   gallon frozen nonfat vanilla yogurt
     Maraschino cherries (optional)

1. Preheat oven to 350°F. Spray 8-inch square baking pan with nonstick cooking spray.

2. In large bowl, combine flour, granulated sugar, ¼ cup cocoa, baking powder and salt. Add milk, apple sauce and vanilla; stir until well blended. Pour batter into prepared pan.

3. In medium bowl, combine hot water, brown sugar and remaining ¼ cup cocoa. Pour over batter. *Do not stir.*

4. Bake 40 minutes or until center is almost set. Cool completely on wire rack. Cut into 12 bars. Top each bar with ½-cup scoop of frozen yogurt; spoon sauce from bottom of pan over yogurt. Garnish with cherry, if desired.

Makes 12 servings

NUTRIENTS PER SERVING			
Calories	300	Fat	3 g
Cholesterol	5 mg	Sodium	200 mg

Fudge Brownie Sundae

Chocolate-Banana Sherbet

2 ripe medium bananas
1 cup apricot nectar or peach or pineapple juice, divided
½ cup HERSHEY'S Semi-Sweet Chocolate Chips
2 tablespoons sugar
1 cup lowfat 2% milk

Into blender container or food processor, slice bananas. Add ¾ cup apricot nectar. Cover; blend until smooth. In small microwave-safe bowl, place chocolate chips, remaining ¼ cup apricot nectar and sugar. Microwave at HIGH (100%) 30 seconds; stir. If necessary, microwave at HIGH an additional 15 seconds at a time, stirring after each heating, just until chips are melted and mixture is smooth when stirred. Add to banana mixture in blender. Cover; blend until thoroughly combined. Add milk. Cover; blend until smooth. Pour into 8- or 9-inch square pan. Cover; freeze until hard around edges, about 2 hours.

Into large mixer bowl or food processor, spoon partially frozen mixture; beat until smooth but not melted. Return mixture to pan. Cover; freeze until firm, stirring several times before mixture freezes. Before serving, let stand at room temperature 10 to 15 minutes until slightly softened. Scoop into 8 individual dessert dishes.

Makes 8 servings

NUTRIENTS PER SERVING			
Calories	130	Fat	4 g
Cholesterol	5 mg	Sodium	15 mg

372

Acknowledgments

• • • • • • • • • •

The publisher would like to thank the companies and organizations listed below for the use of their recipes and photographs in this publication.

Alpine Lace Brands, Inc.

American Lamb Council

California Prune Board

California Tree Fruit Agreement

Delmarva Poultry Industry, Inc.

Dole Food Company, Inc.

Florida Department of Citrus

Golden Grain/Mission Pasta

Grandma's Molasses, a division of Cadbury Beverages Inc.

Guiltless Gourmet, Inc.

Healthy Choice®

Heinz U.S.A.

Hershey Foods Corporation

Kraft Foods, Inc.

Louis Rich Company

McIlhenny Company

Minnesota Cultivated Wild Rice Council

MOTT'S® U.S.A., a division of Cadbury Beverages Inc.

Nabisco, Inc.

National Broiler Council

National Cattlemen's Beef Association

National Fisheries Institute

National Pork Producers Council

National Turkey Federation

Nestlé Food Company

Norseland, Inc.

Perdue Farms Incorporated

The Procter & Gamble Company

Sargento Foods Inc.®

The J.M. Smucker Company

StarKist Seafood Company

The Sugar Association, Inc.

USA Rice Council

Washington Apple Commission

Index

• • • • • • • • • •

A Lighter Chocolate
  Decadence, 294
Alpine Fettuccine, 280
Angel Food Cake with
  Pineapple Sauce, 308
Angel Hair Pasta with
  Seafood Sauce, 196
Apples
  Apple Barbecue Sauce, 134
  Apple-icious Lamb Kabobs,
    132
  Apple-Potato Pancakes, 270
  Apple Strudel, 342
  Baked Apple Crisp, 356
  Breakfast S'Mores, 79
  Carefree Golden Oven
    Stew, 165
  Crunchy Apple Salsa with
    Grilled Chicken, 140
  Fruit and Nut Bars, 334
  Golden Apple French
    Toast, 63
  Golden Apple Oatmeal, 78
  Golden Apple Stuffed
    Fillets, 207
  Oatmeal Apple Cranberry
    Scones, 98
  Pumpkin Apple Tart, 348
  SMUCKER'S® Double
    Apple Turnovers, 351
  Soft Apple Cider Cookies,
    326
  Spiced Turkey, Squash and
    Apple Medley, 176
  Stuffed Pork Tenderloin,
    106
  Tomato Chutney Chicken,
    158
Apple Sauce Cinnamon Rolls,
  84
Apple Sauce Coffee Ring, 92

Artichokes
  Fresh Vegetable Lasagna,
    282
  Risotto with Vegetables,
    275
  Salad Primavera, 236
  Santa Fe Chicken Pasta
    Salad, 227
  Seafood Paella, 192
Athenian Rice with Feta
  Cheese, 276

Baked Apple Crisp, 356
Balsamic Chicken, 154
Bamboozlers, 336
Bananas
  Breakfast S'Mores, 79
  Caribbean Jerk-Style Pork,
    109
  Chocolate-Banana Sherbet,
    372
  Frozen Chocolate-Covered
    Bananas, 368
  Light Banana Cream Pie,
    361
  PB & J French Toast, 58
  Pineberry Smoothie, 53
  Sunrise Pizza, 62
Barbecue Bacon Meatloaf,
  176
Barbecued Shrimp with Spicy
  Rice, 186
Barbecued Turkey Tenderloin,
  177
Bar Cookies (*see also* **Cookies**)
  Bamboozlers, 336
  Cappuccino Brownies,
    333
  Choco-Lowfat Strawberry
    Shortbread Bars, 328
  Fruit and Oat Squares, 340

PHILLY® FREE® Marble
    Brownies, 333
  Pumpkin Harvest Bars,
    338
  Tri-Layer Chocolate
    Oatmeal Bars, 330
Beans
  Beef & Bean Burritos, 118
  Black Bean Pancakes with
    Salsa, 56
  Cheesy Potato Skins with
    Black Beans & Salsa, 16
  Country Cream of Chicken
    Chowder, 43
  Country Green Beans with
    Ham, 252
  Couscous with Chick-peas
    and Vegetables, 278
  Easy Bean Nachos, 10
  Festive Chicken Dip, 30
  Five-Layered Mexican Dip,
    36
  Hot to Go Thai Salad,
    218
  Old-Fashioned Beef Stew,
    120
  Polenta with Black Bean
    Salsa, 258
  Roasted Red Pepper, Corn
    & Garbanzo Bean Salad,
    240
  Seafood Paella, 192
  South-of-the-Border Pizza,
    266
  Spicy Orzo and Black Bean
    Salad, 232
  Spinach-Tomato Salad, 234
Beef (*see also* **Beef, Ground**)
  Beef & Bean Burritos, 118
  Beef Cubed Steaks
    Provençale, 122

374

Beef (*continued*)
Grilled Flank Steak with Horseradish Sauce, 124
Healthy Chef's Salad, 222
Hot to Go Thai Salad, 218
Mighty Hero Sandwich, 121
Old-Fashioned Beef Stew, 120

Beef, Ground
Beef Burgers with Corn Salsa, 130
Chili con Carne, 127
Lasagna, 126
Mediterranean Meatballs and Couscous, 128

Beverages
DOLE® Juice Spritzer, 52
Easy Chocolate Pudding Milk Shake, 53
Hot Cocoa with Cinnamon, 54
Pineapple-Mint Lemonade, 50
Pineberry Smoothie, 53
Slimming Chocoberry Splash, 48
Black Bean Pancakes with Salsa, 56
Black Forest Chocolate Fudge Cake, 288
Black Pepper Patties, 73

Breads (*see also* **Muffins**)
Apple Sauce Cinnamon Rolls, 84
Apple Sauce Coffee Ring, 92
Apricot Carrot Bread, 88
Chili-Cheese Cornbread, 95
Cranberry Poppy Seed Loaf, 82
Oatmeal Apple Cranberry Scones, 98

Breakfast Burritos, 72
Breakfast Risotto, 78
Breakfast S'Mores, 79
Broccoli
Broccoli, Scallop and Linguine Toss, 182
Fresh Garden Dip, 26
No-Fuss Tuna Quiche, 202
SMUCKER'S® Mandarin Shrimp and Vegetable Stir-Fry, 198
Broiled Lemon Chicken, 146
Brunch Quesadillas with Fruit Salsa, 76
Brunch Rice, 74
Busy Day Oven-Fried Chicken Breasts, 164
Butterflied Shrimp Parmesan, 190

Cakes
A Lighter Chocolate Decadence, 294
Angel Food Cake with Pineapple Sauce, 308
Black Forest Chocolate Fudge Cake, 288
Chocolate Roulade with Creamy Yogurt Filling, 300
Four Way Fudgey Chocolate Cake, 303
HERSHEY'S Slimmed Down Chocolate Cake, 298
Mocha Marble Pound Cake, 292
Pineapple Upside-Down Cake, 304
Polenta Apricot Pudding Cake, 306
Sensibly Delicious Chocolate Chip Snacking Cake, 296

Sensibly Delicious Chocolate Pound Cake, 297
Trimtime Chocolate Cake Roll, 291
Cappuccino Brownies, 333
Caramel Sauce, 366
Carefree Golden Oven Stew, 165
Caribbean Jerk-Style Pork, 109
Carrots
Apricot Carrot Bread, 88
Brunch Rice, 74
Country Cream of Chicken Chowder, 43
Fresh Garden Dip, 26
Garden-Style Risotto, 272
Healthy Chef's Salad, 222
Honey-Dijon Salad with Shrimp, 226
Mandarin Pork Stir-Fry, 102
Microwave Flounder with Carrots, 210
Old-Fashioned Beef Stew, 120
Cheesecakes
Chocolate Swirled Cheesecake, 308
Key Lime Cheesecake, 314
Luscious Chocolate Cheesecake, 312
Trimmed Down Chocoberry Cheesecake, 311
Cheesy Potato Skins with Black Beans & Salsa, 16
Cherry Chocolate Chip Walnut Cookies, 324
Chicken
Balsamic Chicken, 154
Broiled Lemon Chicken, 146

Chicken (*continued*)
Busy Day Oven-Fried Chicken Breasts, 164
Carefree Golden Oven Stew, 165
Chicken & Tortilla Casserole, 148
Chicken Breasts with Orange Basil Pesto, 171
Chicken Chop Suey, 160
Chicken Florentine with Lemon Mustard Sauce, 166
Chicken Nachos, 12
Chicken Sesame with Oriental Crème, 8
Chicken with Mandarin Orange and Water Chestnut Sauce, 155
Chicken with Zucchini and Tomatoes, 146
Country Cream of Chicken Chowder, 43
Crunchy Apple Salsa with Grilled Chicken, 140
Festive Chicken Dip, 30
Grilled Chicken Sienna, 162
Honey-Orange Chicken Legs, 170
Lemon-Dilly Chicken Sauté, 147
Maui Chicken Sandwich, 150
Oven Chicken & Rice, 170
Party Chicken Tarts, 14
Pot Stickers, 13
Rosemary Chicken with Asparagus Lemon Rice, 152
Santa Fe Chicken Pasta Salad, 227
Skillet Chicken Pot Pie, 156

Spicy Marinated Chicken Kababs over Rice, 142
Spinach-Stuffed Chicken Breasts, 144
Tomato Chutney Chicken, 158
Chili-Cheese Cornbread, 95
Chili con Carne, 127
Chili con Queso con Surimi, 27
Chilled Poached Salmon with Cucumber Sauce, 200
Chocolate
A Lighter Chocolate Decadence, 294
Bamboozlers, 336
Black Forest Chocolate Fudge Cake, 288
Cappuccino Brownies, 333
Cherry Chocolate Chip Walnut Cookies, 324
Chocolate Almond Biscotti, 318
Chocolate-Banana Sherbet, 372
Chocolate-Filled Meringue Shells with Strawberry Sauce, 346
Chocolate Roulade with Creamy Yogurt Filling, 300
Chocolate Swirled Cheesecake, 308
Choco-Lowfat Muffins, 87
Choco-Lowfat Strawberry Shortbread Bars, 328
Easy Chocolate Pudding Milk Shake, 53
Four Way Fudgey Chocolate Cake, 303
Frozen Chocolate-Covered Bananas, 368

Fudge Brownie Sundaes, 370
HERSHEY₁S Slimmed Down Chocolate Cake, 298
Hot Cocoa with Cinnamon, 54
Luscious Chocolate Cheesecake, 312
Microwave Chocolate Pudding, 364
Mocha Marble Pound Cake, 292
Mocha Yogurt Glaze, 292
PHILLY® FREE® Marble Brownies, 333
Rocky Road Pizza, 360
Sensibly Delicious Chocolate Chip Snacking Cake, 296
Sensibly Delicious Chocolate Pound Cake, 297
Slimmed Down Cocoa Frosting, 298
Slimming Chocoberry Splash, 48
Sweet Holidays Pizza, 358
Tiramisu, 352
Tri-Layer Chocolate Oatmeal Bars, 330
Trimmed Down Chocoberry Cheesecake, 311
Trimtime Chocolate Cake Roll, 291
Choco-Lowfat Muffins, 87
Choco-Lowfat Strawberry Shortbread Bars, 328
Chunky Hawaiian Spread, 34
Cider Glaze, 326
Citrus-Caper Dressing, 236

Cookies (*see also* **Bar Cookies**)
Cherry Chocolate Chip Walnut Cookies, 324
Chocolate Almond Biscotti, 318
Gingersnaps, 320
Low Fat Molasses Jumbles, 316
Mocha Cookies, 323
Oatmeal Cookies, 322
Soft Apple Cider Cookies, 326
Cool Summer Gazpacho Salad, 244
Corn
Beef Burgers with Corn Salsa, 130
Chili-Cheese Cornbread, 95
Country Cream of Chicken Chowder, 43
Healthy Chef's Salad, 222
Iowa Corn Pudding, 268
Margarita Pork Kabobs, 104
Polenta with Black Bean Salsa, 258
Roasted Red Pepper, Corn & Garbanzo Bean Salad, 240
Savory Corn Cakes, 22
South-of-the-Border Pizza, 266
Spicy Mexican Frittata, 64
Country Cream of Chicken Chowder, 43
Country Green Beans with Ham, 252
Couscous with Chick-peas and Vegetables, 278
Creamy Garlic Dressing, 250
Creamy Macaroni and Cheese, 285
Creamy Yogurt Filling, 302

Crunchy Apple Salsa with Grilled Chicken, 140

Dilled Vichyssoise, 42
Dips & Spreads
Chili con Queso con Surimi, 27
Chunky Hawaiian Spread, 34
Festive Chicken Dip, 30
Five-Layered Mexican Dip, 36
Fresh Garden Dip, 26
Fresh Tomato Eggplant Spread, 28
Lemon Dill Seafood Spread, 34
Light and Zippy Dip, 35
PHILLY® FREE® Salsa Dip, 32
DOLE® Juice Spritzer, 52
Dressings & Marinades
Citrus-Caper Dressing, 236
Creamy Garlic Dressing, 250
Microwave or Roasted Red Bell Pepper Dressing, 249
Mock Blue Cheese Dressing, 248
Mustard-Tarragon Marinade, 239
Southwest Salsa Dressing, 248

Easy Bean Nachos, 10
Easy Chocolate Pudding Milk Shake, 53
Easy Fruit Tarts, 344
Egg Dishes
Asparagus-Swiss Soufflé, 70
Breakfast Burritos, 72
Brunch Rice, 74
Eggs Santa Fe, 68

Mini Vegetable Quiches, 254
Potato and Pork Frittata, 116
Spicy Mexican Frittata, 64
Vegetable Strata, 262
Western Omelet, 66

Festive Chicken Dip, 30
Fiesta Quesadillas with Fruit Salsa, 24
Fillings & Toppings
Chocolate Filling, 346
Creamy Yogurt Filling, 302
Mixed Berry Topping, 60
Yogurt Topping, 312
Fish (*see also* **Shellfish**)
Angel Hair Pasta with Seafood Sauce, 196
Chilled Poached Salmon with Cucumber Sauce, 200
Golden Apple Stuffed Fillets, 207
Microwave Flounder with Carrots, 210
No-Fuss Tuna Quiche, 202
Ragoût of Tuna, 208
Salmon Steaks with Lemon Dill Sauce, 212
Snapper Veracruz, 206
Southern Breaded Catfish, 204
Three-Pepper Tuna Salad, 220
Wisconsin Tuna Cakes with Lemon-Dill Sauce, 214
Five-Layered Mexican Dip, 36
Four Way Fudgey Chocolate Cake, 303
Fresh Fruit with Peach Glaze, 354
Fresh Garden Dip, 26
Fresh Tomato Eggplant Spread, 28

Fresh Tomato Pasta Soup, 38
Fresh Vegetable Lasagna, 282
Frostings & Glazes
Chocolate Drizzle, 290
Cider Glaze, 326
Mocha Glaze, 290
Mocha Yogurt Glaze, 292
Powdered Sugar Glaze, 82
Slimmed Down Cocoa
Frosting, 298
Vanilla Chip Drizzle, 328
Frozen Chocolate-Covered
Bananas, 368
Fruit (see also individual
listings)
Black Forest Chocolate
Fudge Cake, 288
Breakfast S'Mores, 79
Brunch Quesadillas with
Fruit Salsa, 76
Cherry Chocolate Chip
Walnut Cookies, 324
Chicken with Mandarin
Orange and Water
Chestnut Sauce, 155
Easy Fruit Tarts, 344
Fiesta Quesadillas with
Fruit Salsa, 24
Fresh Fruit with Peach
Glaze, 354
Fruit and Oat Squares,
340
Fruity Wild Rice Side Dish,
274
Mandarin Pork Stir-Fry,
102
Mixed Berry Topping, 60
Peach-Melon Cooler, 52
Spumoni Pizza, 360
Summer Fruit Salad, 246
Sunrise Pizza, 62
Tandoori Pork Sauté, 114
Tossed Rice Salad with
Balsamic Vinaigrette, 228

Fruit and Nut Bars, 334
Fruit and Oat Squares, 340
Fruity Wild Rice Side Dish,
274
Fudge Brownie Sundaes, 370
Fusilli Pizzaiola with Turkey
Meatballs, 178

Garden-Style Risotto, 272
Gingersnaps, 320
Golden Apple French Toast,
63
Golden Apple Oatmeal, 78
Golden Apple Stuffed Fillets,
207
Grilled Chicken Sienna, 162
Grilled Flank Steak with
Horseradish Sauce, 124
Ground Turkey Chinese
Spring Rolls, 18

Ham
Country Green Beans with
Ham, 252
Healthy Chef's Salad, 222
Spinach-Stuffed Chicken
Breasts, 144
Healthy Chef's Salad, 222
Hearty Tortilla Chip Soup,
46
Herbed Stuffed Tomatoes, 20
HERSHEY®S Slimmed Down
Chocolate Cake, 298
Honey-Dijon Salad with
Shrimp, 226
Honey-Orange Chicken Legs,
170
Hot Cocoa with Cinnamon,
54
Hot to Go Thai Salad, 218

Indian-Style Vegetable Stir-
Fry, 261
Iowa Corn Pudding, 268

Jelly Donut Muffins, 90

Key Lime Cheesecake, 314

Lamb
Apple-icious Lamb Kabobs,
132
Pronto Pizza, 136
Spring Lamb Skillet, 135
Lasagna, 126
Lemon
Broiled Lemon Chicken,
146
Chicken Florentine with
Lemon Mustard Sauce,
166
Lemon Dill Seafood Spread,
34
Lemon-Dilly Chicken
Sauté, 147
Rosemary Chicken with
Asparagus Lemon Rice,
152
Salmon Steaks with Lemon
Dill Sauce, 212
Wisconsin Tuna Cakes with
Lemon-Dill Sauce, 214
Light and Zippy Dip, 35
Light Banana Cream Pie, 361
Linguine with White Clam
Sauce, 199
Low Fat Molasses Jumbles,
316
Luscious Chocolate
Cheesecake, 312

Mandarin Pork Stir-Fry, 102
Margarita Pork Kabobs, 104
Marinated Vegetable Spinach
Salad, 239
Maui Chicken Sandwich,
150
Mediterranean Meatballs and
Couscous, 128

Mediterranean Pasta Salad, 216
Mexican Lasagna, 172
Microwave Chocolate Pudding, 364
Microwave Flounder with Carrots, 210
Microwave or Roasted Red Bell Pepper Dressing, 249
Mighty Hero Sandwich, 121
Mini Vegetable Quiches, 254
Minted Fruit Rice Salad, 242
Mixed Berry Topping, 60
Mocha Cookies, 323
Mocha Marble Pound Cake, 292
Mocha Yogurt Glaze, 292
Mock Blue Cheese Dressing, 248
Muffins
Blueberry Muffins, 96
Choco-Lowfat Muffins, 87
Jelly Donut Muffins, 90
Peach Gingerbread Muffins, 80
Mushrooms
Alpine Fettuccine, 280
Brunch Rice, 74
Carefree Golden Oven Stew, 165
Chicken Chop Suey, 160
Honey-Dijon Salad with Shrimp, 226
Marinated Vegetable Spinach Salad, 239
Party Chicken Tarts, 14
Pot Stickers, 13
Risotto with Vegetables, 275
Spinach-Stuffed Chicken Breasts, 144

Spring Lamb Skillet, 135
Stuffed Shells Florentine, 286
Mustard-Tarragon Marinade, 239

Nacho Salad, 230
New England Style Vegetables with Garlic-Cream Sauce, 260
New Orleans Pork Gumbo, 112
No-Fuss Tuna Quiche, 202
Nutty Rice, 114

Oatmeal Apple Cranberry Scones, 98
Oatmeal Cookies, 322
Oats
Baked Apple Crisp, 356
Barbecue Bacon Meatloaf, 176
Fruit and Nut Bars, 334
Fruit and Oat Squares, 340
Golden Apple Oatmeal, 78
Oatmeal Apple Cranberry Scones, 98
Oatmeal Cookies, 322
Tri-Layer Chocolate Oatmeal Bars, 330
Old-Fashioned Beef Stew, 120
Onion Soup with Crouton Crust, 40
Orange
Chicken Breasts with Orange Basil Pesto, 171
Honey-Orange Chicken Legs, 170
Minted Fruit Rice Salad, 242
Salad Primavera, 236

Smoked Turkey & Fruit Salad, 224
SMUCKER'S® Orange Chili Barbecue Sauce, 168
Oven Chicken & Rice, 170

Party Chicken Tarts, 14
Pasta
Alpine Fettuccine, 280
Angel Hair Pasta with Seafood Sauce, 196
Broccoli, Scallop and Linguine Toss, 182
Couscous with Chick-peas and Vegetables, 278
Creamy Macaroni and Cheese, 285
Fresh Tomato Pasta Soup, 38
Fresh Vegetable Lasagna, 282
Fusilli Pizzaiola with Turkey Meatballs, 178
Lasagna, 126
Linguine with White Clam Sauce, 199
Mediterranean Meatballs and Couscous, 128
Mediterranean Pasta Salad, 216
Pineapple Noodle Pudding, 284
Pork with Sweet Hungarian Paprika, 110
Santa Fe Chicken Pasta Salad, 227
Shrimp Classico, 189
Spicy Orzo and Black Bean Salad, 232
Spicy Pasta Del Mar, 188
Stuffed Shells Florentine, 286
PB & J French Toast, 58

379

Peaches
Fresh Fruit with Peach Glaze, 354
Peach Gingerbread Muffins, 80
Peach-Melon Cooler, 52
Peach Sauce, 302
Sweet Holidays Pizza, 358
Peppy Snack Mix, 6
PHILLY® FREE® Marble Brownies, 333
PHILLY® FREE® Salsa Dip, 32
Pies & Tarts
Easy Fruit Tarts, 344
Light Banana Cream Pie, 361
Party Chicken Tarts, 14
Pumpkin Apple Tart, 348
Pineapple
Angel Food Cake with Pineapple Sauce, 308
Chunky Hawaiian Spread, 34
Cool Summer Gazpacho Salad, 244
Maui Chicken Sandwich, 150
Mediterranean Pasta Salad, 216
Minted Fruit Rice Salad, 242
Pineapple-Mint Lemonade, 50
Pineapple Noodle Pudding, 284
Pineapple Upside-Down Cake, 304
Pineberry Smoothie, 53
Smoked Turkey & Fruit Salad, 224
Sweet Holidays Pizza, 358
Pineberry Smoothie, 53

Pizza
Pronto Pizza, 136
Rocky Road Pizza, 360
South-of-the-Border Pizza, 266
Spumoni Pizza, 360
Sunrise Pizza, 62
Sweet Holidays Pizza, 358
Sweet Valentine Pizza, 360
Polenta Apricot Pudding Cake, 306
Polenta with Black Bean Salsa, 258
Pork
Caribbean Jerk-Style Pork, 109
Mandarin Pork Stir-Fry, 102
Margarita Pork Kabobs, 104
New Orleans Pork Gumbo, 112
Pork Tenderloin with Raisin Sauce, 108
Pork with Sweet Hungarian Paprika, 110
Potato and Pork Frittata, 116
Stuffed Pork Tenderloin, 106
Sweet and Spicy Pork Tenderloin, 100
Tandoori Pork Sauté, 114
Tossed Rice Salad with Balsamic Vinaigrette, 228
Potatoes
Apple-Potato Pancakes, 270
Cheesy Potato Skins with Black Beans & Salsa, 16
Country Cream of Chicken Chowder, 43
Dilled Vichyssoise, 42
Old-Fashioned Beef Stew, 120

Potato and Pork Frittata, 116
Southwestern Twice-Baked Spuds, 264
Vegetable Potato Salad, 238
Pot Stickers, 13
Powdered Sugar Glaze, 82
Pronto Pizza, 136
Prune Purée, 90
Pumpkin
Pumpkin Apple Tart, 348
Pumpkin Harvest Bars, 338
Sensibly Delicious Chocolate Pound Cake, 297

Ragoût of Tuna, 208
Rice
Athenian Rice with Feta Cheese, 276
Barbecued Shrimp with Spicy Rice, 186
Breakfast Risotto, 78
Brunch Rice, 74
Fruity Wild Rice Side Dish, 274
Garden-Style Risotto, 272
Hot to Go Thai Salad, 218
Minted Fruit Rice Salad, 242
Nutty Rice, 114
Oven Chicken & Rice, 170
Pot Stickers, 13
Rice Pudding, 362
Risotto with Vegetables, 275
Rosemary Chicken with Asparagus Lemon Rice, 152
Seafood Paella, 192
Shrimp Curry, 194
Shrimp in Tomatillo Sauce over Rice, 180

Rice *(continued)*
Shrimp Pita, 184
Southern Breaded Catfish, 204
Spicy Marinated Chicken Kababs over Rice, 142
Spicy Rice, 186
Spring Lamb Skillet, 135
Summer Fruit Salad, 246
Tandoori Pork Sauté, 114
Tossed Rice Salad with Balsamic Vinaigrette, 228
Risotto with Vegetables, 275
Roasted Red Pepper, Corn & Garbanzo Bean Salad, 240
Rocky Road Pizza, 360
Rosemary Chicken with Asparagus Lemon Rice, 152

Salads, Main Dish
Healthy Chef's Salad, 222
Honey-Dijon Salad with Shrimp, 226
Hot to Go Thai Salad, 218
Mediterranean Pasta Salad, 216
Nacho Salad, 230
Santa Fe Chicken Pasta Salad, 227
Smoked Turkey & Fruit Salad, 224
Three-Pepper Tuna Salad, 220
Tossed Rice Salad with Balsamic Vinaigrette, 228

Salads, Side Dish
Cool Summer Gazpacho Salad, 244
Marinated Vegetable Spinach Salad, 239

Minted Fruit Rice Salad, 242
Roasted Red Pepper, Corn & Garbanzo Bean Salad, 240
Salad Primavera, 236
Spicy Orzo and Black Bean Salad, 232
Spinach-Tomato Salad, 234
Summer Fruit Salad, 246
Vegetable Potato Salad, 238
Salmon Steaks with Lemon Dill Sauce, 212

Sandwiches
Grilled Flank Steak with Horseradish Sauce, 124
Maui Chicken Sandwich, 150
Mighty Hero Sandwich, 121
Shrimp Pita, 184
Turkey Gyros, 174
Santa Fe Chicken Pasta Salad, 227

Sauces
Apple Barbecue Sauce, 134
Caramel Sauce, 366
Peach Sauce, 302
Raspberry Sauce, 296
SMUCKER'S® Orange Chili Barbecue Sauce, 168
Savory Corn Cakes, 22
Seafood Paella, 192
Sensibly Delicious Chocolate Chip Snacking Cake, 296
Sensibly Delicious Chocolate Pound Cake, 297

Shellfish *(see also* **Fish**)
Angel Hair Pasta with Seafood Sauce, 196
Barbecued Shrimp with Spicy Rice, 186

Broccoli, Scallop and Linguine Toss, 182
Butterflied Shrimp Parmesan, 190
Chili con Queso con Surimi, 27
Honey-Dijon Salad with Shrimp, 226
Lemon Dill Seafood Spread, 34
Linguine with White Clam Sauce, 199
Seafood Paella, 192
Shrimp Classico, 189
Shrimp Curry, 194
Shrimp in Tomatillo Sauce over Rice, 180
Shrimp Pita, 184
SMUCKER'S® Mandarin Shrimp and Vegetable Stir-Fry, 198
Spicy Pasta Del Mar, 188
Shrimp Classico, 189
Shrimp Curry, 194
Shrimp in Tomatillo Sauce over Rice, 180
Shrimp Pita, 184
Silver Dollar Pancakes with Mixed Berry Topping, 60
Skillet Chicken Pot Pie, 156
Slimmed Down Cocoa Frosting, 298
Slimming Chocoberry Splash, 48
Smoked Turkey & Fruit Salad, 224
SMUCKER'S® Chilled Berry Soup, 44
SMUCKER'S® Double Apple Turnovers, 351
SMUCKER'S® Mandarin Shrimp and Vegetable Stir-Fry, 198

SMUCKER'S® Orange Chili Barbecue Sauce, 168
Snapper Veracruz, 206
Soft Apple Cider Cookies, 326

Soups & Stews
Carefree Golden Oven Stew, 165
Country Cream of Chicken Chowder, 43
Dilled Vichyssoise, 42
Fresh Tomato Pasta Soup, 38
Hearty Tortilla Chip Soup, 46
New Orleans Pork Gumbo, 112
Old-Fashioned Beef Stew, 120
Onion Soup with Crouton Crust, 40
SMUCKER'S® Chilled Berry Soup, 44
Southern Breaded Catfish, 204
South-of-the-Border Pizza, 266
Southwest Salsa Dressing, 248
Southwestern Twice-Baked Spuds, 264
Spiced Turkey, Squash and Apple Medley, 176
Spicy Marinated Chicken Kababs over Rice, 142
Spicy Mexican Frittata, 64
Spicy Orzo and Black Bean Salad, 232
Spicy Pasta Del Mar, 188
Spicy Rice, 186

Spinach
Chicken Florentine with Lemon Mustard Sauce, 166
Fresh Vegetable Lasagna, 282

Garden-Style Risotto, 272
Marinated Vegetable Spinach Salad, 239
Shrimp Classico, 189
Shrimp Pita, 184
Spicy Orzo and Black Bean Salad, 232
Spinach-Stuffed Chicken Breasts, 144
Spinach-Tomato Salad, 234
Stuffed Shells Florentine, 286
Spinach-Stuffed Chicken Breasts, 144
Spinach-Tomato Salad, 234
Spring Lamb Skillet, 135
Spumoni Pizza, 360

Squash (*see also* **Zucchini**)
Spiced Turkey, Squash and Apple Medley, 176
Spicy Marinated Chicken Kababs over Rice, 142
Spring Lamb Skillet, 135
Stacked Burrito Pie, 256

Strawberries
Brunch Quesadillas with Fruit Salsa, 76
Chocolate-Filled Meringue Shells with Strawberry Sauce, 346
Choco-Lowfat Strawberry Shortbread Bars, 328
Pineberry Smoothie, 53
Slimming Chocoberry Splash, 48
SMUCKER'S® Chilled Berry Soup, 44
Sweet Holidays Pizza, 358
Sweet Valentine Pizza, 360

Tossed Rice Salad with Balsamic Vinaigrette, 228
Trimmed Down Chocoberry Cheesecake, 311
Stuffed Pork Tenderloin, 106
Stuffed Shells Florentine, 286
Summer Fruit Salad, 246
Sunrise Pizza, 62
Sweet and Spicy Pork Tenderloin, 100
Sweet Crumb Crust, 358
Sweet Holidays Pizza, 358
Sweet Valentine Pizza, 360
Spumoni Pizza, 360
Tandoori Pork Sauté, 114
Three-Pepper Tuna Salad, 220
Tiramisu, 352
Tomato Chutney Chicken, 158

Tortilla Dishes
Beef & Bean Burritos, 118
Breakfast Burritos, 72
Brunch Quesadillas with Fruit Salsa, 76
Chicken & Tortilla Casserole, 148
Chicken Nachos, 12
Easy Bean Nachos, 10
Eggs Santa Fe, 68
Fiesta Quesadillas with Fruit Salsa, 24
Five-Layered Mexican Dip, 36
Hearty Tortilla Chip Soup, 46
Mexican Lasagna, 172
Mini Vegetable Quiches, 254
Nacho Salad, 230
Stacked Burrito Pie, 256

Tossed Rice Salad with
Balsamic Vinaigrette, 228
Tri Layer Chocolate Oatmeal
Bars, 330
Trimmed Down Chocoberry
Cheesecake, 311
Trimtime Chocolate Cake
Roll, 291
Turkey
Barbecue Bacon Meatloaf,
176
Barbecued Turkey
Tenderloin, 177
Black Pepper Patties, 73
Breakfast Burritos, 72
Country Green Beans with
Ham, 252
Fusilli Pizzaiola with Turkey
Meatballs, 178
Ground Turkey Chinese
Spring Rolls, 18
Healthy Chef's Salad, 222
Mediterranean Pasta Salad,
216
Mexican Lasagna, 172
Mighty Hero Sandwich, 121
Smoked Turkey & Fruit
Salad, 224
Spiced Turkey, Squash and
Apple Medley, 176
Spinach-Stuffed Chicken
Breasts, 144
Turkey Gyros, 174
Western Omelet, 66

Vanilla Chip Drizzle, 328
Veal in Gingered Sweet Bell
Pepper Sauce, 138
Vegetables *(see also
individual listings)*
Alpine Fettuccine, 280
Athenian Rice with Feta
Cheese, 276

Chicken & Tortilla
Casserole, 148
Chicken Chop Suey, 160
Chili con Carne, 127
Chilled Poached Salmon
with Cucumber Sauce,
200
Cool Summer Gazpacho
Salad, 244
Couscous with Chick-peas
and Vegetables, 278
Fresh Vegetable Lasagna,
282
Grilled Chicken Sienna,
162
Ground Turkey Chinese
Spring Rolls, 18
Healthy Chef's Salad, 222
Herbed Stuffed Tomatoes,
20
Indian-Style Vegetable Stir-
Fry, 261
Marinated Vegetable
Spinach Salad, 239
Mediterranean Pasta Salad,
216
Mini Vegetable Quiches,
254
New England Style
Vegetables with Garlic-
Cream Sauce, 260
New Orleans Pork Gumbo,
112
Onion Soup with Crouton
Crust, 40
Potato and Pork Frittata,
116
Ragoût of Tuna, 208
Risotto with Vegetables,
275
Shrimp Pita, 184
Skillet Chicken Pot Pie,
156

SMUCKER'S® Mandarin
Shrimp and Vegetable
Stir Fry, 198
Spicy Marinated Chicken
Kababs over Rice, 142
Spicy Orzo and Black Bean
Salad, 232
Spicy Rice, 186
Spinach-Tomato Salad, 234
Three-Pepper Tuna Salad,
220
Tomato Chutney Chicken,
158
Vegetable Potato Salad, 238
Vegetable Strata, 262
Vegetables in Garlic-Cream
Sauce, 260
Western Omelet, 66

Western Omelet, 66
Wisconsin Tuna Cakes with
Lemon-Dill Sauce, 214

Yogurt Cheese, 302, 310
Yogurt Topping, 312

Zucchini
Beef Cubed Steaks
Provençale, 122
Chicken with Zucchini and
Tomatoes, 146
Couscous with Chick-peas
and Vegetables, 278
Fresh Tomato Eggplant
Spread, 28
Santa Fe Chicken Pasta
Salad, 227
Three-Pepper Tuna Salad,
220

METRIC CONVERSION CHART

VOLUME MEASUREMENTS (dry)

⅛ teaspoon = 0.5 mL
¼ teaspoon = 1 mL
½ teaspoon = 2 mL
¾ teaspoon = 4 mL
1 teaspoon = 5 mL
1 tablespoon = 15 mL
2 tablespoons = 30 mL
¼ cup = 60 mL
⅓ cup = 75 mL
½ cup = 125 mL
⅔ cup = 150 mL
¾ cup = 175 mL
1 cup = 250 mL
2 cups = 1 pint = 500 mL
3 cups = 750 mL
4 cups = 1 quart = 1 L

VOLUME MEASUREMENTS (fluid)

1 fluid ounce (2 tablespoons) = 30 mL
4 fluid ounces (½ cup) = 125 mL
8 fluid ounces (1 cup) = 250 mL
12 fluid ounces (1½ cups) = 375 mL
16 fluid ounces (2 cups) = 500 mL

WEIGHTS (mass)

½ ounce = 15 g
1 ounce = 30 g
3 ounces = 90 g
4 ounces = 120 g
8 ounces = 225 g
10 ounces = 285 g
12 ounces = 360 g
16 ounces = 1 pound = 450 g

DIMENSIONS

1/16 inch = 2 mm
⅛ inch = 3 mm
¼ inch = 6 mm
½ inch = 1.5 cm
¾ inch = 2 cm
1 inch = 2.5 cm

OVEN TEMPERATURES

250°F = 120°C
275°F = 140°C
300°F = 150°C
325°F = 160°C
350°F = 180°C
375°F = 190°C
400°F = 200°C
425°F = 220°C
450°F = 230°C

BAKING PAN SIZES

Utensil	Size in Inches/Quarts	Metric Volume	Size in Centimeters
Baking or	8×8×2	2 L	20×20×5
Cake Pan	9×9×2	2.5 L	22×22×5
(square or	12×8×2	3 L	30×20×5
rectangular)	13×9×2	3.5 L	33×23×5
Loaf Pan	8×4×3	1.5 L	20×10×7
	9×5×3	2 L	23×13×7
Round Layer	8×1½	1.2 L	20×4
Cake Pan	9×1½	1.5 L	23×4
Pie Plate	8×1¼	750 mL	20×3
	9×1¼	1 L	23×3
Baking Dish	1 quart	1 L	—
or Casserole	1½ quart	1.5 L	—
	2 quart	2 L	—

PLASTICS

FOR ARTISTS
AND CRAFTSMEN

PLASTICS

FOR ARTISTS
AND CRAFTSMEN
By Harry B. Hollander

WATSON-GUPTILL PUBLICATIONS / NEW YORK
PITMAN PUBLISHING / LONDON

To my wife, Rufus,
who involved us in the crafts
over twenty years ago.

Edited by Margit Malmstrom
Designed by James Craig
Set in 10 point English 49 by JD Computer Type Inc.
Printed and bound in Japan by Toppan Printing Company Ltd.

Acknowledgments

The largest stimulation in gathering material for this book has come from the hundreds of enthusiastic and inventive students who have participated in my workshops. I should like to give special thanks to all of them. I would also like to thank all those who participated in the demonstrations for sharing their ideas and contributing their time: Juanita May, Lil Morris, Virginia McClure, Arch Gregory, Jan Gelb, Professor Oliver M. Coleman, Jr., Lamont Anderson, Gloria Hall, Richard Adams, Jim Cooper, Carolyn LePage, Esther Werthheimer, and Blanche Plafson. My thanks, too, to *Modern Plastics Encyclopedia* Editor-in-Chief Sidney Gross for giving permission to borrow material from this excellent reference work.

The draft of this book was read and corrected by my father-in-law, Dr. Floyd G. Ballentine, Professor Emeritus of Classical Languages at Bucknell University. It is with gratitude and amazement that I acknowledge his skill in plowing through a technical vocabulary some distance from Greek and Latin! Without the generous help and friendship of Walter and Dorothy Wenninga, originators of Waldor Enterprises in Montreal, it is doubtful that I would have been introduced to the exciting world of plastics. Bill Brown, Director of the Penland School of Crafts, should know how indebted I am to him for his part in liberating me from the "rinky-dink" arena of the marketplace. For his encouragement and counsel over the years, I am heartily grateful.

Grover Cole, Director of the Miami Art Center, has, over the past three years, made many valuable suggestions in the framing of projects for my workshops, many of which are included in this book. To him, and especially to my efficient and ever-patient typists, Bonnie Burnham and Sister Joan Rowan, go many thanks. Finally, and strongly, an enormous *merci beaucoup* to Watson-Guptill Editorial Director Don Holden, who paced the floor with me and held my hand while I was "having my book," and to editorial "nurse" Margit Malmstrom and her associate Diane Casella Hines, who straightened out the manuscript and polished the pieces.

Contents

Acknowledgments, 5

Introduction, 11

POLYESTER RESINS, 13

Polyester Resins, 15
What is a Polyester Resin?, 15
Catalysts, 15
Inhibitors, 15
Accelerators, 15
Casting Resins, 16
Characteristics of Polyester Casting Resins, 16
Cautions When Using Polyester Resins, 20
Range of Polyester Resins, 21
Kinds of Additives, 24
Table of Polyester Resin Additives, 25

How to Use a Balance, 27
Ohaus Triple Beam Balance, 27
Using the Balance, 27
Balance Tally Sheet, 27
Pouring and Balancing, 28
Notes and Cautions, 28

Project 1: Internally Decorated Polyester Resin Panels, 31
Materials, 31
Assembling the Glass Mold, 31
Polyester Resin Formula, 31
Pouring and Curing the Panel, 31
Removing the Panel from the Mold, 32
Variations, 32

Project 2: Three-Dimensional Polyester Resin Windows or Murals, 37
Materials, 37
Assembling the Glass Mold, 37
Polyester Resin Formula, 37
Cutting the Polyester Resin, 37
Making "Fractured Glass," 37
Constructing a Three-Dimensional Window or Mural, 37
Polyester Adhesive Formula, 38
Bonding, 38
Variations, 38

Project 3: Casting Polyester Resin Reliefs, 43
Materials, 43
Making a Clay Negative Mold, 43
Polyester Resin Formula, 43
Pouring and Curing, 43

Removing the Polyester Resin Cast from the Mold, 43
Finishing, 43
Metallic Coating, 44

Project 4: Gelatin Molds for Polyester Resins, 47
Materials, 47
Preparing Gelatin Mold-Making Mixture, 47
Relief Molds, 47
Formula for Clear Castings, 47
Formula for Filled Metal Castings, 47
Formula for Filled Non-Metal Castings, 48
Formula for Large Castings, 48
How to Cast, 48
Notes, Variations, and Cautions, 48

Project 5: Cellulose Acetate Molds for Polyester Resins, 51
Materials, 51
Making a Cellulose Acetate or Mylar Mold, 51
Formula for Rotational Casting, 51
Rotational Casting, 51
Formula for Still Casting, 53
Still Casting, 53
Notes, Variations, and Cautions, 53

Project 6: Microcrystalline Wax as an Engraving Mold and Medium for Polyester or Epoxy Resins, 59
Materials, 59
Melting the Wax, 59
Engraving and Embossing, 59
Applying Silicone Release, 59
Polyester Resin Formula, 59
Epoxy Resin Formula, 59
Curing, 62
Mat Finish for Polyester Resin Plate, 62
Mat Finish for Epoxy Resin Plate, 62
Notes, Variations, and Cautions, 62

Project 7: Polyester Resin Sculpture, 65
Materials, 65
Making an Armature, 65
Polyester Resin Formula, 65
Applying Polyester Resin, 65
Using Fiberglass Mat, 65
Using Fiberglass Cloth, 65
Finishing, 66

Project 8: Translucent Polyester Resin Sculpture, 70
Materials, 70

Making a Cardboard Pattern, 70
Transferring the Pattern to Acetate Sheet, 70
Bonding, 70
Polyester Resin Formula, 70
Applying Fiberglass, 70
Additives and Colors, 71
Notes, Variations, and Cautions, 71

Project 9: None-Glare Polyester "Glass" Coating for Photo and Graphic Prints, 73
Materials, 73
Stretching Polyvinyl Film, 73
Stretching Mylar Mat Film, 73
Polyester Resin Coating Formula, 73
Applying Polyester Resin Coating, 73
Removing "Print," 74
Notes, Variations, and Cautions, 74

Project 10: Painting with Polyester Resins, 77
Materials, 77
Polyester Resin Paint Formula, 77
Mixing Paint and Peroxide, 77
Painting on Plexiglas, 77
Additives for Painting on Plexiglas, 77
Making a Larger Panel for a Plexiglas Mural, 77
Painting a Plexiglas Panel, 77
Applying Decorations to Your Panel, 79
Painting on Masonite, 79
Painting on Polystyrene, 79

Project 11: "Plastique" Dyeing, Bleaching, and Painting, 85
Materials, 85
Testing Your Fabric, 85
Applying Resist, 85
Dyeing, 85
Bleaching, 87
Applying Poly-paint Medium, 87
Notes, Variation, and Cautions, 87

Project 12: Combining Batik or "Plastique" with Polyester or Epoxy Painting Medium, 89
Materials, 89
Polyester Resin Saturant, 89
Epoxy Resin Saturant, 89
Poly-paint Modified Medium, 89
Epoxy Paint Modified Medium, 89
Curing, 90
Applying Resin Paint Medium, 90
Notes, Variations, and Cautions, 90

EPOXY RESINS, 91

Epoxy Resins, 93
What is an Epoxy Resin?, 93
Uses for Epoxy Resins, 93
Additives, 93
Kinds of Epoxy Resins, 94
Epoxy Curing Agents, 94
Characteristics of Epoxy Curing Agents, 95
Different Epoxy Curing Agents for Different Uses, 95
Relatively Nondermatitic Formulas, 101
Table of Epoxy Curing Agents, 95
Description of Epoxy Curing Agents, 95

Preparing Surfaces for Coating, Bonding, or Enameling with Epoxy Resins, 102
Metal Surfaces, 102
Wood Surfaces, 102
Cement Surfaces, 102
Plaster of Paris Surfaces, 102
Stone and Unglazed Ceramic Surfaces, 102
Glass and Vitreous Surfaces, 102

Project 13: Epoxy Enameling, 105
Materials, 105
Preparing Surfaces for Enameling, 105
Epoxy Resin Enamel Formula, 105
Applying Epoxy Resin Enamel, 105
Finishing the Enameled Surface, 105
Curing Agents for Thicker Surfaces, 106
Various Finishes, 106
Advantages of Epoxy Enamel, 106
Disadvantages of Epoxy Enamel, 106

Project 14: Epoxy-Metal Jewelry, 109
Materials, 109
How to Begin, 109
Epoxy-Metal Formula, 109
Preparing Epoxy-Metal, 109
Shaping Your Jewelry, 109
Finishing Your Jewelry, 110
Epoxy Resin Enamel Formula, 110
Plique à Jour, 110
Formula for Plique à Jour, 110
Variations, 110

Project 15: Epoxy Resins in Ceramics, 129
Materials, 129
A Five-Minute Adhesive Formula, 129
A Two-Hour to Three-Hour Adhesive Formula, 129
Repairing Ceramicware, 129
Bonding Pieces of Ceramic Sculpture, 130
Matching Finishes, 130
Mat Finish Formula, 130
Waterproofing the Inside of Pots, 130
Waterproofing Formula, 130
Glazes for Special Effects, 130

Formula for Ceramic Glazes, 130
"Stained-Glass Window" Effects, 130
Fast Cure Formula, 131
Slow Cure Formula, 131
Making "Stained-Glass Windows," 131
Notes, Variations, and Cautions, 131

Project 16: "Stained-Glass" Reliefs, 135
Materials, 135
How to Build and Use a Light Box, 135
Selecting Colored Glass, 135
Cutting Glass, 135
Overlapping Pieces of Colored Glass, 138
Gluing Your Glass Pieces, 138
Hints for Assembling Your Relief, 138
Mixing Your Own Epoxy Adhesives, 139
Short Pot Life Adhesive Formula, 139
Long Pot Life Adhesive Formula, 139
Notes, Variations, and Cautions, 139

Project 17: Transferring Color Reproductions to Epoxy Film, 143
Materials, 143
Epoxy Resin Film Formula, 143
Making an Epoxy Film Transfer, 143
Formula for Bubble-Free Transfer, 143
Formula for Less Flexibility, 143
"Colorless" Formula, 144
Notes, Variations, and Cautions, 144

Project 18: Casting an Epoxy-Polymercaptain Plate on Methyl Methacrylate Sheets, 147
Materials, 147
Preparing Your Methyl Methacrylate Sheets, 147
Epoxy-Polymercaptain Resin Formulas, 147
Formula No. 1, 147
Formula No. 2, 147
Formula No. 3, 147
Formula No. 4, 147
Formula No. 5, 147
Casting with Epoxy-Polymercaptain Resins, 147
Notes, Variations, and Cautions, 148

Project 19: Epoxy-Metal Casting, 150
Materials, 150
Building a Mold, 150
Washing and Drying Your Mold, 150
Epoxy-Metal Formula, 150
Mixing in Powdered Metal, 151
Casting Your Sculpture, 151
Curing and Finishing, 151
Formula for Mat Finish, 151
Other Metals, 151

Project 20: Epoxy Resin "Oil" Paints, 156
Materials, 156
Epoxy Resin "Oil" Paint Formula, 156
Curing Agent Formula, 156

Adding Color to Epoxy Resin Paints, 156
Using Epoxy Resin Paints, 156
Creating a Mat Finish, 157
Mat Finish Formulas, 157
Notes, Variations, and Cautions, 157

SILICONES, POLYURETHANES, EXPANDED POLYSTYRENE, 163

Silicone Polymers, 165
What are Silicone Polymers?, 165
Characteristics of Silicone Polymers, 165
Release Agents, 166
Artists' Paints, 167
Adhesives and Caulking Compounds, 167
Molds, 167
Dispersions, 167
Anti-Tarnish Coatings, 168
Clear Blocks, 168
Polishes, 168
Self-Extinguishing Fluids, 168
Silicone-Soluble Dyes, 168
New Breakthroughs in Silicone Polymers, 168

Project 21: Making Silicone Rubber Molds, 169
Materials, 169
Making Your Pattern, 169
Release Coating, 169
Mixing Silicone Rubber and Catalyst, 170
Making a Skin Mold, 170
Table of Curing Rates, 171
Making a Holding Mold, 171
Making a Cast Mold, 171
Making a Cellulose Acetate Box, 172
Making a Plywood Box, 172
Pouring the Mold, 172
Removing the Mold, 172
Making Multiple-Piece Molds, 173
Why Use Silastic E or G?, 173
Comparative Data Table, 173
Preserving Molds, 174
Notes, Variations, and Cautions, 174

Polyurethane Resins, 183
Uses, 183
A Few Words About Polyurethane Resins, 183
Cautions When Using Polyurethane Resins, 183
Foams, 184
Conathane UF 3: Rigid Urethane Foam, 184
Molds, 186
Coatings, 186
Adhesives, 186

Project 22: Expanded Polystyrene for Relief Murals, 188
Materials, 188
Transferring Design to Styrofoam, 188

Repairs, 188
Epoxy Resin Paint Formula, 188
Additives, 188
Painting with Epoxy Resins, 188
Metalized Area, 189
Notes, Variations, and Cautions, 189

Project 23: Expanded Polystyrene Armature for Epoxy-Fiberglass Sculpture, 192

Materials, 192
Keep it Simple, 192
Cutting Tools, 192
Bonding Your "Baby" Model, 192
Epoxy Resin Adhesive Formula, 192
Epoxy Resin Adhesive Curing Agent Formula, 192
Commercial Adhesive, 192
Bonding Larger Sculpture, 192
Epoxy Resin Combination Formula, 193
Applying Epoxy Resin Combination and Fiberglass, 193
Finishing, 193
Metalizing Formula, 193
Metalizing, 193
Notes, Variations, and Cautions, 193

APPENDIX, 197

Colors for Polyester, Epoxy, Silicones, and Polyurethanes, 198

Pigments, 198
Lightfastness of Pigments, 198
Transparency of Pigments, 198
Dyestuffs, 199
Lightfastness of Dyestuffs, 199
Buying Colorants, 199

Fire and Health Problems of Resins, 200

Precautions, 200
List of Reference Works, 200

Interesting Products, 202

Oderless Polyester Resin HH 571, 202
Characteristics of Oderless Polyester Resin HH 571, 202
Epoxy Brighteners, 203
Epoxy Curing Agents, 203
Epoxy Fillers, 203
Epoxy Flexibilizers, 203
Epoxy Flow-out Aids, 203
Epoxy Accelerators, 203
Diluents, 204

Adhesives, 204
Release Agents, 204
Thickening Agents, 204
Resists, 205
Colorants and Decorative Additives, 205
Ultraviolet Light Absorbers, 205
Clays, 205
Waxes, 205
Mold-Making and Reinforcing Materials, 205
Self-Releasing Reddi-Mold HH 871, 206
Polyurethanes, 206
Polyurethane Protective Finishes, 206
Transparent Plastic Sheets, 206
Buffing and Polishing Materials, 206
For the Painter, 206
Workshop Equipment, 207

Suppliers and Manufacturers, 208

Resin Suppliers in the U.S., 208
Resin Suppliers in Canada, 208
List of Manufacturers, 208

Glossary, 211

Index, 222

Chair by Allen Jones. Photo courtesy Richard Feigen Gallery, New York and Chicago. The media are many and include polyester resin and fiberglass, leather, Plexiglas, a wig, metal, vinyl fabric, and acrylic paints.

Introduction

The artist-craftsman of today is finding himself as frustrated as he is intrigued by the profusion of materials that technology and industrial development have put at his disposal. Along with his experiments and successful creative efforts with resins and plastics, has come puzzlement regarding new combinations of materials which he does not fully undertand. He finds that if he wishes to use polyesters, epoxies, silicones, or polyurethanes, he needs to know more about their very nature, what they are capable of doing, and *why* a catastrophe occurs! He must not only know how to accurately weigh and modify ingredients, but he must also know how to avoid exposing himself unnecessarily to the health hazards they pose. Rarely is the artist-craftsman a trained chemist, and for this reason he often finds that he is over his head in materials he does not understand. Also, he is unaware of the endless possibilities of compounds which behave so differently from traditional art and craft materials.

My interest in plastics came about when I decided to investigate the possibilities of using epoxy resin "enamel" in cloisonné as part of gold and silver jewelry. I approached a resin supplier in Montreal, and the door opened! After that initial discovery, I spent twelve years applying resins in the industrial and architectural fields and testing information about the decorative use of epoxy resins for murals over plaster walls, asbestos panels, and even cement blocks. Later on, I worked with bonding glass to glass for three-dimensional interior stained-glass windows, using an epoxy resin system. Along with the application of resins in the industrial and architectural areas, I have always been interested in the part the plastics family might play in the arts and crafts. Back in 1954, epoxy "enamel" on gold and silver pins was, of course, just an eye opener. Now, however, that situation has changed. Some idea of the varied ways in which plastics or resins can stand alone as art forms or be integrated with the traditional media of artists and craftsmen can be seen in a glance at the index.

Over the years, I have collected information on resins which would be applicable in the art and craft field. Manufacturers of basic resins have generously furnished the most up-to-date technical literature and evaluation samples. The plastics industry is presently becoming more and more interested in making materials which can be of direct use to the artist-craftsman, and I have been invited into laboratories in the United States and Canada for a view of compounds of special interest. Hundreds of dollars' worth of samples are being supplied by resin manufacturers for evaluation in my plastics workshops all the time. Some of the companies that have been so very helpful are CIBA, a pioneer in epoxy resins, Dow Corning Corporation, one of the first companies to market silicones, and Diamond Shamrock Company, now especially active in polyesters, urethanes, and polymercaptains.

The greatest source of information for this book however, has come from projects developed during plastics workshops at institutions such as the Penland School of Crafts in Penland, North Carolina, the Miami Art Center, the Philadelphia Museum School, the University of Georgia Art Department, and Sheridan College School of Design, Mississauga, Ontario. A large number of the ideas presented are the result of student creativity and of suggestions from participating artists and craftsmen.

In framing these projects, it has been my intention to present the material in such a way as to equip the reader with sufficient information to apply it successfully in his particular art or craft field. There has been no attempt to present a complete reference list of all the available resins, hardeners, additives, colors, etc. As a general reference book of that kind, I highly recommend *Modern Plastics Encyclopedia,* which I have drawn on for much of the information in this book, especially in the polyester resin additives section.

POLYESTER RESINS

Totem *by Maya Lightbody. 28" high. Photo courtesy of the artist. This is a casting from a leather-hard clay mold. The mold is covered with oil (in this case, mineral oil was used), and the polyester resin is poured into it. For this piece, stove ashes were sifted into the resin for texture and tone. After the polyester resin is cured, the clay mold, which does not stick at all, is removed. According to the artist, the polyester casting made in this way requires very little finishing.*

Polyester Resins

Polyester resins came into the industrial marketplace in the late 1930's and with the impetus of World War II began being used in large quantities in the 1940's. Since the 1950's, millions of pounds annually of these unsaturated polyester resins have been reacted with, cross-linked with, or catalyzed by organic peroxides (as distinguished from the hydrogen peroxide we can all buy in the drugstore), such as methyl ethyl ketone peroxide, which I abbreviate as MEK-Px. We are all familiar with polyester-fiberglass boats, TV trays, corrugated translucent roofing, surfboards, and so forth. All of these items and hundreds of others are made from polyester resin combinations, commonly called general-purpose polyester resins.

WHAT IS A POLYESTER RESIN?

Artists and craftsmen may find it helpful to understand how synthetic polymers, known as *unsaturated* polyester resins, are converted from liquids to solids. (Incidentally, the *saturated* polyester resins are the industrial fibers made for use in the textile industry.) You had the courage to buy this book, so hang on and we will briefly discuss what a polyester resin is made of. First, let's define terms. Throughout this book when we say polyester resins, we mean *unsaturated polyester resins*. Polyester resins, as we use them, are polymers which consist of a great number of small units called *mers*. These units, or building blocks, are synthesized from organic (generally, anything that burns and contains carbon) raw materials, such as phthalic anhydride, meleic anhydride, and ethylene or propylene glycol. These chemicals are fused, reacted, or cooked together under very controlled conditions of mixing, temperature, and time. A blanket of nitrogen is also necessary to keep out the oxygen in the air. This cooking is done in such a way that the chemicals are only permitted to hook up with one another to make molecules (chains) of certain lengths. After cooling, the resin molecules are then mixed and dissolved in about 30% styrene, which is a low viscosity (water-thin) liquid.

CATALYSTS

The story of how these polyester resin chains are made to join up chemically is really very fascinating. The repulsion of the two identical bodies, or electric charges, for one another and the attraction of plus to minus, or male to female, all come into play. Although these relatively small similar molecules of polyester resins cannot easily be made to join up with one another, they have an affinity for the different styrene molecule, which, under the proper conditions, can "join hands" with two polyester resin molecules. If enough of this "socializing" takes place in the presence of a catalyst, the polyester resin mixture goes from its liquid state through a series of stages until it becomes a solid. Many factors are necessary to create the proper conditions under which this solidification, or, as the chemists say, "cross-linking," can take place. Simply stated, a catalyst, or an "initiator," is needed for things to happen. In the case of the polyester-styrene mixture, organic peroxides such as MEK-Px (methyl ethyl ketone peroxide) will do the job. In nonchemical terms, the MEK-Px puts the polyester resin molecule into such a state that it will join up with a molecule of styrene. When this happens, the styrene molecule gets so activated that it joins up with another polyester resin molecule. And on and on goes the molecular dance.

INHIBITORS

Impurities and minute amounts of peroxides which may be formed or are present in this mixture during its storage time, before the MEK-Px is added, could set off the chemical reaction just described. To prevent this premature cross-linking (polymerization, or "hooking-up"), the manufacturer adds what is called an *inhibitor*, or reducing agent. Inhibitors keep small quantities of oxidizing agents and other impurities from initiating any reactions between the polyester resin molecules and the styrene molecules. Sometimes, however, the inhibitors are overpowered. In this case, you lose your can of resin! They are the restrainers which prevent the styrene "boys" and the polyester resin "girls" from "holding hands" before the allotted time. The most common inhibitor is *hydroquinone*.

ACCELERATORS

But there is more to the story than this. The MEK-Px catalyst, since it is an oxidizing agent, easily knocks out

So I Said—So She Said by Arlene Love, lifesize. Photo courtesy of the artist. This flesh-colored polyester fiberglass reinforced figure is part of three nudes, all "yacking" busily.

the inhibitor. The peroxide, however, works very slowly in getting the polyester resin molecules to react with the styrene unless an accelerator is present. This accelerator is either a special organic compound, a metal-organic compound, or a mixture of both. The most common accelerator is called *cobalt naphthenate*. Its function is to activate, or accelerate, the decomposition of the MEK-Px so that the peroxide will perform its appointed job according to plan. Incidentally, the presence of this accelerator makes the hydroquinone inhibitor even more necessary to stabilize the uncured polyester resin.

So, briefly, here is what happens when you add your MEK-Px to your polyester resin. The MEK-Px knocks out the hydroquinone on contact. *Flash*: "Oxidizing agent destroys reducing agent!" Now the plot thickens. The accelerator goes to work and turns on (activates) the catalyst (the MEK-Px oxidizing agent). The MEK-Px begins its decomposition, which starts the polyester molecules reacting with styrene molecules, which, in turn, react with other polyester resin molecules to form one big, solid, happy family. Here are the various steps after you add your MEK-Px: Liquid-in-the-can stage to liquid "A" stage (early in the reaction) to "B" stage (softens with heat but doesn't dissolve in solvents) to the final solid or thermoset "C" stage (does not dissolve in solvents and does not melt).

CASTING RESINS

The polyester resin which I principally use and discuss in this book is called a *casting resin*. There are a number of manufacturers making casting resins. I use one called 32-032 made by Reichhold Chemical Company. (I also use a new "oderless" polyester resin, called HH 571. Details of its discovery and characteristics can be found in Interesting Products section of Appendix.) This polyester resin 32-032, which has a bluish cast when reacted with MEK-Px, changes from light blue to light green to colorless. The blue color, incidentally, comes from the accelerator. For the artist and craftsman generally, the polyester resins commercially available do not have all of the properties which may be needed. Such properties as flexibility, translucency, opacity, transparency, non-sticking to nonporous vitreous surfaces, color, texture, tensile strength, etc. should all be under the control of the user. No supplier could possibly dish up, in separate cans, all of the different variations which the user might call for. This book endeavors to show you how to formulate your polyester resin so that you can achieve your desired results.

CHARACTERISTICS OF POLYESTER CASTING RESINS

Here are the important characteristics of polyester casting resins (see Interesting Products section of Ap-

Clear casting (*Left*) *by Cristos Gianakos. Photo courtesy of the artist. Notice not only the various layers of polyester resin which were poured at different times, but also how the sculptor has achieved surface texture by not overfinishing and polishing. Part of the esthetics of working with plastics is this controlled transparency and translucency.*

Black Serpent / Black Rocks (*Below*) *by Brenda Minisci, 3½' x 5'. Photo courtesy of the artist. This fountain is made from polyester resin reinforced with fiberglass. The armature is made from hardware cloth.*

Uncle Joe and His Friends *by Arlene Love, 31" x 41". Photo courtesy of the artist. This sepia-toned polyester resin relief panel is reinforced with fiberglass.*

Detail of mural. (*Above*) *This closeup shows some of the various textures in the mural by John Menihan seen below.*

Mural for the Security Trust Company, Rochester, New York (*Left*) *by John C. Menihan, 11' x 130'. Photo courtesy of the artist. Polyester resins, lightfast colors, and other additives were used on top of wooden construction board for this impressive mural.*

Adagio *by Gwynyth Young, approximately 22' high. Photo by Paul Smith. The metal skin of this sculpture is a mixture of 300-mesh nickel powder and polyester resin catalyzed with about 2% MEK-Px. Although polyester resins do work with metal powders, the resulting mixture is much weaker than the same skin done in epoxy resin.*

pendix for the characteristics of HH 571, a newly discovered "odorless" polyester resin):

1. They are extremely water-clear and transparent.

2. They are less yellowing generally than epoxy resins.

3. They are cheaper than epoxy resins.

4. Shrinkage of the unfilled cured polyester resin is around 7%.

5. For any type of structural strength and shrinkage control, fiberglass or other reinforcement is needed.

6. They make poor adhesives—in part because of this shrinkage.

7. They are excellent for certain special effects, such as crushed or broken "glass," or a magnifying or "lens" effect.

8. They can be used where curing or hardening time is not critical.

9. The various stages of curing the resin yield certain results if the polyester is manipulated purposefully during the curing.

10. They have less degradation (at the moment) in direct sunlight than epoxy resins.

11. For our purposes, we use one catalyst whose proportions may be varied from 1/4% to 2% (see Table of Polyester Resin Additives, p. 25).

CAUTIONS WHEN USING POLYESTER RESINS

The major cautions which should be observed when using polyester casting resins are these:

1. *Good ventilation.* Work with windows open if possible. If not, try to make sure that the air in your workroom or studio is changed by an exhaust fan at least six times per hour. Industrial health experts claim that the styrene vapor from polyester resins should be in no greater concentration than 100 PPM (parts per million) when one is exposed to the resin throughout the day. (See Interesting Products section of Appendix for details of the "non-smelly" new polyester resin HH 571.)

2. *Do not smoke.* Not only are polyesters generally flammable, but this is a good way to get polyester resin in your mouth. Besides, tobacco may be worse for you than styrene vapor!

3. *Wear gloves when possilbe.* The resin is sticky, irritating, and hard to remove from your hands without the use of solvents which are flammable and which tend to dry out your hands. Also, when using fiberglass as a reinforcement for the polyester resin, the use of gloves is a *must*.

4. *Remove fiberglass cuttings and fibers from clothing and body with masking tape.* Blowing off these glass "needles" may land them into the pores of your skin or into your bloodstream. They could possibly kill you, according to the experts at the Cook Paint and Varnish Company, manufacturers of polyester resins.

5. *Accelerators in their pure state are explosive when mixed with the MEK-Px catalyst.* Although there is no reason to have any around, if you do, be sure to keep the two chemicals in different parts of your studio. The amount of accelerator present in the polyester you are using presents no hazard in this respect.

6. *Thoroughly mix all ingredients needed into the resin, especially the MEK-Px.* If you do not mix them well, you will get either no cure or uneven curing.

7. *Do not overcatalyze.* This is not only wasteful, but you will alter the properties of your polyester if you go to extremes. See Table of Polyester Resin Additives for average correct proportions.

8. *Store your polyester resin in the coolest area you can find.* Freezing will make it keep best. Store below 70° F.

9. *Your MEK-Px should also be store in a cool place.* Remember that this is a strong oxidizing agent and therefore it is a possible fire hazard if the spills are not wiped up. All trash from use with polyester resins should be put in a metal garbage can outdoors.

10. *Keep your containers of polyester resin covered except when pouring.* This will not only keep out dirt but will help your resin last longer.

RANGE OF POLYESTER RESINS

There are many types of polyester resins used in industry which have no great value for the artist and craftsman. However, it is good to know what resins are available. They are:

1. *Fire-retardant or fire-resistant self-extinguishing.* These will burn when a direct flame is applied but the fire will be extinguished when the flame is removed.

2. *Chemical resistant.*

3. *Mixable or emulsfiable with water,* generally up to around 50%. Ashland Chemical Company calls them WEP resins. Reichhold calls them water-fillable (32-180 is one).

4. *Light-stabilized,* for outdoor use.

5. *Rigid, resilient, flexible, thixotropic.*

6. *Rigid, clear, tack-free,* gloss surfaces.

7. *General purpose,* for use with reinforcements such as fiberglass. Have pink cast. Used with opaque colors.

Catalyst #2 by Sidney Simon, 36" x 24" x 14". Collection Mr. and Mrs. Richard Shields. Photo courtesy of the artist. This piece is made from water-clear polyester resin similar to 32-032. Note the texture of the exterior areas. These were chiseled, using a ½" solid steel bar, the end of which was cut on a 45° angle.

Tubelo #4 by Jacques Schnier, 22" x 13". Photo courtesy of the artist. Although acrylic casting is not covered in this book, it is interesting to compare the transparency of the acrylic resin forms with polyester resin forms (above).

Rockyhill Twanger (*Above*) *by Gene Kangas, 7½' x 20' x 104'. Photo courtesy of the artist. This outdoor sculpture is constructed of fiberglass, polyester resin, Plexiglas, aluminum, and stainless steel cable.*

Cast polyester resin sculptures (*Right*) *by Marjorie P. Benua, approximately 8" to 10" high. Photos by Ralph Dicks. This series of sculptures beautifully illustrates the simple use of polyester casting resins. These pieces are cast solid. They are originally sculpted in modeling clay, then a mold is made in plaster and the inside of the plaster mold is waxed. The polyester resin is poured into the waxed plaster mold, and when the resin is cured the mold is removed and the piece sanded, buffed, and polished.*

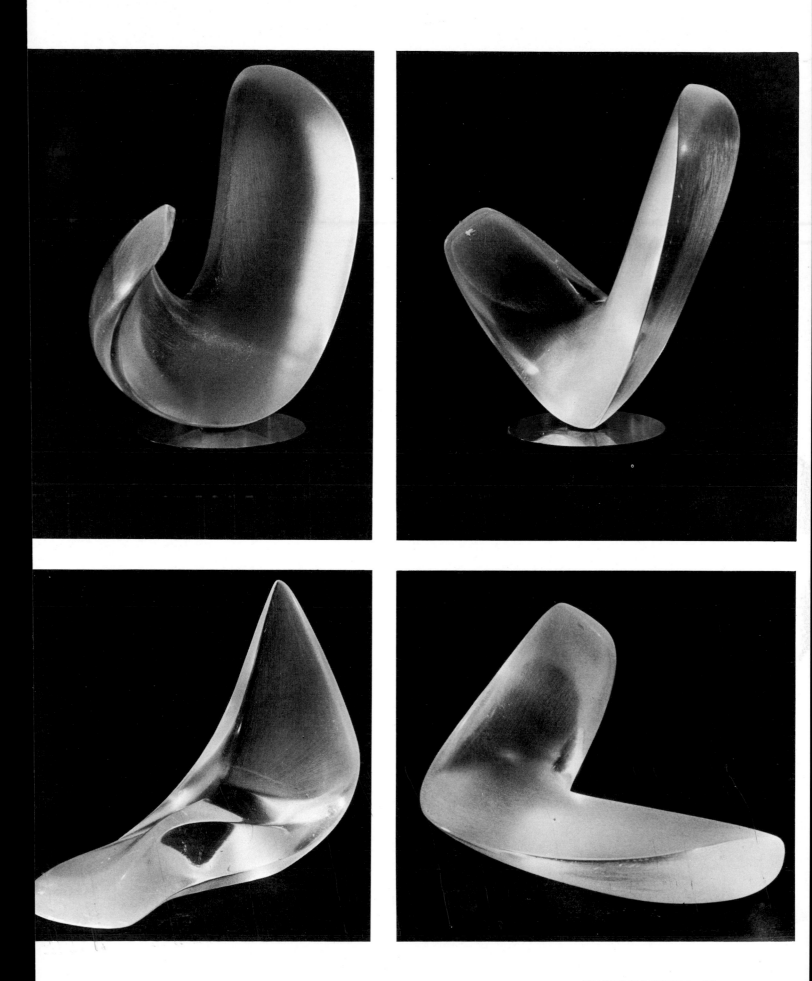

For any special uses, check with your resin supplier, the *Modern Plastics Encyclopedia*, or the polyester resin manufacturers. Artists executing murals or panels for public buildings should be sure to use fire-resistant polyesters, such as the Hetrons manufactured by Hooker Chemical Corporation.

KINDS OF ADDITIVES

There are many additives which can be considered for polyester resins. They are mainly the same as those used for epoxy resins. At the present writing, the ultraviolet screeners—protectors against the ravages of sunlight—are more effective when used with polyesters than with epoxies. Here is a partial list of additives for polyesters. Check with the manufacturers if you are involved with art or craft work requiring certain specifications for architects or builders or government officials, or just for your own desire to do the best possible work with what is available.

1. *Thixotropic agents:* Asbestos 244 or Cabosil (M-5). The addition of either of these relatively inert materials produces non-runny, easily moveable gels if the viscosity of the polyester resin is low.

2. *Opaciffiers and fillers:* Talc, dried clay such as kaolin, and powdered sand (called flint) which is about 200-mesh.

3. *Silica sands:* All mesh sands from 1-mesh to 200-mesh.

4. *Miscellaneous fillers:* Pumice, mica, grog, silica carbide chips, stones, rocks (all of which must be dry).

5. *Colors:* Either dry pigments or ground up in a compatible vehicle, opaque or transparent pigments, or dyes (see Colors section of Appendix).

6. *Internal release agents:* Internal Release 54 or Zelec UN from Dupont De Nemours Co., Inc.

7. *Reactive diluents:* Styrene, vinyl, toluene for lower volatility, methyl methacrylate for better weathering, along with U-V absorbers, alfa-methyl styrene (which along with styrene reduces high exotherm, or heat give-off), and methyl acrylate (which when mixed with styrene gives cured polyesters which are more glasslike in transparency).

8. *Flame retardants:* It is estimated by the National Fire Protection Association that, in the U.S., a fire starts every two seconds. Every 44 minutes someone dies from fires and the property damage caused by these fires amounts to 1/5 to 1/8 billion dollars annually. (Chemicals which contain chlorine, bromine, antimony, and phosphorous are the basis of additives to make polyesters fire retardant or self-extinguishing. For fire-retardant resisns, check with the manufacturers for

suggestions and try out their recommendations. *The claims of the manufacturers are not always accurate!* For a description of the test for fire-retardant resins, see *Modern Plastics Encyclopedia.*

9. *Flexibilizers:* There are a huge number of organic chemicals which will make polyesters more flexible. I have found that Benzoflex 9-88 works well.

10. *Ultraviolet light absorbers:* Resins and polymers such as polyesters are degraded by ultraviolet light from the sun, in particular where the energy content is such that it will destroy most organic molecules. The addition of ultraviolet light absorbers to the polyester resin absorbs the ultraviolet incident light or screens it out. Normally they are used in concentrations from 1/4% to 1% (get specifications from your resin supplier).

11. *Organic peroxides:* The one which we use is called MEK-Px (methyl ethyl ketone peroxide). Although it is safe to use, it should be stored in a cool place. If spilled, wipe up with nonburning compounds, such as perlite or vermiculite. In any case, after wiping up, take the peroxide-soiled material outdoors and burn up. *Do not mix* directly with polyester resin accelerators such as cobalt naphthenate—it will probably *explode!* Use *only* the recommended amounts.

12. *General additives:* Usually any inert dry chemical may be added to the polyester resins. If there is any doubt, however, be sure to check with your resin supplier, plastics reference book, or plastics expert.

13. *Air driers:* The polyester resin which we work with, 32-032, is a very slow, air-drying resin surface. If you are willing to sacrifice clarity, you may add about 1 oz. per gallon of polyester resin of a wax-styrene solution which is available from your resin supplier. The wax is ordinary paraffin wax which is used for canning. General-purpose polyester resins usually all contain paraffin wax.

POLYESTER RESIN ADDITIVES

In order to simplify the use of polyester resins for the artist and craftsman, we have settled on the use of Polylite polyester resin 32-032, manufactured by the Reichhold Chemical Company, for the table which follows. With the use of several simple additives, we can give the water-clear polyester resins quite a number of interesting properties. These additives and their uses are:

1. *Benzoflex 9-88*	For varying flexibility.
2. *Asbestos 244, or Cabosil*	For varying thixotrophy.
3. *Internal Release 54*	For non-stick to glass.
4. *Styrene monomer*	For lowering viscosity.
5. *Various amounts of MEK-Px*	For varying thicknesses of resin.

TABLE OF POLYESTER RESIN ADDITIVES

The polyester resin additives shown in this table should be added to 100 grams of Reichhold Polylite polyester resin 32-032 at 70 F. Use less polyester resin if you add styrene; for example, 90 grams of 32-032 to 10 grams of 32-032 to 10 grams of styrene = 100 grams of relatively diluted polyester resin. (I have drawn liberally in this section from *Modern Plastics Encyclopedia*, Vol. 46, No. 10A. McGraw-Hill, 1969.)

USE	POLYESTER RESIN ADDITIVES, IN GRAMS				
	Benzoflex 9-88	Asbestos 244	Internal Release 54	Styrene	MEK-Px
Thin coatings (the thickness of 1-4 sheets of paper: 4-20 mils)	5			0-10	2
Heavy coatings (the thickness of 10-60 sheets of paper: 40-250 mils)	5-7.5			0-10	¾-1
Thick castings, ¼"-3" (release from glass)	7.5-10		¼	0-10	¼-½
Decorative panels cast between glass (Project 1)	5		¼		2
Poly-paint medium for Plexiglas (Project 10)	5	3		10	½
Non-glare semimat coatings on mat side of PVA film stretched on canvas stretcher (Project 9)	5				2
Rotational casting (Project 5)	5				1-2

An Ohaus triple beam balance (Step 1). *Demonstration photos courtesy Ohaus Scale Corporation. For this demonstration, we will be weighing polyester resin, but this balance may be used to weigh out all the formulas in this book. The following materials will be weighed in the same cup: 125 grams of polyester casting resin 32-032, 6.2 grams of Benzoflex 9-88, 0.3 gram of Internal Release 54, and 1.2 grams of MEK-Px.*

How to Use a Balance

A balance, or a scale, is a must when working with polyester, epoxy, silicone, and urethane resins. With polyester resins, there is some chance of avoiding the expense of buying a balance since the catalyst amounts used do have some leeway. However, in the long run, you will find that you pay for a balance out of the cost of the materials you waste by not being able to weigh the correct amount needed.

OHAUS TRIPLE BEAM BALANCE

One of the most reasonably priced balances now available is the Ohaus Triple Beam Balance Model 750S, capacity 2610g. This balance can be purchased through chemical laboratory supply companies. A very nice feature of this balance is a permanent magnetic damping, which brings the balancing mechanism quickly to rest.

Look at the balance illustrated here. Notice that the first beam of three is marked for 0-to 1/10-gram units. The back beam is divided into 10-gram units up to 100 grams. The central beam is marked from 0 to 500 grams in 100-gram units. Three additional weights which hang at the ends of the beams may be purchased along with the balance. These weights will give you an additional 2000 grams. The technique used for weighing is explained briefly below.

USING THE BALANCE

Start your weighing with all of your weights in the "0" position (see Step 1). Place your weighing cup and a clean mixing stick on the balance pan and rebalance the scale by moving the weights (see Step 2). Remember that when using the 100-gram and the 500-gram weights, they must be placed exactly in the appropriate notches. Always begin weighing materials of unknown weight by moving the middle 500-gram weight until the beam tilts to its lower, or overweight, position. Next, move the 500-gram weight back one notch and move the rear 100-gram weight notch by notch until the beam again tilts. Back up one notch on the 100-gram weight beam. Now, on the front sliding scale, which weighs from 0 to 10 grams, lightly push the weight until the white mark on the beam pointer corresponds to the white mark "0" on the right-hand column.

You have thus tared, or balanced, the cup. You are now ready to weigh your resins. An Ohaus Model 760 Triple Beam Balance, which has a tare poise (weight) for this purpose, is available at a cost slightly greater than that of Ohaus Model 750S.

As an example, let's weigh the following materials in the same cup (see Step 1): 125 grams of polyester casting resin 32-032, 6.2 grams of Benzoflex 9-88, 0.3 gram of Internal Release 54, and 1.2 grams of MEK-Px (methyl ethyl ketone peroxide). Although there are many different ways to weigh, this one is the most foolproof. List the following calculations on a sheet of paper and check off as you finish weighing each item. Your tally sheet should look something like this.

MATERIAL	WEIGHTS	CHECK ADDITIONS MADE
1. Cup and mixing stick	99.9g	. . . .
2. 32-032	125.0g	. . . .
	Subtotal 224.9g	
3. Benzoflex	6.2g	. . . .
	Subtotal 231.1g	
4. Internal Release 54	.3g	. . . .
	Subtotal 231.4g	
5. MEK-Px	1.2g	. . . .
	Total 232.6g	. . . . Final Check

POURING AND BALANCING

First set the balance at 224.9 grams. Pour the resin with your right hand (if right handed) slowly into the cup while
pushing the pan down gently with your left finger (Step 3). In this manner, you will feel when you are approaching the balance point. At this stage, pour your resin drop by drop. An eye dropper may be useful here (see Step 4). With this technique, you should not overshoot.

Check off the 125.0 grams of 32-032 you have just

added and reset the scales to 231.1 so that you can add the 6.2 grams of Benzoflex right into the same cup. Pour from a cup with the lip crimped to a V shape (Step 5). As you pour your Benzoflex slowly, push-tap lightly with your left finger until your scale balances (Step 6). Overshooting by 1 gram, for example, will necessitate adding 20 more grams of 32-032.

Again, check off the Benzoflex 6.2-gram addition and reset the scale to 231.4 for the addition of the Internal Release 54. Here again, the use of an eye dropper is most helpful (Step 7). Remember, the 28 drops of such a liquid, or of MEK-Px, is approximately 1 gram. In this case, the addition of 0.3 grams of Internal Release 54 is approximately 8 to 10 drops, depending upon your dropper.

When balanced, check off the Internal Release 54 and set the balance beams to 232.6 for the final 1.2-gram addition of MEK-Px (see Step 8). This catalyst, too, may be added by dropper. Approximately 34 drops should balance for your final check off.

NOTES AND CAUTIONS

Your balance should be clean at all times. The top of the balance pan should be protected with a piece of Saran Wrap cut to size or, in any case, waxed with a good paste wax. It is an excellent idea to wax the whole balance from top to bottom even before starting to work. Should resin fall on any of the bearings, the bearings should be cleaned before the resin has a chance to dry. When you are storing your balance, it is wise to put the rubber grommet back where it was over the "O" on the right-hand side of the balance. In addition, you might very well make a polyethylene cover to keep out the dirt and dust. A low-cost, vinyl dust cover, Ohaus Model 706, is available.

Step 2. *Start your weighing with all your weights (poises) in the "0" position, as shown here. Place your weighing cup and a clean mixing stick on the balance pan and rebalance the scale by moving the weights.*

Step 3. *Set the balance at 224.9 grams and pour in the 125 grams of polyester resin slowly. Push the pan down gently with your finger so that you will be able to feel when you are reaching the balance point.*

Step 4. *When you get close to the balance point, you may want to use an eye dropper to get the exact amount of polyester resin.*

Step. 5. *Reset the scales to 231.1 and add the 6.2 grams of Benzoflex. Crimp the lip of the cup to facilitate pouring.*

Step 6. *Tap the pan gently until you have the scale balanced.*

Step 7. *Reset the scale to 231.4 and add your 0.3 gram of Internal Release 54. Here again, an eye dropper is most helpful in getting the exact amount to balance the scale.*

Step 8. *Reset the scale to 232.6 and add the 1.2 grams MEK-Px. You can pour it in gently, as shown here, or you can use an eye dropper.*

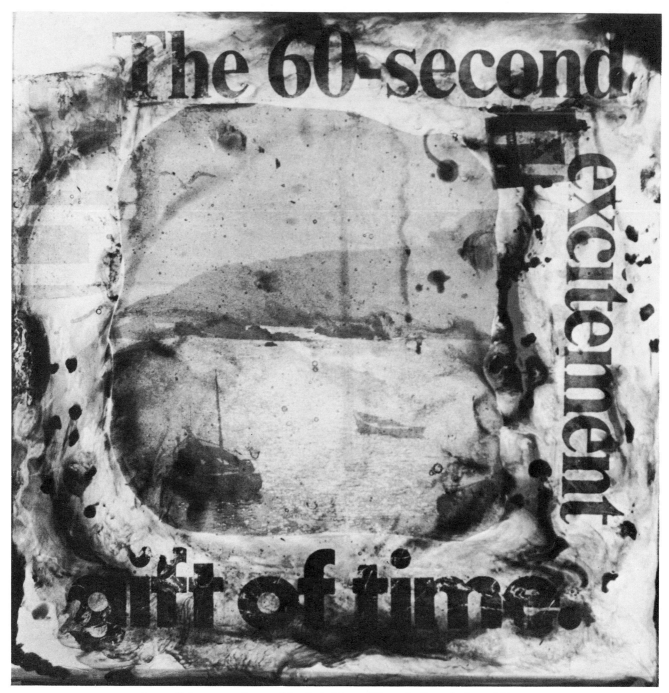

Polyester resin panel *by Jack Morse. Photo by Pete Steiner. This panel and the one on p. 32 illustrate how an epoxy resin lift, or transfer (described in Project 17), can be integrated. In this case, the polyester resin was not poured between two sheets of glass, but rather, internally released resin was poured over MirrorGlazed, polished, and waxed double-strength glass closed in with masking tape.*

Internally Decorated Polyester Resin Panels

Any design, painting, collage, or color combination may be imbedded in a rigid plastic panel of almost any size or shape. The panel may be cast from liquid polyester resins with any desired degree of transparency, texture, and flexibility. The designs, paintings, and collages themselves should also be done in polyester as described.

MATERIALS

1. Two sheets of double-strength window glass, say 1' square.

2. 3 1/2" approximately 3/16" thick plastic-coated clothesline.

3. 1" to 2" wide spring glamps.

4. Roll of 1/2" masking tape.

5. 400 to 500 grams of water-clear polyester resin, such as Reichhold Polylite polyester resin 32-032 or equivalent.

6. MEK-Px (methyl ethyl ketone peroxide) catalyst.

7. Polyester color pastes.

8. Benzoflex 9-88 flexibilizer.

9. Internal mold release, such as Internal Release 54 or Dupont Zelec UN.

10. MirrorGlaze wax.

ASSEMBLING THE GLASS MOLD

Thoroughly sand the edges of the glass panels to remove sharp cutting edges.

Clean both sides of the glass panels, if dirty, with a weak liquid synthetic detergent solution, followed by rinsing them under running water.

Dry well and wax both sides of the glass with Mirror Glaze wax. Polish the glass immediately with a clean, soft, turkish towel, until the wax disappears. Repeat the waxing and polishing.

Sandwich the plastic clothesline, which acts as a gasket, between the glass panels, approximately 1" from each of three sides, leaving the two ends of this gasket extending a few inches from the fourth or top side. Clamp the panels together with the spring clamps, using three on each side and four on the bottom. With masking tape, cover the top 1/4" of the two glass panels, thus making a pouring trough. Stand the panels vertically and securely. This is the mold into which you will pour your polyester resin.

POLYESTER RESIN FORMULA

All formulas given in this book are based upon 100 grams of liquid resin. This formula is based on 100 grams of Reichhold Polylite polyester resin 32-032, or equivalent.

Polyester resin 32-032: 100 grams.

Benzoflex 9-88: 5 grams.

Internal Release 54 or Dupont Zelec UN: 1/4 grams.

MEK-Px: 2.0 grams.

Weigh four to five times the above formula, depending upon the thickness of your gasket, into a clean tin can. Mix well until the liquid is completely clear.

Pour the mixture into as many hot drink cups as you need for your various colors. Add the desired amounts of transparent color paste to the liquid in the cups and stir.

POURING AND CURING THE PANEL

Although there are an infinite number of variations on this basic technique, this is the simplest:

Pour the colorless or colored resin mixture between the two panels—through the open end of the glass sandwich—in any way you choose. (Although this method is inevitably controlled by gravity and diffusion, you can exert considerable control by careful pouring or by mixing the poured colors with a long, thin wire.)

When the channel between the sheets of glass is filled, you may harden (or cure) the resin in either of two ways: (1) let the panel remain standing as it is overnight at room temperature; (2) place two infrared heat lamps, one on each side of the panel, at a distance of 2 1/2'.

You can tell when the resin is adequately cured by pushing a slender wooden stick through the open end of the sandwich; when you cannot push the stick 1/8" below the top resin surface (which will remain sticky for a long time), the cure is complete.

REMOVING THE PANEL FROM THE MOLD

Remove the clamps and the gasket, and carefully wedge open the glass panels with a wide strip of hard wood. Remove one of the glass sheets, then wax the polyester panel with MirrorGlaze wax, and polish immediately.

If you wish to cut your panel, use a sharp mat knife or an X-acto knife. Should the resin be too gelatinous, let it cure an additional hour.

Leave the cut panel on the other glass sheet for three or four hours before removing, waxing, and polishing. If the resin is too hard to cut, remove it from the glass and wax and polish the other side.

VARIATIONS

If you wish to have a highly controlled painting or design, then use the basic formula, colored and thickened to your taste with small amounts of Cabosil or Asbestos 244. Apply your colors directly to one of the waxed and polished glass sheets. Remember to leave about 1" free on three sides of the glass sheet. Let your resin cure to the non-runny state. Close up your panels of glass with the clothesline gasket and clamps as described earlier, and carry on as recommended above. If this technique intrigues you, you will discover an infinite number of variations.

Polyester resin panel *by Jack Morse. Photo by Pete Steiner.*

Step 1. *Demonstration photos by Robert J. McCauley. The mold for a decorative panel made from polyester resin cast between sheets of glass is shown here. A plastic-covered clothesline is sandwiched between two 1' square sheets of double-strength, twice-waxed glass which has been immediately highly polished with MirrorGlaze wax. The pressure clamps are readily available in any stationery store.*

Step 2. *The polyester resin mixture is poured between the sheets of glass. The color pastes which are used are generally transparent and are mixed with resin mix in different 7 oz. paper cups. Notice the pouring spout made from masking tape. The LOF label was left on the glass to indicate which side of the glass had not been waxed.*

Step 3. *The pouring continues. Different colors are added in infinite variations until a desired height is obtained. The room temperature determines the curing speed of the resin. If you wait too long, the resin will gel. This gel, however, may be forced in between the panels for novel effects.*

Step 4. *After the panel is poured to the desired height, the resin is left to cure until it is quite impossible to push a coffee stirrer into the resin from the top. Usually, this takes about four hours at room temperature. First the clamps are removed and then the gasket. After this, as shown in the picture, the panels are carefully separated by using a long piece of thin but firm metal.*

Step 5. *Once the air lock is broken, the glass sheets separate relatively easily. At this stage, the polyester panel is usually very delicate and should be waxed and polished with MirrorGlaze wax.*

Step 6. *The waxed and polished polyester panel is shown here as it is carefully lifted from the glass sheet.*

Step 7. *After removing the panel completely from the glass sheet, the other side of the plastic is also waxed. The edges of the panel may be sticky because of contact with the plastic clothesline. These edges may be cut off or they may be left to cure further. The stickiness will eventually disappear.*

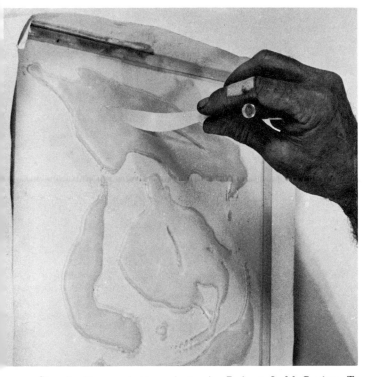

Step 1. *Demonstration photos by Robert J. McCauley. To make a more interesting panel, with additional intaglio dimension, microcrystalline wax 1290 Y is melted and poured upon the double-waxed and polished glass sheet. This wax can be cut, engraved, and sprayed with silicone release 1711.*

Step 2. *This illustration shows the waxed panel closed up and filled with a single monochromatic pouring of polyester resin mixture.*

Step 3. *After the resin has cured out, the glass sheets are opened up and the polyester panel is waxed and polished with MirrorGlaze wax.*

Step 4. *If the microcrystalline wax has been adequately sprayed with the silicone release 1711, it is easily removed, as can be seen in this photograph.*

Step 1. *Demonstration photos by Robert J. McCauley. A gelatin mixture of weight of ⅓ Knox and Kind edible gelatin, ⅓ permanent antifreeze, and ⅓ water, can also be used to create negative space. Here, the hot gelatin mixture is being poured upon a MirrorGlazed, double-strength, 1' square glass panel. This will be used in the same way as the microcrystalline waxed panel. The polyester resin cures but does not adhere to the gelatin.*

Step 2. *(Above) Decorative panels can be cast directly on a flat, twice-MirrorGlazed and polished glass plate. The possibilities are endless. Here is the beginning of one such plate, using the gelatin mixture for the creation of negative space.*

Step 3. *(Below) Here is a finished panel in polyester resin, after the gelatin has been removed.*

PROJECT 2

Three-Dimensional Polyester Resin Windows or Murals

Polyester resin castings, as described in Project 1—with certain modifications may be cut, sawed, or broken into chips which may then be reassembled to make three-dimensional relief windows or murals.

MATERIALS

1. Two sheets of double-strength window glass, say 1" square.

2. 3 1/2" of approximately 3/16" thick plastic-coated clothesline.

3. 1" to 2" wide spring clamps.

4. Roll of 1/2" masking tape.

5. 400 to 500 grams of water-clear polyester resin, such as Reichhold Polylite polyester resin 32-032 or equivalent.

6. MEK-Px (methyl ethyl ketone peroxide) catalyst.

7. Polyester color pastes.

8. Benzoflex 9-88 flexibilizer.

9. Internal mold release, such as Internal Release 54 or Dupont Zelec UN.

10. MirrorGlaze wax.

ASSEMBLING THE GLASS MOLD

Take two (1" square) of double-strength glass or antique glass, wax them several times, and polish immediately with MirrorGlaze wax. You are now ready to assemble this mold for the polyester sheet.

Gasket the two sheets together (see Project 1) and clamp with spring clamps. The resin formula follows.

POLYESTER RESIN FORMULA

Internal Release 54 or Zelek UN: 1/4 gram.

MEK-Px: 2 grams.

Benzoflex 9-88: 5 grams (if you wish to make fractured glass, omit the Benzoflex).

Add the usual colors to the polyester resin and mix well; pour the sheets in the manner described in Project 1.

CUTTING THE POLYESTER RESIN

When the resin has reached a leather-hard, or "B," stage, it may then be cut with a sharp mat knife or X-acto blade. You will know when the resin is in the leather-hard stage by pushing a coffee stick down into the surface of the resin.

At this point, open the glass sheets and cut the polyester resin into the desired shapes. Should cutting be impossible (the resin may have cured too completely), the sheet should be thoroughly cured, removed from the glass sheet, and cut with a jeweler's saw or a band saw. Naturally, a jeweler's saw will give better cuts.

MAKING "FRACTURED GLASS"

Should you wish to have crystal-clear, fractured edges, the polyester sheet would be cast and colored exactly as in Project 1, with the exception of leaving out the Benzoflex. Once the polyester resin has gelled, or cured, it is a good idea to remove the sheet from the glass mold and heat-cure the resin. Use an infrared heat lamp placed a couple of feet away. The temperature may be controlled by checking it with a cooking thermometer. In this way, the resin will become more brittle as the molecules tighten up. The sheet should then be placed in a deep freeze or the freezer part of the refrigerator until the plastic is very cold. It may then be cracked, broken, crunched with a hammer or other heavy object. The cracked pieces of polyester will then have a glasslike appearance. This cracking also can be done at room temperature with almost the same results.

CONSTRUCTING A THREE-DIMENSIONAL WINDOW OR MURAL

Make a drawing on translucent paper. Place it upon a table made of a translucent sheet of plastic or glass on improvised wooden legs or saw-horses, below which are some floor lights. On top of the drawing, place another sheet of glass or Plexiglas, or a cast sheet of your own polyester resin, to which you will bond the polyester pieces. If you use the sheet of glass, then bond the polyester pieces to the surface with a silicone rubber adhesive such as Silastic 140, made by Dow Corning, or the equivalent.

If you plan to bond the pieces to a polyester resin or Plexiglas (acrylic sheet), you may then adhere your glasslike polyester resin shards, or pieces, with polyester resin 32-032, Benzoflex, and MEK-Px in the following polyester adhesive formula.

POLYESTER ADHESIVE FORMULA

Polyester resin 32-032: 100 grams.

Benzoflex 9-88: 5 grams.

MEK-Px: 1/2% to 2%, depending upon the speed with which you wish the resin to cure.

BONDING

In any of the three panel methods, glass, polyester, or Plexiglas, after the first pieces of the polyester are placed upon the panel, you may then bond with the polyester

adhesive described just above. Applying the rest of the pieces of polyester is now purely a matter of art and craftsmanship, which you can only learn by yourself.

After the bonding polyester resin has cured, the panel is finished. It obviously needs no cover glass to prevent injury to anyone who touches the panel, but a cover glass might be indicated if you have a dust problem.

VARIATIONS

Naturally, should you wish to paint with polyester resin or overlay a design upon the polyester resin pieces with the polyester formulas covered in this book, there certainly is no problem. Interesting effects can also be achieved by applying polyester resin in drops or by pouring carefully with no color in the resin at all, which gives optical, or "lens" effects. Naturally, care should be taken in the selection of the colors for this type of mural, especially if it will be used as a window decoration where sun is liable to hit the resin.

Step 1. *Demonstration photos by Robert J. McCauley. This is a sketch done on translucent paper which is placed below the Plexiglas panel that is lying on the lighted transparent table top.*

Step 2. *After casting different color sheets of polyester resin, as shown in Project 1, the glass molds are opened up while the resin is leather hard. Although the text mentions hardening and then fracturing the polyester resin into pieces, the technique shown here is equally valid. The cast polyester resin, in this cuttable stage, is cut with a mat knife in even or uneven strips. These strips are assembled upon a sheet of Plexiglas or other acrylic sheeting. The sketch to be followed is placed below the transparent Plexiglas, on a base-lighted transparent table top. The pieces are bonded to the Plexiglas with the same formula used to produce the sheets in the first place (with the exception of the Internal Release 54, which is omitted). Notice the polyester resin adhesive being squeezed onto a polyester fragment which will then be applied either to the acrylic sheet or to another piece of polyester resin.*

Step 3. *Cutting pieces of polyester resin is quicker and safer than cutting glass with a glass cutter. The cut pieces of polyester resin, even though they look like glass, will not require that the "toucher" apply Band-Aids to his bloody fingers after moving them over the cut-glass piece!*

Step 4. *The assemblage continues. In the text, I mention that silicone adhesives, such as Silastic 140 or Silastic 732, may be used instead of the polyester resin. This is an especially good idea when a large mural (5' x 20', for example) is contemplated. Since the Silastic RTV adhesive is flexible, there will be less chance that the panel will warp, and less chance of any pieces dropping off in moving the work.*

Step 5. *During this assembling, the applicator should be sure that his hands are very clean. If he gets any resin on his hands, they should be washed immediately since these resins are tacky, and sticky fingers will leave marks and fingerprints everywhere.*

Step 6. *The pieces of "antiqued" plastic which can now be seen in the light areas were cast between sheets of glass upon which microcrystalline wax 1290 Y had been dropped from a height. After the microcrystalline wax was applied, the wax was coated lightly with silicone oil applied with a cotton swab, so that the wax could easily be removed after the resin was separated from the casting sheets of glass. These polyester panels are lightly wiped down with mineral spirits to remove any excess silicone oil. Effects like antique glass can also be obtained by casting polyester sheets between sheets of real antique glass.*

Step 7. *Here is the finished panel of polyester resin assemblage.*

Polyester resin panel *by Robert J. McCauley. Photo courtesy of the artist. This panel was cast between sheets of MirrorGlaze waxed glass. Before the glass panels were closed, they were lightly dripped with microcrystalline wax to give a type of cut-glass texture to the polyester resin sheet. The 1290 Y waxed panels were lightly sprayed with release agent 1711. The panel was cut with a mat knife while the resin was leather hard.*

Relief sculpture (*Above*) *by Xavier Gonzales. Photo courtesy of the artist. This relief was sculpted directly in wet clay negative molds. Subsequently, polyester resin was poured into the molds, and panels were cast. Bronzing powders and colors were used as a patina for these panels, and finally, they were assembled into this large frame.*

Transparent polyester bowl (*Right*) *by Ron Garfinkle. Photo by Evon Streetman. This bowl was cast between two wheel-thrown wet clay molds made by the artist during the summer of 1970 at the Penland School of Crafts in North Carolina. The resin was allowed to cure in continually wet clay for 24 hours. After this period of time, the clay was removed and scrubbed from the cured resin under running water. Notice the holder's fingers through the bowl.*

PROJECT 3
Casting Polyester Resin Reliefs

With the usual molding techniques practiced by crafts-men and sculptors, a negative mold may be made from damp water-based modeling clay. Into this negative mold, polyester resin (and certain epoxy resin combinations, to be mentioned in Project 19) may be poured, cured, and easily removed as a semifinished piece. The usual finishing procedures may be utilized.

MATERIALS

1. Slabs of damp ceramic clay of any type.

2. A board on which to work the clay.

3. Some type of hand sprayer to mist water over the clay before pouring in the polyester resin.

4. Polylite polyester resin 32-032.

5. Benzoflex 9-88 flexibilizer.

6. MEK-Px (methyl ethyl ketone peroxide) catalyst.

7. Additives, such as color pastes, metals, etc.

MAKING A CLAY NEGATIVE MOLD

Wet water-based modeling clay is the material recommended for this project. Perhaps the simplest way to begin such a project is to make a slab of wet clay about 1" to 2" thick, and approximately 4" x 6". Flatten the top.

After you have planned the relief design that you wish to make in this negative mold, begin cutting and gouging with the usual modeling, woodcarving, or linoleum block cutting tools. You can also use other tools, such as spatulas, coffee sticks which have been sharpened, etc. Do not cut away the edges of the block, but leave 1/2" intact all around the design so that when you pour in the polyester resin, it will not run out the sides. Remember that every bit of clay you remove from the inside of this bowl is negative space; that is, the polyester resin will replace the clay which has been removed.

When you have finished preparing your negative mold, lightly spray the entire clay area with water before adding the polyester resin. The light spray is not to soak the clay, but to ensure its dampness so that the polyester resin will not adhere.

The polyester formula recommended for this project is

as follows (see the end of this project for the formula for a metallic coating which can later be buffed or polished).

POLYESTER RESIN FORMULA

Polyester resin 32-032: 100 grams.

Benzoflex 9-88: 5 grams.

MEK-Px: 1 gram.

POURING AND CURING

Mix the polyester and other additives thoroughly, including whatever colors and solid materials you wish to add. Pour in your resin mixture and cover the polyester resin, as well as the clay, with Saran Wrap—completely, if possible. Let this system cure slowly at room temperature. Do not place the mold near heat, but in the coolest part of the room. Do not touch the mold once you have placed it aside. You will find that it generally takes a day or two before the resin is well cured.

REMOVING THE POLYESTER RESIN CAST FROM THE MOLD

When the resin has cured, take the entire piece to a sink, or put it in a bucket of water, and remove the clay as well as you can. If the clay is sufficiently moist, as it is supposed to be, you will have a relatively simple time cleaning the piece.

Should you wish to have a *transparent* relief in polyester resin, clean the piece thoroughly and let it dry with or without a heat lamp until the surface tackiness goes away. However, if you wish to dust powders or other additives on the surface, place the polyester cast near the heat lamp only until the water has evaporated; remove the lamp while the tack still remains. The tack may be useful in adhering such things as metal glitters (shiny metal flakes).

FINISHING

Even though the finishing of the piece depends upon your particular taste, the following suggestions may be helpful:

1. For complete transparency, you may find it helpful to

brush on an additional thin coating of polyester resin 32-737. This polyester will give a non-tacky surface. The formula is 100 grams of polyester resin 32-737 and 1 to 2 grams of MEK-Px.

2. Remember, when you are finished with your brush, wash it well in lacquer thinner or acetone.

METALLIC COATING

If you want metallic coatings which can later be buffed and polished, your *original* polyester mix should be:

Polyester resin 32-032: 100 grams.

Benzoflex 9-88: 5 grams.

MEK-Px: 1 1/2 grams.

Enough metal powder (300-mesh) to make a heavy but flowable paste.

After the above mixture is poured into the wet clay, cured, and the clay washed off, let the resin cure under a heat lamp to remove the final tack. After this, the piece may be buffed and polished.

Wet clay mold *by Juanita May. Photo by Robert J. McCauley. A wet clay mold is an excellent release material for polyester resin. This mold has been lightly sprayed with release agent 1711.*

Clay castings taken from plaster molds *by Juanita May. Photo by Robert J. McCauley. Equally effective is a wet plaster mold for casting polyester resins. This is, of course, of interest to those wishing to make many copies of a piece. The plaster mold is made by pouring casting plaster into a wet clay mold such as the one shown in the preceding illustration. Once this plaster positive mold has set, it can be used to make a second plaster mold which will be identical to the original wet clay mold. Seen here are fragments of clay castings which have been taken from plaster molds.*

Step 1. *Demonstration by Juanita May. Photos by Robert J. McCauley. Here, the polyester resin is being poured into a wet plaster mold. As you can see, the plaster mold is surrounded by water in order to make sure the resin does not become overheated. Immediately after the pouring, the resin is covered with Saran Wrap to keep out dirt and dust. This also hastens the curing of the exposed surface of the casting.*

Step 2. *Here, the cured polyester resin casting is being removed from the plaster cast.*

Step 3. *These polyester resin slabs were cast from plaster molds, but the same results can be obtained by using wet clay molds. These slabs can be used in murals and assemblages. They can be combined with bisqued and glazed ceramic slabs cast from plaster molds (see the clay castings taken from plaster molds opposite). Epoxy resin adhesive is a good grout to hold polyester and ceramic slabs together.*

Sterling silver pendant in Glygel mold. *Photo by Robert J. McCauley. The clarity of the Glygel mold is shown here surrounding this piece of sterling silver pendant. A mixture of catalyzed polyester resin and 300-mesh metal powder was subsequently poured into the mold.*

PROJECT 4

Gelatin Molds for Polyester Resins

When edible gelatin is mixed in equal proportions by weight with glycerin (or ethylene glycol, permanent antifreeze) and water, it provides an excellent mold-making material into which polyester resins can be cast.

MATERIALS

1. 275 Bloom Edible Porkskin Gelatin from Kind and Knox.

2. Glycerin, for use by children, or

3. Ethylene glycol (permanent antifreeze), for use by adults.

4. Water, stove, and double boiler.

5. Polylite polyester resin 32-032.

6. Benzoflex 9-88 flexibilizer.

7. MEX-Px (methyl ethyl ketone peroxide) catalyst.

8. Additives.

PREPARING GELATIN MOLD-MAKING MIXTURE

Polyester resins do not adhere and will cure well given sufficient time in the presence of wet clay, wet plaster, or other wet or damp surfaces. Another mold-making substance having the two salient properties of containing water and releasing this water slowly from a damp surface is gelatin. The following procedure for preparing this gelatin mold-making mixture works well:

To the top of a double boiler add by weight 1/3 gelatin, 1/3 very cold water, and 1/3 very cold glycerin or ethylene glycol. Immediately stir the mixture into a smooth slurry and begin boiling the water. Stir the gelatin mixture occasionally and slowly until the gelatin is dissolved. Keep "stewing" until you have a clear to translucent bubble-free viscous liquid with only a small amount of froth on the top which may be skimmed off.

Pour into clean, dry, coffee cans that have been lightly greased with petroleum jelly, such as Vaseline. Cover with the polyethylene covers that these coffee cans come with.

When you wish to use your gelatin mixture (which we will call *Glygel*), open the bottom end of the coffee can and push out what you need, cut off a slug of Glygel, and

remelt it in the double boiler. The melted Glygel can be poured over any form which does *not* contain free water. Best results are achieved on nonporous objects, such as metals, stone, glazed ceramic, glass, plastics, high-melting wax such as 1290 Y, and Plasticine.

RELIEF MOLDS

If you plan to make a relief mold, place the piece you wish to copy in a plastic or other nonporous container which is at least 1/2" larger and higher than any side or height of the item to be duplicated.

Warm the container and the piece (which we will call the "first" original) to about 110° F. and pour over it the Glygel, which has been warmed to 140° F. The Glygel should be poured at least 1/2" above the highest part of the first original.

Let cool slowly. You should have no air bubbles in the mold. When cold and at room temperature, remove the gelatin mold from the first original.

Although the Glygel mold will tend to hold on to its moisture because of the glycerin or ethylene glycol, both of which are humectants, it is a good idea to wrap your mold in some type of plastic film, such as Saran Wrap, until you are ready to use the mold. This will also keep it clean. The polyester resin casting formulas follow.

FORMULA FOR CLEAR CASTINGS

Polyester resin 32-032: 100 grams.

Benzoflex 9-88: 5 grams.

MEK-Px: 1 gram, for 1/8" to 1/4" thick castings, or
        1/2 gram, for 1/4" to 1" thick castings, or
        1/4 gram, for 1" to 3" thick castings.

Other non-reactive additives: Q.S.*

FORMULA FOR FILLED METAL CASTINGS

Polyester resin 32-032: 100 grams.

Benzoflex 9-88: 5 grams.

MEK-Px: 2 grams, for fast cure, or

MEK-Px: 1 gram, for slow cure.

---

*Quantum sufficit: as much as suffices, or use your own judgment.

300-mesh powdered metal: Q.S.* to make a thick but flowing paste.

Color: Q.S. if you wish to have a certain type of patina in the incised areas after buffing.

Other non-reactive additives: Q.S.

FORMULA FOR FILLED NON-METAL CASTINGS

Polyester resin 32-032: 100 grams.

Benzoflex 9-88: 5 grams.

MEK-Px: 1 gram.

Fillers such as talc, flint, kaolin, sawdust, wood flour, beach sand: Q.S.* to make a thick but flowing paste.

Other non-reactive additives: Q.S.

FORMULA FOR LARGE CASTINGS

If you wish to make larger castings than 4" to 5", you will find that making your formula up as follows will give a firmer mold.

Gelatin: 40 grams.

Glycerin or ethylene glycol: 40 grams.

Water: 20 grams.

HOW TO CAST

Whichever polyester mixture you use, be sure that the gelatin mold is cold. If you are about to do a large casting, say over 4" x 6" x 1", two procedures are indicated:

1. Coat the mold twice with the polyester mixture you require and let it cure. This will help to protect the gelatin from distortion either by weight or by heat.

2. Place the Glygel mold in an open waterproof box which may then be surrounded by water for cooling. In this way, you can prevent the melting of the Glygel mold from an overheated polyester resin casting.

After you have taken the above precautions, pour in your polyester resin mixture and then cover the box with a plastic film to keep out any dirt. Covering the surface directly with 20-mil acetate sheet (on top of which you have brushed some of your polyester mixture to relieve the acetate sheet from stress) or with 1 1/2-mil Mylar will give you a non-tacky surface in a relatively short time. In any case, leave your polyester casting in the mold for at least 24 hours.

To remove the casting from the Glygel mold, carefully separate the gelatin from the polyester "second" original. You can then use the mold again.

MAKING A TWO-PIECE MOLD

If you wish to make a two-piece Glygel mold rather than a relief mold, you should proceed in the following way:

Pour 1/4" to 1/2" of Glygel into your waterproof box and let it cool. At the same time, cover the bottom half of the "first" original you wish to duplicate with Glygel. Let this cool also.

Now pour a thin overall coating of Glygel on top of the already-cooled Glygel in the waterproof box and place the 1/2 Glygel-coated original with the coated side resting on the newly-poured Glygel. Let it cool.

Add more Glygel until your form is half covered. Let it cool well; then grease all the horizontal areas of the Glygel lightly with petroleum jelly. Following this, pour (and let cool in between pourings) multiple layers of Glygel no more than 1/16" thick. Continue pouring until you have filled your box at least 1/4" to 1/2" above the highest point on the original. Let it cool thoroughly. Carefully open the mold and remove the "first" original.

Cut a 1/4" to 1/2" pouring channel between the two sides next to the bottom of the piece. Close the mold.

Seal the mold with hot Glygel where the mold halves meet. Let it cool.

Pour in the polyester resin. Remember that polyester resins shrink, so fill to excess if possible.

NOTES, VARIATIONS, AND CAUTIONS

Because the Glygel is so rubbery and flexible, you can often make a one-piece mold instead of a two-piece mold. Undercuts are almost never a problem.

Your gelatin molds may be used many times. When they become distorted, merely remelt them in your double boiler. If the gelatin appears too thick and heavy, merely add a small amount of water to replace that which has evaporated. Stir in the new water until it is completely mixed. Caution: do not keep the gelatin on the fire any longer than necessary as you may destroy its gelling properties.

If you wish to make cellulose acetate boxes to hold your molds, see Project 21.

Plaster "mother" molds over the gelatin mold will give added strength to the gelatin.

*Quantum suffict: as much as suffices, or use your own judgment.

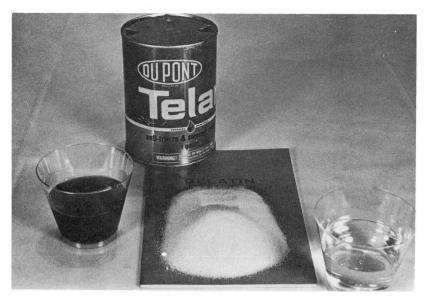

Step 1. *Demonstration photos by Robert J. McCauley. This first illustration shows the three ingredients which go to make up Glygel (a name coined by the author).* ⅓ *pure gelatin, by weight, is stirred into* ⅓ *by weight, of any brand of permanent antifreeze, then* ⅓ *water is stirred in last, and the entire mixture is placed in a double boiler. This "stew" is stirred on occasion and after several hours a clear gelatin solution results.*

Step 2. *Here, the Glygel is being poured over a small polyester resin casting which has been placed on the bottom of an aluminum box.*

Step 3. *Once the Glygel has re-gelled to room temperature—or below if you wish to speed the cooling in a refrigerator—it is easily removed from its container. In this illustration, catalyzed polyester resin is being poured into the Glygel mold.*

Step 4. (*Above*) *Once the polyester resin has been well cured, it is easily removed from the Glygel mold. The surface of the polyester resin may be slightly hazy upon removal from the mold, but as soon as the surface is completely dry, it will clarify. It is important, when using this type of mold, that the exothermic curing of the resin be negligible, otherwise the mold may melt. These molds may be reused or re-melted for further use.*

Variation. (*Right*) *Here is a mixture of ½ water and ½ Reichhold polyester resin 32-180 being poured into a Glygel mold. The system works well in this type of mold.*

PROJECT 5

Cellulose Acetate or Mylar Molds for Polyester Resins

Forms may be cast in containers made from cellulose acetate or Mylar sheet filled with polyester resin, clear or colored. After the resin has cured, the non-adhering form is easily removed, revealing the final finished piece.

Containers, or molds, may also be made from glass. Glass is good if you want a flat, rigid surface and if your form is relatively simple. The *Glass mold demonstration* illustrates this glass mold technique. For a glass mold, add Internal Release 54 to your polyester resin formula.

MATERIALS

1. A sheet of Bristol board or other cardboard the thickness of shirt cardboard.

2. 20-gauge cellulose acetate sheet to be used for items under 18" high and 50-gauge cellulose acetate sheet for items over 18" to 36" high. (7 1/2-gauge or 10-gauge Mylar may be substituted.)

3. Adhesive tape and Scotch tape.

4. Polylite polyester resin 32-032.

5. Benxoflex 9-88 flexibilizer.

6. Transparent colors.

7. MEK-Px (methyl ethyl ketone peroxide) catalyst.

MAKING A CELLULOSE ACETATE OR MYLAR MOLD

On a piece of paper, draw a design for a container with the same dimensions that you want the container itself to have. For the first try at this project, the form should be as simple as possible. In this way, you will be able to handle any complications which may arise. The procedure follows:

Once you have your design, make a container out of Bristol board or sheet cardboard. To do this, copy the exact measurements of your paper design onto the Bristol board; cut out the Bristol board and reassemble it with Scotch tape to make sure that all the sides fit.

Now, open up the mold, or box, and cut pieces of cellulose acetate or Mylar to fit the pieces of the mold you have just made. In this way, you can make an exact duplicate of your Bristol board box.

Next, assemble the acetate or Mylar pieces carefully, adhesive-taping one next to another on the outside edge until you have reconstructed the second "original" box out of cellulose acetate or Mylar. All edges must fit together well; otherwise, you will end up with polyester resin running out of some fissure and down the side of your sleeve. Cut an equilateral triangular hole (each side of the triangle should be approximately 1/4") with a razor on whichever side is to be the base of your form. You are now ready to fill your construction with polyester resin. There are two basic techniques: *rotational in-motion casting* and *still casting*. They can be used separately or together. The following rotational casting formula is suggested for a shape whose dimensions are 6" x 6" x 6".

FORMULA FOR ROTATIONAL CASTING

Polyester resin 32-032: 100 grams.

Benzoflex 9-88: 5 grams.

MEK-Px: 1 to 2 grams.

(For a glass mold, add 1/4% Internal Release 54.)

ROTATIONAL CASTING

Carefully pour this resinous mixture into your container and seal the hole up with adhesive or Scotch tape. If you are still concerned with leakage, you can put your form inside a Baggie and seal this up.

This next step is the one which separates the patient people from the restless ones. Rotate your container in all directions slowly until the resin has gelled. If the day is cool, you can use 2 grams of MEK-Px. On warm days, you will find that 1 gram per 100 polyester resin 32-032 is adequate. This step of sealing the sides and corners takes about 20 minutes to 1/2 hour.

Trying to rush this curing operation will not give nice, smooth results. The next charge should really be the same as the first (without color) to make sure that you have a sealed polyester resin box inside of your acetate one. To recharge your construction, open up the hole, fill, and reseal with more adhesive or Scotch tape. Rotate again. You will now find that each time you refill, the rotating cycle gets shorter since the container becomes a little warmer from each charge.

Vinyl-Look Crystal by Brenda Minisci, approximately 14"
high. Photo courtesy of the artist. This water-clear polyester
resin casting was done in a technique similar to the acetate
mold technique shown in the cellulose acetate mold
demonstration which follows.

Fractured Wedge in Aqua by Brenda Minisci, 3' high. Photo
courtesy of the artist. The general method of casting this
water-clear polyester resin piece is using a cellulose acetate
mold as shown in the cellulose acetate mold demonstration
which follows. Notice the cast head at the top.

For the remaining fillings, it is suggested that you cut down successively on your charges. About 10% to 15% less each time you refill. Now each time you add color, you should make the next batch darker than the previous one. Start with a very light color on your third filling. The number of fillings is up to you. The important thing to remember is that the beauty of these "sculptures" is in their internal air spaces where there is no resin. Solid castings are often lackluster; they have no mystique. Once you have stopped filling and rotating and your resin has gelled, it is wise to let the resin cure for at least several hours before removing the acetate mold.

As you remove the acetate or Mylar, wax and polish each freshly opened side with MirrorGlaze wax to protect the surfaces against scratches and tacky resins. The following still casting formula is suggested for a shape with the same dimensions as before, 6" x 6" x 6".

FORMULA FOR STILL CASTING

Polyester resin 32-032: 100 grams.

Benzoflex 9-88: 5 grams.

MEK: 1/2 to 1 gram, depending on the weather.

(For a glass mold, add 1/4% Internal Release 54.)

STILL CASTING

The procedure for casting without rotating is similar to that of rotational casting in the first and second steps. You must seal the container first; otherwise, your resin will possibly leak out. Since you are about to cast without turning, there will be a greater mass of resin settling at one place. You must, therefore, cut down on the catalyst MEK-Px. A good rule is to halve the quantity which you use for rotation, as is shown in the formula above.

Once your resin has gelled, let it stand for at least 1/2 hour so that it will not tear itself loose from any side. If the casting should begin to feel hot, don't hesitate to *run* to the sink to cool it off with cold water! You will not ruin anything. You merely slow down the chemical reaction.

Your next addition of polyester resin, turning your container to another angle, should contain a little less MEK-Px if you are around the 1% amount. It is not necessary to ever cut down to below 1/2%.

Continue in the same way as above until you have added and gelled your resin to your satisfaction. Again, remember that the voids in the resin often make the piece. Let the figure set at least several hours before you dismantle your acetate or Mylar box. Wax and polish as before.

NOTES, VARIATIONS, AND CAUTIONS

Patience brings results, as I mentioned before. Also, you will be learning what happens when the polyester resin changes from a liquid to a solid.

Chips of acrylic sheeting, chunks of cured polyester resin, and other foreign materials may be added to your container before or during your additions of polyester resins. Hot liquid microcrystalline wax may be painted on the inside of your sculpture mold to give you "lost wax" areas. If you do use this approach, remember to lightly apply silicone oil over your microcrystalline wax areas so that it will be easy to remove the wax from the finished sculpture.

Remember not to overcatalyze with the MEK-Px. If you do, dunk the piece in cold water to slow down the reaction if it gets too hot.

Cellulose acetate mold

Step 1. *Demonstration by Lil Morris. Photos by Brian J. Merritt. Here are pencil designs for a cellulose acetate mold as well as a cardboard maquette (left) and the finished cellulose acetate mold (right).*

Step 2. *After the preliminary drawing is completed, a cardboard maquette, or model, is made.*

Step 3. *Once the cardboard maquette is done, it is duplicated in 20-mil cellulose acetate. All the outside edges may be attached either with adhesive tape, masking tape, or Scotch tape.*

Step 4. *Next, the edges are painted and sealed with MEK-Px catalyzed polyester resin 32-032. After the resin hardens, the acetate mold is placed upside down in a container filled with vermiculite, so that the mold will not be distorted in the casting process. The polyester resin is then poured into this mold.*

Step 5. (*Left*) *After the polyester resin casting has thoroughly cured, the cellulose acetate mold is easily removed. Here you see the form which has just been removed from the transparent mold.*

Step 6. (*Below*) *Since the sides of the polyester casting are glass clear, very little finishing is needed. The edges may be carefully sanded with special papers and cloths which go down to a grit of 8000. These very fine wet or dry sanding cloths are manufactured by Micro-Finishing Products, Inc., P.O. Box 481. Wilton Junction, Iowa 52778. This final step shows the piece mounted on a plate of polished chromium bonded to an ebony base.*

Step 1. *Demonstration by Virginia McClure. Photos by Patricia Ling. Here, a glass mold is being assembled. The sheets of glass have been polished with MirrorGlaze wax.*

Step 2. *After closing up the five-sided glass mold, a thin coating of catalyzed Reichhold polyester resin 32-032 is applied to all the sides and corners of the mold. This is done so that, after the polyester resin has cured out, the mold will be leakproof upon further filling.*

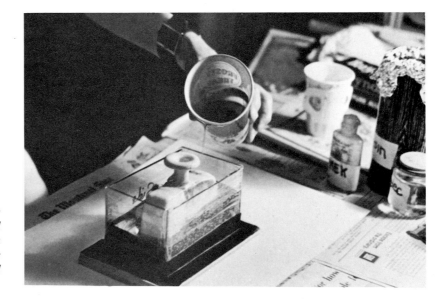

Step 3. *A mixture of polyester resin 32-032, internal release Zelec UN (or Internal Release 54), Benzoflex, and MEK-Px is being poured into the glass mold which contains a stoneware ceramic pot. After it is poured, the resin mixture is left to cure slowly in a cool place.*

Step 4. *When the polyester resin has completely cured, the glass sides and bottom are easily removed. The external faces of the resin have the exact surface shine of the glass mold.*

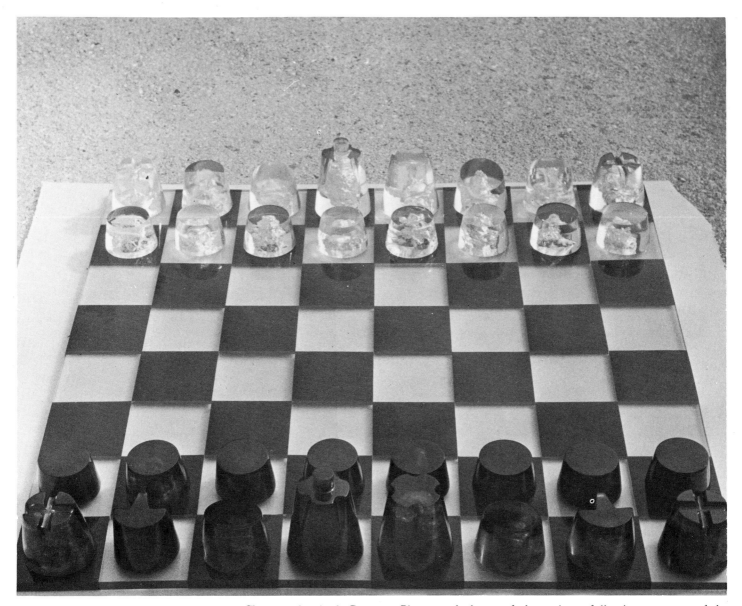

Chess set *by Arch Gregory. Photo, and photos of chess pieces following, courtesy of the artist. An ingenious use of microcrystalline wax 1290 Y is shown in this cast polyester chess set. The board is made from black Plexiglas squares set in poured epoxy resin (90 grams of Dow's water-clear epoxy resin DER 332, 10 grams of Epoxide 7, and 20 grams of Benzoflex). The curing agent for this resin formula was 60 grams of B-001. A detailed description of how these chess pieces were made follows.*

*Quantum sufficit: as much as suffices, or use your own judgment.

Microcrystalline Wax as an Engraving and Mold Medium

An inexpensive wax called microcrystalline wax 1290 Y, whose melting point is 178° F., may be easily cast into sheets of any thickness which may be engraved and embossed with additional wax. Polyester or epoxy resin may then be poured over these sheets to produce decorative panels or printing plates.

MATERIALS

1. Microcrystalline wax 1290 Y.

2. Cookie tin or other metal container whose sides are at least 1" high.

3. Silicone release oil or silicone aerosol spray.

4. Polylite polyester resin 32-032 (or Araldite epoxy resin 502 and epoxy curing agent RC 125).

5. Benzoflex 9-88 flexibilizer.

6. MEK-Px (methyl ethyl ketone peroxide) catalyst.

7. Additives.

MELTING THE WAX

Melt the required amount of microcrystalline wax in the top of a double boiler. In this way, you will not overheat your wax and create a possible fire hazard. The procedure follows:

Into a warmed (approximately 125° F.), clean, new, and shiny metal container, wipe in sparingly a small amount of undiluted liquid detergent or silicone oil. Let the water evaporate from the soap. You should see no visible film.

Pour in the microcrystalline wax to fill the pan about 1/4" to 1/2" and let cool as slowly as poosible. This will give you a more uniform surface.

When the wax has solidified or reached room temperature, you can begin to work on it. The underside should be smooth and glossy, the top dull and not quite so even.

ENGRAVING AND EMBOSSING

Using burins (engraver's tools), linoleum block cutters, or other knives, you are now ready to engrave your design. You should not overlook the possibility of embossing by adding additional wax to your plate A tjanting tool, used for putting down controlled wax lines in batik, is useful. You may also use a brush, or any other means, for that matter, to add the hot wax. Remember, too, that you can cut into these embossings. The more "hills and valleys" your plate has, the more dimensional the relief will be.

APPLYING SILICONE RELEASE

When you have finished engraving and embossing the wax plate, apply a very thin coating of silicone oil with a cotton swab dipped in either silicone oil or silicone-oil spray. This treatment allows the polyester or epoxy resin to be released most easily from the microcrystalline wax. Do not forget to oil the sides of your container with silicone oil as well. You are now ready to pour the resin of your choice.

For a highly decorative, non-yellowing panel, polyester resin is most adequate. For a stronger printing plate, epoxy resin is preferred. Both work for both uses. Formulas for both follow.

POLYESTER RESIN FORMULA

Polyester resin 32-032: 100 grams.

Benzoflex 9-88: 5 grams.

MEK-Px: 2 grams.

Ultraviolet light screener: Q.S.* (if the plate is to be put outdoors).

Color and additives: Q.S.

EPOXY RESIN FORMULA

Epoxy resin 502: 100 grams.

Curing agent RC 125: 25 grams.

Benzoflex 9-88: 5 grams.

Color and additives: Q.S.*

The plate made with epoxy resin should be made in two pourings, at least, and of no more than 1/8" each, since heat that develops may tend to melt the wax.

Casting a chess piece. *The first piece on the left is carved wax, originally a small block of 1290 Y wax cast in a paper cup sprayed with silicone release agent. The form was removed from the cup and lightly coated with concentrated liquid detergent. Next, the piece was brushed with melted wax. The first few coats were hot enough so that the wax had a chance to thoroughly coat the surface of the "released" wax form before hardening. After the original wax form was coated with ⅛" to ¼" of wax (the thickness depends upon the size of the piece), the mold was cut open with a sharp knife. The two mold pieces (second and third from the left) were internally sprayed with release agent, fitted together, and then carefully held in place with rubber bands. Melted 1290 Y wax was applied at the joints to seal them. To achieve the internal air space present in the chess piece, Glygel ⅓ gelatin, ⅓ permanent antifreeze, ⅓ water) was manipulated into forms and skewered on a toothpick as shown here. The resin formula which was used to cast the piece was 100 grams of polyester resin 32-032, 5 grams of Benzoflex, and 0.5 grams of MEK-Px. After the resin mixture was poured into the mold, it was covered with Saran Wrap to keep the air from the surface of the resin, thus speeding the cure. Once the resin was cured, the mold was opened and the piece was extracted. The fourth piece from the left shows the knight removed from the mold. The piece was sanded by hand with a series of wet-and-dry papers, starting with 180 grit and going up to 240, 400, and 600 grit. After this, a Polysand TR-34 sanding kit was used, with grits going up to 8000. The finished piece is on the right.*

One of each. (*Above*) *This photo shows one of each of Arch Gregory's chess pieces. Notice the difference in all of their centers, caused by the different ways the Glygel insert was molded. The clear pieces were made with no color pastes added, the black pieces were cast with black color paste mixed into the polyester resin formula.*

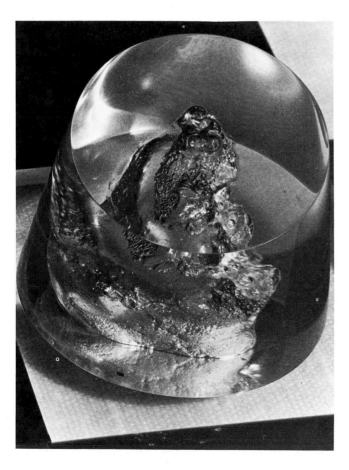

A pawn. (*Left*) *This closeup of one of the pawns from Arch Gregory's chess set shows the typical transparency of the finished, polished pieces. Here, the center air space left by the Glygel insert is very clear. This gelatin center is easily removed from the polyester piece after it has been taken out of its wax mold.*

CURING

Once the resins have cured out, the plates may be separated from the wax quite easily. The polyester plate will take longer to cure since the 32-032 is a slow air-curing resin. If you are in a hurry, cover the resin with a sheet of either Saran Wrap or cellulose acetate. However, if you don't wish problems with covering the resin once it has gelled, you may use a heat lamp held about 2' away. This will hasten the curing of the top surface of the polyester resin 32-032 without melting the microcrystalline wax.

Should you desire dull mat finishes on sections of either of the two types of resin plates, paint on one of the following suggested formulas.

MAT FINISH FOR POLYESTER RESIN PLATE

Polyester resin 32-032: 70 grams, to which you add the following well-stirred mixture,

Styrene: 30 grams.

Cabosil: 5 to 8 grams, depending upon the amount of "matting" desired. Small test samples are in order here.

MEK-Px: 1 gram.

MAT FINISH FOR EXPOXY RESIN PLATE

Epoxy resin 502: 10 grams.

Curing agent 956: 2 grams.

Epoxy paint thinner: 72 grams.

Cabosil: 3/4 to 1 gram, depending upon the amount of "matting" desired. Again, small test samples are in order.

NOTES, VARIATIONS, AND CAUTIONS

Should you wish to have certain areas of your plate carefully designed in any controlled colors, you should consider the use of the polyester painting medium (Project 10) or the epoxy painting medium (Project 20) with appropriate addition of color pastes. Either of these media can be applied directly on top of the "siliconed" wax plate. The medium should, of course, be gelled before pouring your plate.

Remember that since epoxy resins are adhesives, it is conceivable to use the polyester painting medium upon the silicone wax plate and then follow this with a pouring of epoxy resin.

If you wish to have a more rigid plate of either resin, this is easily accomplished by putting the plate in an oven at 125° F. for about five to 10 hours.

For printing, you may treat your resin plate as you would a linoleum block or a somewhat fragile, ordinary etched metal plate. The microcrystalline wax may be modified to give sharper cutting lines by the addition of varying quantities of special polyethylene pellets made by USI Chemical Company called Ultrathene Copolymers. The pellets are merely stirred and melted into the microcrystalline wax. The rest of the steps are carried out as above.

Step 1. *Demonstration by Jan Gelb. Photos by the author. Microcrystalline wax 1290 Y, which melts at about 170° F., is seen here being poured into a cookie pan that has been lightly wiped with a small amount of concentrated liquid detergent. To make a wax casting slab for engraving and or embossing to be followed by pouring a printing plate made from epoxy resin, it is well to cast the 1290 Y plate at least ¼" to ½" thick. The reason for this thickness is that should there be any warming up of the epoxy resin system, there will be less chance of melting the wax.*

Step 2. *There are many ways of engraving into the wax. A linoleum block cutter, as shown here, or a burin both cut nicely. Spraying the wax with a release agent such as 1711 can make it easier to cut the wax.*

Step 3. *The wax slab is worked upon while the wax is still quite warm and somewhat soft, but not liquid. Several shavings of Styrofoam cut on a hot-wire cutter are sprayed with a generous amount of silicone release agent 1711. They are then pushed into the soft wax and held in position until the wax cools. After the removal of the Styrofoam, the wax plate is further shaped and cut. The negative here has just been sprayed again with release agent. It is now ready for pouring the epoxy resin system.*

Step 4. *Here is the first pouring of the epoxy resin system over the released wax. The mixture is poured over the wax plate and spread evenly to a thickness of about ⅛" (no more, because of the heat developed). Any surface air bubbles may be removed by lightly spraying with acetone, which immediately flashes off.*

Step 5. *Here is the cast epoxy resin plate. Note that not only is this a printing plate but it also is a decorative transparency.*

Step 6. *Here is the original epoxy plate. It was first well sprayed with release agent and then the mirror-image plate below was made.*

Step 7. *This plate was made from the plate above. It is now ready to be inked and printed.*

Polyester Resin Sculpture

This convenient method for making sculpture begins with wire mesh, such as chicken wire, stapled or bound to a rigid armature of wood or other material. The wire mesh is then filled with crumpled newspaper or sawdust, dipped or saturated with polyester resin. After the resin has cured, areas are sanded and refilled with sawdust and resin. Finally, the surfaces are coated or painted with any type of paint or epoxy resin paint.

MATERIALS

1. Rubber gloves and/or protective creams.

2. Stand, armature, and wire mesh (such as chicken wire).

3. Newspaper, sawdust, and cotton wads.

4. Wire, string, or thread.

5. General-purpose polyester resin may be used, as well as Reichhold polyester resin 32-032.

6. MEK-Px (methyl ethyl ketone peroxide) catalyst, in quantities of 1/4% to 2%, depending upon the speed with which you wish to use the resin.

7. Color pastes, additives, fillers, etc., which are usually employed with polyester resins.

MAKING AN ARMATURE

After you have given considerable thought to a single design for the sculpture you wish to make, it is an excellent idea to fashion a small model out of Plasticine. When you are satisfied with the model, you can begin confidently to construct your armature. The armature can be built on top of a wooden stand to which a wooden stick or metal rod is attached. The skeleton form of the shape is constructed with wood, binding wire, chicken wire, string, etc.; the larger the piece, or course, the heavier all of these components must be. For your initial piece of sculpture in this technique, I suggest that you make a form no more than 2' high.

Once the armature is completed, it should be internally reinforced. Make this reinforcement out of tightly crumpled newspaper dipped in general-purpose catalyzed polyester resin. The suggested formula for polyester resin sculpture follows.

POLYESTER RESIN FORMULA

General-purpose polyester resin: 100 grams, into which is stirred

MEK-Px: 1/2 gram.

APPLYING POLYESTER RESIN

It is a good idea to cover the base of the armature with aluminum foil which can act as a drip pan. In this way, should resin run off the newspaper, you can pour it back into your container and reuse it. The method of application follows:

Stuff the crumpled newspaper, saturated with polyester resin, into the wire mesh areas that form the figure. When this is done, let the resin cure.

Next, mix up a non-runny slurry of sawdust and general-purpose catalyzed polyester resin, containing no more than 1/2% catalyst. Using a spatula or a serrated grapefruit knife, fill in all the voids with this mixture. When you are finished, let the shapes harden; then saw, sand, repair, and shape the desired contours.

For the figures under 2' high, there is no need for additional reinforcement except in forms that are long and thin. Reinforcement for such forms—or for larger figures and forms—is generally made with fiberglass mat and/or cloth.

USING FIBERGLASS MAT

Caution: *when using fiberglass mat, be sure to wear rubber gloves and tightly woven shirts*. To reinforce with this type of mat, pull it apart into small 1" to 4" squares. Dip the squares into catalyzed resin and apply them to the form. All the pieces should overlap slightly by at least 1/4 of their area. This will build a very strong, tight, reinforced structure when cured.

USING FIBERGLASS CLOTH

Large areas of a form, however, may be covered with fiberglass cloth of different thicknesses depending upon the contours. If there are many contours and sharp turns, the RC 181 airplane-grade type of fiberglass cloth is recommended, since it drapes beautifully. If the cloth is cut and a second piece laid next to it, be sure to overlap the second (and any subsequent) piece by approximately 1/4" to 1/2".

FINISHING

When the resin has cured to the "B" stage, or leather-hard stage, it may be cut with a mat knife or with a rough, heavy pair of scissors. When the resin has become hard, you may then saw, file, sand, and repair the form as needed.

The figure or form may be finished by a great number of different methods. Here are a few:

1. Conventional latex paint acrylics.

2. Spray painting with standard materials, among them automobile body paints of the acrylic solvent type.

3. Epoxy formula coatings.

4. Polyester formula coatings.

5. Urethane formula coatings.

6. Standard artists' oil paints.

Reclining Sun Worshipper *by Claire Hogenkamp, half lifesize. Photo courtesy Rothman's Art Gallery, Stratford, Ontario. This Montreal sculptor has been working with polyester resins for quite a few years. These figures and the two which follow, are basically made from filled chicken wire armatures covered with polyester resin mixed with fillers such as talc, sawdust, and fine sand. If thickening agents such as Cabosil and Asbestos 244 are added to the mixture, the slurry does not run.*

Female Sun Worshipper (No. 1) *by Claire Hogenkamp, 48" x 15". Photo courtesy Rothman's Art Gallery, Stratford, Ontario.*

Male Sun Worshipper (No. 2) *by Claire Hogenkamp, 34½" x 23½". Photo courtesy Rothman's Art Gallery, Stratford, Ontario.*

Step 1. *Demonstration by Oliver Coleman. Photo courtesy of the artist. This wire mesh armature is made with ¼" hardware cloth that is wired together. The intruding-extruding form is made by placing the hardware cloth over a form and shaping it. It is then wired to the main form, in which a hole has been cut.*

Step 2. *The armature is stuffed with wads of newspaper which have been dipped in catalyzed polyester resin. The plastic pail and rubber gloves are used for the dipping process. Saran Wrap is employed to keep the armature from sticking to the table.*

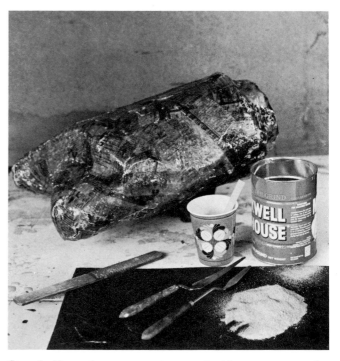

Step 3. *Here we see the armature in the process of being covered on the outside with newspaper strips dipped into the polyester resin. Notice the cut-off plastic milk carton used for holding the polyester resin. Strips of paper are drawn through the catalyzed polyester resin and then pulled between two touching gloved fingers to remove excess resin and assure an even coat.*

Step 4. *Here, the armature is coated with newspaper strips dipped in polyester resin. The uneven places have been filed off and the armature is now ready for sawdust coating.*

Step 5. *A rather stiff sawdust coating, made with fine cherry sawdust mixed with a small amount of polyester resin, is applied with a palette knife.*

Step 6. *After curing, the sawdust-coated piece is filed and drill sanded. Where necessary, additional resin and sawdust are applied. These may be seen here as dark spots which, after curing, are re-filed and re-sanded.*

Step 7. *The final picture shows the completed piece painted with polyester resin. The sanded piece was painted over with several shades, ranging from yellow to orange. When this coating had dried, a dark raw umber colored polyester resin mixture was wiped over the piece with a cloth.*

PROJECT 8

Translucent Polyester Resin Sculpture

Cellulose acetate sheet (equivalent to five sheets of paper) is easily cut, shaped, and bonded into three-dimensional transparent forms which can then be covered and encased in polyester resin reinforced with fiberglass.

MATERIALS

1. 20-mil cellulose acetate sheet.

2. Acetone.

3. Polylite polyester resin 32-032.

4. Benzoflex 9-88 flexibilizer.

5. MEK-Px (methyl ethyl ketone peroxide) catalyst.

6. Colors and additives.

7. Fiberglass surfacing mat or fiberglass cloth.

8. Rubber gloves.

9. Plastic or glass syringe and needle.

10. Metal clamps.

11. Rubber cement.

12. Cheap 1" brush.

MAKING A CARDBOARD PATTERN

To learn the technique, make something very simple for your first attempt (see *Translucent sculpture demonstration*). Start with a sheet of 10" x 15" flexible cardboard.

Make four cuts in the sheet, one cut from each of the four sides (Step 1). Now start turning, twisting, and trimming the fan sections until they fit together.

When you have found a dimensional form which pleases you, temporarily cement with rubber cement, overlapping pieces when necessary to hold the shape. Where one piece of cardboard is bonded to another, draw a line through both pieces and number them.

TRANSFERRING THE PATTERN TO ACETATE SHEET

Open up the cemented areas of the cardboard and cut out your piece of cellulose acetate sheet to duplicate your pattern. At the same time, cut out two identical pieces of fiberglass mat or cloth having the same internal cuts as

the original cardboard pattern (Step 2). The exterior dimensions should be at least 1/4" larger than the pattern. (*Note: be sure to wear gloves when handling fiberglass.*)

BONDING

You are now ready to bond your acetate sheet with acetone to the same shape as your original pattern. It might be wise to cement your cardboard original again, using rubber cement (Step 3), thus giving you a model from which to work. The bonding of the acetate to itself is most easily done by clamping the acetate pieces together where they should be and squirting acetone from your syringe between the acetate sections (Step 4).

After 10 minutes, remove the clamp; you will find that the acetate is bonded. Actually, it is glued in about one minute, but if you open your clamp too soon, the acetate will be too tender. Any trimming or slight modifying of your form should be done now before you start laying up the polyester resin and fiberglass. (Note: put on rubber gloves for sure, otherwise you will suffer when glass fibers work their way into the pores of your skin. A convenient device is to clamp your piece with metal clamps suspended from the ceiling with nylon fishing line.)

Mix well the following simple polyester resin formula.

POLYESTER RESIN FORMULA

Polyester resin 32-032: 100 grams.

Benzoflex 9-88: 5 grams.

MEK-Px: 1 gram.

Asbestos 244: Q.S.*

Additives: Q.S.

APPLYING FIBERGLASS

Brush the above polyester resin mixture over all of both sides of the acetate armature. Lay up the precut and trimmed fiberglass cloth on both sides of the armature which has just been coated with the polyester mix. With your brush dipped into the polyester resin, dab the resin on all over the fiberglass until it is saturated with polyester resin, *but not dripping*. Let the resin cure.

*Quantum sufficit: as much as suffices, or use your own judgment.

ADDITIVES AND COLORS

You may next add more of the polyester resin formula with whatever colors and additives you choose. If you wish relief decorations, drawings, or painting, use the Poly-paint medium described in Project 10, with desired colors. In order not to have shrinkage distortion, try to balance your polyester resin additions on both sides of your piece. You naturally do not have to add color to both sides. Once the resin is cured, it may be filed, sanded, drilled, or sawed (Step 6).

NOTES, VARIATIONS, AND CAUTIONS

Be sure to wear rubber gloves when cutting, handling, and impregnating fiberglass cloth. There is no reason not to add more fiberglass to certain individual areas. Remember, however, that whatever amount you add to one side you must add to the other side. Otherwise your lamination will not be balanced and your piece might warp.

It is also possible to make up a thick acetone slush/cellulose acetate solution which may be then daubed on as an adhesive for bonding cellulose acetate to fiberglass to cellulose acetate. Collodion should also work. This will enable you to spot-glue your fiberglass cloth or mat to your acetate sheet before you bond it together into its sculptural form. Once the acetone has evaporated, form your piece of sculpture. Sandwich by spot-gluing some of the acetone/cellulose acetate "goop" between fiberglass and acetate or fiberglass and fiberglass, and clamp with a metal clamp until dry. You are then ready to apply polyester resin to the pre-attached fiberglass.

More complicated sculpture can naturally be made if you cut and edge-bond different pieces of cellulose acetate to cellulose acetate with syringed acetone. In this approach, make duplicate fiberglass pieces as you go along.

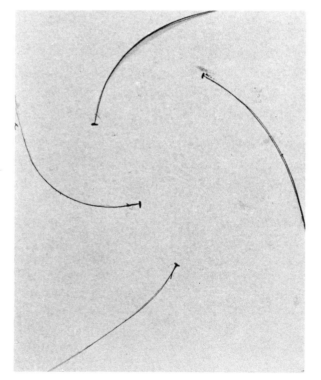

Translucent sculpture (Step 1). *Demonstration photos by Robert J. McCauley. Using a piece of cardboard which is easily shaped, cuts are made with a knife or scissors. This becomes the pattern for the form which is made in the next step.*

Step 2. *20-mil cellulose acetate sheet is cut to the exact pattern of the cardboard. Next, two sheets of fiberglass surfacing mat are cut to be about ½" larger, in both dimensions, than the pattern.*

Step 3. *This form is fabricated by temporarily bonding sections together with rubber cement. Once the desired form has been constructed, adjoining sections are numbered so that, if it is necessary to open up the construction, it can be easily reassembled.*

Step 4. *The acetate form is "welded" together with acetone in a syringe, as shown in Project 21. Following this, the fiberglass mat is applied to both sides; it can be "spot-welded" with a solution made from acetone and cut-up pieces of cellulose acetate.*

Step 5. *This view shows the fiberglass saturated with catalyzed polyester resin, 5. Benzoflex, and 1. MEK-Px. A convenient spreader for the resin is a piece of foam rubber, which will not be attacked by the polyester resin mixture.*

Step 6. *After the resin has cured, the fiberglass and polyester resin is sanded and trimmed. Colors and other additives are mixed with the polyester mixture and applied.*

PROJECT 9

Non-Glare Polyester "Glass" Coating for Photo and Graphic Prints

Pictures, photographs, or other paper *objets d'art* may be coated and protected with non-glare resin covering. By casting a film of polyester resin on a releasing surface, such as a mat-finish polyvinyl alcohol film or Mylar, and adhering your photographic or graphic print, etching, silkscreen, etc., you can make a permanent, protective covering for your artwork.

Photographic black and white or colored prints lend themselves nicely to this process. In the area of the graphic arts, generally, etchings, silkscreen or lithographs, etc., may be successfully given non-glare coatings on other than handmade paper. Prior testing should be made, however, on small samples of the material you wish to coat.

MATERIALS

1. 4-mil/or 6-mil polyvinyl alcohol film (PVA), or 5-mil to 7 1/2-mil Mylar mat film.

2. Canvas stretcher frame, silk screen frame, or other frame made from 3/4" thick x 2 1/2" wide plywood.

3. Staple gun.

4. Polylite polyester resin 32-032.

5. Benzoflex 9-88 flexibilizer.

6. MEK-Px (methyl ethyl ketone peroxide) catalyst.

7. Plexiglas or Masonite backing for picture, print, etc.

8. Rubber inking roller, or brayer.

9. Infrared heat lamps (optional).

STRETCHING POLYVINYL FILM

Take a sheet of 4-mil or 6-mil polyvinyl alcohol film (PVA) and give it a slight misting of water on its shiny side from a spray gun or other device.

Lay your frame (inside dimensions approximately 18" x 24") flat on a table. Place your polyvinyl alcohol sheet mat-side down and stretch and staple it to the wood frame. One way of doing this is to staple the sheet tightly to the middle of each end. Two people working together make this job much simpler.

Next, pull the film hard and staple out from the center of each side. Now stretch and staple the polyvinyl film to

the center of each of the long ends. Pull forcefully and staple out from the center on both sides.

When your film is uniformly stretched smooth all over, it is wise to staple the film to the outside edges. You will see that as the film which has been premoistened dries out, it will begin to tighten, much as a rawhide drum will. If the day is very humid, the extremely moisture-sensitive polyvinyl film will not really tighten unless you put your frame near heat. An infrared heat lamp will serve very well for this purpose.

STRETCHING MYLAR MAT FILM

With a staple gun, attach 5-mil to 7 1/2-mil Mylar mat film, mat-side down, to your frame (with inside dimensions of 18" x 24") which is lying flat on a table. Next place the frame in a 350° F. to 450° F. oven for 30 to 60 seconds. Remove the frame; cool it, and observe how well the Mylar film has shrunk. Repeat if necessary until the film is drum-tight. The film will remain this way since it is not moisture sensitive as PVA film is. Mylar film, however, is more expensive than PVA film.

You are now ready to run your test non-glare coating, or covering. The following formula is suggested where you are not overly concerned with direct sunlight exposure. Add ultraviolet light screeners according to manufacturer's suggestions for outdoor exposure.

POLYESTER RESIN COATING FORMULA

Polyester resin 32-032: 100 grams.

Benzoflex 9-88: 5 grams.

MEK-Px: 2 grams.

APPLYING POLYESTER RESIN COATING

Mix the above ingredients well and evenly. Brush or roll the resin directly onto the mat-finish side of the polyvinyl alcohol or Mylar film (see Steps 1 and 2 of *Coating a photograph demonstration*). Here you have a choice: you may place your "print" face down into the wet resin, or let the resin cure to its "B," or tacky, stage. You should try both alternatives to see whether you prefer the thinner or the heavier coating. For the latter, once the first coating has become tacky, roll an additional coating or the same polyester mixture over it. Here, too, place your "print" face down into the resin.

After this operation, in both cases, apply the polyester resin mixture to the back of the "print" and then back this up with a piece of Plexiglas or 1/4" thick tempered Masonite—smooth side against the uncured resin.

Then turn the PVA or Mylar stretched frame over, having placed a block of well-waxed wood the size of the Plexiglas or Masonite backing underneath. This well-waxed block should be thicker than the wooden frame so that the PVA or Mylar will be tightly stretched over the "print." Fasten the frame to a table with a C-clamp.

Now, with a rubber inking roller, or brayer, roll out the air bubbles, working your way in all directions out from the center of your "print," as shown in Step 3. Once this has been done, leave everything just as it is for at least 12 hours. If you are pressed for time, place infrared heat lamps 2' away for about six hours.

REMOVING "PRINT" FROM POLYVINYL FILM

When the polyester is well cured, you may *very carefully* remove your non-glare coated "print" from the PVA or Mylar film (Step 4). If you try to rip the print too quickly from the film, you may leave the cured polyester resin upon it. Naturally, should this happen, recoat the PVA or Mylar film with the polyester mixture and start again. With patience, you'll arrive at your goal!

NOTES, VARIATIONS, AND CAUTIONS

Interesting variations may be made using transparent colors either plain or mixed. Polyester resin may be applied and cured completely upon the PVA or Mylar film. Drawings may be done in India ink upon the "dried" polyester. An additional coat of polyester resin mix may then be applied as described above. Another variation might be the application of Poly-paint medium as described in Project 10 to certain sections of the finished non-glare coating.

The main caution is not to try to remove the non-glare coating too quickly from the polyvinyl alcohol or Mylar film. If you are working with paper which is porous to the polyester resin mixture, you should experiment with additional nonporous paper backings.

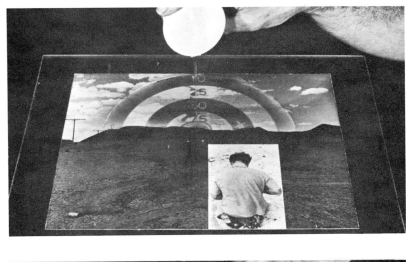

Step 1. *Demonstration photos by Robert J. McCauley. Polyester resin 32-032 is easily formulated for laminating a photograph print to Plexiglas, Masonite, wood, etc. To demonstrate this, we shall look at a photograph by Robert J. McCauley and follow the process of covering it with a non-glare protective polyester resin coating. Here, the catalyzed polyester mixture has been spread directly upon the photograph and upon the Plexiglas sheet that the photograph is glued to. Additional resin is being poured over the photograph. Although the print we are working with is black and white, this process works successfully on color prints as well.*

Step 2. *Now the polyester resin mixture is being spread over the print. Any handy spreading device, such as a small paintbrush, may be used. The stretcher frame you see underneath the Plexiglas sheet is not in use at this stage; the Plexiglas is merely being supported on it.*

Step 3. *Here the canvas stretcher that you saw in Step 2 is being used. This stretcher, a ⅜" plywood frame, is covered with a film of 4-mil to 6-mil polyvinyl alcohol film (PVA). The film, which is moisture sensitive, is "softened" in an atmosphere of high humidity, such as a hot shower room. The "softened" film is staple-gunned to the stretcher with the mat side of the polyvinyl alcohol film facing in. After the stapling, stretcher and film are removed to normal humidity and the PVA tightens like a drum. This mat side of the PVA film is placed over the "polyesterized" print. The air bubbles are removed from between the photographic print and the PVA film with a rubber roller (brayer). The print and the film are left pressed tightly together for at least 12 hours. Infrared heat lights playing 1½' from the print will keep the humidity away from the PVA. Mat-finish 5-mil Mylar may be substituted for PVA film. The Mylar is staple-gunned to the wood frame and stretched by being placed in an oven set at 450°F for 30 to 60 seconds one or more times.*

Step 4. *The infrared heat lamps are cooled or turned off. When the system has come to room temperature, you can carefully peel the Plexiglas and print from the PVA or Mylar film; the film can be used again immediately. The finished lamination is shown here.*

Same photograph covered with glass. *To show the amount of non-glare achieved by this process, a glass sheet was placed over the non-glare coating of polyester resin. Notice the glare on the right-hand side of the photo.*

Polyester Composition C-13 *by Claude Blin, 2' x 2' x ½". Photo by J. Varry. This polyester painting is done and cast on Masonite which is backed with ¾" plywood.*

PROJECT 10
Painting with Polyester Resins

Polyester resin 32-032 may be modified in a simple way to be used as a painting medium. It may be used for painting on top of Plexiglas, polyester resin sheets, polystyrene, or Lexan.

MATERIALS

1. Polylite Polyester resin 32-032.

2. Styrene.

3. Benzoflex 9-88 flexibilizer.

4. Asbestos 244.

5. Transparent or opaque colors.

6. Additives which may be used with polyester resins.

7. Plexiglas, Lexan, polystyrene, or polyester resin sheets.

8. Masonite, plywood, etc.

POLYESTER RESIN PAINT FORMULA

Polyester resin 32-032: 900 grams.

Styrene: 100 grams, into which is stirred

Benzoflex 9-88: 50 grams, and

Asbestos 244: 3 grams.

Stir the entire mixture slowly and well until there are no lumps (see *Adding styrene to polyester mixture demonstration* for details). Then put it in a quart can to preserve it for future use. (Note: if you wish to thin the polyester resin painting medium somewhat, there is no objection to adding up to 10% styrene.)

MIXING PAINT AND PEROXIDE

When you are ready to paint, mix 10 grams of the polyester painting medium and 4 drops of MEK-Px. This will give you a 2% peroxide mix. With no more than 1 to 3 drops of MEK-Px, you will find that you can work most leisurely. On the other hand, if you wish to speed curing, use 8 drops of MEK-Px and there will be approximately 10 to 15 minutes working time (at 70° F. room temperature).

PAINTING ON PLEXIGLAS

If your "canvas" does not exceed 12" x 18", it is not generally necessary to paint on both sides of the canvas to overcome the 7% polyester resin shrinkage. The use of 2% or 3% Asbestos 244 prevents the polyester resin 32-032 from running. If you find that the polyester resin medium is not clear enough for your purposes, you must then work on flat panels, and, as you will learn, you cannot use too thick a coating of the resin medium.

ADDITIVES FOR PAINTING ON PLEXIGLAS

For greater flexibility of the polyester resin medium, use up to 10% Benzoflex; for less transparency and greater translucency, add either more Asbestos 244 or Cabosil. For a great deal more translucency to opacity, you may use flint, a finely powdered sand of approximately 200 mesh. Flint does not have the thickening property that Asbestos 244 or Cabosil has. Many painters are adding pearlescence and other materials such as mica flakes to their polyester resin paints. Pearlescence gives the typical pearl-like look of the buttons on a shirt. (Incidentally, these buttons are now generally made of polyester resins.) For metallic colorings along with transparent paints, add metal glitters (shiny flakes) —bronze, aluminum, etc.—which are available in paint stores.

MAKING A LARGER PANEL
FOR A PLEXIGLAS MURAL

To insure a problem-free panel of 10' x 5', my students in Miami have devised a scheme of applying a thin fiberglass surfacing mat bonded to the Plexiglas with the 32-032/MEK-Px combination and 5% Benzoflex. In this way, they are relatively sure that there will be no separation of the polyester resin from the Plexiglas. It is a good idea in this type of thing to put the thin fiberglass surfacing mat on both sides of the Plexiglas. The use of the Plexiglass in this case yields a good firm panel to which decorations can be applied with no warping.

PAINTING A PLEXIGLAS PANEL

Once the fiberglass and polyester resin has set, proceed with the polyester resin painting on top of this. If you

Polyester Composition A-11 *by Claude Blin, 2' x 2' x ½". Photo by J. Varry.*

plan, however, to use very thick coatings on any one side of the Plexiglas mural, try to balance the other side as well so that there will be no uneven strains on your large sheet. Uneven strains may cause warping.

For this type of mural work, it is wise to include an ultraviolet light screener, such as Tinuvin 328 or American Cyanamid's U.V. 9. If your mural is going to be exposed frequently to sunlight, such as there is around Florida, the use of Rohm and Haas' P 444 A (plus the correct accelerator), which has been thoroughly tested with good results in Florida sunlight, is recommended by many painters I know.

APPLYING DECORATIONS TO YOUR PANEL

Polyester painting medium thickened with an additional 2% to 3% Asbestos 244 is an effective technique for applying decorations to your panel. This mixture, once catalyzed, is placed in a squeeze bottle (like a mustard dispenser) or in an Evenflo dispensable polyethylene bottle with a bottom corner cut minutely off on the bias to make a pinhole, and lines are squeezed to make the desired cloisonnés or designs that will later hold a clear resin material. When the resin that has been squeezed out is cured, you may then apply clear resin in the cloisonnés, or closure areas. Rather interesting "stained-glass" window effects may be obtained in this manner.

Be sure to add an equal amount of polyester resin on the reverse side of the panel even if you add no color to the catalyzed polyester medium.

The methods of painting described above may be done on Lexan or sheets of polyester resin which you cast yourself.

PAINTING ON MASONITE

Another technique which has been used by several artists in Canada is as follows:

Cut a sheet of untempered Masonite bonded to 3/4" plywood the size of the canvas you wish and edge it with 2" wood stripping so that you have a boxtop.

Paint the entire inside of the Masonite and sides with styrene-thinned polyester resin painting medium as described at the beginning of this project. In order to have a "white canvas," add titanium dioxide color paste to your polyester resin painting medium.

When the painting has cured, begin building it up, using the regular polyester painting medium and an additional amount of Asbestos 244. This will yield a relief-type painting with your polyester painting medium.

Let this cure and then, as you will notice, by the application of clear, non thickened 32-032/Benzoflex and MEK-Px/resin mixtures, you will begin to see hill-and-valley, watery-type reliefs in your resin pool painting.

The use of such materials as pearlescence, glitters, transparent colors, thickeners, etc., in combination with craftsmanship and your artistic ability will enable you to achieve some rather startling results—that is, if you are willing to pursue this track diligently.

PAINTING ON POLYSTYRENE

Another interesting technique which was explored at the Miami Art Center was the use of polystyrene sheet as a "canvas" material (see *Painting on relief canvas demonstration*). This, perhaps, is the most satisfactory of the painting materials upon which to apply polyester resins, since polystyrene is so closely related to polyesters. While I was teaching at the University of North Carolina in Chapel Hill, Gene Kangas, one of the professors there, was kind enough to show the following technique:

Clamp a 1/8" thick sheet of polystyrene between a 1' x 1' double frame made from two 1/2" pieces of plywood (Step 2). Warm this polystyrene sheet over an electric hotplate, electric oven, gas oven, or other heat source, and with asbestos gloves shape it with a can or any other item that you can roll over the surface (Step 2). In this way, you may make a relief canvas upon which you can paint a picture (Steps 3, 4, and 5).

Step 1. *Demonstration photos by Robert J. McCauley. When a water-clear polyester resin such as Reichhold's polyester resin 32-032 is mixed with 10% styrene, its viscosity is considerably lowered. Here, the sytrene is being added to the polyester. This addition of more styrene to a system which already contains sizable quantities of styrene is done in order that a thixotropic mixture may be made which is easy to handle as a non-runny painting medium for painting upon acrylic sheets, polystyrene, or polyester resin panels. 5 grams of Benzoflex per 100 grams of polyester resin are also added to give more flexibility to the painting medium.*

Step 2. *One of the most interesting agents for causing a resin such as polyester to become non-runny, or thixotropic, is Asbestos 244, manufactured by Union Carbide. 4 grams per 100 grams of the polyester resin mixture is being added to the mixture of polyester resin 32-032, styrene, and Benzoflex. The resin will then remain where it is placed until it is easily pushed to another location where it again remains until "molested."*

Step 3. *An ordinary paint stirrer attached to a ¼" electric drill is adequate to mix in the Asbestos 244. Try not to beat in any more air than necessary, since air bubbles tend to make the medium less transparent. As can be seen here, the Asbestos 244 wets in easily.*

Step 4. *This final picture shows that most of the Asbestos 244 is dispersed in the resin mixture. This thixotropic, or jellylike, mixture will remain in this condition if kept in a cool place, until at least 2 drops of MEK-Px are added per 10 grams of the mixture. Any of the color pastes sold by such resin suppliers as mentioned in Suppliers and Manufacturers section of Appendix can be added to this polyester painting medium.*

Step 1. *Demonstration by Lamont Anderson. Photos by Robert J. McCauley. Here is a 16" x 16" sheet of polystyrene which has been bolted and clamped between two sheets of pressed wood with wing nuts. Poly-paint medium bonds perfectly to polystyrene sheets. It also works well as a painting medium for acrylic sheeting, such as Plexiglas.*

Step 2. *The frame and polystyrene sheet is placed in an oven at 350° F. until the polystyrene is soft enough to feel rubbery. At this point, the frame is taken out of the oven, placed upon the edge of two chairs, and three tin cans are pressed and held into the warmed polystyrene sheet until it cools off.*

Step 3. *Here, the first coloring has been applied to the polystyrene-formed sheet with Poly-paint medium. 2% catalyst was added so that the system gelled quite rapidly.*

Step 4. *Poly-paint medium has now been applied to the opposite (raised) side of the polystyrene sheet. The color pastes which are used must always be well mixed into the medium, since these colors are not paints in themselves and will never dry. If too much color is used and the surface will not dry, then it will become necessary to cover over the "wet" surface with additional medium, with or without color. For cleaning brushes with a solvent system which will not interfere with the curing of the Poly-paint medium, use 100 grams of styrene and 2 grams of MEK-Px.*

Step 5. *This final picture shows additional application of Poly-paint medium.*

Embossed plate by Richard Adams. Photo by Pete Steiner. Adams used Poly-paint medium, described in this project, to emboss his ¼" thick Plexiglas plate. According to Adams, the use of the Poly-paint medium enables him to achieve effects which are quite different from the standard materials in use by graphic artists.

Finished print by Richard Adams. Photo by Pete Steiner. This finished print "State I" is, according to the artist, an inked and wiped intaglio. The rolled relief has two colors separated by using two different viscosity inks. The print was made on handmade paper which was passed through an etching press.

"Plastique" Dyeing, Bleaching, and Painting

When a fabric has been waxed and dyed with cold-water temperature dyes, the process is called *batik*. When a fabric is treated with a resist, such as Remyzist, manufactured by Resin Coatings Corporation, and dyed with dyes from 150° F. to boiling temperature, this is called *"Plastique"* dyeing. Remyzist is a mixture of organic materials which are soluble in cold water and insoluble in water over 125° F. Because of this property, Remyzist is an excellent resist for any combination of two-color changing methods: the hot bleaching out of a fabric dyed with chlorine bleachable dyes and the dyeing of a fabric at temperatures as low as 125°F.

With the use of Remyzist, it is possible to brush or paint a batik-like waxless dye or bleach-resist surface on top of material ordinarily used for batik, such as cotton or shantung silk. The textile dye or bleach must be applied at a temperature at least above 150° F. Upon completion of the dyeing or bleaching, the resist material is removed by washing the fabric in cold running water.

MATERIALS

1. Remyzist.

2. Cotton or silk, etc., used for batik.

3. Textile dyes, such as Rit, Putnam, or other hot-water dyes.

4. Sodium hypochlorite or Clorox bleach.

5. Poly-paint medium (see Project 10).

6. Colors and additives (optional).

7. Batik wax—1/2 beeswax, 1/2 paraffin (optional).

8. Wax spreader, such as a tjanting tool (optional).

9. Batik dyes (optional).

TESTING YOUR FABRIC

Brush or drip a small amount of Remyzist on a small sample of your fabric. Put half the sample in a Baggie to keep it moist and let the other half dry. If your sample is already dyed, your first test may be evaluating how the piece bleaches. Place the wet and dry samples in a chlorine bleach adjusted to about 150° F. with 1 part Clorox and 4 parts water.

Stir the bath and samples for 15 to 60 seconds to see if bleaching takes place. Leaving your fabric too long in the bleach can noticeably degrade the fibers.

If you want to test a dyed or undyed fabric in a dye bath, take your samples which have been treated with Remyzist and place them in an 150° F. dye bath made with such dyes as Putnam, Rit, etc.

Proper rinsing is most important after bleaching or dying your sample. In either case, give a short rinse in hot running water to get rid of the bleach or dye without solubilizing the resist. Next rub and agitate your samples well in cold running water to remove the Remyzist.

Your bleached or dyed test samples or swatches may further be used to test the effect of successive dye baths on top of one another.

APPLYING RESIST

After you have selected a design, stretch a piece of white cotton or silk cloth as shown in Step 1 of the *Plastique demonstration*. Apply the Remyzist where you do not wish the dye to penetrate. Remyzist can be applied to either a wet or a dry fabric, using any method you wish. This includes the application of the resist by brush, rubber or other stamps, syringes, squeegees through a silk screen, etc. If you find that the consistency of Remyzist is too thick for your method of application, you may thin it with either denatured or wood alcohol (which is fast-evaporating) or with water (which will slow down the drying time).

At this point, you have two options: you can immerse your fabric in the hot dye bath *before* the resist solution has dried out completely, or you can immerse your fabric in the hot dye bath *after* your fabric is thoroughly dry. The drier your resist solution is when you dye your fabric, the sharper the lines will be. To dry your resist material, let the fabric stand at room temperature or place it under an infrared heat lamp at least 2' to 3' away. Remyzist is available as a water solution and as an alcohol solution. The alcohol-based solution will, of course, dry faster than the water-based solution.

DYEING

The dyeing system to begin with should be simple see *Plastique demonstration*). As with all new techniques

which the artist-craftsman uses at the outset, you cannot learn to use your tools properly if you are going to try to do everything at once. Don't try to be the "bride at the wedding and the funeral corpse all at the same time!" For example, try a yellow dye first. Make up your dye bath with Putnam, Rit, etc., which will dye preferably around 150° F. Enter your "resisted" fabric and stir constantly for about five to 10 minutes holding the temperature between 125° F. and 150° F. When the fabric has been dyed to the required shade, place it immediately in a bath of clear, running hot water. This bath will rinse out the excess dye while the resist will continue to protect the undyed areas. When the hot rinse bath is quite clear, you may wring out your fabric and wash and rub out the resist in cold running water.

Should you desire to stop after the yellow dyeing, fine. Merely dry the fabric. You may continue the hot dyeing at any time thereafter.

If you want the marbleized effect associated with batik, let the fabric completely dry out, and dye it in the usual batik cold-dye method available in any book on batik.

BLEACHING

Hot bleaching with Clorox (sodium hypochlorite) may be done using Remyzist as the bleach resist. If you take a black-dyed piece of cotton cloth and apply the resist in the areas you wish to keep black, you will find that it will enable you to produce some interesting results. After you have applied the resist, immerse the fabric in the hot bleach (temperature should be no higher than 150° F.) When the black has been bleached to your satisfaction, wash and rinse your fabric in hot water. If you wish to be more exact in stopping the action of the bleach, immediately rinse your fabric in a 1/2% solution of sodium bisulfiite or hypo for about a minute. This solution

should also be hot, so that the resist will not be disturbed during this step.

Next wash and rub the fabric well in cold water to remove the Remyzist (which is quite harmless to your hands). Keep doing this until there is no more sticky feeling to the cloth. If you wish not to remove the resist from the fabric, in preparation for a following dye, go directly from the hot wash, rinses, and wringing into the dye. Naturally, you may dry your fabric after wringing before you enter it in the dye bath, if you wish.

APPLYING POLY-PAINT MEDIUM

You may desire to explore the possibility of applying Poly-paint medium in certain areas on your dried fabric. If so, the particular areas to be treated should be blocked in with wax. A convenient tool is a tjanting tool. Make a wax line around the desired area to be Poly-painted. Since the hot wax penetrates right through the fabric, the catalyzed Poly-paint medium will not bleed beyond the wax line. During this operation, the fabric should be held suspended and horizontal.

Once the Poly-paint has been applied, cure it at room temperature in order not to risk melting the wax. Try not to use very much, if any, color in the painting medium; instead, apply the catalyzed medium as thick as possible with a palette knife, but no more than 1/16" thick. In this way, you will see the interesting translucent effects possible when the cloth is "wet" with the polyester resin.

NOTES, VARIATIONS, AND CAUTIONS

There are so many possibilities open in this new approach to dyeing and application of plastic to materials that you should proceed very slowly. Try numerous simple experiments and keep a notebook. Give your fabric swatch numbers which will correspond to the information in your notebook.

Batik wall hanging (*Left*) *by Margaret Pelton. Photo by Robert J. McCauley. This batik was impregnated, in the dark areas, with a modified Poly-paint medium. In the hands of the creative Batik artist, there are many ways in which resins such as polyester, epoxy, and polyurethane may be used.*

"Plastique"

Step 1. *Demonstration by Gloria Hall. Photos by Robert J. McCauley. A simple batik design is stapled to a canvas stretcher, prior to the application of the liquid resist which becomes a waterproof "Plastique" at temperatures around 150°F. When the temperature of the bath is lowered to room temperature, the Plastique again returns to its water-soluble state. This synthetic chemical mixture, the newly developed Remyzist, penetrates fibers more readily and is also hot-bleach resistant.*

Step 2. *Remyzist has been applied to the fabric, and since it is a small piece, it was put wet into the dye. According to Sister Remy Revor of Mount Mary College, Milwaukee, Wisconsin, who helped work out the formula now called Remyzist, the best results are achieved when the resist is thoroughly dried; the lines are then sharper.*

Step 3. *Here is seen the further addition of Remyzist.*

Step 4. *The fabric, in this case cotton, has been immersed into a dye bath whose temperature was held at approximately 150° F. The dye used was Rit blue-black, and the dyeing time was 10 minutes. After the fabric was dyed, it was washed in cold running water until the resist was completely removed. Here is the result of the dyeing, after cold-water washing and drying.*

Combining Batik or "Plastique" with Polyester or Epoxy Painting Medium

After fabrics which have been batiked or "Plastiqued" are dry, they may be treated with polyester or epoxy resins for added dimension or laminated together to achieve new and novel effects.

MATERIALS

1. Fabrics which have been batiked or Plastiqued.

2. Poly-paint medium modified, and/or

3. Epoxy paint medium modified, and/or

4. Epoxy paint medium combined with curing agent RC 303 and Asbestos 244.

5. Transparent colors (optional).

6. Asbestos 244 (optional).

7. Curing agent B-001 (optional).

8. Frame to hold the batik or Plastique.

The first batiks that were combined with polyester resin were done by Thérèse Guité, a student of mine and a teacher in Montreal. In this case, the wax drawing was left in the fabric so that it would act as a barrier to prevent the liquid polyester resin from running from one area to another. In this technique, therefore, there are certain areas which are pure batik and other areas which contain the Poly-paint medium.

In order to learn how to combine resins with either of the two dyeing techniques, it is suggested that either you make a batik and remove all the wax or make a Plastique and dry it out thoroughly.

Next you should stretch your dyed fabric on a frame stretcher similar to that used for canvas. The simplest method to start with is to impregnate the entire cloth with your resin. The resin, whichever you use, should be applied sparingly all over so that the feel of the fabric is maintained once the resin has cured out. The formulas which follow are for saturating the cloth. Your choice can be either epoxy or polyester.

POLYESTER RESIN SATURANT

Polyester resin 32-032: 100 grams.

Benzoflex 9-88: 10 grams.

MEK-Px: 2 grams.

EPOXY RESIN SATURANT

Epoxy resin 502: 90 grams.

Benzoflex 9-88: 5 grams.

Epoxide 7: 10 grams (to lower viscosity).

Curing agent B-001 or B-002: 50 grams (not moisture sensitive).

Either resin mix can be colored. I would suggest that you use the resins without color initially to learn the esthetics of these transparent "wetting" resins. Once the resin has cured, then consider applying additional resin to obtain interesting reliefs. Naturally, you should use the same type of resin on top of the base resin. However, since the epoxies are good adhesives, you can use epoxy paint medium on top of polyester resin. *The reverse will not work!* Polyesters are not good adhesives.

It is a good idea to select certain areas of your impregnated fabric for application of either of the resin paints. Whichever one you use should be applied as thickly as possible so that you may learn what effects are possible with this type of translucent relief. I have found that by far the most elegant results were achieved on shantung silk.

POLY-PAINT MODIFIED MEDIUM

Styrene: 10 grams.

Benzoflex 9-88: 10 grams.

Asbestos 244: 4 grams.

The above mixture is then added to

Polyester resin 32-032: 90 grams.

Stir the entire batch carefully with an electric paint stirrer. It can be done by hand, but it takes considerably longer to remove the Asbestos 244 lumps.

Depending upon how fast you wish to work, use 10 grams of Poly-paint medium and 2 to 8 drops of MEK-Px to cure the Poly-paint medium.

EPOXY PAINT MODIFIED MEDIUM

Epoxide 7: 10 grams.

Benzoflex 9-88: 5 grams.

Asbestos 244: 4 grams.

Mix well and add to

Epoxy resin 502: 90 grams, which has been heated slowly to 212° F. in a double boiler.

Stir the entire batch carefully with an electric stirrer to remove the lumps in the Asbestos 244.

CURING

To cure the epoxy paint modified medium, you can use either curing agent 956 or the less moisture-sensitive B-001 or B-002 as follows: 11 grams of epoxy paint modified medium and either 2 grams of 956 or 5 grams of B-001 or B-002.

APPLYING RESIN PAINT MEDIUM

The resin painting mediums should be applied either with a palette knife or coffee stick. Try to get as much texture as possible. If your resin is not thixotropic (non-runny) enough, you may, of course, add small amounts of Asbestos 244. Too much asbestos will cut down on the translucency.

NOTES, VARIATIONS, AND CAUTIONS

After you have evaluated the different resins and have seen what each does, you should, if you are still interested, try some of the following variations:

1. After you have waxed and batik-dyed your fabric, leave in the wax and apply resin where there is no wax. Let the resin cure and then remove the wax. Here you will see the interesting contrast between "dry" and "wet" fabric.

2. After you have removed your wax from your last batik dyeing, apply wax with a tjanting tool to form cloisonnés of wax. You may then apply either of the saturating resins or either of the modified painting mediums in the cloisonnés. This technique will naturally work with your Plastique dyeing method, too.

3. There is nothing which says that you cannot cut out areas of your fabric, back them with Saran Wrap, and then make "windows" of either epoxy resin saturant, epoxy paint modified medium, or the 50/50 mixture of epoxy resin 502 and RC 303 to give flexible "windows." Thin windows of polyester will not be very satisfactory since they will tend to shatter and shrink.

4. Try laminating or making collages of different pieces of your batik and Plastique using either of the resins described above.

Remember to have good ventilation when you work with either polyester resins or epoxy resins. Keep these

materials off your hands. If resin contact is made, unhysterically wash your hands well with soap and water. Dry them, and apply small quantities of silicone oil DC 200 or Silicare, made by Revlon, which contains silicone oil. If you find that you cannot work without being sloppy, wear gloves or at least apply some sort of barrier lotion as mentioned above.

Fabric design *by Bernadette Merkel. Photo by Pete Steiner. This dyed fabric design was created using Remyzist. Different Rit dyes were applied at 150° F. The whole procedure took only several hours.*

EPOXY RESINS

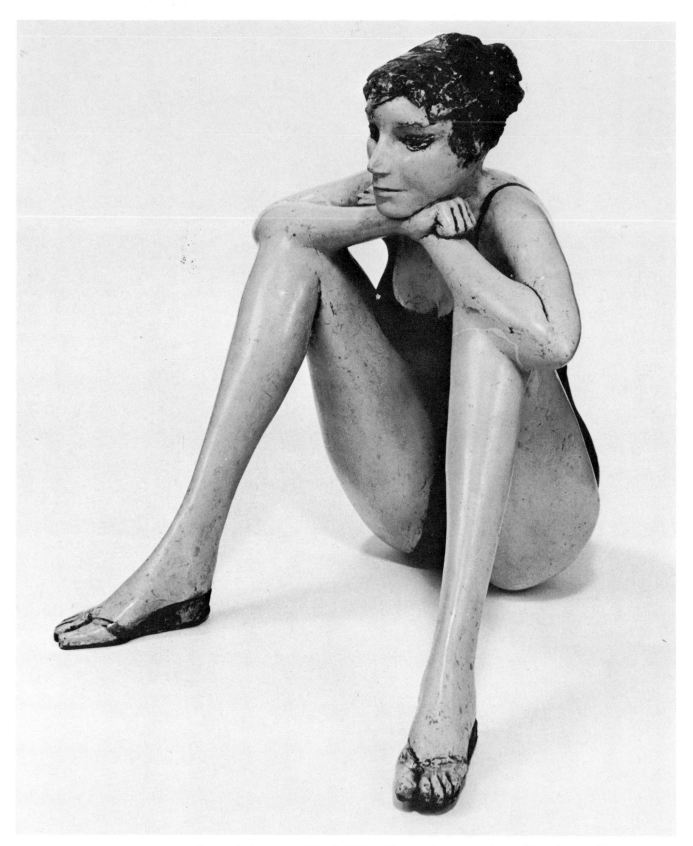

Sitting Swimmer *by Frank Gallo, lifesize. Collection Louis Hubschman. Photo courtesy Fulton and Partners, Inc. Frank Gallo produces sculptures made from epoxy resin such as the one shown here and on the following pages. For the past few years, he has worked in modeling clay from which he makes a wax or plaster mold. See Project 19 for a more complete description of the process.*

Epoxy Resins

Why should the artist and craftsman use epoxy resins? Perhaps for many of the same reasons that so many different industries throughout the United States use over 100,000,000 lbs. of epoxy resins per year—they are among the most versatile of today's synthetic resins. They are used in four-engine jet aircraft, for "stained-glass collages," and in restoration work. The Sydney Opera House in Sydney, Australia (see p. 96) is "glued together " in huge, wedge-shaped concrete segments with a layer of epoxy resin which maintains a uniform load distribution over the area of contact. Even a replica head of Guy, the London Zoo's gorilla, has been made from epoxy resin (see p. 97).

WHAT IS AN EPOXY RESIN?

The word *epoxy* comes from the chemical name given by chemists to a particular grouping in a molecule of elements of carbon and oxygen called an *epoxide linkage*. Epoxy resins began to be used commercially in substantial quantities in the early 1950's. There is now a huge amount of information available on this relatively new family of synthetic resins. (If you are interested in the subject, you will find a world of information in Henry Lee and Kris Neville's book, *Handbook of Epoxy Resins*, published in 1967 by McGraw-Hill.)

Since definitions are often helpful, I shall use the definition of epoxy resin given in Lee and Neville's book: ". . . An epoxy is defined as any molecule containing more than one epoxy group . . . which is capable of being converted to a useful thermoset *non-meltable* form. The term is used to indicate the resin in both the thermoplastic *meltable* (uncured) and thermoset *non-meltable* form. The term is used to indicate the resin in both the thermoplastic *meltable*(uncured) and thermoset *non-meltable* (cured) state." (The italics are mine.)

USES FOR EPOXY RESINS

Again, let's ask, "Why should the artist and craftsman use epoxy resins?" Epoxy resins combined with their proper curing agents, or hardeners, have the following properties, which make them of great interest to the artist and craftsman:

1. They are excellent adhesives.

2. They have transparency similar to that of water-clear or transparent colored glass.

3. They may be obtained as low-viscosity liquids which are easily converted to solids having almost any desired properties.

4. They have less shrinkage than Sanforized shirts, below 1/2%. This makes them useful for accurate, clear castings. ("Actually, shrinkage, as measured in the laboratory, is greater than this—it is more like 5% to 6%. But it must be remembered that when people measure shrinkage in the laboratory, they go to a lot of trouble to make sure that they get it all, and the measured value implies a lot worse mold adaptation than you get in practice.")*

5. They are very strong and have high mechanical properties, which make them one of the strongest resins.

6. They have good chemical resistance and appear to have good long-term aging properties.

7. They may be readily modified with various additives to give an extremely wide range of useful materials for the areas covered by the artist and craftsman.

ADDITIVES

A partial list of the additives which can be used to modify epoxy resins follows:

1. *Relatively lightfast transparent and opaque pigments and dyes*. All colors are intermixable.

2. *Thixotropic agents, such as Cabosil or Asbestos 244.* These are chemically inert substances, producing jelly-like epoxy resin systems which remain in the form they are given until moved or pushed to another place. Unless moved again, the epoxy resins retain their newly acquired shape until they have cured to solids.

3. *Viscosity-lowering special thinners called reactive diluents, which in themselves are usually epoxies.* These reactive diluents, if not used in excess generally of more than 10% of the epoxy resin, will not cause any great amount of additional shrinkage.

4. *Flexibilizers, such as Benzoflex 9-88. These give varying amounts of flexibility and stretchability.*

*My thanks to Kris Neville, co-author of *Handbook of Epoxy Resins*, for this clarification.

Figure, 1970 *by Frank Gallo, lifesize. Photo courtesy Fulton and Partners, Inc.*

5. *Lacquer thinners, such as xylene, MIBK, and toluene.* These can be added to the epoxy resin combinations to yield thin coatings and/or mat or dull finishes with the addition of Cabosil.

6. *Fillers, such as dry and various-mesh sand, talc, stones, clay, metal powders, glass chips, sawdust, etc.*

7. *Accelerators, such as Mod-Epox (triphenyl phosphite) or DPM 3-800 LC.* These will make the epoxy resin/hardener combinations harden or cure in much shorter time.

Don't let the chemical names and numbers scare you! Remember, you have already learned to live with such chemical names as stannous fluoride in toothpaste, and numbers such as 205-657-109 on your Social Security number!

KINDS OF EPOXY RESINS

Of the many epoxy resins available, there is one that has been successfully used in the art and craft area for 16 years, CIBA Araldite epoxy resin 502. The following information is taken from the CIBA Company, Inc. *Technical Bulletin 4*: "Araldite epoxy 502 is a light, amber-colored liquid modified epoxy resin of medium viscosity at room temperature. The viscosity may be substantially lowered by heating. The resin has been modified with a flexibilizer called dibutyl phthalate to increase its resistance to low-temperature cracking. Cured Araldite epoxy 502 displays good mechanical and electrical characteristics, good chemical resistance, and excellent adhesion to metal and ceramics . . . ." The working temperature range of the unfilled, cured epoxy resin is claimed by the manufacturer to be between 140° F. to 158° F.

If you want to use a less flexible epoxy resin, I suggest CIBA epoxy resin 6004 or equivalent. (As a matter of fact, throughout this book whenever I mention a trade name or a company name, the "or equivalent" is *always* implied!) You must remember, however, that different epoxy resins require different amounts of curing agents, or hardeners, to change them from liquids to solids. In this book, most of the data on amounts of curing agents is based on CIBA Araldite epoxy resin 502. For example, I use 20 grams of Araldite curing agent 956 with 100 grams of Araldite epoxy resin 502. Use 20% more hardener (curing agent) when using epoxy resin 6004, or 24 grams of curing agent.

If you wish to develop a formula with epoxy resins which have no color at all, use Dow Chemical's DER 332. For curing agents which have no color, contact your retail resin supplier.

EPOXY CURING AGENTS

For the epoxy resins to become useful solids, or plastics, it is necessary to combine them with chemicals which are called *hardeners*, or *curing agents*. As there are many different epoxy resins, ranging from liquids to solids, so there are scores of curing agents or hardeners. I have used six to 12 throughout the book which will fulfill most art and craft requirements. The ones which are of the most interest to the artist and craftsman are those which are related in some way to ammonia. They are usually very alkaline, as is household ammonia. Often they are caustic, like lye. If they come in contact with hands or skin over a period of time, many of them may cause a dermatitic rash similar to that caused by poison ivy.

If you should happen to get any of these curing agents in your eyes, flush your eyes out with cold running water for at least 15 minutes. Following this, *get medical attention.*

CHARACTERISTICS OF EPOXY CURING AGENTS

All of these curing agents have a number of properties in common:

1. They are almost all alkaline materials which more or less may provoke dermatitic skin reactions similar to that caused by poison ivy over relatively long periods of actual contact. Remember: *no contact, no dermatitis!*

2. They must be combined with the epoxy resins in exact proportions, otherwise the results will generally be unfavorable. Do not add more or less curing agent than recommended by the text unless it is so specified. Either your resin may not cure or you will not obtain optimum properties.

3. All of the curing agents we are using give off heat when they react with epoxy resins. Because epoxy resins cure more rapidly with heat, and since the addition of curing agents to the epoxy causes a reaction which gives off heat (exothermic), it is wise to mix up only what you need. 100 grams of epoxy resin 502 mixed with 20 grams of curing agent 956 turns solid at 70° F. (room temperature) with much dissipation of heat in about 20 to 30 minutes. 12 grams of this mixture will last at least several hours. Mixing should be done at 70° F. The heat of reaction must be taken into account when you are making thick castings. Too much exothermic heat will probably yellow your resin, distort the shape you are making, and shrink your final shape.

There are some curing agents which are claimed to be relatively nontoxic upon external application to the skin. Such curing agents as Versamid 140 or CIBA 840, and the Ajicure series including B-001 are considered nondermatitic by their manufacturers. However, if they come in contact with your eyes you should still wash your eyes for 15 minutes in cold running water and then get medical attention.

Over the last 16 years, I have evaluated many of the curing agents for epoxy resins as they have been developed. For our purposes, the backbone of the curing

agents used with Araldite epoxy resin 502 is CIBA Araldite curing agent 956, which is manufactured by Union Carbide under the Bakelite brand name of ZZL-0816.

DIFFERENT EPOXY CURING AGENTS FOR DIFFERENT USES

Curing agents and other additives determine many of the final properties of the cured epoxy resin. In order to simplify the use of epoxy resin for the artist and craftsman, the table which follows lists different curing agents that cure at different rates. The uses of some of the curing agents are shown in the same table.

TABLE OF EPOXY CURING AGENTS

The curing agents shown in this table should be added to 100 grams of CIBA Araldite epoxy resin 502.

USE	CURING AGENT	AMOUNT IN GRAMS	CURING TIME
Adhesives	RC 303	100	5 min.
	RC 125	25	20 min.
	956	20	1-3 hr.
	HH 1065 B*	25	8-12 hr.
Coatings	RC 125	25	20 min.
or	956	20	1-3 hr.
enamels	HH 1065 B	25	8-12 hr.
Sculpture	RC 125	25	20 min.
	956	20	1-3 hr.
	HH 1065 B	25	8-12 hr.

*Do not use HH 1065 on Styrofoam or Dylite. This curing agent contains menthane diamine, which dissolves expanded polyurethanes.

DESCRIPTION OF EPOXY CURING AGENTS

A description of each of the various curing agents used in this book follows.

RC 303 is a curing agent system developed by the Diamond Shamrock Company. It is a mixture of DPM 3-800 LC, manufactured by Diamond Shamrock, and DMP-30, manufactured by Rohm and Haas: 90 gr. DPM 3-800 LC + 10 gr. DMP-30 = 100 gr. RC 303. Mixing instructions follow:

Mix well and place in a closed container. When ready to use, mix by weight equal parts of RC 303 with epoxy resin 502. Stir well one minute. Apply in two to three minutes. Adhesive is hard in about five minutes. This 303/502 combination is a very flexible adhesive when

The Sidney Opera House. *Photo courtesy CIBA. The Sidney Opera House (shown under construction above, completed below) is one of the most ambitious and controversial buildings inthe world. The soaring arches, which together form a roof weighing 21,000 tons, are built up from wedge-shaped concrete segments. Between adjacent segments, a layer of Araldite epoxy resin maintains uniform load distribution over the area of contact.*

cured at room temperature. The DPM 3-800 LC is a liquid polymer which gives rapid cure properties to epoxy resins in combination with certain curing agents.

For those artists and craftsmen who desire to modify this curing system, the suppliers mentioned in the Suppliers and Manufacturers section of the Appendix will gladly supply them with pure DPM 3-800 LC and DMP-30. The most interesting modification is the varying of the DPM 3-800 LC from 30 PHR (parts per hundred by weight of epoxy resin 502 or other epoxy resin) to 100 PHR. At any of these proportions, the speed of cure is roughly five minutes. The cured epoxy resin 502 has the following properties with less DPM 3-800 LC:

1. It is more brittle.

2. It has lower adhesive strength.

3. It has higher chemical resistance, such as water absorption.

4. It has a higher heat-distortion point—the temperature at which the epoxy resin softens.

5. Last but not least, the adhesive is cheaper.

According to the manufacturer's literature, there are many other variations. For those who are interested in these, the Diamond Shamrock Company will gladly send literature. Samples and orders must be obtained from the specified suppliers mentioned in Suppliers and Manufacturers section of Appendix.

RC 125 is a curing agent which I learned about from the Resin Coatings Corporation. It is a product of the Jones-Dabney Company No. 87 (Celanese Corporation). It is not particularly moisture sensitive and cures in about 20 minutes. It bridges the time gap between the RC 303 and 956. Although RC 125 gives out a considerable amount of heat (exothermic) while curing, coatings about 1/16" to 1/8" thick appear to offer no problems. *Use with good ventilation and keep it off your hands.*

956 is a curing agent which has been promoted by the CIBA company, and is considered to be a safety hardener. I have been using it since the middle 1950's with excellent results. It was developed in part because of the dangerous characteristics of the early curing agents such as diethylene triamine (DETA, CIBA 950) and triethylenetetramine (TETA, CIBA 951): their vapors are hazardous, they are extremely caustic, and they often give allergies to the careless user.

But even 956 must be used with caution. *Have good ventilation*, even though the curing agent is not very volatile. *Do not allow it to get on your hands or to come in contact with your body. When handling 956, use gloves and/or brushes, mixing sticks, rollers, etc. If the hardener gets on your hands, wash it off as soon as possible.* If your observe these precautions, you should not have problems with this hardener.

Guy, the Gorilla. *Photo courtesy CIBA. This replica head of Guy, the London Zoo's gorilla, was made from Araldite epoxy resin by an enthusiastic pattern-maker, Mr. J. Parker, of Bedworth, Nuneaton. Guy's dimensions were given to Parker by zoo officials, and with the help of photographs, a clay model was made. A two-piece plaster mold was made from the clay model. Then the mold was removed and a black-pigmented epoxy resin Araldite gel-coat was applied to the inside of the plaster mold and backed up with an Araldite fiberglass laminate to a thickness of about ½". When the epoxy resin had cured, the plaster was chipped away and the joint line removed. Sculptures made in this manner are strong, durable, light, and can be made in any desired color.*

Step 1. *Demonstration photos by Hugh Stovall. Here is a dramatic demonstration of the fast curing (45 seconds) properties of an epoxy resin system based upon CIBA Araldite epoxy resin 502 and curing agent DP 116. (DP 116 is a specialty item which has limited practical use—it cures so fast!) After having mixed 100 parts by weight of the resin with 50 parts per weight of the curing agent, I pour the mixture from one cup to another.*

Step 2. *This is what happens to the mixture after 45 seconds. The resin suddenly hardens with a great evolution of heat.*

The proportions of 956 suggested for use with epoxy resin 502 is 20 PHR (parts per hundred of resin by weight). The proportions have been varied and tested over long periods of time for glass-to-glass bonding (gluing). 20 PHR is not to be tampered with! If you must experiment, this is not the place to do creative evaluations.

B-001 and others in the same family were first shown to met at the plastics show in Chicago several years ago. The manufacturer, the Ajinomoto Company, Inc., of Tokyo, claims that these curing agents, which he calls Ajicure, have the following features:

1. Direct contact with the skin produces no irritation.

2. When mixed with epoxy resins, they result in transparent resins which do not turn brown.

3. There is very little shrinkage in the cured epoxy resins.

4. They cure epoxy resins to clean, clear, glossy surfaces.

5. They cure epoxy resins completely even in the presence of water.

6. They have excellent adhesive properties.

7. They have a long pot life.

Other claims are made, but for the artist and craftsman the above are adequate. For additional information, write for literature to the Ajinomoto Company. See address in the Suppliers and Manufacturers section of Appendix.

The proportion of B-001 to CIBA Araldite epoxy resin is 50 PHR (parts per hundred of resin by weight). If you need a product with approximately half the viscosity, with half as short a pot life, and almost double the exotherm, B-002 will do the job. As far as I can tell after two years of trials, B-001 appears to be very interesting for use as a curing agent with epoxy "oil" paints (see Project 20).

HH 1065 B was developed by the author for 1/2" to 1" castings of epoxy resins for decorative purposes. This curing agent has the following properties:

1. Low viscosity to get rid of air bubbles during the curing of the epoxy resin.

2. Long pot life and low exotherm in order not to have distortion, yellowing, and shrinkage.

3. Good aging characteristics. Not brittle.

The following formula used in the proportions of 25 PHR (parts per hundred of resin by weight) to epoxy resin 502 gives excellent results and has been used successfully over the last five years: 12 grams menthane diamine (Rohm and Haas) +12 parts ZZL-0822 (Union Carbide) + 1 part 956 (CIBA).

Ceramic tile plaque by Myldred Dingwall. Photo courtesy of the artist. This plaque is bonded to ½" plywood with an epoxy resin grout and adhesive made from 502 / 956 and mixed with dry pigments of yellow ochre and burnt umber. The resin joint is about ⅛" below the tile surface.

Wooden bowl by Tage Frid. Photo by Evon Streetman. This turned bowl was rotationally coated with epoxy resin. An electric potter's wheel was used.

Glass bowl by James Turner. Photo by Evon Streetman. The feet of this glass bowl are made of epoxy resin. They were cast in forms made of 20-mil cellulose acetate which were attached to the bowl.

Pàpier mâché duck (*Above*) *by Grover Cole. Photo by Robert J. McCauley. Cole, the director of the Miami Art Center in Florida, used epoxy resin "enamel" to heavily coat his duck with its découpage skin. The heavy coating of the resin gives an interesting optical quality to the piece.*

Field Marshall #3 (*Left*) *by Frank Gallo, lifesize. Collection Louis Hubschman. Photo courtesy Fulton and Partners, Inc.*

All the curing agents listed have relatively little color and will yield clear, transparent, light straw-colored resins when mixed with epoxy resin 502.

To repeat, a good rule to remember when you are handling curing agents is the industrial admonition given to workers: *no physical contact, no dermatitis*. This is also the case when using epoxy resins. However, CIBA Araldite 502 appears to be one of the least sensitizing.

RELATIVELY NONDERMATITIC FORMULAS

As I have already mentioned, there are certain manufacturers who claim that their curing agents are relatively safe and nonsensitizing to use. This does not mean that they can be safely swallowed! Such curing agents are Versamide 140 or CIBA 840 and the Ajicure series including B-001, B-002, N-001, and N-002. Based on the manufacturers' literature, I would consider these curing agents to be relatively safe for short-exposure handling. Formulas using 840 are described in Project 14, which discusses epoxy-metal jewelry. Many of my students have made jewelry with this particular formula with no ill physical results. But still, take care! *Wash your hands after using!* This formula is very similar to the ones sold in the hardware stores.

Preparing Surfaces for Coating, Bonding, or Enameling with Epoxy Resins

In a short paragraph or two, I will briefly describe the procedures necessary for preparing various kinds of surfaces prior to applying epoxy resins.

METAL SURFACES

When preparing a piece of metal for coating with epoxy resins, sand the metal with wet-and-dry sandpaper to remove its surface oxides. After sanding the piece of metal, wash it well with a synthetic detergent and water, then rinse in clear water. Dry and re-clean the metal with a solvent such as lacquer thinner or xylene. The surface of the metal is now ready.

WOOD SURFACES

The wood's surface must be dry and free from soap, oil, or wax. After the wood has been dried (if necessary) sand those areas which you wish to coat, completely cleaning any area which appears to be soiled with grease or dirt.

Since wood is such a porous material, there is generally no problem in adhering plastics to its surface. Should you wish to coat the wood heavily, it is most important that you seal it with coats of epoxy resin.

CEMENT SURFACES

Cement or concrete really presents no problem when it has not been used previously. It should never be coated until it is at least 28 days old. This is the point at which cement or concrete is mature enough to be stable for coatings. For excellent cleaning, the surface of the cement or concrete should be scoured with a steel brush, using 10% muriatic or hydrochloric acid. After the acid has reacted with the cement (or concrete), the surface should then be hosed down and scrubbed with a steel brush. Dry the surface thoroughly. The first coat of resin should certainly be one which has been thinned down so that there will be good adhesion to the cement surface.

PLASTER SURFACES

Work on new plaster which is thoroughly dry. It takes approximately six months at room temperature before plaster is "bone" dry. Should the plaster be old or used, make sure that it is sanded below the soiled areas. The first coatings of epoxy resin should be thinned down with solvent or lacquer thinner, using 1 part resin to 6 to 10 parts thinner by weight. In this way, you will insure good penetration and bonding to the plaster.

STONE AND UNGLAZED CERAMIC SURFACES

If they are dirty, both stone and unglazed ceramic should be well cleaned with chlorinated solvents, such as trichlorethylene. The first coat of epoxy resin should be thinned down 6 to 10 times by weight with lacquer thinner.

GLASS AND VITREOUS SURFACES

Glass and vitreous surfaces should be washed with a 25% alcohol and water solution and thoroughly dried. After drying, it is a good idea to rub down the surface with a clean cloth saturated with a chlorinated solvent such as trichlorethylene. Do not use carbon tetrachloride, since it is a health hazard when used in a room that does not have adequate ventilation.

Coatings over glass and vitreous surfaces should be composed of epoxy resin systems which have a certain amount of flexibility at the temperature at which they will be used. For example, if glass is bonded to itself with the usual epoxy resin formulas, my experience has been that the bond will break at temperatures of 20° to 40° below zero. The reason for this is that the epoxy shrinks more than the glass does; being a powerful adhesive, the plastic tears the glass away from both sides of the bond and the glass shatters and falls down. It is possible, however, to develop special epoxy resin systems which will work.

Preparing a wood surface. *Photo, and those following, by Robert J. McCauley. The best way to clean a wood surface is to remove all old paint, grease, or soil, and then sand or steel wool. From bitter experience, I've found that only unsoiled or epoxy, the wood surface should be sealed with thin coats of the same resin until the surface is nonporous. If this is not done, air may "leach" into a heavy coating while it is curing, and air bubbles can be trapped there which will mar the coating.*

Preparing a stone or cement surface. *Stone, slate, or cement should be well cleaned with wet-and-dry sandpaper or steel wool. From bitter experience, I've found that only unsoiled or new surfaces of cement, stone, or slate should be treated with epoxy resins; otherwise, they may not adhere very well. Cement should be at least 28 days old and be completely dry. In this illustration, a very clean, dry piece of slate is being cleaned with steel wool. When cleaned, the slate is sealed in the same way as the wood surface, using the same formula. Once the resin cures out, the slate becomes very hard. I have made many cufflinks with this system.*

Scouring a metal surface. *As this illustration shows, the best way to clean a metal surface is to remove soil and metal oxides with steel wool.*

Preparing a metal surface. *After metal has been cleaned with steel wool, use a clean rag or cloth and wipe the metal surface with lacquer thinner or paint thinner; be sure to keep your fingers off the surface. There is often enough natural oil on your fingers to prevent the best of adhesives from bonding well to metallic surfaces. Even highly polished surfaces, when well cleaned with lacquer thinner applied with clean rags, can be bonded with epoxy resins.*

"The End" bracelet (*Above*) *by Walter Schluep. Photo by Brian J. Merrett. Artist Walter Schluep who designs, makes, and sells jewelry in Montreal, combines epoxy resins with platinum, gold, silver, and precious stones. This bracelet, which he makes in both 18 carat gold and sterling silver, is deeply "enameled" with an epoxy resin system which was developed during a workshop-seminar which Walter attended at the Visual Art Center in Westmount, Quebec. A curing agent was required which, when mixed with the epoxy resin, would harden slowly and give off very little heat during the curing. After the workshop, Walter and his associates further modified the epoxy resin "enamel" to produce exactly the nuances desired: hardness and clarity of color, without air bubbles.*

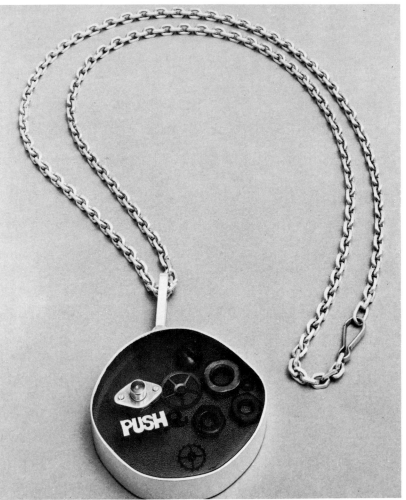

Dingle-dangle (*Right*) *by Walter Schluep. Photo by Brian J. Merrett. This "dingle-dangle" is made of precious metal, small found objects, and epoxy resin "enamel."*

Epoxy Enameling

With the use of an epoxy resin and the selection of proper curing agents and additives, it is relatively simple to apply this "enamel" to metal, wood, stone, etc. When cured, it can have any transparency, color, texture, hardness, etc. that you wish. The epoxy enamel may be stoned, pumiced, or polished to finishes comparable to those of vitreous enamels. This combination of epoxy resin and curing agent will adhere to properly prepared metal, wood, stone, and ceramic surfaces; these surfaces must be dry and not oily.

MATERIALS

1. Araldite epoxy resin 502.

2. Araldite curing agent 956, for thin coatings of enamels, or

3. Curing agent HH 1065 B or B-001, for heavy coatings, between 1/8" and 1/4" thick, or

4. Curing agent N-001, for coatings approximately 1/2" to 1" thick.

5. Non-oily solvent, such as acetone. It is convenient to use some kind of spray device when using acetone.

6. Additives, such as talc, bentonite, sand, color pastes, pumice, or any other fillers.

PREPARING SURFACES FOR ENAMELING

Naturally, the first step is to prepare the surface of the wood, stone, or metal you wish to coat or cover with the epoxy enamel. Metal surfaces must be sanded or rubbed with steel wool to remove surface metallic oxides and then cleaned thoroughly with some type of solvent.

Wood must be thoroughly dry and non-oily. By the same token, perhaps the best cleaning method is to sand the wood areas down to their raw surfaces. Stone or other vitreous surfaces should be thoroughly abraded or sanded to below the virgin surface. The basic epoxy resin enamel formula follows.

EPOXY RESIN ENAMEL FORMULA

Epoxy resin 502: 10 grams.

Curing agent 956: 2 grams.

PREPARING EPOXY RESIN ENAMEL

Mix the formula well and let it stand five minutes after thorough mixing. If you use larger quantities of these materials, you should, after thorough mixing, divide the system into smaller units so that you have no more than approximately 20 grams per cup. In this way, the reaction will not overheat to the point where you will lose your resin.

The application of these materials seems to work best when you allow the 502/956 mixture to stay in the cup in very small quantities, such as 10 to 20 grams for about 1/2 hour. After that time, it will have reacted sufficiently to become twice as viscous.

APPLYING EPOXY RESIN ENAMEL

To apply this resin combination with the appropriate colors and fillers, use a small, metal spatula or toothpicks. Carefully apply the epoxy resin combination to the areas which are to be "enameled" and allow the resin to cure no closer than 12" from an infrared heat lamp. Should you have any air bubbles appearing on the surface of the resin, touch the surface with a drop of acetone or spray acetone from a Preval power unit made by the Precision Valve Corporation. This will remove the bubbles. Should new ones form before the resin is cured, these too may be easily removed.

Allow the resin to cure under the heat lamp for at least an hour at temperatures no more than 140° F. In order to have some sort of consistency, a cooking thermometer would be helpful. The standard colors which I use and recommend in this book (see Colors section of Appendix) should also be used in jewelry to obtain the best light-fastness.

FINISHING THE ENAMELED SURFACE

Once the resin has cured and imperfections are noticeable, it is very simple to sand the affected areas to remove the blemish with wet wet-and-dry sandpaper. After sanding, the 502/956 combination can be reapplied in the same way as before. Remember that 502/956 is an excellent adhesive; therefore, there is no problem of adhesion from one application to another.

The curing of the 502/956 under the heat lamp makes

a tougher, tighter resin system. My experience in jewelry making over the past 15 years shows that these "enameled" pieces hold up extremely well.

CURING AGENTS FOR THICKER SURFACES

When you want to enamel thicker surfaces, approximately 1/8" to 1/4", a low-viscosity curing agent, such as HH 1065 B, should be used. The proportions are 100 grams of epoxy resin 502 to 25 grams of curing agent HH 1065 B. Cure the enamel from four to eight hours at 125° F.

Another extremely helpful curing agent for surfaces with a 1/8" to 1/4" thickness is B-001; it is made by the Ajinomoto Company in Tokyo but is also available through Ajinomoto in New York City (or through other suppliers mentioned in this book) and is most interesting. This curing agent is nontoxic and relatively non-yellowing. It also cures slowly under heat lamps and doesn't emit too much heat which can distort the curing resin system. The basic formula follows.

FORMULA FOR SURFACES 1/8" TO 1/4" THICK

Epoxy resin: 10 grams.

Curing agent B-001: 5 grams.

The resin is mixed with the hardener and allowed to stand for 1/2 hour. It is not necessary to divide the system into smaller units since this reaction is a very slow one. The application of the resin/hardener system is the same as with the 502/956; curing is done as previously mentioned using the heat lamp held about 1' away from the piece in question.

For curing sections 1/2" to 1" thick, use Ajicure curing agent N-001. The formula follows.

FORMULA FOR SURFACES 1/2" TO 1" THICK

Epoxy resin 502: 10 grams.

Curing agent N-001: 5 grams.

Methods of application and curing for this system are the same as for the previous formula. Unlike the 502/956 system, it is not necessary to divide the resin and hardener into smaller units. The N-001 is an extremely slow curing agent and usually does require heat.

VARIOUS FINISHES

The epoxy enamels are easily finished with wet-and-dry sandpaper used wet. Pumice stone or other wet stones may be used for sanding equally well. Use the finest grade of sandpaper which will achieve the desired effect. Should you wish highly lustrous surfaces, in many cases you need do no finishing at all. (See Project 14 for more detailed and specific information on polishing and sanding.)

For mat or satin finishes, the sandpaper technique is the best. Once you have sanded down the surface to the desired level, you may then use buffing methods which are described in Project 14. Remember that epoxy enamels do not have the heat resistance of vitreous enamels. Therefore, when you are buffing or sanding you must be sure that the piece is cool so that you do not soften the resin. Should the resin soften, you will get poor results in your polishing.

ADVANTAGES OF EPOXY ENAMEL

There are many differences in this type of enameling from "fired" enamels. You should remember the advantages of the epoxy resin systems over the vitreous enamel systems. They are as follows:

1. Organic materials may be mixed and added to the epoxy enamel system because temperatures are low enough so that they do not destroy the organic materials.

2. If you do not like what you have applied, you can remove it. Merely place a heat lamp 1" or 2" from your metal, wood, or stone piece for a short time, then the epoxy resin may be picked out of the spaces and reapplied.

3. Epoxy resin enamels are less brittle. The short time factor in application and curing over traditional enameling is, of course, an obvious one.

4. Epoxy resins and curing agents are cheaper than the vitreous enamels. Other effects which are impossible with vitreous enamels can be achieved with resins, such as *plique à jour. Plique à jour* means the casting of a clear enamel unsupported by the backing of the metal, wood, or stone. In other words, a "window" is the achieved effect.

DISADVANTAGES OF EPOXY ENAMEL

The following are some disadvantages of epoxy enamel over vitreous enamel:

1. Since heat resistance is not present, epoxy enamels cannot be used for cookware, ashtrays, or other objects where high heat-resistant applications are needed.

2. Vitreous enamel colors are fired-on colors and, therefore, more lightfast.

3. A piece of jewelry made of epoxy enamel might last only 100 years. Jewelry made of vitreous enamel, if not dropped upon a concrete or other hard floor, should last indefinitely.

Plique à jour jewelry (*Above*) *by Bob Stoetzer. Photo by Robert J. McCauley. These copper pieces with their plique à jour inlays were designed, then soldered and welded. A light yellow transparent color paste was added to the basic epoxy formula (see Project 2). When plique à jour epoxy enamel is to be poured into any metal, wood, or stone opening, it is convenient to use a sheet of self-releasing Mylar to work on.*

Detail of plique à jour jewelry. (*Left*) *When the resin system used to produce this technique begins to get warm (determined by feeling the resin left in the mixing cup), you can create an "antiqued" finish by stirring air bubbles into the mix with some type of mixing stick as the resin hardens.*

Silver pendant with epoxy-lead enamel insert (*Above Left*) *by Harry B. Hollander. Photo by Evon Streetman. This sterling silver pendant is filled with powdered lead and epoxy-metal. A sgraffito technique was produced on the epoxy-metal insert with a dentist's bit mounted in a flexible shaft drill.*

Silver pendant with plique à jour insert (*Above Right*) *by Harry B. Hollander. Photo by Evon Streetman. This chased sterling silver pendant has an unsoldered back of sterling. The inserts are solid, clear epoxy resin made from a 502/B-001 mixture. This system works well for thick (¼" to ½") castings, whether a plique à jour or cloisonné technique is used.*

Epoxy-metal brooch (*Right*) *by Harry B. Hollander. Photo by Pete Steiner. When aluminum, copper, and brass are mixed into the epoxy-metal jewelry formula described, what comes out of this "modeling-claylike" mixture depends upon the artist-craftsman. For this brooch, mille-fiori glass chips were added to the resin system. When the piece had cured out, it was buffed and polished on a regular soft-cotton buffing wheel. The polishing compounds were obtained at Sears Roebuck; they work well as long as very little pressure is applied to the metal-resin piece while it is being buffed. The surface of this handmade jewelry is pure metal, because the surface resin was removed in the buffing.*

Epoxy-Metal Jewelry

Using a highly flexible, very adhesive, low-viscosity, relatively nontoxic epoxy resin formula, epoxy-metal alloy jewelry may be cast by hand from any metal, depending upon which powdered metal is added to the formula. The powdered metal may be lead, copper, brass, aluminum, bronze, etc., and any jewelry such as brooches, rings, pendants, earrings, etc., may be cast by hand relatively easily.

MATERIALS

1. Polyethylene sheets on which to fashion your hand-made jewelry.

2. 300-mesh powder metals such as copper, aluminum, brass, lead, tin, nickel, etc.

3. Infrared heat lamp with holder and stand.

4. Protective gloves and/or protective hand creams (optional).

5. Araldite epoxy resin 502.

6. Curing agent DMP-30.

7. Araldite curing agent 840, or

9. Curing agent RC 125, for *plique à jour*.

10. Epoxide 7.

11. Asbestos 244.

HOW TO BEGIN

Naturally, the first step is to have some general idea of what you would like to make. Besides drawing with black pencil on a white paper, it is often helpful to use white crayon on black paper. You may also make models from modeling clay.

At this point, let's assume you are now ready. Mix the following epoxy-metal formula.

EPOXY-METAL FORMULA

Epoxy resin 502: 10 grams.

Epoxide 7: 1 gram.

Curing agent 840: 5.4 grams.

Curing agent DMP-30: 0.3 gram.

Asbestos 244: 0.2 gram.

PREPARING EPOXY-METAL

The simplest method of preparing the formula is to mix together the Epoxide 7, curing agent 840, and DMP-30; stir in Asbestos 244. When this is all well mixed, add the epoxy resin 502. In this way, you will have a good dispersion of the Asbestos since you are adding it to a liquid of low viscosity (see *Epoxy-metal pendant demonstration*). Mix the resin mixture for at least two minutes.

Mix in as much of the desired metal powder or metal powder mixtures as you can, until you have a non-runny, heavy paste which will be about the consistency of Vaseline or not-too-damp wet clay.

Next, take some of the dry metal powder; sprinkle it on a polyethylene sheet, and knead in the resin mixture by hand until it is an almost dry, heavy putty. When evenly mixed, let the resin mixture stand for one hour at room temperature to give the reaction a chance to start. Meanwhile, wash your hands well. Now the mixture will be less runny and more easily worked.

SHAPING YOUR JEWELRY

From the demonstration, you can see one method of making a piece of jewelry, such as a pendant. In this technique it is very helpful to use such forming tools as bits, wood-carving equipment, linoleum-cutting knives, nails, screw heads, etc.

Ronald Pearson, a well-known jeweler in Rochester, New York, has tried the epoxy resin formula. He suggests that you think of your pendant as a slab whose workable surface is 1/3 down inside the slab. Cut into the uncured epoxy-metal mixture and work up and down from this imaginary plane. In this way, you will create a piece of jewelry that has both hills and valleys, ups and downs, and is free.

When you have shaped your piece, let the resin cure without heat. Once it is almost hard, you can put it under the heat lamp without danger. However, if you are in a hurry and do put the piece of jewelry under the heat lamp (at least 1' away) you must continually watch it, because as it is setting, it may tend to distort. If it does run, you must reshape it. When the resin has begun to set, then the infrared will no longer distort the resin.

Once the resin has cured, you can study your piece and see how you want to modify it. You may very well find areas in your piece that you would like to modify. In that case, it is suggested that you file, cut with a jeweler's saw, or grind away at undesirable areas. You will notice a great freedom of expression in this technique once you start cutting into your piece.

FINISHING YOUR JEWELRY

When you have finally decided on a shape that you like, then comes the problem of buffing it. Generally, I have found that your buffing wheel should be made of cotton; whichever buffing compounds are used should be applied freely. Craftsman Buffing Compounds, available from Sears Roebuck and Company, are good. They should be used with a power-driven cotton buffing wheel: use the brown bar (tripoly) on one buffing wheel, and the white bar (white rouge) for the finishing buffing wheel.

Oxides used for buffing by hand are aluminum oxide and tin oxide. These must be mixed with a small amount of water and rubbed on with a soft cloth. As a final buff, use a white rouge block. It is very important to remember not to let your piece get overheated. It is not a bad idea to have a container of water next to your piece so that you can dip it and continually cool the plastic. Another important warning: *hold your jewelry as tightly as possible when you are grinding or buffing*, so that it does not fly from your hand and damage you or itself.

Once you have finished buffing your jewelry, you must make sure that you are down to the raw, bare metal. Then you may use jewelry techniques for applying patinas to your creation. Liver of sulfur (called potassium sulfide) is the most common patina for copper or sterling silver; such chemicals may be obtained at a drugstore. A small piece of liver of sulfur is added to warm water, and once it has dissolved you may immerse your jewelry five to 10 minutes in the solution.

When you are satisfied with your piece of jewelry, remove it, and wash with cool water. Buff off the areas which you wish to brighten. After you have done whatever finishing you want, you may wish to add some epoxy enamel in certain areas. The formula follows.

EPOXY RESIN ENAMEL FORMULA

Epoxy resin 502: 10 grams.

Curing agent 956: 2 grams.

The usual epoxy color pastes may be used to color the resins. The infrared light (for clear, shiny surfaces) should be used no closer than 2' from the piece. See details of how to prepare and apply epoxy resin enamel in Project 13.

PLIQUE A JOUR

Combinations of the preceding technique may be also used in a *plique à jour* technique. *Plique à jour* is a clear, transparent glaze or enamel with no backing, held only on the sides. The following formula can be used to produce such *plique à jour* techniques.

FORMULA FOR PLIQUE A JOUR

Epoxy resin 502: 100 grams.

Curing agent RC 125: 25 grams.

Color paste (not necessary for sealing): Q.S. *

Before casting the epoxy enamel, a thin layer of the epoxy resin should first be poured into the opening to seal the area to be enameled. The above formula can be used for this purpose, minus the color paste.

VARIATIONS

Should you wish to bond something to your piece of jewelry, the best formula to use is the one for making the epoxy-metal jewelry itself.

After your piece of jewelry is finished, another effective variation is produced by brushing on the 502/956 formula in certain areas. Then blow on some glitter (shiny metal flakes). It will stick only where the wet resin has been placed. Then, you can cure the coating with or without heat.

*Quantum sufficit: as much as suffices, or use your own judgment.

Step 1. *Demonstration photos by Robert J. McCauley. The ingredients pictured here are used to create the epoxy-metal resin system. In the glass on the left, the epoxy resin 502, curing agent 840, Epoxide 7, and the DMP-30 are mixed together. The glass in the middle contains Asbestos 244, which is added as a thixotropic agent. The glass on the right contains various metal powders, such as aluminum for lightness, copper and brass for the bronzing element, and a small amount of talc (optional) for filling and lightness.*

Step 2. *Here, the Asbestos 244 is added and the mixture is about to be stirred until it is dispersed.*

Step 3. *Here, the Asbestos 244 is completely mixed into the epoxy resin mixture. Asbestos 244 is one of the best thixotropic agents for use with epoxy and polyester resins.*

Step 4. *Once the resin mixture and the Asbestos 244 are thoroughly mixed, the 300-mesh, powdered metals (such as copper, brass, and aluminum) and the small amount of talc can be added to the resin / hardener system. Additional metal powders are added to the mixture until it becomes like a heavy dough, as pictured here.*

Step 5. *The epoxy-metal "dough" can be shaped by hand or with such tools as mat knives, nails, and dentist's tools. When shaping the piece, it should be placed on a sheet of polyethylene from which it easily releases as soon as it becomes hard. When the piece of jewelry is completed, it may be left to dry at room temperature or heat-cured under infrared heat lamps which are placed 1½' away.*

Step 6. *After the epoxy-metal "alloy" has cured out or hardened, fine steel wool will remove the excess resin and polish the metal mixture. The eye in the center of this pendant is a mille-fiori glass chip, embedded in the epoxy-metal before the form had hardened. If a minimum of approximately 10 copper powder is added to any resin-metal mix, it is quite easy to give the piece a patina with a weak solution of liver of sulfur.*

Colorado Girl *by Frank Gallo, 27" high. Photo by Lee Boltin. This piece, as well as the figure on p. 120, is cast epoxy resin with a polyurethane foam core. It was originally modeled in water clay, then a plaster waste mold was made into which the epoxy resin was poured. The surface is sanded, buffed, and polished to produce a translucent glow. The colors come from carbonization (that is, the sculptor used an acetylene torch to burn the surface, bringing out "trace" colors that he has mixed into the resin).*

Titiopoli's Lighthouse *by Bruce Beasley, 34 ¼" high. Photo by Joanne Leonard. This sculpture, and the one which follows, is made of Lucite cast from a multiple-piece, fabricated aluminum plate mold. The cast Lucite form was polished with a milling machine (used in heavy industry) to achieve the perfectly smooth and crystal-clear surface. In the background, you can see San Francisco Bay.*

Dodecker *by Bruce Beasley, 16" high. Photo by Joanne Leonard*

Column *(Right) by Dennis Byng, 15 ¾" x 7" x 6". Photo courtesy Martha Jackson Gallery, New York. This piece is bonded Plexiglas glued with PS 30 acrylic adhesive. The colored inclusions are strips of Plexiglas. The parts of this block are so well glued and so painstakingly polished that you cannot see the seams.*

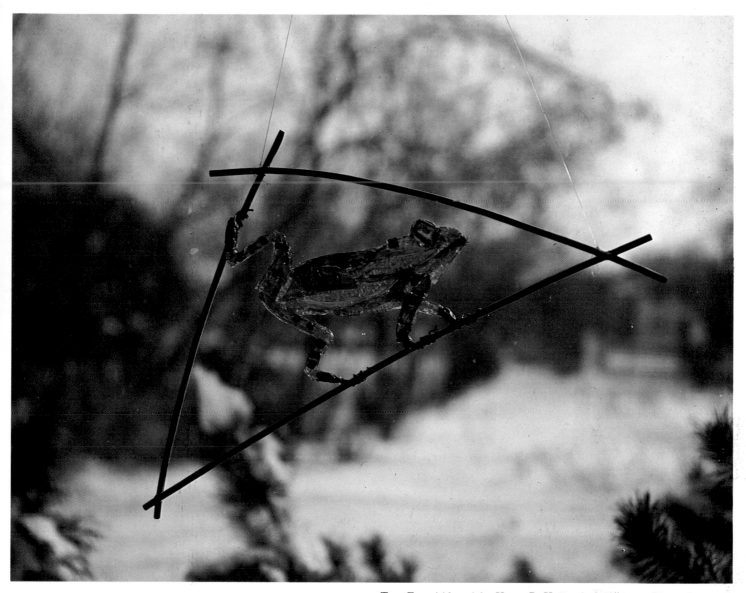

Tree Frog (*Above*) *by Harry B. Hollander, 10" long. Photo by The author. This frog is made of bits of antique glass glued together with an epoxy resin 502/956 adhesive system. The frog's feet are made out of sterling silver wire. The cross pieces from which he is suspended are lengths of hollow brass tubing. See Project 16 for details on how to cut and assemble glass pieces and for adhesive formulas.*

Three Figures (*Left*) *by Hollis Holbrook, lifesize. Photo courtesy of the artist. This group was cast from multiple-piece molds taken from living figures. The sections of the mold are made by laminating 6" to 8" lengths of 4" wide surgical plaster tape to the models, then backing it with a polyester and fiberglass jacket. The parts of the mold are then removed and the insides are given a coat of Part-all (similar to PVA). A gel-coat layer of polyester resin is applied to the inside of the mold, followed by a coat of colored polyester resin, followed by a polyester and fiberglass reinforcement. This cast is removed from the mold, and the parts are welded together with polyester and fiberglass and painted carefully to hide the seam, or joint line.*

Stained-glass mural (*Above*) *designed by Alfred Pellan and executed by the craftsmen at L'Art Kaleiray Ltee, Montreal, 4' x 4'. Photo by the author. See Project 16 for details on the technique used.*

Stained-glass collage (*Right*) *designed by Jean-Paul Mouseau and executed by the craftsmen at L'Art Kaleiray Ltee, Montreal, approximately 4' x 2'. Photo by the author. See Project 16 for details on the technique used.*

Broken Environs: Walking Man Series *(Above) by Eugene Massin, 5" x 10" x 5½". Photo by Tom McCarthy. This was made as a single polyester resin cylinder, containing acrylic inclusions which have been cut out on a jigsaw, heated, and bent to take the shapes of dancing, running, walking "men." The single piece was then fractured in two, and mounted on a 1" piece of acrylic sheet.*

Small Nude Figure *(Left) by Frank Gallo, 16" high. Photo by Lee Boltin. Cast epoxy resin.*

State I   ARTIST Proof   R Adams

Intaglio print (*Left*) *by Richard Adams, 3' x 2'. Photo courtesy of the artist. The plate for this print was made by pouring epoxy resin into a wax and Plexiglas mold. See Project 18 for details on the technique used.*

Detail of resin resist on cotton (*Above*) *by Sister Remy Revor, 11" x 8". This closeup shows just part of a much larger 45" x 108" textile made with Remyzist in the method shown in detail in Project 11.*

Polyester Composition C-28 *by Claude Blin, 2' x 2'. Photo by J. Varry. This painting, and the one which follows, was done with polyester resin mixed with color pastes and additives such as talc, Cabosil, etc. See Project 10 for details on the technique used.*

Polyester Composition D-12 *by Claude Blin, 4' x 4'. Photo by J. Varry.*

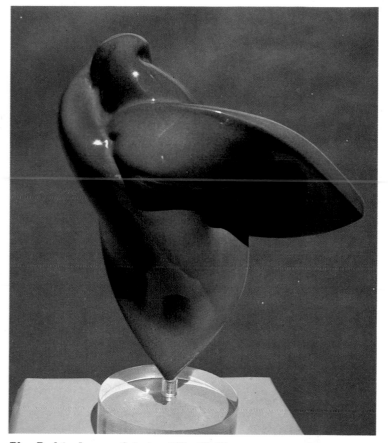

Red Chair by Hollis Holbrook, 43" high. Photo courtesy of the artist. The body of the chair (without the legs) was originally built up with plaster on a chicken-wire armature. A polyester and fiberglass mold was made from which a polyester and fiberglass cast was taken. The human leg was cast from a live model, also in polyester and fiberglass, and the other three legs of the chair were cast in water-clear polyester resin. All the legs were then attached to the cast chair. The color is polyester and dry pigments dissolved in styrene. The stripes were made using masking tape to get the straight lines. The piece was sanded and buffed to produce a high gloss.

Blue Bud by Jacques Schnier, 13" x 9". Photo courtesy of the artist. This is a built-up sculpture. The core is made of polyurethane foam covered with several layers of fiberglass mat saturated with polyester resin. Refinements in the form were made from an auto-body type plastic filler and abraded to the final configuration. The piece was then primed, wet sanded, and sprayed with acrylic lacquer. Color was sprayed onto the lacquered surface, then a final polish was given with an auto-body compound.

Hot Ice (*Left*) by Carol R. Levy, 36" x 27½" x 4½". Photo by Arthur Swoger. This sculpture, which can either be free-standing or hung on the wall, was made by vacuum-forming a vinyl sheet and then re-heating it in areas to produce its explosive forms. Flourescent lights enclosed in the black acrylic frame are fitted with color filters to create an iridescent play of light and color over the surface of the piece.

Mom and Pop (*Overleaf*) by Arlene Love, lifesize. Photo courtesy of the artist. The piece on the following page is polyester resin and fiberglass cast from a plaster waste mold. The original work was modeled in water clay. The colors were obtained by adding color pastes to the resin mixture before it was poured into the mold. The cast piece was sanded with wet-and-dry sandpaper, then buffed with white buffing compound and an electric cotton-pad buffer and rouge to produce its glowing patina.

PROJECT 15

Epoxy Resins in Ceramics

Epoxy resins have been found to be excellent adhesives and decorative finishes for patching and repairing ceramicware or ceramic sculpture. Epoxy resins are extremely useful in any situation where the piece to be treated is not exposed to heat over 150° F. Epoxy resins have many more uses in ceramics than you may think. In quick order, here are some of them: adhesives, patching glazes, waterproofing the insides of pots, glaze and "stained-glass window" effects, and overglazes on top of ceramic glazes.

MATERIALS

1. Araldite epoxy resin 502.

2. Five-minute curing agent RC 303, or

3. 1/2 hour curing agent RC 125, or

4. Two-hour to three-hour Araldite curing agent 956, or

5. 12-hour curing agent B-001.

6. Additives, such as talc, powdered pumice, grog, flint, sand, etc.

7. Asbestos 244.

8. Color pastes.

FIVE-MINUTE EPOXY ADHESIVE FORMULA

Epoxy resin 502: 10 grams.

Curing agent RC 303: 10 grams.

Asbestos 244: .05 to 2 grams.

Additives: Q.S.*

Color: Q.S.

TWO-HOUR TO THREE-HOUR EPOXY ADHESIVE FORMULA

I have used this tried and true adhesive for the past 15 years for patching my wife's ceramic pots and *objets d'art*. It produces an adhesive that cures in two to three hours.

Epoxy resin 502: 50 grams.

Curing agent 956: 10 grams.

Asbestos 244: .05 to 2 grams.

Additives: Q.S.*

Color: Q.S.

REPAIRING CERAMICWARE

About 10 years ago, an irreplaceable ceramic salad bowl, 1 1/2' in diameter (made by Rosalie Namer of Montreal) was dropped and broken by one of our daughters. The pieces were carefully gathered up, washed in the dishwasher, and dried. The 502/956 adhesive combination above was made up with a small quantity of Cabosil (which works like Asbestos 244 in the formula just given). This mixture was then divided into 20-gram batches.

The glaze on the broken salad bowl was not a solid color. A great deal of blending of shades and hues was needed. Therefore, I added small amounts of pigment color pastes with toothpicks to these batches of adhesive until the exact colors of the glaze were matched.

The smaller pieces were first bonded together into larger ones and rested on top of pieces of Plasticine to hold them until these larger pieces were glued together. Sharpened toothpicks made excellent tools. After putting the colored and thickened resin mixture on both sides of the piece to be adhered, I squeezed two pieces together. I wiped off the excess with the rounded end of the toothpick. I took care not to get any adhesive on any areas which were not immediately to be bonded to others. The pieces were left to rest comfortably until they were well adhered. Without heat, this adhering was achieved overnight.

If the pieces had been held about 1 1/2' to 2' from the infrared light, it would have taken about 1/2 to one hour to adhere them. This adhering procedure was repeated until all the shards had been glued. The same procedure was carried out in bonding the glued pieces to the main bowl pieces. Masking tape or Scotch tape was very helpful in properly holding the pieces in position. This operation was continued until the bowl was rebuilt. I did have pieces missing and areas where the glaze had chipped off. Taking both time and patience, these, too, were replaced or matched in. (See also *Repairing a ceramic pot demonstration*.)

---

*Quantum sufficit: as much as suffices, or use your own judgment.

BONDING PIECES OF CERAMIC SCULPTURE

Often two or three units of sculpture will not fit in the kiln. These units may be bonded or glued together after they are completely glazed and fired. For hasty bonding, a 502/RC 303 combination is most helpful.

Remember that this type of 502/956 or 502/RC 303 adhesion will not take any heat greater than hot dishwasher water. If you wish to make sure that your resin combination will have the highest heat resistance, you should try to cure the entire piece in an oven for at least eight hours at 125° F.

MATCHING FINISHES

When you repair ceramics with the 502/956 combination mentioned, your patch will have a glossy finish, a glaze. If you wish to produce a patch with a mat finish, use the following formula.

MAT FINISH FORMULA

Epoxy resin 502: 10 grams.

Curing agent 956: 2 grams.

Epoxy paint thinner, xylol, or similar solvent: 72 grams.

Cabosil: 05. to 1 gram.

By varying the amount of Cabosil, you can weaken or intensify the mat finish of the area upon which you are working.

If possible, you should run a series of tests, varying the Cabosil in the preceding formula. Once the resin has cured, you may also find it advantageous to recoat with the same mixture. When the resin/hardener system is thinned with this much solvent, you will find that you can keep this combination for at least seven to 10 hours. Using a baby-food jar as a container, you can put this mixture in the freezer and keep it for several days. However, if you do this, do not open your jar until the resin mixture has come to room temperature. When things are very cold, they condense, or collect the moisture in the air.

WATERPROOFING THE INSIDE OF POTS

The following formula will easily seal the inside of a very porous Raku pot and make it waterproof. It is designed to be very fluid, so that you may swish the resin/hardener combination around the inside of the pot and pour out the excess. The best results will be obtained by repeating this procedure several times, allowing time for it to cure between coatings. After the final cure, if you want the most heat resistance, put your pot in the oven for about five to 10 hours at a temperature no higher than 125° F. The formula follows.

WATERPROOFING FORMULA

Epoxy resin 502: 45 grams.

Epoxide 7: 4.5 grams (never exceed 10%).

Curing agent 956: 10 grams.

Color: Q.S.*

Mix well. Let the mixture stand about 10 minutes. Pour it in the pot and roll it around. Pour out the excess. When most of the mixture has stopped running out, leave the pot upside down, resting on three or four well-waxed nails imbedded in a piece of polyethylene. Now, let the pot cure. If you wish to drink from a coated Raku cup, post-cure your cup for 12 hours in an oven set at 125° F. This will make the coating more chemical resistant.

GLAZES FOR SPECIAL EFFECTS

Sometimes you may wish to decorate your piece of ceramic in a way that is impossible with ceramic glazes. For example, you may not wish to refire your piece of ceramic, or you may wish to add ebony, locust, or thibet wood chips to your glaze. Perhaps you may wish to add a section of a black and white negative or a collage of newsprint to give a particular effect. You might even wish to imbed precious or semiprecious stones, such as opals, which will not stand much heat, into your ceramicware. You may also wish to do *plique à jour* (see Project 14) work in certain areas. In all these instances, glazes can be useful.

Suppose you have a need for a certain bright red glaze which, I am told by my ceramist wife, is not always easy to achieve. (At this writing, nickel oxide is in extremely short supply.) Red glazes made with nickel oxide can surely be duplicated with epoxy glazes. You may wish to overglaze with these epoxy glazes on top of conventional ceramic glazes. As you can see, the options are many. The basic formula for these glazes is always the same.

FORMULA FOR CERAMIC GLAZES

Epoxy resin 502: 100 grams.

Curing agent RC 125: 25 grams.

Fillers, such as talc, flint, pumice, grog: Q.S.*

Translucent to transparent thickeners, such as Cabosil or Asbestos 244: Q.S.

Colors: Q.S.

"STAINED-GLASS WINDOW" EFFECTS

If you wish to make thick "windows" or heavy *plique à jour*, the following formulas are recommended. Many

---

*Quantum sufficit: as much as suffices, or use your own judgment.

variations have been tried over the past 10 years for making "stained-glass windows" in ceramic containers. Here are the latest formulas which have been found to be successful over a period of years (see *Ceramic with a "stained-glass window" demonstration*).

FAST CURE FORMULA

Epoxy resin 502: 100 grams.

Curing agent RC 125: 25 grams.

Color: Q.S.*

Do not apply this mixture thicker than 1/8", so that you do not build up too much heat. Curing time is about 1/2 to 3/4 hour.

SLOW CURE FORMULA

Epoxy resin 502: 100 grams.

Curing agent B-001: 50 grams.

Color: Q.S.*

This is a slow curing system which requires about 12 hours to cure out. You may pour as thick a window as you wish with little problem of exothermic heat.

MAKING "STAINED-GLASS WINDOWS"

To make your "stained-glass windows," use rubber cement to adhere a sheet of polyethylene film to the outside of your ceramic container, right over the "window," or opening. With no adhesive, you may also "stick" Saran Wrap over the hole. Next, lay the side with this window flat down. Mix up a small amount of 502/RC 125 and apply this at the edge where the ceramic meets the polyethylene or Saran Wrap. Let the resin cure. You have now made a container into which you can pour your "window."

Mix up either of the preceding formulas with the colors you desire. Stir well and pour in the resin mixture from the top. If you are in a hurry, the RC 125/502 will be the best formula. Don't add it too thick or you will melt your polyethylene film or Saran Wrap. If you wish to have an "antique glass" look, you can lightly scratch the plastic film with a nail. When the resin has cured, you may very easily remove the polyethylene or Saran Wrap. Repeat this procedure for each of your "windows."

An important part of this procedure is to learn when the resin is about to cure. At 70° F. (room temperature), this takes approximately 1/2 hour. When the resin begins to feel warm, the reaction is well on the way. If, at this point, the resin is stirred while it hardens, beautiful "antique glass" effects can be obtained. Refer to Project 13 for illustrations of this same type of effect in jewelry.

NOTES, VARIATIONS, AND CAUTIONS

If you are not used to epoxy resin, the biggest problem is to keep your fingers out of it. If the warning of "no contact, no dermatitis" goes unheeded, there is an excellent chance that you may become allergic to these chemicals. This would be unfortunate since once you become sensitized, you do not lose this sensitivity.

So remember: *keep your hands away from the resin mixture. Wash your hands well if they get contaminated. If the resin mixture gets in your eyes, flush them with water for 15 minutes. The curing agents are alkaline. In any case, get medical attention.*

Potters, in particular, are often interested in experimenting with different glazes. If you are interested in exploring this new medium, it is strongly suggested that you run a series of small test tiles or fired ceramic, 1/4" thick "doughnuts" with and without glaze. You will find many interesting variations of your own.

"Stained-glass window" ceramic. *Photo by Robert J. McCauley. This ceramic piece with its epoxy resin "stained-glass window" can be safely used as a screen for candles. As long as the burning candle is at least 2" from any of the epoxy windows, there will be no problem. Although this epoxy resin formula is not fire resistant, it is not highly flammable. Check it yourself to see what I mean.*

Step 1. *Demonstration photos by Robert J. McCauley. The mending of ceramics with epoxy resins, colors, and talc requires little equipment aside from a 250-watt infrared clear glass industrial lamp and fixture. This very damaged pot is first stuffed with newspaper; then casting plaster is placed over the paper. When the plaster is hard, an epoxy resin and grog grout is prepared, using the following simple epoxy resin system: 90 grams of epoxy resin 502 and 10 grams of Epoxide 7; to this mixture is added 25 grams of RC 125.*

Step 2. *Just enough epoxy resin mixture is added to the grog to make a dense, non-running paste. Then the paste is applied with a spatula to the damaged area. After the epoxy grout (seen in this picture) has cured, a fresh resin mix is made up and color pastes are added to it. The colors are blended to match the ceramic glaze of the pot.*

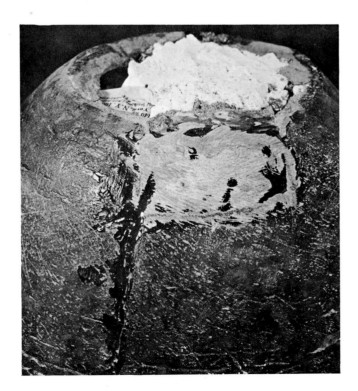

Step 3. *(Left) When the colored epoxy glaze has cured, it is sanded and rubbed with steel wool to bring the surface to the level of the pot.*

Step 4. *(Right) With the judicious use of color pastes and talc, mixed with the epoxy resin system, an epoxy resin glaze is finally made which is impossible to distinguish from the real ceramic glaze. However, the finish was too highly glossed. It was easily made more mat by light rubbing with fine steel wool.*

Step 1. *Demonstration photos by Robert J. McCauley. Epoxy resins make excellent "stained-glass windows" or insets for ceramic pots or forms. Shown here is a simple clay container with openings which will eventually hold the windows. These openings are cut after the clay has become leather hard.*

Step 2. *After the pot has been bisqued, glazed, and fired, a thin sheet of polyethylene is bonded to the outside of the opening with double-thick Scotch tape. Additional adhering, as can be seen here, is accomplished with masking tape. Then the pot is placed with the polyethylene side down, on a table. The epoxy resin mixture is poured into the cavity.*

Step 3. *This illustration shows the epoxy resin "stained-glass windows." Notice that some of the epoxy resin has leaked from the bottom of the polyethylene mold. Since this is a highly glazed pot, the excess resin can be removed with a mat knife. The thermosetting epoxy resin will not melt but will soften under heat. Therefore, the pot is placed about 12" from a heat lamp for a short time; afterward it is very easy to cut away the temporarily soft resin. Once the heat has dissipated, the resin will regain its hardness.*

Stained-Glass Reliefs

Stained glass—either antique or cathedral—may be cut, fused, slumped (softened), or broken and reassembled with proper adhesives on top of a glass sheet. In this way, you can produce a permanent decorative relief panel. The one described in this project has maximum dimensions of approximately 10' x 5'.

MATERIALS

1. Antique stained glass (handmade) or cathedral stained glass (machine-made, and cheaper).

2. Araldite epoxy resin 502.

3. Araldite curing agent 956.

4. Color and additives.

5. Dow Corning Silastic 140 adhesive or RTV silicone rubber adhesive/sealant which is now available from resin suppliers or from paint and hardware stores.

6. A small kiln or an air acetylene torch (optional, but helpful for attaining special effects).

7. If you are going to use a kiln or torch, you will need kiln wash—a mixture of water with an equal mixture of kaolin and powdered beach sand (also called flint).

8. A glass-topped table with fluorescent lighting fixtures underneath or a light box (optional).

9. Infrared lamps, glass cutters, protective goggles, and Band-Aids.

10. Theatrical, colored gelatin sheets (optional).

11. Well-cleaned, double-strength glass for your transparent "canvas," or backing sheet.

HOW TO BUILD AND USE A LIGHT BOX

After you have looked at the stained-glass work shown in color on pp. 118 and 119, you may be inspired to work in this most fascinating medium. Unless painting is your "thing," you should begin by designing some very simple overlapping forms on translucent paper. It is also helpful to use overlapping pieces of thin, colored gelatin sheets.

Lay the paper down on top of a lighted, glass-topped table, or a light box. If neither of these are readily available, you can make your own light box. You can use any 8" high box that has its top and bottom removed. It can be any width and legnth; 18" x 24" is a convenient size.

First, fasten a piece of pegboard to the bottom, or back, of this box. Attach three fluorescent fixtures (about 10" long) to the pegboard inside the box. Now cover the top with 1/4" thick glass. If convenient, it should be diffusing glass (ground, non-glare) with the shiny side up. The glass ought to be waxed as soon as possible with several coats of MirrorGlaze wax.

SELECTING COLORED GLASS

The selection of colored (stained) glass will be your hardest problem. In a large city, the local glass companies will often have at least a small stock of cathedral glass. Connoisseurs in this field say that this type of stained glass should be relegated to the W.C., because it doesn't have the real handmade beauty of antique glass, which is basically handblown and shaped. Try, if you can, to get the antique stained glass, which has slightly different thicknesses, uneven surfaces, and noticeable air bubbles.

Initially, two square feet each of light and dark transparent red, yellow, blue, green, amber, violet, and water-clear antique glass will give you a good palette of colors. Remember that you are going to be adding one piece of glass upon another which, since the glass is transparent, will give you a fantastic color range.

CUTTING GLASS

When you have chosen your colored (stained) glass, first practice cutting on some cheap, old window glass. Buy yourself an ordinary glass cutter which costs something around $1.00. If you can remember a few simple rules and are willing to practice a bit, you will find that cutting glass is not only easy but lots of fun (see *Cutting and assembling stained glass demonstration*):

Hold the cutter as you would a pencil (Step 1).

Press the cutting wheel firmly into the glass to actually break into its surface. Next, draw or push the wheel along, relaxing your pressure until you are just scarring the surface of the glass. The stresses set up by this pressure will make the glass break easily (Step 2).

Let your arm be nice and loose, as it should be for

Antique glass pieces. (*Above*) *Photo by Robert J. McCauley. Here, pieces of antique glass (made by the Blenco Glass Company of Milton, West Virginia) are assembled and ready to bond with Silastic 140 adhesive sealant to a ¼" plate glass "canvas."*

Glass cleaning material. (*Left*) *Photo by Robert J. McCauley. In fabricating a stained-glass relief, the glass must be thoroughly cleaned. Such cleaners as lacquer thinner or rubbing alcohol also work well. Once the glass is cleaned and wiped dry, you must not get your fingers on the surfaces that will receive the glue.*

Glass and epoxy relief. (*Right*) *Photo courtesy CIBA. Bold effects, particularly suited to modern architecture, are achieved with large slabs of glass assembled and held in place with an Araldite epoxy mixture. The glass slabs are first cut, then positioned, and finally the Araldite epoxy is used as a grout and poured to fill the space. This photo relief is shown under construction in the studio of A.H. Associates Limited.*

drawing. In this way, you will quickly find that you can cut freehand curves with little or no difficulty. With a pencil, draw a curve on a sheet of paper. Next, put your glass on top of this paper and lightly trace the penciled curve with your glass cutter. You can either push the cutting wheel or pull it on the glass over the curve—whichever feels more comfortable.

After you have made your cut, or scar, lightly tap the underside of the glass directly below your cut with the end of your cutter. You will quickly see a crack in the glass. For straight line cuts, one fissure is sufficient to break the glass along your cut line (Step 3).

With the cut line up, hold the glass with both hands between your thumb and forefinger. With your knuckles touching (as in Step 4), roll your knuckles so that the thumbs recede from each other and the glass breaks. If it doesn't break easily, don't force it. Tap the glass again from the underside and repeat the procedure described.

It is well to remember that only freshly scored glass can be readily cut. When the cutting wheel is rolled across the glass and scores it, temporary strains are set up. This makes it easy to cut the glass. If you wait a number of hours to break the glass after you have scored it, the strains will have dissipated and the glass may not break along the scored line.

Never go over the same cut twice with your cutter. You will surely spoil it.

To preserve your cutter, place some cotton soaked in turpentine or mineral spirits in the bottom of a bottle. When you are finished with your cutter, put it in this bottle. To sharpen your wheel, put some cup grease on a piece of slate. At an angle of 45°, roll your wheel back and forth over the slate. Turn the wheel around and repeat the procedure on the other side.

Now that you are an expert cutter of window glass, you will find that the cutting of stained glass is a cinch. Antique glass is much softer than window glass and easier to cut. Cathedral glass is another matter; it is machine-made and generally much tougher (Step 5).

OVERLAPPING PIECES OF STAINED GLASS

Now you are ready to cut your stained glass. It is suggested that you cut a whole bunch of thin slivers, or shards, of different colors. If you have trouble cutting thin sections, lay your glass on a table after you have cut into it. Tap the glass until you see a fissure appear. You can break the thin piece away from the rest of the glass using the proper channel in your cutter or a special pair of vise grips with very wide jaws.

When you have cut enough colored glass slivers, start laying one color partly on top of another. Notice that blue on top of red appears black. Green is produced naturally when blue lies on top of yellow. Different shades of green will occur when more than one piece of blue is laid on top of yellow. As you will shortly learn, the

nuances of color you can produce are endless as you become more proficient.

GLUING YOUR GLASS PIECES

You are now ready to try your first panel. The simplest adhesive to use is the RTV silicone translucent adhesive. To get a general idea of what your panel will look like, try, at first, to assemble its glass sections without any adhesive. In this way you will learn what some of the problems are before they become permanent mistakes. If you like, arrange your glass pieces on one master sheet of glass. Starting on another separate sheet you can take your glass pieces from the first and glue them to this second sheet following the same arrangement as on the unglued relief (Step 6).

When gluing your pieces, you should run the glue along the bias on the piece's bottom edge, the edge to be glued to the glass "canvas," or sheet. Run the silicone adhesive sparingly over at least two edges. Once you place your glass piece down on the master glass sheet or on top of another piece of colored glass, try not to move it. If you do, it will become smudgy (Steps 7 and 8).

HINTS FOR ASSEMBLING YOUR RELIEF

Here are a few points to keep in mind when making your stained-glass relief:

1. Most painters are used to working with opaque colors applied on a non-transparent surface. In glass, you are working with transparent colors—a very different situation.

2. In order to have the greatest feeling of depth in your stained-glass relief, the darkest colors should be nearest the observer. Therefore, place the lightest color glass pieces next to the master sheet and arrange the darker colors on top of them.

3. The most brilliant use of this structural, cut-glass technique is displayed in window panels which are exposed to sunlight. When the "pencils," or undiffused rays of light, hit an edge of handcut glass, there is really a dazzling refractive light "explosion." Take any piece of glass that you have cut and compare its appearance under diffused fluorescent light and under sunlight or an incandescent, unfrosted bulb.

4. Remember that the source of illumination for window panels is the sun; the sun is a moving fission fire-ball, emitting rays of light and is always at a different position each day of the year. Under these conditions your picture or collage is not static, but ever-changing.

5. For greater depth, you can build up your stained glass on both sides of the master glass panel.

6. If your relief is in a position where it can be touched

you will have to cover it. A glass cover can be taped over your relief with a canvas contact adhesive tape. The glass cover is separated from your stained-glass relief with a simple wood frame made from 1" x 1 1/2" pine. Several 1/4" holes are drilled into the wooden frame to act as vents. These holes are filled with glass wool to keep out the dust. This technique has been successfully in use in the Province of Quebec for the past 12 years.

7. If you seek effects that differ from the sharp crystalline fractures obtained from the glass cutter, you may fuse the glass pieces of your relief in a kiln on top of a kiln-washed shelf (that is, a shelf coated with a mixture of 1 part kaolin clay, 1 part flint, and enough water to make a paste). Your glass cuts will soften until their sharp edges are gone. Then you will not have to use a glass cover over your relief.

MIXING YOUR OWN EPOXY ADHESIVES

If you do not have a commercially prepared adhesive, such as RTV silicone (transparent) rubber adhesive or Silastic 140, you can mix up either of the two epoxy glass adhesives described in the formulas which follow. Note: do not use these epoxy adhesives on windows which will be exposed to freezing weather conditions.

The first adhesive for glass-to-glass bonding has a short pot life and is the most tested. The formula follows.

SHORT POT LIFE ADHESIVE FORMULA

Epoxy resin 502: 100 grams.

Curing agent 956: 20 grams.

Asbestos 244: 0 grams to Q.S.* (depending on how non-runny you want your adhesive to be).

If you want your adhesive less runny, make it up with more Asbestos 244. If you would like a more flexible adhesive, add 5% Benzoflex. If you do add more Asbestos 244, it is suggested that you warm your epoxy resin 502 to 212° F. and add the Asbestos to the hot resin. Stir well; then let the mixture cool. You should also add at least 1% Asbestos 244 to the curing agent 956. If you heat the 956 as you did the 502, do so where there is *extremely good ventilation. The vapors of hot 956 are toxic.*

The following formula will produce a flexible adhesive for glass-to-glass bonding which has a long pot life. It has less chance of yellowing, but has been less thoroughly evaluated than the first.

LONG POT LIFE ADHESIVE FORMULA

Benzoflex 9-88: 5 grams.

Epoxy resin 502: 90 grams.

Epoxide 7: 10 grams.

Asbestos 244: 5 grams.

Curing agent B-001: 50 grams.

Cabosil: 2 grams.

Combine Benzoflex with the epoxy resin 502 that has been warmed to 212°F. Add the Asbestos 244 to the Epoxide 7 and stir the mixture well. Then add the Asbestos 244/Epoxide 7 mixture to the 502/Benzoflex mixture and let the whole thing cool to room temperature. Heat the curing agent B-001 to 125° F. and add the Cabosil, stirring well. Let the B-001/Cabosil cool.

When ready to use, mix 10 parts of the 502/Benzoflex/Asbestos 244/Epoxide 7 mixture to 5 parts of the B-001/Cabosil mixture. For convenient application, this adhesive may be put in a squeeze bottle.

NOTES, VARIATIONS, AND CAUTIONS

In the kiln, glass may be slumped, or softened, over various heat-resistant forms. If the pieces are not too large (bigger than 8"), it is not necessary to anneal (temper) the glass after softening and reshaping it. The windows of the chapel at St. Foy, Quebec, were done in 1960 to 1961 with such slumped pieces of glass. These pieces were bonded to both sides of the master glass which in this case is made of plate glass, since it is over 5' long. The adhesive used was Dow Corning Silastic 140°.

For indoor murals, you may drip a 502/956 combination with or without color on top of your glass to give it additional lens-like (that is, magnified) areas.

For areas where there must be no breakage of the main glass plate, an acrylic or a polycarbonate sheet, such as Lexan, may be used. The adhesive in this case must be RTV· Silastic 140 or the equivalent.

Although 502/956, as with all epoxy resins, does tend to yellow, my experience over the last 12 years shows that for indoor use, glass-to-glass collages (or reliefs) protected by a glass cover exhibit a relatively small amount of yellowing.

Be sure that your glass is well cleaned before you do any gluing or bonding. A good cleaner would be rubbing alcohol or any solvent such as xylene or lacquer thinner. *Use these solvents in well-ventilated areas, without sparks or flames about, since they are highly flammable.*

If any of these resins come in contact with your hands, wash them well. Remember: *no contact, no dermatitis.* Good ventilation is always a must.

If you are working with 502/956 on warm, humid days, you may find it necessary to use infrared lamps at least 2' away from your piece, in order to ensure a non-sticky resin surface. If you should get a sticky resin surface, when the resin is hard you can wash off this tacky surface with rubbing alcohol and all will be O.K.

*Quantum sufficit: as much as suffices, or use your own judgment.

Step 1. *Demonstration photos by Robert J. McCauley. A new or undamaged glass cutter is needed to cut antique (handmade) or cathedral (machine-made) stained glass. Although it is not apparent from this illustration, the cutter is first pushed firmly into the glass at the very edge. Then, as the cutter is rolled along the desired cutting line, the pressure is relaxed so that the cutting line becomes very thin and light. Notice how the cutter is held almost like a pencil. The arm must be held very loosely so that you can follow any pencil or ink line.*

Step 2. *Here, the cut is being made. If there are places where the cutter does not cut the glass, do not retrace the cut line with your glass cutter. This is a good way to ruin it.*

Step 3. *It is far better to tap the glass gently under the cut line as shown than to use force. This tapping will often break those small areas where the glass was not cut.*

Step 4. *Notice here how the knuckles of both hands are held next to each other while the thumbs are firmly pressing the glass piece to be cut against the first coiled fingers of both hands. Slowly and deliberately the thumb and first fingers are rolled away from each other, always keeping at least one set of knuckles touching until you get to the knuckles of the little finger. By this time, the glass should be broken apart. If this is not the case, tap again lightly with the end of the glass cutter below the cut mark in the glass. It must eventually work. It is not necessary to use brute force and thus cut your fingers. It is said that cutting glass is like riding a horse: if you are not in control, both the horse and the glass seem to know it—and you will get hurt.*

Step 5. *This illustration shows how neat a cut can be made in antique glass with very little effort. Cathedral stained glass or standard window glass is a little more difficult to cut. Plate glass is even harder. Be sure to practice on scraps before you begin on your good pieces.*

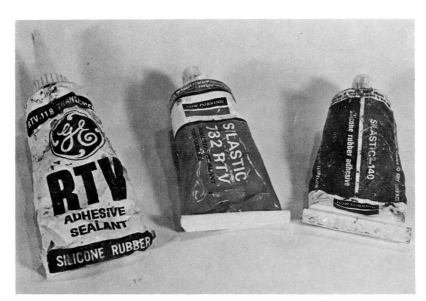

Step 6. *Shown here are several types of equally effective, silicone RTV (room-temperature vulcanizing) adhesives made by General Electric and Dow Corning. A silicone RTV rubber adhesive which will do the same job can be found in hardware stores.*

Cutting and assembling stained glass

Step 7. (*Right*) *Here, silicone RTV adhesive is applied at the edge of a glass section which is to be glued or adhered to the clear glass master plate (or "transparent canvas") or another piece of colored glass. When the decorative panels made by L'Art Kaleiray Ltée were assembled, each glass piece was usually glued on at least two sides in the same manner as shown.*

Step 8. *Here are a few pieces of antique glass bonded together with the silicone adhesive. Although close up the glue line is apparent, at a distance of over several feet the adhesive is hardly noticeable.*

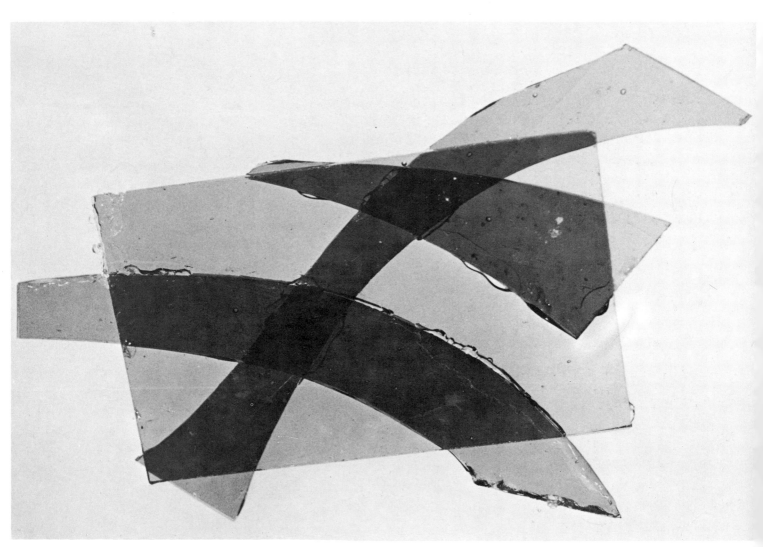

Transferring Color Reproductions to Epoxy Film

With quick-curing, epoxy resin systems, you can produce epoxy films and transfer any printed matter from clay-coated paper onto these films. This transfer technique can be useful for doing transparent collage or transferring printed matter to a different surface.

MATERIALS

1. Any magazines printed on clay-coated paper.

2. Araldite epoxy resin 502, for flexible castings, or

3. Epoxy resin 6004 or 6010 (which has a higher viscosity than 6004) for semiflexible castings, or

4. Epoxy resin DER 332, for semiflexible colorless castings.

5. Epoxide 7 reactive diluent for bubble-free castings.

6. DPM 3-800 LC.

7. Any of the following curing agents: Jeffamine 230, Ajicure B-001, CIBA 956, or DMP-30.

8. MirrorGlaze wax.

9. Acetone spray.

EPOXY RESIN FILM FORMULA

Epoxy resin 502: 50 grams.

DPM 3-800 LC: 45 grams.

Curing agent DMP-30: 5 grams.

MAKING AN EPOXY FILM TRANSFER

For the moment, without worrying about the art or craft forms involved, select a page from *Time, Life,* or *Playboy*—any of which are printed on clay-coated paper. Tape the edges of the paper to a flat surface with masking tape (see *Making an epoxy transfer demonstration*). Next, mix up the above formula in the order given or use 50 grams of epoxy resin 502 and 50 grams of curing agent RC 303, which is the equivalent of the first two substances (Step 1). Stir the mixture for one minute (Step 2), and then apply a 1/16" coating over the magazine page as evenly as possible (Step 3). Immediately (no later than two minutes) after the first

application of the resinous ingredients, spray them lightly with acetone (Step 4). *Remember that acetone is highly flammable, so do not smoke*! The acetone will break many of the air bubbles which are locked in the resin/hardener system. Approximately five minutes after first mixing the ingredients, the resin will become gelled and practically non-tacky. Spray lightly with mold release 1711.

Approximately 15 minutes from this point you may wash off the paper from the resin in warm running water (Step 5). Rubbing with your fingers will aid the process (Steps 6 and 7). Do not scratch the paper off with your fingernails since you will remove the ink from the resin. Once you have taken off all of the paper, as well as its loosely bound clay coating, gently dry your resin-printing ink transfer. Once the resin is dry, then coat the printing ink side with additional fresh 502/RC 303. This will give a clearer impression and also seal in the image (Step 8).

Once you have mastered this technique you may want to use it as an art or craft form. Remember, you can bond one resin-printing ink transfer to another with the same "adhesive" 502/RC 303 combination used to create the transfer film itself. If you wish to have a bubble-free transfer, the following formula is suggested.

FORMULA FOR BUBBLE-FREE TRANSFER

Epoxy resin 502: 85 grams.

Epoxide 7: 15 grams.

DPM 3-800 LC: 70 grams.

Jeffamine curing agent 230: 30 grams.

Naturally, you will not wish to use all of this material; therefore cut it down proportionately. This formula has an additional variation from the original. It takes about 1/2 to one hour, thus giving plenty of time for the bubbles of air to escape.

If you wish to have the preceding formula with less flexibility, substitute lower viscosity epoxy 6004 or epoxy 6010 for 502 as follows.

FORMULA FOR LESS FLEXIBILITY

Epoxy resin 6004: 85 grams.

Epoxide 7: 15 grams.

DPM 3-800 LC: 70 grams.

Jeffamine curing agent 230: 30 grams.

If you wish to make the preceding formula almost colorless, substitute epoxy resin DER 332 for the epoxy resin 502 as follows.

"COLORLESS" FORMULA

Epoxy resin DER 332: 85 grams.

Epoxide 7: 15 grams.

DPM 3-800 LC: 70 grams.

Jeffamine curing agent 230: 30 grams.

NOTES, VARIATIONS, AND CAUTIONS

There are obviously many other variations which you can make, but I am sure that you will probably not wish to take the time to do this. If you do, you can write to the manufacturers of these materials for their technical literature. You can most easily obtain these products from suppliers mentioned in this book (see Suppliers and Manufacturers section of Appendix).

To "paint" over these "transparent transfers" you can use the epoxy painting medium (see Project 20) with whatever colors you desire. You should, however, add an additional 5% to 10% Benzoflex to the epoxy painting medium to increase its flexibility in bonding to the flexible transparency you have made.

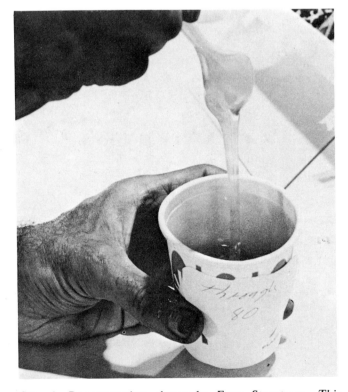

Step 1. *Demonstration photos by Evon Streetman. This illustration shows 50 grams of 502 being mixed with 50 grams of RC 303 in preparation for lifting or transferring a colored printed surface from clay-coated paper to an epoxy film.*

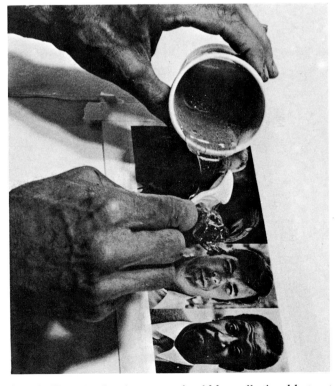

Step 2. *The mixed resin system should be well stirred but not whipped, since air bubbles, which can be seen here, will occlude the final transfer.*

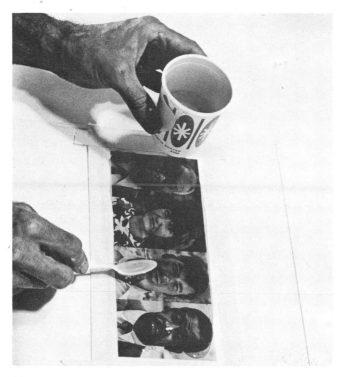

Step 3. *Since the curing system is a five-minute one, it is important to spread the resin mixture as quickly as possible. A relatively thin coating (¹⁄₃₂") should be applied so there will be few air bubbles and the heat developed will be kept at a minimum so as not to yellow the resin and mar the finish.*

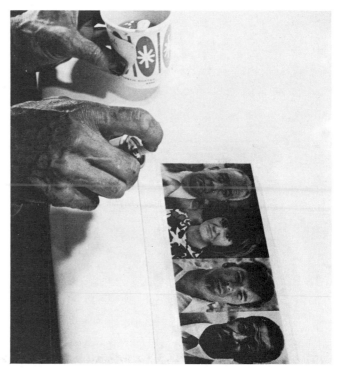

Step 4. *Here, acetone is sprayed on the freshly applied 502 / RC 303. This should be done no later than three after the mixing in of the ingredients, otherwise the surface bubbles may not be removed.*

Step 5. *After the resin has cured for ½ hour, the exposed surface is waxed and polished with MirrorGlaze wax to prevent this fresh surface from sticking to itself. Next, the paper, print, and resin are washed in warm water.*

Step 6. *Once the cellulose fibers of the clay-coated paper (Time, Newsweek, Playboy, etc., are all printed on such paper) are saturated with water, the paper is easily removed by gentle rubbing with the thumb.*

Step 7. *The resin, print, and paper unit is turned over in the water bath and a breakthrough, caused by massaging with the thumb, is found.*

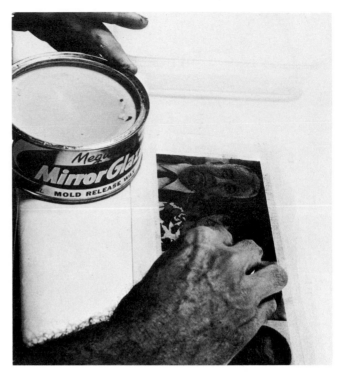

Step 8. *Once the entire paper backing is gone, the transparency is thoroughly and gently dried. An additional thin coating of 502 / RC 303 is next applied to the ink side. After the resin has cured for approximately ½ hour, the entire resin surface is waxed and polished with MirrowGlaze wax.*

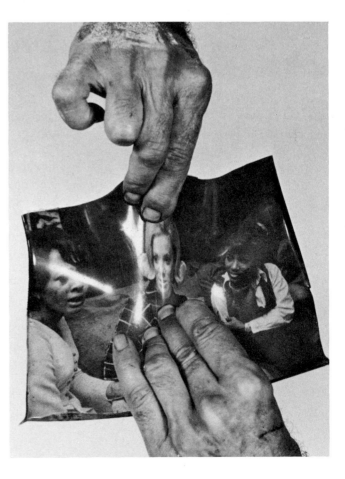

A urethane transfer. *Photo by Robert J. McCauley. This lift was made in exactly the same manner as shown in the demonstration for making a transfer with 502 / RC 303. However, here urethane coating and mold-making system TU 75, manufactured by Conap, Inc. of Allegheny, New York, and distributed by the resin distributors mentioned in this book, was used instead. Notice the rubbery stretch of this urethane rubber transfer.*

PROJECT 18

Casting an Epoxy-Polymercaptain Plate on Methacrylate Sheets

Methyl methacrylate sheets, such as Plexiglas, are excellent self-releasing sheets of plastic upon which to cast certain epoxy-polymercaptain resin combinations and other additives to produce plates for printing.

MATERIALS

1. Plexiglas, Lucite, or other methyl methacrylate sheet.

2. Microcrystalline wax 1290 Y (melting point 180° F.).

3. Silicone oil, DC-200 (50 centistokes viscosity), or spray mold release 1711.

4. Araldite epoxy resin 502, or

5. Epoxy resin 6004, for less flexibility.

6. Curing agent RC 303 (DPM 3-800 LC and DPM-30).

7. Epoxide 7, for fewer air bubbles in the resin mixture.

8. Araldite curing agent 956, for a more rigid second sheet.

9. Additives.

PREPARING METHYL METHACRYLATE SHEETS

Place your design under the sheet of Plexiglas or Lucite and temporarily glue it with rubber cement. If you wish to cast something other than a dead, flat sheet of epoxy resin, you may scratch, drill, sand, or cut into the Plexiglas sheet (see *Casting an epoxy-polymercaptain plate on a Plexiglas sheet demonstration*). In addition, you may pour hot microcrystalline wax 1290 Y on the Plexiglas sheet, cool the wax, and cut back into it with a burin or linoleum-block cutter (Step 1).

Coat the microcrystalline wax with silicone oil, applied sparingly with a small cotton swab or spray lightly with mold release 1711. When you have finished embossing on top of and/or engraving into the methyl methacrylate sheet, you are ready to put some sort of frame around the sheet so that the resin you are going to pour will not run over its side. Masking tape works well (Step 2).

EPOXY-POLYMERCAPTAIN RESIN FORMULAS

Mix any one of the following five epoxy-polymercaptain resin formulas. Each will give you a different result, so choose your formula according to what characteristics you want your sheet to have. Formula No. 1 is a fast cure, flexible formula which may produce air bubbles. Formula No. 2 is the same, but will produce fewer air bubbles. Formula No. 3 is a less flexible formula which may produce air bubbles. Formula No. 4 is the same, but will produce fewer air bubbles. Formula No. 5 will produce as few air bubbles as 3 and 4, but is even less flexible.

FORMULA NO. 1

Epoxy resin 502: 100 grams.

Curing agent RC 303: 100 grams.

FORMULA NO. 2

Epoxy resin 502: 80 grams.

Epoxide 7: 20 grams.

Curing agent RC 303: 100 grams.

FORMULA NO. 3

Epoxy resin 502: 120 grams.

Curing agent RC 303: 80 grams.

FORMULA NO. 4

Epoxy resin 502: 100 grams.

Epoxide 7: 20 grams.

Curing agent RC 303: 80 grams.

FORMULA NO. 5

Epoxy resin 6004: 100 grams.

Epoxide 7: 20 grams.

Curing agent RC 303: 80 grams.

CASTING EPOXY-POLYMERCAPTAIN RESINS

Pour your resin mixture about 1/8" thick all over your Plexiglas plate. If the waxed areas are higher than 1/8" above the Plexiglas plate, cover the wax with additional 1/8" pourings by at least 1/16". Cool the sheet between pourings of the mixture. Remove the cast epoxy-polymercaptain resin sheet after the last pouring has cooled. If you wish a more rigid sheet, you may cast epoxy resin 502/curing agent 956 combination in 100 gram/20 gram proportions right on top of the freshly set epoxy sheet that you have just cast and removed from the Plexiglas form. (See Steps 3 and 4 for cast plate and finished print.)

NOTES, VARIATIONS, AND CAUTIONS

If you wish to have controlled color areas, you may, of course, mix small quantities of any of the preceding formulas with whatever colors and additives you desire.

Step 1. *Demonstration by Richard Adams. Photos by Pete Steiner. 1290 Y microcrystalline melted wax is applied to the surface of the acrylic sheet. Once the wax has cooled, certain areas of the Plexiglas are engraved with a dentist's drill while other sections of the wax are melted with a blowtorch.*

Step 2. *The entire Plexiglas sheet is now boxed in on its sides with two or three layers of masking tape so that the epoxy resin to be poured will not run over. Prior to applying the resin, the entire plate is lightly sprayed with release 1711. The following formula is used for the first two flexible layers of the epoxy printing plate: 216 grams of epoxy resin 6010, 24 grams of Epoxide 7, and 160 grams of polymercaptain-curing agent blend RC 303. The resin mixture is stirred and spread as described in the text. In five or six minutes, the resin is cured. A second batch of the above resin is prepared and applied. With the wax on the Plexiglas now completely covered, the third and final semirigid coating is applied to the plate: 400 grams of epoxy resin 502 and 100 grams of curing agent RC 125. These components are mixed well and applied evenly over the entire plate. They are sprayed with acetone to remove air bubbles. The resin takes between 30 to 60 minutes to cure. The epoxy-polymercaptain is left on the wax and cured at 120° F. for 12 hours for a more rigid plate.*

Step 3. *The cast plate is removed from the wax negative, inked, and pulled through the etching press. Here, the deeply embossed print is peeled from the epoxy resin cast plate.*

Step 4. *Here, the finished print—which was printed intaglio— is touched up with two different viscosity relief colors.*

PROJECT 19

Epoxy-Metal Casting

You can easily make a two-piece wax mold from a piece of sculpture made of water-based clay. After you remove the still-wet clay, powdered metal and epoxy resin are put in the wax mold and cured. Following the curing of the epoxy-metal "alloy," the sculpture is removed from the wax mold, buffed, and polished. Chemical patinas may then be applied.

MATERIALS

1. Water-based clay.

2. Microcrystalline wax 1290 Y (melting point 180° F.).

3. Nylon monofilament (fishing line).

4. Empty 5-gallon metal paint and two empty 1-gallon metal cans.

5. Araldite epoxy resin 502.

6. Epoxide 7.

7. Asbestos 244.

8. Araldite curing agent 956.

BUILDING A MOLD

Take a 1" x 1/2" dowel stick and drill several holes in one end; snugly fit 1 1/4" nails in these holes. Then start building up your form over the nailed end. To learn the technique I suggest that you make something no larger than 6" long by about 5" in diameter (see *Epoxy-metal casting demonstration*). For easier working, you should be able to fit the other end of the dowel in a stand or clamp it to a table with a C-clamp. Sculpt your form without regard to the undercuts. As you will see, this is no problem.

Once you have made your sculpture, *do not let the clay dry out*. Spray it all over lightly with a silicone mold release such as 1711. Attach a nylon filament to your piece. This nylon line should be draped so that it contacts the clay all over, vertically dividing the sculpture in half. About 6" of nylon should be hanging free from the base of your form. Tie the loose ends around the armature stick so that they do not get in the way of your dipping (Step 1).

Now immediately dip your sculpture into the microcrystalline wax which has been previously melted in the 1-gallon can. This can should be hung in the 5-gallon pail which you half fill with boiling water (Step 2). Hold your figure in the melted wax for a second or two (Step 3). Then carefully remove the figure from the wax and plunge it into cold water in the other 1-gallon can (Step 4). Let your sculpture remain in the cold water about six seconds. Keep repeating this procedure (Step 5).

WASHING AND DRYING YOUR MOLD

After you have built up a wax coating of about 1/4" on your mold (a pin sticking out 1/4" from your clay figure will help you determine the thickness; the larger your sculpture, the thicker your wax mold should be. There are spray guns available for applying hot wax. This becomes important when you are going to do larger pieces.) Let the wax cool slowly at room temperature. While the mold still feels slightly warm, pull the ends of the nylon line firmly and slowly upward. This operation will divide the mold in half (Step 6).

Remove the wet clay carefully (Step 7). Wash out any remaining clay with a garden hose. A "Water Pik" (used for cleaning teeth) works magnificently well. Be sure to use cold water.

Once all of your clay has been washed out, carefully dry the inside of your wax mold. When it is dry, spray or wipe the inside of the mold lightly with silicone oil. This will prevent the epoxy-metal alloy from sticking to the microcrystalline wax (Step 8).

Now mix up the epoxy-metal formula which follows. The Epoxide 7 is added to lower the viscosity of the epoxy resin 502.

EPOXY-METAL FORMULA

Epoxy resin 502: 90 grams.

Epoxide 7: 10 grams.

Asbestos 244: 3 grams.

Curing agent 956: 20 grams.

For a more liquid formula, modify the formula by using 85 grams of epoxy resin 502 and 15 grams of Epoxide 7. As a general rule, try not to go over 10% on the reactive diluent Epoxide 7, since it does have a slight weakening effect on the epoxy resin 502. Naturally, the thinner the resin, the more metal powder can be added. I add the Asbestos 244 so there will be less tendency for the metal-resin mixture to run. Asbestos 244 does not increase the viscosity of the epoxy/hardener combination.

MIXING IN POWDERED METAL

Once you have mixed all of the ingredients well (Step 9), add your powdered metal or metals. For your first pieces, use aluminum powder: it is not only the cheapest of the metals, but it is the lightest as well. Mix in your powdered metal until you have a metal-resin mixture with the consistency of very heavy cream. It should just flow slightly (Step 10).

CASTING YOUR SCULPTURE

Now smear the epoxy-metal mixture into both sides of the mold (Step 11). It is not necessary to solidly fill each half. Once you have thoroughly covered both sections, put the mold pieces together and hold them tightly in place with rubber bands, string, or masking tape.

Immediately pour warm, dry sand (100° F.) into the bottom of the mold and fill completely (Step 12). This will suck up the excess resin and give you a richer metal "skin." Pouring in warm sand (100° F., if this is possible) will help cure the resin more rapidly.

CURING AND FINISHING

Once the epoxy-metal is hard, pour out the non-adhering sand and mix up a small quantity of the epoxy resin 502, Epoxide 7, and curing agent 956. Now pour this resin mixture into your mold and swish it around well. Pour out the excess and immediately add the warmed sand again. Repeat this procedure one more time after the resin has again cured. Let your mold remain with the sand filling until the resin is again cured a third time.

Leave the mold overnight where it will be at a temperature of about 125° F. Otherwise, do not open up the casting for several days.

After you have removed the wax mold (Steps 13 and 14), you may then buff and polish your sculpture (Step 15). Do not try to put a chemical patina on your aluminum sculpture. Not many people have had any success with this. If you do wish to put a chemical patina on aluminum, you should be sure that you have added at lease 10% lead to the aluminum. In this way, once you have buffed and polished your metal-epoxy sculpture down to the raw metal, such chemical patinas as liver of sulfur or ammonia and salt will give interesting effects.

However, patinas can be made with India ink and later sealed in with a mat-finish formula such as the following.

FORMULA FOR MAT FINISH

Epoxy resin 502: 10 grams.

Curing agent 956: 2 grams.

Cabosil: 1 gram.

Lacquer thinner: 72 grams.

Let this epoxy matting solution cure very well before touching.

OTHER PATINAS

If you wish to put patinas on brass, be sure you have added either copper or lead to the brass. If you want a nice bronze-looking piece of sculpture, use about 1/3 each of lead, brass, and copper. Again, here is a good opportunity to experiment with different metals. Silicon powder should not be overlooked. It is cheap, ebony black, and hard. Tin, which is now about $2.50 per lb., is a beautiful, powdered metal when incorporated with the epoxy and then cured, buffed, and polished.

Step 1. *Demonstration photos by Robert J. McCauley. Making a quick microcrystalline wax mold for casting begins with the sculpting of a wet clay form over an armature of heavy aluminum. The clay figure is sprayed with release agent 1711 so that the clay will release more readily from the wax mold. Not shown is the attaching of a single strand of at least 12 lb. nylon fishing line. It starts at the bottom of the form and goes completely around the perimeter and back to the bottom. About 6" of nylon should be hanging free from the bottom to subsequently open up the wax mold.*

Step 2. *When the modeling is completed, the head is dipped into the melted 1290 Y wax which is at a temperature of about 190° F.*

Step 3. *After several seconds, the figure is removed from the melted wax.*

Step 4. *The waxed head is next plunged into cold water.*

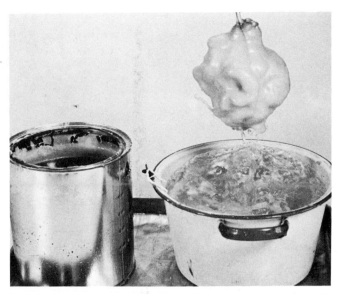

Step 5. *After six seconds, the head is removed from the cold water. This plunging into cold water is repeated again and again until there is a coating of wax approximately ¼" in thickness all over the clay. A toothpick is inserted into the wet clay figure in such a way that ¼" of the toothpick is exposed to act as a guide for wax thickness.*

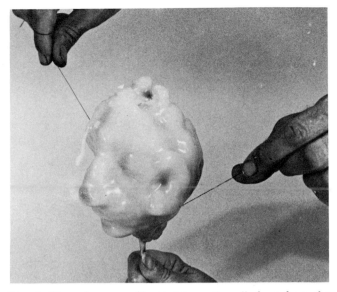

Step 6. *The nylon monofilament is gently pulled up from the base of the wax mold, which is at 100° F. The monofilament emerges from the top of the figure, thus cutting the mold in half.*

Step 7. *The removal of the wet clay from the wax mold is usually accomplished quite easily, as can be seen here.*

Step 8. *The wax mold must be completely cleaned of clay. Sometimes it may be necessary to wash out the remainder of the clay with water, using either a toothbrush or a "Water-Pik." Then, the mold should be well dried and sprayed with silicone mold release 1711.*

Step 9. *This sculpture of epoxy-aluminum contains the following formula: 90 grams of epoxy resin 502, 10 grams of Epoxide 7, and 20 grams of curing agent 956. These ingredients are then well mixed.*

Step 10. *Next, 300-mesh aluminum powder is added to the epoxy resin system in such a quantity as to yield a paste which will just about stay where it is placed. About 10% 300-mesh lead powder may be added to the aluminum powder before mixing with the epoxy resin and curing agent. This will subsequently permit the application of a patina (chemical coloring) with a weak solution of liver of sulfur, after the piece has been buffed to a high shine and cleaned off.*

Step 11. *Here, the epoxy-aluminum mixture is spread into the wax mold.*

Step 12. *After the inside of the mold is completely covered with the epoxy-metal mix, the pieces of the mold are reassembled and either sealed together with wax or pressure-closed with rubber bands. Then dry powdered sand or grog (aggregate) is poured into the cavity (see text). Once the epoxy-aluminum mixture has cured, the excess aggregate is poured out and fresh epoxy-hardener mixture is poured in, swished around, and the excess poured out. Fresh aggregate is poured into the cavity and then allowed to remain until the epoxy has again set. The larger the figure, the more coatings of aggregate and epoxy resin-aluminum are used.*

Step 13. *Once the epoxy-aluminum mixture has cured hard, the wax mold is removed.*

Step 14. *If there is any difficulty in removing the mold, it may be placed in hot water (125° F.) for 15 minutes; then the wax can be easily pulled away from the figure.*

Step 15. *Finally this epoxy resin-aluminum head is buffed on a soft-cotton buffing wheel, using the usual buffing compounds sold in any hardware store or in Sears Roebuck. This final photo shows the finished head.*

Epoxy Resin "Oil" Paints

With the proper formulation of epoxy resins, you may make an epoxy resin painting material which handles exactly like oil paint. Epoxy resin paint has the additional advantage of providing any degree of transparency you desire; also, with heat, you can cure the painting at any time you desire.

MATERIALS

1. Araldite epoxy resin 502.

2. Epoxide 7.

3. Asbestos 244.

4. Cabosil.

5. Curing agent B-001 or HH 1065 B.

6. Color pastes (transparent or opaque, as you wish).

7. Brushes, palette knives, etc.

8. Epoxy paint thinner: xylene, toluene, or acetone (primarily for cleaning brushes).

EPOXY RESIN "OIL" PAINT FORMULA

Epoxy resin 502: 90 grams.

Epoxide 7: 10 grams.

Asbestos 244: 4 grams.

Heat the epoxy resin 502 to a temperature of 180° F. To this hot resin add Epoxide 7, into which you have already stirred the Asbestos 244. After the Epoxide 7 and Asbestos 244 mixture has been thoroughly stirred into the resin, it is a good idea to keep this formula at 125° F. for an additional 1/2 hour, stirring continually until all the lumps have disappeared and there is a relatively translucent to transparent, thixotrophic, gelatin-like mass.

The formula for the curing agent side of the reaction is as follows.

CURING AGENT FORMULA

Curing agent B-001: 50 grams.

Asbestos 244: 1.5 grams.

Warm the B-001 to 150° F. in a well-ventilated area. Add Asbestos 244 to the B-001 curing agent, stirring well. When the Asbestos 244 is well stirred in, do not heat further.

If you use curing agent HH 1065 B, which has a lower viscosity than B-001, add 1 gram of Cabosil to 25 grams of HH 1065 B without heating. The epoxy resin part of the system is the same, but omit the Epoxide 7 and use 100 grams of epoxy resin 502 and 4 grams of Asbestos 244. In this case, proportions are 100 grams of thickened epoxy resin 502 and 25 grams of thickened HH 1065 B.

ADDING COLOR TO EPOXY RESIN PAINTS

When you are ready to paint with your epoxy "oil" paints, combine 10 grams of the above epoxy resin parts formula with 5 grams of the B-001 and Asbestos 244 you prepared (or 10 grams of the alternate mixture to 2 1/2 grams of the HH 1065 B mixture). Stir the two ingredients very well and divide the mixture into small batches. The color pastes should then be thoroughly stirred into these epoxy resin/curing agent batches.

Remember that unless the color pastes are mixed well with the epoxy resin/curing agent systems, they will never cure. The working time for this epoxy system is at least five hours. If the weather is not exceptionally warm, it will take longer. Curing systems using curing agent B-001 are very slow and practically no heat is given off.

USING EPOXY RESIN PAINTS

Epoxy resin paints such as described may be used on all canvases or boards that are used with traditional oil paint. If you want a more flexible epoxy resin curing system, you can add up to 10% Benzoflex—or for every 100 grams 502/Epoxide 7 or 502 alone, 10 grams of Benzoflex.

When working with epoxy oil paints, remember to select the most lightfast colors possible. Briefly, the use of phthalocyanine blue and green is a must for transparent colors. CIBA's Microlith T colors are needed for this type of transparent to translucent paint. Color pastes made from these pigments are most satisfactory. Again, the use of ultraviolet light screeners or absorbers is recommended for combination with epoxy resin systems.

The American Cyanamid Company has an ultraviolet light screener called Cyanasorbe 207. It would be well to evaluate this product or similar products. Since the field of resin chemistry and additives is always changing, by the time this book reaches you there may be screeners which will be even more effective than Cyanasorbe 207.

If you want your picture to dry in less than a 12-hour to 24-hour period, you may put it under infrared lights, but be sure that these lights are at least 1 1/2' to 2' away from the picture. Otherwise, there will be a chance of the resin burning or yellowing.

MAT FINISH FORMULA

Epoxy resin 502: 10 grams.

Curing agent 956: 2 grams.

Lacquer thinner: 72 grams.

Cabosil: 1 gram.

Combine the epoxy resin 502 and curing agent 956. Mix well. After 10 to 15 minutes, add a lacquer thinner. Such lacquer thinners as xylene, toluene, MIBK, or the usual lacquer thinners may be used here. After this is well mixed, add the Cabosil. This concoction is painted thinly

CREATING A MAT FINISH

After your paints have hardened, you may wish to have a mat finish over a particular or total area; the following formula will work beautifully to produce such a finish.

over the areas you wish to have a mat finish. Let the resin cure well before touching it.

NOTES, VARIATIONS, AND CAUTIONS

You must remember that you are not using standard oil paints and that you are probably painting with your good brushes. Therefore, it is important that you wash your brushes well with epoxy paint thinner or the usual lacquer thinners when you are finished using them. Following this cleaning, wash the paintbrushes with soap and water. Although the formula which you are using for your epoxy paint is relatively nontoxic, be sure to scrub well with soap and water any skin area that has been in contact with an epoxy resin.

Should you wish to have the epoxy resins more textural or more thixotrophic, you may add additional Asbestos 244 at any point, or if you do not mind losing a certain amount of transparency, add powdered flint which is 200-mesh silica sand. This will do an excellent job.

The use of pearlescent materials (available from Resin Coatings, see address in Suppliers and Manufacturers section of Appendix) provides effects that are rather foreign to the usual oil painting media. If you wish to give a metallic cast to your oil paints, you may do so with 300-mesh aluminum, copper, chrome, zinc, or tin metal powders. These particular powders are made by Alcan Metal Powders, P.O. Box 290, Elizabeth, New Jersey, and other companies. They must be buffed and polished, once the resin has cured, for a truly metal finish. However, you can settle for the glitter-type powders, which are available in hardware or paint stores; these do not have to be polished.

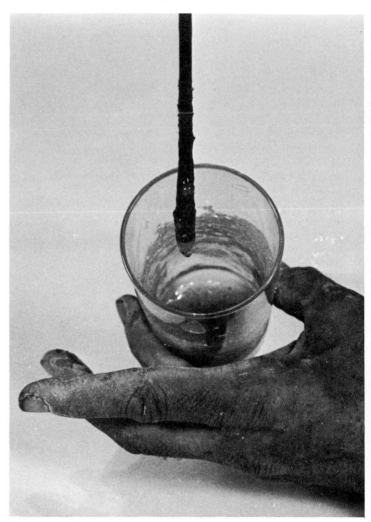

Step 1. *Demonstration photos by Robert J. McCauley. The use of Cabosil as a thickener or thixotropic agent is shown here in conjunction with HH 1065 B, an epoxy resin curing agent of low viscosity. The action of from 1% to 8% Cabosil (depending upon the viscosity and chemical nature of the liquid to be thickened) will make the curing agent completely non-runny.*

Step 2. *After good agitation for several minutes, the thickened epoxy curing agent, HH 1065 B, appears as shown. Asbestos 244 is used to thicken epoxy resin 502 because it produces a mixture with greater clarity than Cabosil. However, in this case, for thickening HH 1065 B curing agent, Cabosil gives a greater clarity.*

Step 1. *Demonstration by Jim Cooper. Photos by Robert J. McCauley. The following formula was used to create the epoxy paints which are employed in this painting like ordinary oil-based paints: 90 grams of CIBA epoxy resin 502, 10 grams of Epoxide 7, and 4 grams of Asbestos 244. The curing agent formula was: 25 grams of HH 1065 B and 1 gram of Cabosil (Cabosil is a thixotropic agent like Asbestos 244, but produces a clearer mixture than 244 when used with HH 1065 B). The thinner used for these epoxy paints was produced from 90 grams of CIBA epoxy resin 502 and 10 grams of Epoxide 7. These two ingredients were then mixed with 25 grams of HH 1065 B to produce the thinner. Both the epoxy paints and their corresponding thinners are workable for at least three or four hours. The artist's first brushstrokes are seen here.*

Step 2. *The painting progresses. Here, the artist is firming up his design.*

Step 3. *Artists enjoy using epoxy "oil" paints because they remain as brilliant when dry as they were when applied. At this stage, the painting begins to show real structure.*

Step 4. *The following day, the artist continues with his painting. Because it is an adhesive, fresh epoxy paint naturally adheres to the old or cured epoxy paint.*

Step 5. (*Right*) *Here is the finished painting in epoxy "oil" paint. Should you wish a slightly more flexible epoxy paint, add 5 grams of Benzoflex to the epoxy curing agent.*

SILICONES, POLYURETHANES, AND EXPANDED POLYSTYRENE

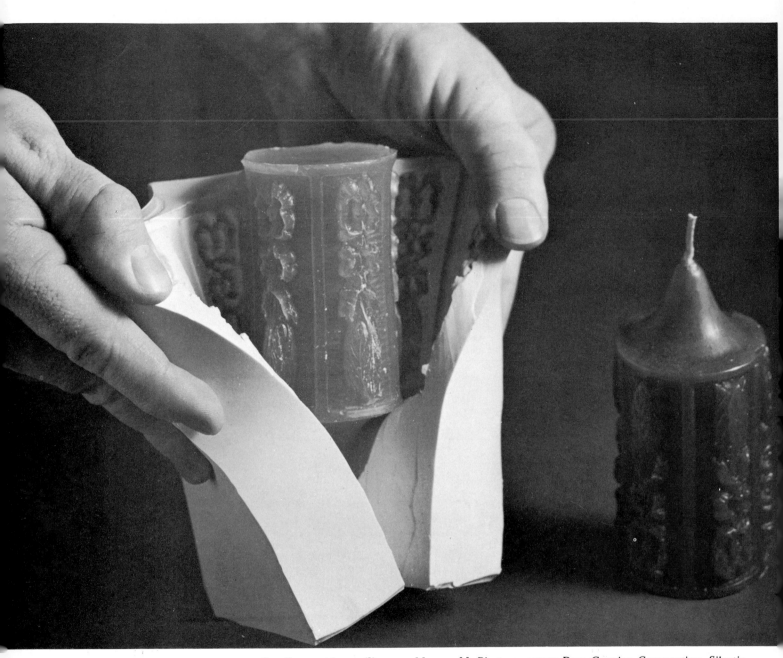

Candles cast from silicone rubber mold. *Photo courtesy Dow Corning Corporation. Silastic E RTV (room-temperature vulcanizing) rubber is now being used as a mold-making material for manufacturing wax candles. The original candle, shown on the left, is bonded to the base of a 20-mil acetate, or a lightly greased plywood box. Silastic E RTV rubber, which has been catalyzed and degassed (vacuumed), is poured slowly around the base of the candle until the wick is covered. The rubber is then allowed to cure at room temperature for approximately 24 hours. The mold is removed from the box and the candle extricated from the silicone rubber by cutting the mold along one side and part of the bottom, as shown in this picture. A wick is threaded through the hole left by the original wick and knotted at the end; the other end of the wick is held taut in place. Candle wax is then poured into the top of the Silastic E mold, and when the wax is cooled a new candle emerges, as shown here.*

Silicone Polymers

Silicone polymers are made into so many different types of products that it is impossible to give them a single classification. They are made into and marketed as fluids, oils, rubbers, greases, adhesives, compounds, and mixtures of themselves and other materials.

WHAT ARE SILICONE POLYMERS?

The starting substance for making silicones is sand or quartz, which contain silicon and oxygen atomically bound together by nature in the form of silicon dioxide. The extraction of the silicon from the sand or quartz by means of the electric-arc furnace is the first of a series of complicated chemical reactions. Finally, the manufacturer produces products containing many repeated units made up mostly of atoms of silicon, oxygen, carbon, and hydrogen. These products have been given the general name of *silicones*. To indicate the repetitive joining of similar units, the prefix *poly* is added to the designation and we end up with the name *polydimethylsiloxane*. The polydimethylsiloxanes are basically fluids. These fluids, or oils, are called DC 200 fluids by Dow Corning and SF 96 and SF 97 by General Electric.

CHARACTERISTICS OF SILICONE POLYMERS

Silicone polymers have the following useful and often unusual properties:

1. Physical characteristics such as viscosity vary little in temperature changes from 50° F. to 450° F. Because of this, silicone oils and greases are used to lubricate machinery in sub-zero climates.

2. Practically nothing sticks to silicones except other silicones. Paper coated with silicones and molds made from silicone rubbers are self-releasing. Minute quantities of DC 200 fluids prevent even such excellent adhesives as epoxies from adhering to surfaces treated with these oils.

3. Silicones are relatively not affected by ultraviolet light (sunlight) or weather, and therefore coatings or paints made with these polymers deteriorate less rapidly than the usual paints now on the market. Such materials as glass, ceramics, and metals may be permanently glued or bonded with silicone adhesives. I have had experience in bonding glass to glass in three-dimensional stained-glass window collages with silicone adhesives such as Silastic 140. Thousands of dollars worth of these windows have been installed over 10 years ago with no failures.

4. Extreme water repellency is one of the outstanding properties of silicones. Even when they are applied on porous surfaces such as cement blocks or clothing, drops of water are repelled. General Electric's Dri-Film 103 is one such product available for making masonry water-repellent and yet breathable.

5. Silicones are superior non-staining lubricants for metals, rubber, and plastics. Textile machinery might well be oiled with DC 200 fluids.

6. The physiological inertness of silicones is another noteworthy property. Silicones are, of course, being implanted more and more in the human body to replace defective human parts. The polymers used are mainly silicone rubbers. Silicone fluids, such as the DC 200 series, are considered completely safe to handle. They are extensively used in hand and face lotions. I have been formulating such a lotion for the past 20 years. These silicone oils are excellent barriers for protecting the skin from contact with polyesters, epoxies, and urethane resins.

7. Silicones have excellent electrical insulating properties. For example, covering electrical connections with silicone adhesives such as Silastic 732 from Dow Corning provides instant insulation.

8. When they can be dissolved in a substance like polyurethane, silicones act like a soap and therefore can wet and make the material foamy. They are extensively used in the manufacturing of urethane foams.

9. The extreme insolubility of silicones in water leads to another interesting property. They are foam breakers. In processes where foaming is a problem, minute quantities of silicone fluids may be sprayed on top of the foam, or 1/10 to 100 parts of silicone polymer per million parts of foaming liquid may be added to prevent the foam from forming. Such products are available from either Dow Corning or General Electric, or others. Dow Corning has products which can be used, for example, in the food

manufacturing industry, such as DC Antifoam A compound, food grade, for non-water systems, and DC Antifoam AF emulsion for water systems.

10. Silicones are being synthesized to have extremely high chemical resistance. The newest fluorsilicone sealing compounds also have exceptional resistance to fuels and hydraulic and engine oils, and they resist splash and fume exposure from liquid fuels.

RELEASE AGENTS

Silicone fluids or oils are most useful as release agents which prevent resins such as epoxies, polyesters, and polyurethanes from adhering to surfaces upon which the fluids or oils are applied. Available in all viscosities are such silicones as Dow Corning's DC 200 fluids and General Electric's SF 96 or SF 97 fluids. Since these synthetic polymers are highly inert chemically, they do not react with the surfaces upon which they are applied. Because of their temperature-viscosity stability, they will not tend to run off a surface at high temperatures. These silicone fluids are also used in barrier creams and hand lotions, such as Silicare by Revlon, and as lubricants for plastics, rubbers, and metals.

ARTISTS' PAINTS

It is now possible to build remarkable resistance to weathering, heat and corrosive atmospheres into the vehicles of paints and coatings containing almost all silicone resins and polymers. I have little doubt that silicone paints will be at the top of the list of the really permanent artists' paints in the very near future.

ADHESIVES AND CAULKING COMPOUNDS

Excellent permanent adhesives and elastomeric (rubberlike) sealants or caulking compounds are now available in the silicone family. The easiest to use are the non-runny thixotropic products which are put up in collapsible metal tubes which have a storage life of about six months if kept in a cool place. Besides now being available in hardware and paint stores, they may be bought from such resin suppliers as Resin Coatings Corporation, Polyproducts Corporation, and Waldor Enterprises Ltd. (see Suppliers and Manufacturers section of Appendix for addresses). These bonding agents and sealants are available as Dow Corning's 732, which comes in colorless translucent, black, and white. These products have a stretch of about 4 1/2 times, a tensile strength of about 275 pounds per square inch, and take approximately 24 hours for a 1/8" thick section to cure. They mostly all have a vinegar or acetic-acid odor which disappears upon curing. When these products are full cured, they are relatively inert and they

may be used for very extended periods of time at temperatures of 212° F. (boiling water).

MOLDS

Silicones such as Silastic E and the newest RTV Silastic G, made by Dow Corning, and RTV 662, made by General Electric, are available for mold making. Silastic E is a two-part system composed of a silicone liquid polymer to which a special catalyst is added immediately before use. At room temperature, or with moderate heat, the mixture polymerizes into a solid rubber. Such silicone rubber molds, although expensive (about $8.50 per pound, in single-pound units), have the following properties:

1. They are self-releasing for the life of the mold.

2. They can be cured in five minutes at temperatures of 300° F.

3. They are much less affected by high humidity in curing than the urethane rubber mold-making systems. As a matter of fact, curing Silastic E under infrared heat lamps at a distance of 2' will prevent the stickiness often occurring on the surface of the cured silicone rubber when the humidity is high.

4. They have little or no shrinkage during cure and they enable the artist or craftsman to make completely accurate reproductions.

5. When these molds are properly cared for and precoated with certain silicone or wax preparations, they can be used to make hundreds of polyester and urethane resin castings.

6. Epoxy resins destroy the surface of these silicone molds rapidly, even when the user follows the manufacturer's suggestions. If it is absolutely necessary to use epoxy resins (epoxy resins might be needed because they do not shrink), it is a wise precaution to precoat the mold with polyester resin. Let this coating cure well, then proceed with the curing of the epoxy resin system.

DISPERSIONS

Excellent releasing surfaces for polyester, epoxy, and urethane resins may be obtained by using silicone dispersions, such as Dow Corning's 236 dispersion. This product may be thinned with dry solvents, such as xylene. It may be applied thinly on any dry non-oily surface. This dispersion, or one made from Dow Corning 732, thinned with a dry solvent such as xylene, will air and moisture cure to yield a dry-surface, durable, and rubbery coating which will give excellent releases after many applications of the above polymers.

ANTI-TARNISH COATINGS

Metal protectants and anti-tarnish coatings made from silicone polymers are now available. Such products as Dow Corning's XR 6-2121 (530 fluid), or Marine Anti-Rust are ready to use as supplied and directed. According to the manufacturer, they provide very good resistance to corrosion and tarnish. I have used XR 6-2121 experimentally as a non-tarnish coating over polished copper with good results.

CLEAR BLOCKS

Silicones may be synthesized into low-viscosity polymers which when catalyzed yield transparent, flexible, and bubble-free compounds for embedding or partially submersing art or craft forms. General Electric makes LTU 602, and Dow Corning offers Sylgard 182 and 184.

POLISHES

Detergent-resistant polishes are now possible because of the insolubility of the silicone polymers in washing soaps. Therefore, objects painted with acrylic lacquers, for example, may have their luster preserved by polissing them with products which contain Dow Corning 530 and 531 fluids.

SELF-EXTINGUISHING FLUIDS

Many self-extinguishing silicone-fluid polymers above 50 centistokes (1 centistoke = 1/100 of a stoke) viscosity are now available. This is indeed a comforting aspect for anyone using them in public buildings to know.

SILICONE-SOLUBLE DYES

Various colored, clear silicone fluids may have some art or craft value. Down Corning has evaluated many dyestuffs, and here is a list of their recommended silicone-soluble dyes along with concentrations (data on lightfastness was not given):

DYE STUFF	CONCENTRATION
National Oil Blue BMA	0.01%
National Oil Green M-255	0.002 to 0.01%
American Cyanamid's Calco Oil Red ZD	0.002%
American Cyanamid's Calco Oil Orange Z 7070	0.01%
American Cyanamid's Calco Aviation Oil Blue	0.05%
American Cynamid's Calcofluor Yellow HEB	0.001 to 0.002%

Step 1. *Demonstration photos by Dick Haun. When they developed a foam-in-place silicone rubber, Dow Corning probably never thought of this exotic material in connection with humor or artforms. Here, artist Carolyn LePage has just poured catalyzed room-temperature vulcanizing silastic rubber foam into a "sick" tennis ball's mouth.*

Step 2. *There is a bit of foaming at the mouth, but the reaction is over in about two minutes, and five minutes later a silicone foam rubber ball is being removed from the little old lady's mouth. Industrial products such as these silastic rubber foams are increasingly being used by the artist-craftsman to enlarge his horizon.*

NEW BREAKTHROUGHS IN
SILICONE POLYMERS

The artist-craftsman is now in a position to partake of and use the "goodies" researched for the aerospace era. If he is interested in joining the remaining 3/10 of the 20th century full tilt, it will pay him to eye the synthetic polymers and resins which are skyrocketing from the university, national, and industrial laboratories. Here is a case in point: during my last visit to the Dow Corning Research Laboratories in the spring of 1970, I was shown samples of clear, colorless silicone resins which will not be marred by the lighted end of a cigarette butt whose temperature is about 900° F.

From this observation, we can now add another item to our list of silicone properties: soon to be available on the consumer market are silicones which will withstand temperatures of up to 900° F. This certainly demon-strates new breakthroughs in the area of plastics.

Other desirable properties now nonexistent in silicone polymers are sure to be developed by such companies as Dow Corning, General Electric, and Union Carbide, all of which are specialists in silicones. If there is a large enough national or industrial need for "imagineered" silicone products, the chances are that they will be tailor-made.

For the artist-craftsman, the two most exciting areas to watch in the development of silicone polymers and resins are the paints or coatings for canvas or mural painting and vitreouslike glazes or enamels which can be used in cloisonne jewelry, murals, or sculptures. A starting point for the silicone paint vehicle would be such silicone products as Dow Corning's 804, 805, 806A, 808, and 840. I am now carrying on research along these lines, but it is still too early to know which silicone resins will lend themselves to the formulation of "enamels."

Making Silicone Rubber Molds

One of the most convenient, flexible, accurate, and sturdy molds for duplicating art and craft forms is self-releasing silicone (RTV) curing rubber. These silicone RTV materials are initially liquids which are easily converted with special catalysts into rubbers with low linear shrinkage when cured at room temperature. Almost any dry material can be used as a pattern or model. There are two types of molds, the *skin mold* and the *cast mold*. The skin mold is a thin shell of silicone rubber which is usually reinforced with an open-weave material. The cast mold is formed by pouring the silicone rubber around the pattern. In either type of mold, the silicone rubber is generally housed in some kind of non-adhering, rigid container.

MATERIALS

1. Silastic E or G RTV silicone rubber and catalyst, manufactured by Dow Corning.

2. Silastic RTV thinner for lowering viscosity of Silastic E or G.

3. Petroleum jelly, such as Vaseline.

4. Solvents, such as methylene chloride or acetone.

5. Infrared heat lamp and holder.

6. Heat gun, such as the Model HG-301-J made by Master Appliance Corporation, 1745 Flette Avenue, P.O. Box 545, Racine, Wisconsin 53403 (optional).

7. Disposable polyethylene baby-bottle liners or equivalently thick larger bags.

8. Mixing containers at least four times larger than the amount of Silastic E or G to be vacuumed before use (optional).

9. Laboratory vacuum chamber, such as Duravac 14" x 13" x 10" capable of vacuuming 1000 grams of RTV rubber, manufactured by Ace Glass (see Suppliers and Manufacturers section of Appendix for address).

10. Laboratory vacuum pump, such as Cenco Megavac Cat. 93003 or Hyvac 14, distributed by Central Scientific Company, 4401 West 26 Street, Chicago, Illinois 60623 (optional).

11. Reinforcing open-weave material, such as cheesecloth, Dacron fabric (Dacron tricot) 10, 15, and 25 mils thick.

12. Non-sulfur-material-containing modeling clay, such as Permoplast X-33, manufactured by American Art and Clay Company, or Klean Klay 20 made by Art Chemical Products, Inc. 1019 Salamonie Avenue, Huntington, Indiana 46750.

13. Pattern sheet wax and fillet wax made by the Kindt-Collins Company, 12651 Elmwood Avenue, Cleveland, Ohio 44111 (optional).

14. Mold barrier coatings, such as those made by Contour Chemical Company, 4 Draper Street, Woburn, Massachusetts 01301, or Sherwin Williams, 116 St. Claire Avenue, Cleveland, Ohio 44104.

MAKING YOUR PATTERN

Your model or pattern may be made of almost any clean, dry non-sulfur material. Certain modeling clays and natural rubber do contain sulfur, which inhibits the cure of the Silastic E rubber, leaving it sticky, gummy, and soft at the interface. A few plastics (excluding such synthetics as cellulose acetate, Teflon, polyethylene and Mylar), as well as certain materials containing organometallic salts also may cause trouble. If in doubt, test first. Silicone rubber should *not* be used as a model-making material.

RELEASE COATING

Models or patterns made from clean, dry, oil-free metals, ceramics, plasters, and plastics such as cellulose acetate, Plexiglas, Teflon, polyethylene, and Mylar do not need release coatings. Wood generally does. Such a release coating is 5% petroleum jelly (such as Vaseline) dissolved in methylene chloride or acetone. Stir frequently, since the petroleum jelly tends to settle. If you are in doubt about your model or form material, mix well 1 gram of Silastic E or G and 4 drops of Silastic E or G catalyst and apply this to the pattern. If you are in a hurry, you may heat-cure this test patch in 30 minutes in the oven at 150° F. This temperature is well below the melting point of most thermoplastics such as polyethylene. If you do apply a petroleum jelly release coat to your form or model, apply as thin a coat as possible.

Master Standard Heat Gun. *Photo courtesy Master Appliance Corporation. This heat gun is recommended by Dow Corning for gelling Silastic E RTV rubber when using it to make a skin mold. The price is approximately $45.00 and it is available from Master Appliance Corporation, 1745 Flette Avenue, P.O. Box 545, Racine, Wisconsin 53403. This particular gun, HG 201, has a temperature range of 200 to 300 F; the voltage is 120 v, the amperage is 5 amps, and the shipping weight is 5 lbs.*

MIXING SILICONE RUBBER AND CATALYST

When your pattern is ready for treatment, weight out the Silastic E and catalyst according to the manufacturer's directions into untreated paper containers. If you have no vacuum, weigh your materials into a small, strong polyethylene bag from which you can easily remove the air through a straw taped with masking tape to the inside of the bag.

When you have removed all the air, tightly seal up the bag with a "Baggie wire" and mix in the catalyst by thoroughly kneading the bag. If you have no bag, you can carefully stir the catalyst into the Silastic E or G and not mix in too much air.

Since the Silastic E or G has a relatively high viscosity, you may cut this viscosity to 1/4 its initial value by mixing in and adding no more than 10% Silastic RTV thinner to the Silastic E rubber and Silastic E catalyst. This will somewhat lower the physical properties of the cured rubber, but I have not experienced any difficulty with this thinner addition.

MAKING A SKIN MOLD

The skin-type mold is used when the figure or form is very large and is more readily kept standing. I have suggested the use of Silastic E or G (runny, non-thixotropic) over the other available silicone rubber RTV compounds because of their better physical properties (see Comparative Data Table on p. 157. There is, however, a non-runny, or thixotropic, silicone rubber RTV called Silastic C, whose tear strength is over twice as *low* as that of Silastic E or G. Since the application of the rubber is easiest when it will not run down the form, an ingenious way has been worked out so that Silastic E or G can be successfully used. Here is the procedure:

Prepare the model or form to receive the Silastic E or G by first cleaning it well and drying it. If a petroleum jelly release is indicated, lightly spray or brush the form with 5% petroleum jelly in methylene chloride or acetone, which quickly evaporates.

Next, carefully brush the catalyzed Silastic E or G mixture lightly all over the form. To stop the flow of the Silastic E or G, either a heat gun (as described in the list of materials) or an infrared heat lamp may be used. The heat from either of these tools held close enough to bring the surface of the rubber to at least 200° F. will start the vulcanizing and stop the flow. Once this coating has cured, it is well to repeat the operation.

Now apply a third coating thinly and cover it with either cheesecloth or loosely woven Dacron or fiberglass cloth. *Wear gloves.* With additional Silastic E or G, seal and sandwich in the cloth all over. The thickness of this skin mold should be about 1/8". Let the Silastic E or G cure out well.

TABLE OF CURING RATES

To give you an idea of curing rates, Dow Corning offers the following table for 1/4" thick moldings of Silastic E:

TEMPERATURE	SETUP TIME
77° F.	Less than 24 hours
125° F.	60 minutes
150° F.	30 minutes
200° F.	15 minutes
250° F.	7 minutes
300° F.	5 minutes

MAKING A HOLDING MOLD

Build a 3/4" plywood box assembled with wood screws around the reinforced skin mold. This can then be filled with plaster to make a two-or-more-piece holding mold. If you desire a lighter and stronger holding mold, you might consider using polyester resin highly filled with hollow phenolic microballoons (see Glossary). In this case, the wood box should be well waxed with MirrorGlaze wax. The backup piece mold should be done in sections similar to the multiple Silastic E or G mold described below. Petroleum jelly works well to keep plaster from adhering to plaster. The best separator for the polyester supporting mold pieces is to lightly spray on some 5% RTV thinner in acetone at the edges.

Dura-Vac Vacuum Plastic Plexiglas Dessicator (dryer). *Photo courtesy Ace Glass, Inc. This piece of equipment is recommended by Dow Corning as safe and useful for degassing and removing entrapped air in Silastic RTV rubbers after the catalyst has been thoroughly mixed into the liquid silicone. This transparent, compact, and shatter-resistant plastic vacuum chamber is manufactured by Ace Glass, Inc., 1430 N. W. Boulevard, Vineland, New Jersey 08360. The cost is approximately $51.50.*

MAKING A CAST MOLD

Cast Silastic molds are the most common. A one-piece mold is possible when one side of the surface of the model is flat, such as in a relief figure. If all sides of the form are important, such as in a small sculpture, then a multiple-piece mold must be used. To make a one-piece mold, you need a container whose sides are no greater distance than 1/4" to 1/2" from the model. If there are areas where there is a greater separation, these may be filled with special non-sulfur modeling clay, wax, or wood. If the silicone rubber mold is to be used for casting small forms made of non-foaming polyester, epoxy, or urethane resins, it is generally not necessary to have a strong container to hold the silicone rubber. Pieces no larger than 8" in any direction can be placed flat-side down in a cellulose acetate box, which is quickly and easily made from 20-mil or 30-mil thick cellulose acetate. The "box" does not necessarily have to be box-shaped; it is merely a containing support for the silicone rubber

Dura-Vac Vacuum Plastic Plexiglas Dessicator at work. *Photo courtesy Dow Corning Corporation. A very important part of any mold-making process which uses Silastic RTV mold-making rubbers is removing trapped air in the freshly stirred silicone rubber and catalyst mixture. Under 29.5" of mercury, the entrapped air is removed in a few minutes.*

mold to be poured into. For an example of pouring a mold into a unbox-shaped acetate box, see *Casting a portrait head in a cellulose acetate box demonstration.*

MAKING A CELLULOSE ACETATE BOX

See *Cellulose acetate box demonstration* for how to make the cellulose acetate box. An important thing to remember is that such an acetate box requires no release agent for any of the thermosets discussed in this book except urethane coatings, foams, and rubbers.

First draw a contour line roughly on a piece of paper 1/4" to 1/2" larger all around than the actual size of the relief you wish to duplicate. Place a piece of your cellulose acetate, which will be the bottom of your box, over this sketch.

Next, cut a strip of cellulose acetate 1" higher than the highest point of your relief and a length of about 1/2" longer than the contour length. Overlap the cellulose-acetate strip 1/2" (Step 1). Glue this overlap by carefully squirting a few drops of acetone from a syringe needle placed between the acetate ends (Step 2). Pinch and hold these ends together for about 1 minute, after which they will be bonded (Step 3).

Next, place the sides of the box on top of the acetate sheet which is lying on the contour outline. Bend the acetate loop to fit the contour line. If you experience any trouble, a little Scotch tape will temporarily keep the sides in place. Again, with your syringe filled with acetone, move your needle along the inside bottom edge of the box-to-be (Steps 4 and 5). Be careful to apply no more acetone than necessary, or you may distort your box. (An additional helpful bonding solution is a mixture of acetate scrap pieces and acetone which you let soak overnight. Stir occasionally. This solution, which should be "cream-thick," is handy for bonding acetate to acetate where the joints do not actually fit perfectly.) Hold the freshly "acetoned" cellulose acetate strip to the sheet of acetate for about a minute, until the bond is secure (Step 6). See the finished box in Step 7.

MAKING A PLYWOOD BOX

If a more sturdy container is needed to hold the Silastic rubber, a 1/2" to 3/4" plywood box is indicated (see *Plywood box demonstration* and *Casting a frame in a plywood box demonstration*). The best method of making this box, which can easily be dismantled, is to countersink wood screws in the sides which are attached to edges. The inside measurements of the box should be no more than 1/4" to 1/2" greater than the widest dimensions of the model or pattern. If there are very irregular shapes in the form to be duplicated, pieces of wood, wax, or any non-sulphur modeling clay can be attached to any of the sides, the top, or the bottom. This saves expensive silicone rubber and gives a more

balanced mold. Remember to coat all wood parts which will be in contact with the Silastic E or G lightly with petroleum jelly dispersed in methylene chloride.

A plywood top and bottom of your box that unscrews easily is almost essential. The Silastic E, when cured at room temperature, often has a sticky surface where it comes in contact with the air. A cover with bleeder holes 1/16" in diameter will prevent this. Make approximately one hole every 25 square inches. This will give you a mold with a smooth, level, non-sticky bottom.

POURING THE MOLD

You are now ready to cover your piece with Silastic E or G catalyzed rubber (see *Casting a frame in a plywood box demonstration*). To make sure that there are no voids, or air bubbles, in your mold, carefully brush the silicone over the whole surface. If you have areas of deep undercuts you can fill these spaces air-free by forcing in Silastic E or G through a syringe needle with a 30-mil to 40-mil orifice. Once the entire surface is covered with Silastic E or G, slowly pour the silicone-catalyzed rubber on one side of the box over the highest part of your model (Step 1). This allows the silicone rubber to gently flow around the form. Stop pouring Silastic E or G when the model is half covered, in order to let the liquid level out and any air bubbles coming to the surface escape. If there are any air bubbles coming to the surface, these may be broken by flash spraying with acetone from a Preval aerosol spray unit. Continue filling until the silicone rubber slightly overfills the wooden box.

Screw the cover to the sides, allowing excess silicone rubber to ooze through the 1/16" holes (Step 2). If you should decide not to cover your box with wood, be sure that it is level. For non-sticky surfaces, either cover your Silastic E with Saran Wrap or place the box about 2' from an infrared heat lamp. If you use the latter method, the mold will cure more rapidly (see Table of Curing Rates, opposite page).

REMOVING THE MOLD

Once your Silastic E or G mold is thoroughly cured, remove it from the original model. If you are using the technique of wooden box and cover, merely unscrew the bottom (Step 3), remove the original model (Step 4), and you now have your Silastic E or G mold nicely contained in the plywood box. See finished polyester resin casting in Step 5.

If you are planning to cast any urethane foam in your mold, here are a few important hints. You must calculate the exact amount of catalyzed urethane liquid to add. To find out how much you will need, fill your mold with dry 35-mesh sand. Pour this sand into a volume measure. Having ascertained the amount of polyurethane to add, pour in the mixed resin and catalyst. Clamp the cover on firmly and quickly with Quick Acting Jorgenson C-clamps. The cover of the box should be coated with Dow Corning 236 dispersion, which will stick nicely to the wood and will be an excellent release for the urethane foam. Or else tack some polyethylene or other release paper to your cover. According to Dow Corning, polyurethane foams can create pressure as high as 5 lbs. per square foot. Therefore, the box has to be strong.

MAKING MULTIPLE-PIECE MOLDS

Where a complete figure or form duplication is required, the method of making the silicone rubber mold is slightly more complex. A 1/2" plywood box should be made with wood screws. The model to be copied should be studied so that the parting lines of the multiple-part mold will be where the deepest undercuts would or might prevent the mold from separating from the figure. The number of these parting lines will determine whether you have a two-piece, three-piece, or four-piece mold. If possible and convenient, these lines should be marked on your model.

The size of the box should be such that with the form resting on a 1/2" thick slab which reaches the inside walls of the base and temporarily bonded to the base, no side or top of which is closer than 1/4" to 1/2" from any part of the form. Remember to lightly cover all parts of the plywood box which will come in contact with the Silastic E or G with petroleum jelly dispersed in methylene chloride.

Areas of the original form which are to be blocked off in the first pour may be sealed to the walls of the box with non-sulfur modeling clay, such as Permoplast X-33 or Klean Klay 20, or with pattern sheet wax or any other wax such as paraffine, microcrystalline, or beeswax.

Once the Silastic E or G has cured, remove the barriers. Next, along the edge which was in contact with the barriers cut out a few inverted pyramids of Silastic E or G with an X-acto knife or ream out a deep hole 1/4" square with a cork hole borer. Holes of either type will aid in "keying" the adjoining mold piece. Whenever you do not wish the succeeding Silastic E pouring to adhere, including the "keying" holes, be sure to apply the 5%

petroleum jelly solution. Turn and place the box on the proper angles to prepare for the next pouring of Silastic E or G. If necessary, again block off areas not to be covered in this pouring with the same materials indicated above. Continue this procedure until the mold is complete. The bottom of the wooden box and slab on which the model rests is removed and the top screwed back on so that the second pouring can be made.

Once the multiple-piece mold is thoroughly cured (see Table of Curing Rates, p. 155) open the box, remove the model or form, do whatever trimming is necessary, and cut a *sprue* and a *vent* holes in the bottom of the mold. A sprue is a hole cut into the mold so that the resin or other material may be poured through the mold and into the mold chamber. A vent is a hole made to prevent an air lock from developing when the chamber is being filled. The mold should be left in the box to be sure that there is no distortion in the mold chamber.

WHY USE SILASTIC E OR G?

Although I recommend Silastic E or G, there are other Silastics to choose from, namely, A, B, C, D, which are cured with three types of catalysts used in the ratio of 10 parts of base rubber to 1 part catalyst. Catalyst No. 1 cures in 24 hours at room temperature. Catalyst No. 3 is for heat curing and not to be used with Silastic C, which is thixotropic (non-runny); and catalyst No. 4 is for fast cure.

Silastic G came on the market around April 1970. It can be cured in contact with masking tape, wood resins, or organic rubbers which sometimes inhibit Silastic E or other silicone rubbers.

COMPARATIVE DATA TABLE

A look at Dow Corning's comparative data table will show why Silastic E was chosen. Note tensile strength, elongation, tear strength, and linear shrink. (Below) Linear shrinkage for Silastic A, B, C, and D at 300° F. is 10 times the room temperature linear shrinkage given here, or 3% to 5%. The linear shrinkage for Silastic E at 140° F. is 0.3% to 0.5%.

	Color	Viscosity	Durometer Hardness	Tensile Strength	Elongation	Tear Strength	Linear Shrink	Specific Gravity
Silastic A	White	140 Poise	45	400 PSI	180%	15 PPI	0.3-0.5%	1.17
Silastic B	White	300 Poise	60	600 PSI	120%	30 PPI	0.3-0.5%	1.38
Silastic C	Red	12000 Poise	65	650 PSI	180%	40 PPI	0.3-0.5%	1.47
Silastic D	Red	300 Poise	60	600 PSI	100%	30 PPI	0.3-0.5%	1.50
Silastic E	White	1200 Poise	30	700 PSI	400%	90-115 PPI	0.0-0.1%	1.12
Silastic G	Red	1400 Poise	33-35	850 PSI	300-350%	110 PPI	0.6%	1.10

PRESERVING MOLDS

Silicone rubber molds, like all materials, have their weaknesses. There are certain ingredients in urethanes, epoxies, and polyesters which tend to degrade the Silastic rubbers. Rigid urethane foams contain free amines until cured. Likewise, so do the epoxy resins which we use. Polyester resins are generally constituted with about 40% styrene. All of these substances, to varying degrees, attack the silicone rubbers now on the market. There are a number of things which can be done to help preserve molds made of Silastic rubbers:

1. Leave the resins in the molds no longer than necessary.

2. Coat the molds by spraying, brushing, or wiping on release coatings such as Dow Corning 20 Release or the equivalent made by General Electric.

3. Clean the molds periodically to make sure that there is no resin adhering to them.

4. Heat the molds at 550° F. for about an hour to drive off the amines or styrene which might have been absorbed by them. This should be done after each six castings.

NOTES, VARIATIONS, AND CAUTIONS

I have found that epoxy resins deteriorate silicone rubber more quickly than polyester resins do. For this reason, it may be helpful to apply a thin coat of polyester resin to the mold if you wish to use epoxy resins because of their low shrinkage. Naturally, you should let the polyester resin cure out first before pouring in the epoxy.

Molds may be repaired with the use of silicone RTV adhesive/sealants such as Silastic 732. The surface of the mold cannot, however, be repaired this way.

If you plan to pour low-melting alloys such as pewter or Cero-bend into your silicone rubber molds, you will get the best castings, according to the Dow Corning experts, by lightly dusting the mold with graphite. This yields an exit path for the hot gases formed between the mold and the molten metal.

Since silicone molds are so costly, it is well to know that up to 30% of your old molds which are no longer useable can be used again when mixed with freshly catalyzed silicone rubber. To use the old molds, they should first be heated for an hour at 550° F. to drive out the contaminants. Next wash the rubber well with a chlorinated solvent to remove additional foreign matter. You can now grind up your mold, which you first cut into chunks in a meat grinder. If you are going to use reclaimed mold rubber be sure to apply a skin of Silastic RTV and let it cure. After that you can add up to 30% reclaimed Silastic E to your freshly catalyzed Silastic E.

I have reinforced the outside of silicone rubber molds with cheesecloth, Dacron, or fiberglass cloth saturated with silicone rubber adhesive/sealant 732 or Silastic 140 adhesive.

To know how much silicone rubber will be needed to make a mold of a form or model in the box which will contain the pattern, fill this box with fine sand or salt. This will give you the approximate weight of the Silastic rubber required.

Step 1. *Demonstration photos by Robert J. McCauley. With the use of acetone in a syringe, it is very easy to bond pieces of cellulose acetate together by forcing the liquid between the touching surfaces. Acetone and syringes, as shown here, are usually available from a pharmacy.*

Step 2. *Here, acetone is being forced between strips of cellulose acetate.*

Step 3. *Immediately after the application of the acetone, the pieces of acetate are held together for about a minute, after which they are sealed.*

Step 4. *The next step in making the cellulose acetate box, which in this case will be used to contain a silicone mold, is to run the acetone all around the edge of the sides of the acetate strip touching the acetate sheet.*

Step 5. *If the strip has been carefully made, it will contact the acetate sheet at all places and the acetone will easily spread to both surfaces. If there is trouble, a concentrated solution of pieces of acetate dissolved in acetone will help.*

Step 6. *It is wise to hold the freshly "acetoned" cellulose acetate strip to the sheet of acetate for about a minute, until the bond is secure.*

Step 7. *Here is the finished cellulose acetate container. The excess cellulose acetate sheeting is cut off and the silicone RTV rubber is poured into this self-releasing mold container which will hold not only silicones but also polyester and many epoxy resin systems.*

Step 1. *Demonstration by Esther Wertheimer. Photos courtesy of the artist, unless otherwise indicated. Shown here is Esther Wertheimer's modeling-clay head of Professor Irving Layton of McGill University. Only non-sulfur containing clays will not inhibit the curing of the Silastic. Notice that the cellulose acetate "box" is no more than ¼" to ½".*

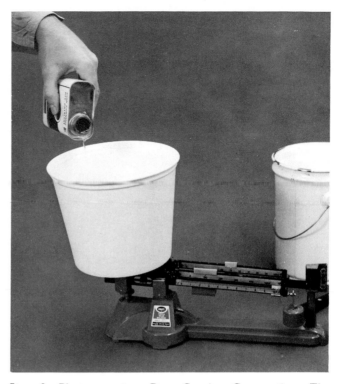

Step 2. *Photo courtesy Dow Corning Corporation. The Silastic E catalyst is here being added to the Silastic E RTV mold-making rubber.*

Step 3. *After carefully weighing out the ingredients and vacuuming out the excess air in the Silastic E silicone rubber mixture, the material is carefully poured 1" above the top of the sculpted head.*

Step 4. *Since heat-accelerated curing cannot be used with modeling clay, the Silastic E is allowed to cure at room temperature for 24 hours. The cellulose acetate "box" is then removed from the silicone rubber.*

Step 5. *The silicone rubber mold is slit down the back, piercing the back of the clay sculpture.*

Step 6. *Here, the clay sculpture is carefully removed from the Silastic E mold. Next, acetone is wiped on the inside of the mold to thoroughly clean out any traces of clay.*

Step 7. *The clean, empty mold is being filled with a slurry of 502/956 epoxy resin system mixed with aluminum powder or bronze powder. Using a vacuum pump helps the artist be certain that there are no air bubbles in the pouring mixture.*

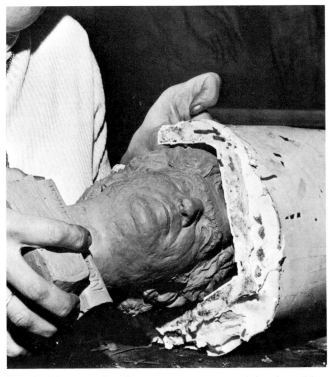

Step 8. *After allowing the epoxy to cure overnight, the rubber bands are removed from the Silastic E mold and the finished epoxy-metal cast sculpture is carefully extracted.*

Step 1. *Demonstration photos courtesy Dow Corning Corporation. One convenient method for containing the Silastic E mold-making rubber while it is being poured is to fabricate a plywood box. The sides can be nailed together lightly, for a small mold, or screwed together for a larger piece. Before the Silastic E is poured, the plywood is lightly covered with a thin coating of petroleum jelly which has been dissolved in a solvent like methylene chloride. This blocks off any dampness in the wood which would inhibit the rubber cure. Here, the Silastic E catalyzed and degassed mixture is being poured.*

Step 2. *After 24 hours at 70 °F. (room temperature) the silicone rubber is cured. The mold is turned upside down, key-in holes have been cut into the silicone rubber to position the next part of the mold to be cast, and the mold is being sprayed with Silastic mold release so that the new pouring will not adhere to the already cast Silastic E.*

Step 3. *More Silastic E catalyzed RTV rubber is being poured over the form to be copied as well as the top of the mold itself. Again, the silicone rubber is left for 24 hours to cure at room temperature. If it is necessary, either this silicone rubber mold casting or the one shown in Step 2 could have been cured at higher temperatures. Should this be done, however, it is essential that the curing take place in a well-circulating air oven so that the heat is evenly distributed.*

Step 4. *The finished molds are shown here. The original form to be accurately copied appears on the left. The copy, or "second original," is on the right. With care, many exact duplicates may be made, using resins such as epoxy, polyester, or polyurethane.*

Casting a frame in a plywood box

Step 1. *Demonstration photos courtesy Dow Corning Corporation. A hand-carved wooden frame is shown lying in a plywood "box" which has been coated with petroleum jelly. The size of the box is ½" larger in every dimension than the frame to be copied. Silastic E, which has been catalyzed, vacuumed, and degassed to remove all entrapped air bubbles, is carefully poured over the frame.*

Step 2. *After adding an additional layer of plywood siding, more Silastic E RTV rubber is added to the point of overflow. The 1" plywood cover, which has ½" vent holes, is being bolted to the box. Notice the silicone rubber bleeding through the holes.*

Step 3. *The Silastic E can either be heat-cured in an hour or more, or room-temperature cured in about 24 hours. Here, the box is being opened for inspection after the silicone rubber is thoroughly cured. This top is then bolted back and the box is turned over on the other side. What was initially the bottom is now removed so that the original frame may be taken out.*

Step 4. *After the polyester resin mixture (in this case, a resin and pecan shell mixture) has been poured into the boxed silicone rubber mold, covered over with the 1" plywood top, and cured out, it is easily removed, as shown in this picture. Notice that the undercuts are no problem with rubber molds.*

Step 5. *There are many ways of finishing such polyester resin frames. Here, a finishing coat of lacquer is being sprayed over the frame. Many sophisticated coatings and finishes have been developed for this ever-expanding field.*

Triologue *by Jacques Schnier, 44" x 33". Photo courtesy of the artist. This foamed polystyrene and fiberglass finished sculpture is spray-coated with acrylic lacquers. Preparations before base and final coats of acrylic are similar to what might be done in an automobile body shop prior to repainting a slightly damaged fender.*

Polyurethane Resins

Polyurethane resins are based on a family of synthetic chemicals which, when mixed together, form a chemical configuration called a *urethane linkage*. This class of synthetic polymers is called *urethanes* or *polyurethanes*. The ones we use start as liquids and are usually two-part systems.

USES

In their cured state, polyurethanes may be used for such varied items as these:

1. Protective coatings (paints), lacquers.

2. Foams, known as urethane foams (solid and flexible).

3. Solid rubber—tires, metal-forming dies, gears, sprockets.

4. Flexible molds for casting epoxies, polyesters, and urethane foams.

5. Adhesives.

A FEW WORDS ABOUT POLYURETHANE RESINS

Although this is not a book on the science of plastics, it is important for the artist, craftsman, or architect to know enough to feel a little "at home" with the new synthetic polymers such as the urethanes. A few technical words may save grief and money when ordering, buying, or specifying materials from the polyurethane family.

The artist and craftsman should be aware that the urethane resins which yellow and lose gloss on exposure to ultraviolet light (sunlight) are called *aromatic* diisocyanates. There are, however, a new group of urethanes now on the market which are called *aliphatic* diisocyanates and cycloaliphatic diisocyanates.

As the 1969-1970 *Modern Plastics Encyclopedia* points out, these newer urethanes not only have the excellent wearing qualities of the conventional polyurethanes, but they also have very good stability to sunlight. Added stability to sunlight, however, can be given to all classes of urethane resins by incorporating ultraviolet light absorbers, which offer limited protection (see Glossary). The science of the polyurethanes is continually improving and so these urethane products will become increasingly important to the painter and sculptor.

Urethanes mentioned in any detail in this book are the two-part rigid urethane foams, urethane "rubbers" for molds, and urethane coatings for painting. In the past, the yellowing property of these urethanes has discouraged me from investigating these polymers in any depth in so far as coatings and paints were concerned. However, there are indications that within a relatively short time the artist and craftsman will be using polyurethane coatings and paints which will be less yellowing than the linseed-oil paints. We should keep our eyes open for developments from companies such as Conap, Inc., Monsanto, Upjohn, and Mobay (a subsidiary of Bayer).

CAUTIONS WHEN USING POLYURETHANE RESINS

The two-part urethane liquid systems which you can mix together on the spot to make foams, molds, coatings, and adhesives have a few cautionary points which should here be mentioned:

1. In the liquid state, urethanes are moisture-sensitive polymers. But once the container is opened, the product will tend to thicken, give off carbon-dioxide gas and lose reactivity unless dry air or nitrogen is put back into the can. Small pressurized cylinders of dry nitrogen are available from such companies as Liquid Carbonic Company. If you are going to do any amount of work with the urethanes, it would be a good idea to keep dry nitrogen on hand.

2. Urethanes sometimes contain small to medium amounts of free diisocyanate (TDI) monomer, which has a pungent odor and may cause breathing discomfort or coughing. According to the American Conference of Governmental Hygienists, a maximum safe threshhold limit of breathing in diisocyanate is 0.02 parts per million. According to Conap, Inc., manufacturers of urethane resins, good ventilation will take care of this. Those polyurethanes which do not have the pungent TDI odor are relatively nontoxic from the breathing angle.

3. *Urethanes should be kept out of contact with the skin.* It is a good idea to apply a protective skin cream to your

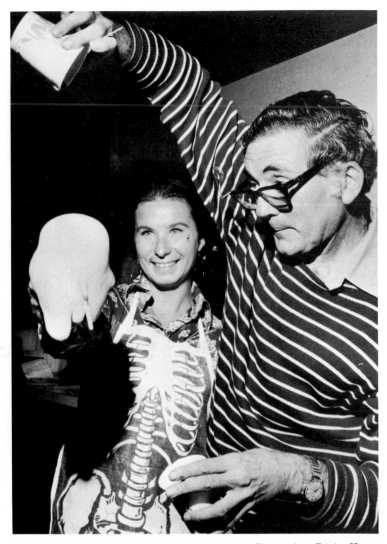

Foam-in-place polyurethane foam. *Photo by Dick Haun. Here, Carolyn LePage helps me demonstrate what happens to foam-in-place polyurethane foam when it's catalyzed. Once the foam has cured and hardened, it can be shaped with an electrical hot-wire cutter or other hand tools.*

hands before starting to work with urethanes. If they get on your hands or body you should wash the soiled areas well with soap and water. For eye contact, be sure to flush with water for 15 minutes. For persistent irritation after washing, see your doctor. If this makes you fearful of using urethanes, remember that you must take the same precautions for household ammonia, lye, or Clorox.

FOAMS

Of particular interest to the artist and craftsman are the urethane foams. The rigid and flexible urethane foams can be described as containing millions of small cells of air or gas evenly trapped in a plastic material formed through the reaction of liquid types of chemicals called *polyols* (alcohols) and *polyisocyanates* in the presence of other chemicals. These other chemicals are the blowing agents, which do the same job as a child does when he blows his soap bubbles. These blowing agents, such as the fluorcarbons and carbon dioxide, which are among the propellants used in aerosol cans, produce the gas which makes the tiny bubbles in the foam. The catalyst, whose function (but not chemistry) is similar to that of the catalyst used for polyester resins, makes the reaction between the polyol and the polyisocyanate go faster. The surfactants, which are related to detergents, control the size of the gas bubbles or cells and they stabilize the rising foam.

The volume of gas in urethane foams can vary from 20 to 80 times the volume of the liquid urethane. Because of this trapped gas, these urethane foams have lightness and floatability. They are strong, can be made fire resistant, and are produced in various densities and flexibilities. They can be readily cut, shaped, and coated with polyester, epoxy, or urethane resins (see Project 23).

CONATHANE UF 3: RIGID URETHANE FOAM

One of the rigid urethane foams which I have recently investigated has been Conathane UF 3. The manufacturer, Conap, Inc., claims that isocyanate compounds such as these give off very few vapors and therefore they are of a minor hazard. Still, they should be used only with adequate ventilation. UF 3, when foamed, is a relatively high-density material of 7.6 lbs. or 7.6 lbs. per cubic foot. The manufacturer claims that UF 3 is unaffected by grease, oils, and most solvents, and is resistant to ozone. Once formed, these foams keep their dimensions—they are dimensionally stable—they do not rot or mildew, and they do not absorb moisture readily.

If you wish to vary the density of UF 3, you may add various proportions of Conathane UR-BA, which is the Conap brand of trichloromonofluoromethane. With this method of adding different amounts of UF-BA, you can get overall densities of from 2.13 lbs. to 7.6 lbs. of foam per cubic foot.

Seashore (*Above*) *by Robert Hunter, 7' x 5' x 8'. Photo courtesy of the artist. This figure was constructed in the following manner: carved polystyrene foam was treated with a barrier coat and then covered with polyester resin and fiberglass. Finishes were of the acrylic type; steel and Plexiglas were also used.*

Sand Wing (*Left*) *by Robert Hunter, 4' 3" x 7' 7". Photo courtesy of the artist. This piece is made from wood, polystyrene, fiberglass and polyester resin, and Plexiglas; the painted finishes are acrylic.*

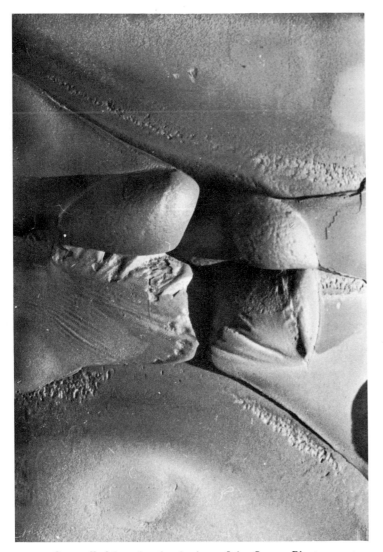

Controlled foaming *by Anthony John Sorce. Photo courtesy of the artist. This sculptor has made a study over the past several years of using polyurethane foams as art forms. Typical of some of the effects is this closeup of one of his controlled foamings.*

Editor's Note: In the projects which follow, expanded polystyrene has been used as an alternative to polyurethane foam because it is less expensive and very readily available to the artist-craftsman. Technically, expanded polystyrene is not in the urethane family; however, when used with epoxies, expanded polystyrene and polyurethane foams are similar in many of their handling properties.

MOLDS

Mold-making polyurethane resins are gaining in popularity because of the high cost of the silicone resins. The urethane two-part mold-making compounds are primarily elastomers or rubbers. They usually have the excellent feature of high tensile strength and high tear strength. Again, these resins are made from polyols and polyisocyanates. They are increasing in the number which are coming on the market. One thing which is generally necessary is to place the freshly stirred mixture of the two-part urethane system under a vacuum to remove air bubbles and moisture. The manufacturer's specifications should be carefully followed. One excellent mold-making polyurethane which I have investigated is TU 75, manufactured by Conap, Inc. The mold made from this mixture was not degassed and yet the results were exceedingly good. Polyurethane mold-making materials are now available with almost any property the artist may require, from transparency to color to hardness to flexibility to elastic strength.

At the present time, polyurethane molds are not self-releasing as are the silicone RTV mold resins such as Silastic E. These urethane molds are made releasing to polyesters, epoxies, and polyurethanes by coating or spraying them lightly with such releasing oils as DC 200 series silicone oils (see Glossary).

COATINGS

The polyurethane coatings which are useful for the painter are almost nonexistent at the moment. Mobay, Monsanto, and USMC, Plastics Division, all are in the process of continually developing urethane coatings. These coatings all contain solvents. What is needed is a 100% resin coating. I have tried TU 75 (Conap, Inc.) as a 100% paint coating on urethane foam. The colors were the same ones used for polyesters and epoxies. Write to the manufacturers if you are interested in such coatings. This may encourage action in research and development of new and better products for the artist and craftsman.

ADHESIVES

One has heard so much about the wonders of the epoxy adhesives. However, there also exists a series of urethane adhesives which have exceptionally high adhesive strength. One, called Conathane AD-1154, was designed for bonding or gluing metals, plastics, and wood to themselves or to each other. The manufacturer claims that this adhesive gives off no monomeric diisocyanate vapors, therefore the possibility of contaminating the work areas with irritating vapors is virtually eliminated.

Homage to a Circle *by Robert Singleton, 68" x 72". Photo courtesy of the artist. The ground for this acrylic painting is Styrofoam which is bonded to canvas. The artist has been working with expanded polystyrene as part of his dimensional canvases for a number of years. Oil paints which are thinned with mineral spirits instead of turpentine also work well on the foamed polystyrene, and will not attack the polystyrene.*

Expanded Polystyrene for Relief Murals

Many painters in the United States are beginning to look for other than two-dimensional surfaces to paint on.

Expanded polystyrene (trade names Styrofoam, Dylite, etc.) may be purchased in almost any size. It can be cut with a hot-wire cutter, an electric knife, or a saw. In addition, it may be burned, or filed, or reshaped merely by pulling out pieces from itself with your fingers. In this way, you can make a relief which can then be covered with epoxy resins, reinforcements, additives, colors, etc. (see *Relief painting demonstration*).

MATERIALS

1. A slab of expanded polystyrene (Styrofoam, Dylite, etc.)

2. Adhesives, such as Elmer's glue, animal glue, Araldite 502/RC 303 adhesive combination, or relatively slow Araldite 502/956 adhesive combination.

3. Araldite epoxy resin 502.

4. Araldite curing agent 956.

5. Additives.

6. A hot-knife cutter (optional).

7. Rasps or files.

8. Any type of saw, including a jeweler's saw for very delicate cuts.

9. Blowtorch (optional).

10. Last, but not least, your fingers!

TRANSFERRING DESIGN TO STYROFOAM

Design on white paper with black pencil, or black paper with white crayon, a simple drawing exactly the size that you wish to interpret in relief.

When the design is finished, place it over a piece of carbon paper on top of the Styrofoam and then transfer the picture to the Styrofoam (Steps 1 and 2).

Cut or shape the Styrofoam in any way you like, using any of the instruments described above for shaping (Step 3). If there are areas or volumes which are to be pushed out or pushed in to form your relief, they should be bonded either with a water-based adhesive such as Elmer's glue, animal glue, or another resin adhesive such

as an Araldite 502/956 combination. These adhesives take more time than the eopoxy resin adhesive 502 mixed in equal proportions with curing agent RC 303. The latter adhesive combination is cured in five minutes; for this reason, only small amounts of the adhesive should be mixed together (Step 5).

After the bonding is completed, the Styrofoam relief can be filed or sanded into its final relief form.

REPAIRS

If there are areas in the course of cutting that are undesirably open, these may be filled with a sealer coat of adhesive combination 502/RC 303. If time is not of great importance, the combination of epoxy resin Araldite 502, 10 parts by weight, and epoxy resin Araldite 956, 2 parts by weight, is very adequate (Step 6). This resin combination can be thickened with Cabosil or Asbestos 244, and it may be filled with talc, clay, or other additives. *You are now ready to paint with epoxy resins.* The following formula is recommended.

EPOXY RESIN PAINT FORMULA

Epoxy resin 502: 100 grams.

Curing agent 956: 20 grams.

Benzoflex 9-88: up to 10 grams may be used for increased flexibility.

ADDITIVES

In addition, any additives may be used which are dry, not oily, and are not plastic materials such as Teflon or cellulose acetate. For colors, use color pastes made for epoxy resins (see Colors section of Appendix). Pigments of any type may be added dry. Thickeners, such as Cabosil or Asbestos 244, may be added to make the epoxy resin non-running.

PAINTING WITH EPOXY RESINS

How one applies these epoxy resins, additives, colors, and reinforcements such as fiberglass to the Styrofoam relief is a matter of personal preference. Cheap brushes, palette knives, coffee sticks, etc., may be used for spreading your resin system over the expanded polystyrene relief mural. It would be wise at the beginning to run a few simple experiments using the 502/956 combination with plain, transparent colors as well as opaque colors. There would be the simple glazes. Next, try adding such additives as beach sand, grog, powdered pumice, gravel, etc. In this way, you will begin to build up experience in what the epoxy resins can do (see finished relief painting in Step 7).

METALIZED AREAS

There are several methods of metalizing with epoxy resins. For painting, however, the most expeditious is to apply the 502/956 in areas which you wish to metalize and then blow metal glitters onto the wet resin. Since the epoxy 502/956 is an excellent adhesive system, the powdered glitters will adhere well. You may also mix large quantities of 300-mesh powdered metals with the 502/956 combination, apply this to your "canvas," let it cure well, and then buff, steel wool, or polish the desired areas.

NOTES, VARIATIONS, AND CAUTIONS

1. *Araldite 502/956 combination should not be allowed to get on the hands*, and, if it does, *wash with soap and water.*

2. Do not use thinners such as xylene, toluene, or methyl ethyl ketone peroxide (MEK-Px), since they dissolve Styrofoam. Reactive diluents such as Epoxide 7 should not be used for the same reason. If a reactive diluent must be used, the only one that I know of at the moment is Mod-Epox, made by Monsanto Chemical Company. Its technical name is tricresyl phosphate (see Interesting Products section of Appendix).

3. Any tools which you wish to continue to use should be washed in lacquer thinner or other solvent for epoxy resins before the resin has cured.

4. If you mix up more than 50 grams of 502/956 at one time and plan to use it over a period of 30 minutes or more, it is recommended that you divide the mixture into amounts of no more than 25 grams each. In this way, you will not run the risk of letting your resins overheat and thus suddenly become hard.

5. If you are going to do a large relief mural using the above technique, it would be very wise to reinforce your Styrofoam with fiberglass cloth. The application of fiberlgass cloth with epoxy resins is covered in Project 7.

6. Remember that since epoxy resins are adhesives, they may be applied over any of your previously done work.

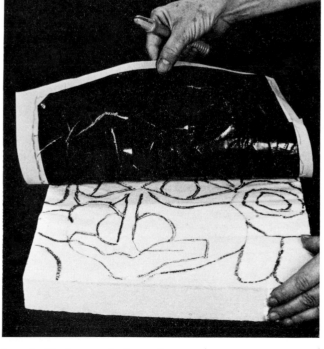

Relief painting (Step 1). *Demonstration by Blanche Plafson. Photos by Robert J. McCauley. A tracing wheel is used on carbon paper to transfer the original design to a piece of expanded polystyrene.*

Step 2. *Having marked up the expanded polystyrene, the carbon paper is removed in preparation for cutting out pieces on a hot-wire cutter.*

Step 3. *A homemade hot-wire cutter is shown being used to cut out the expanded polystyrene pieces; these will then be reassembled and glued into the relief panel.*

Step 4. *Now the cut pieces of expanded polystyrene which are to be glued to the panel are being assembled.*

Step 5. *The following adhesive mixture is used to bond the pieces of expanded polystyrene: 10 grams of epoxy resin 502 and 10 grams of curing agent RC 303. These are mixed well for two minutes and then applied for two or three minutes. After five minutes, the adhesive will be cured. Notice the temporary use of toothpicks to hold the pieces together until the resin has cured out.*

Step 6. *A sealer coat of epoxy resin 502/956 is applied to the piece to keep the Epoxide 7 in the epoxy paint medium from dissolving the expanded polystyrene. In this case, talc plus white and a bit of burnt umber color pastes were added before the epoxy glaze was applied.*

Step 7. *Here is the finished, painted expanded polystyrene relief. The color pastes were thinned with an epoxy medium made up of 85 grams of epoxy resin 502, 15 grams of Epoxide 7, and 20 grams of curing agent 956.*

Expanded Polystyrene Armature for Epoxy-Fiberglass Sculpture

Using expanded polystyrene in the form of Styrofoam or Dylite, you may easily sculpture a form by cutting, sawing, melting, or filing. The foam may then be reinforced with epoxy resin and fiberglass. Following this, you may finish your sculpture with either any combination of epoxy resin and additives or conventional painting materials.

MATERIALS

1. Styrofoam, Dylite, or any expanded polystyrene.

2. Araldite epoxy resin 502.

3. Asbestos 244.

4. Curing agent RC 303 (DPM 3-800 LC and DMP-30 or DION-EH 30).

5. Fiberglass cloth or fiberglass mat.

6. Araldite curing agent 956.

7. Epoxide 7.

8. Additives, depending upon desired effect.

9. Toothpicks and cut-up wire coat hangers.

KEEP IT SIMPLE

As usual, it is suggested that in order to learn with the least amount of problems what is involved in making a piece of sculpture from expanded polystyrene and fiberglass and epoxy resins, do not make anything taller than 18" high by 12" in diameter. Keep it simple. After you have faced the complications of the small form, going to twice the size will often yield some new surprises (see *Covering a Styrofoam armature demonstration*). Unless you are an experienced sculptor, it may pay you to emulate Jacques Schnier and make a "baby" model first. This will use very little Styrofoam and it will give you a chance to get the feel of working with the material. Now for the cutting tools.

CUTTING TOOLS

The electric tools for shaping Dylite or Styrofoam are basically the hot-wire cutter and some form of the soldering iron. The mechanical tools for shaping the Styrofoam, etc. are files, sandpapers, saws, and saw-knives. Don't forget your fingers as another direct tool!

BONDING YOUR "BABY" MODEL

Your "baby" model may temporarily be held together with toothpicks if you are using more than one piece of expanded polystyrene, which from now on will mean either Dylite or Styrofoam. If you wish to glue, however, here is a two-part formula which will last indefinitely, save you a fortune, be easy to make up, and dry in five minutes. The yield is approximately 2 lbs. of adhesive. The proportions are 50/50 resin mixture and curing agent mixture.

EPOXY RESIN ADHESIVE FORMULA

Epoxy resin 502: 400 grams. Warm for 1/2 hour in a coffee can sitting in boiling water. Add

Asbestos 244: 16 grams. Stir well till evenly dispersed (an electric drill with a paint stirrer attached works well). Try not to mix in any more air than necessary.

EPOXY RESIN ADHESIVE CURING AGENT FORMULA

DPM 3-800 LC: 360 grams. Mix well with

DPM-30 or DION-EH 30: 40 grams. Warm to 150° F. in a *well-ventilated area* such as out of doors. Stir well, and evenly mix in

Asbestos 244: 8 grams.

COMMERCIAL ADHESIVE

If you do not wish to make this adhesive up yourself, you may obtain from the suppliers mentioned in this book 1 lb. cans of epoxy resin 502 and RC 303. If the 50/50 mixture is too runny, add about 4% Asbestos 244.

BONDING LARGER SCULPTURE

Having the above adhesive system or some other slower epoxy adhesive available, you are now ready to make your larger piece after you have studied your "baby."

proportions of the epoxy resin and hardener as given above. If you desire lots of texture, use as much Asbestos 244 as is necessary. From 1 to 4 grams will give you a range of textures. If you wish to bulk your resin combination, such additives as talc, kaolin, flint, and sand The gluing, or bonding, is the same as for the "baby." Remember, you are gluing with what might be a 1,000 lb. per square inch tensile strength adhesive. It ought to hold!

Next, *wearing gloves*, cut pieces of fiberglass cloth approximately 1/4" to 1/2" larger than each side. For small pieces of sculpture (1' high at the most), such as you are now making, use one thickness or regular 8 oz. fiberglass cloth or RC 181 airplane cloth, which is more expensive but drapes much more easily. For sculpture which is 2' high, use two thicknesses, for 3' to 4' high pieces, use three thicknesses, and so on.

Now, wearing your gloves for the rest of the fiberglassing operation, mix up the following epoxy resin combination.

EPOXY RESIN COMBINATION FORMULA

Epoxy resin 502: 100 grams.

Curing agent 956: 20 grams.

APPLYING EPOXY RESIN COMBINATION AND FIBERGLASS

Mix well and let stand 10 minutes. Apply a relatively thin coating of the 502/956 combination with brush or roller. Follow this with the proper cut pieces of fiberglass. The excess areas of fiberglass should be draped equally around the sides. Repeat this procedure in such a way that all edges have fiberglass going around them. Apply additional 502/956 all over the fiberglass so that it fills the pores but does not run.

Once your fiberglass is completely covered with epoxy resin combination, let the piece cure. You may hasten things by putting your form no closer than 2' from an infrared heat lamp.

FINISHING

After the 502/956 has cured, you should now file and sand so that you can't feel any fiberglass ridges where there are extra thicknesses. Granted, this is time consuming—but this is where good craftsmanship counts. Once you have your sanding and filing done, you are now ready to coat and color or metalize your piece.

Coating and coloring with 502/956 uses the same

are all cheap and readily available. Colors are the standard color pastes covered and mentioned in this book (see Colors' section of Appendix).

If you wish to finish your piece with acrylic auto-body sprays, sand your piece well. Fill in all imperfections with some sort of crack filler. Then see your friendly family automobile paint man.

If you desire to metalize your sculpture, the following formula will be helpful.

METALIZING FORMULA

Epoxy resin 502: 90 grams.

Epoxide 7: 10 grams (to lower the viscosity).

Curing agent 956: 20 grams.

Asbestos 244: 2 grams (to make the mixture slightly less runny).

METALIZING

Mix well all ingredients and add metal powders of 300-mesh (available from resin suppliers, or see Suppliers and Manufacturers section of Appendix). Add enough powder so the metalized epoxy will not run excessively down the sides of your sculpture. If you have trouble with running, a small amount of aluminum powder added to any of your other metals will help with this problem. For good patinas with such chemicals as liver of sulfur, be sure to have at least 10% copper and/or lead in your metal mixture.

Once you are satisfied with the metal-epoxy application, let the resin cure. Heat from an infrared heat lamp may be used as long as you do not get closer than 2'. When the resin is well cured, your sculpture may then be rubbed with steel wool to remove the excess surface resin. After this treatment, you can then buff and polish your piece (see Project 14 for further information on buffing and polishing).

One other method of metalizing is to lightly brush on a thin coating of 502/956 and then blow on a powdered metal glitter (shiny flakes) of aluminum, brass, copper, etc. Patinas can then be applied using India ink in different colors. These patinas can be sealed in and made permanent with a mat-finish epoxy.

NOTES, VARIATIONS, AND CAUTIONS

Working with fiberglass requires gloves at all times. Remember to have good ventilation. If resin hardener gets on your hands, wash off as soon as possible.

Covering a styrofoam armature

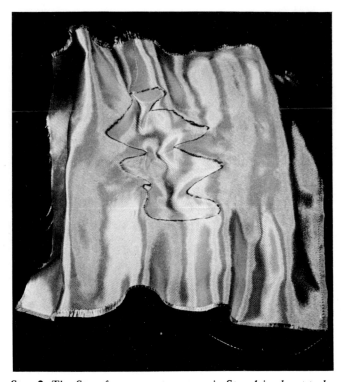

Step 1. *Demonstration photos by Robert J. McCauley. Cutting Styrofoam on the hot-wire cutter presents no real problems. After a little practice any desired shape can be cut. If it is desirable to join pieces together, equal parts of epoxy resin 502 and curing agent RC 303, mixed one minute and applied within three minutes, will bond very adequately in several more minutes. The illustration shows a piece which was cut and bonded with a 502/RC 303 combination. The roller on the left is often available in the kitchen utensil section of any department store. The piece of urethane rubber foam on the right-hand side of the Styrofoam is most useful for spreading an epoxy resin system which, if carefully formulated, may be directly applied over the Styrofoam.*

Step 2. *The Styrofoam armature seen in Step 1 is about to be covered with fiberglass and epoxy resin. The most convenient fiberglass cloth to use is called RC 181 airplane cloth. It is quite expensive, but it is easy to work with since it drapes so easily, and this advantage outweighs the added cost.*

Step 3. *Toothpicks are very helpful when it comes to carefully fitting the fiberglass to the hills and valleys of the Styrofoam. A china marking pencil, lightly used, easily marks the fiberglass.*

Step 4. *In this step, the epoxy resin combination is being applied, using the urethane foam rubber pad. The epoxy resin combination is 100 grams of epoxy resin 502 and 20 grams of curing agent 956. Blue and white pastes and talc were added to this mixture. It is well to let the resin/curing agent mixture stand about 10 minutes before using. This "sweat-in" tends to make the resin combination less moisture sensitive. If you make a large batch, be sure to divide it into about 50-gram units so that there will be less heat build-up. In this way you will lose less resin.*

Step 5. *The epoxy 502/956 combination has been applied over the fiberglass, and any air bubbles which may have been trapped have been squeezed out. The piece is then put under one or more infrared heat lamps, placed at a distance of 1½' from the piece so that the resin does not cure too fast, and so that the Styrofoam does not melt. It is wise to watch the piece carefully while the resin is curing. At a critical point, the resin becomes leather hard and, as can be seen here, certain areas may be easily cut out with a mat knife. If the resin has become too hard, drills, saws, and files may be needed.*

Step 6. *This final picture shows the piece after a white color paste and talc has been mixed with the 502/956. Sanding, filing, and recoating with additional 502/956 and color would help to put a better finish on the piece.*

APPENDIX

Colors for Polyester, Epoxy, Silicones, and Polyurethanes

Over the past 16 years, I have evaluated many pigments and dyestuffs for use with epoxy, polyester, silicone, and urethane polymers. Naturally, it has been impossible to thoroughly test the hundreds of products available. What I have done, however, is to test a few pigments and dyestuffs, which, from the submitted data, appeared to be the most outstanding. If the reader is searching for a complete list of such dyes and pigments, I would like to refer him again to the *Modern Plastics Encyclopedia.*

PIGMENTS

The most convenient, lightfast, essentially transparent pigments to make into non-settling color pastes are the Microlith "T" series of CIBA. These are prepared pigments which can be dispersed quickly in organic solvents, lacquer thinners, and plasticizers such as dibutylphthalate or Benzoflex 9-88 without the necessity of grinding. For example, if 100 grams of Benzoflex 9-88 are heated to 212° F. in a double boiler, 50 grams of any of the Microlith T colors may be stirred in (using a paint stirrer attached to an electric drill) for about 1/2 hour, gradually letting the temperature drop. This dispersion of the Microlith T color will be very stable.

The reason for this stability is the organic resinous carrier in which the pigments are dispersed. The transparency of the Microliths is due to the selection of extremely small, particle-size pigments. However, the main advantage of these pigments is their high lightfastness.

LIGHTFASTNESS OF PIGMENTS

I have tested the following Microlith T pigments dispersed in Benzoflex 9-88 and then mixed with CIBA Araldite epoxy resin 502 and curing agent 956. The proportions of resin to hardener were 100:20. These Microlith pigments in epoxy resin were then exposed for 1000 hours in the Fadeometer at the CIBA Laboratory in Dorval, Quebec, over 10 years ago. Allowing for the slight yellowing which is characteristic of epoxy resins, there was no color change in the following Microlith T pigments which were tested:

Microlith Yellow 2GT

Microlith Red RT

Microlith Blue 4GT

Microlith Green GT

Microlith Black GT

The question usually asked is how many years 1000 hours exposure to the carbon arc or the Fadeometer is equivalent to. Exact answers are impossible, since such testing is only really comparative to another test with a colored resin sample whose actual exposure fastness in the environment which interests us is known. It is correct, however, to say that any pigment which holds up 1000 hours is extremely lightfast.

TRANSPARENCY OF PIGMENTS

Emphasis is on transparent pigments and dyestuffs, because one of the principal esthetic values of the thermosetting polymers is their transparency.

The Microlith Blue 4GT and the Microlith Green GT are essentially as transparent as dyestuffs. The remaining Microliths in the T series are definitely not as transparent as the yellow and red dyes. All the Microliths are intermixable not only with themselves but also with the dyestuffs mentioned further on.

I have had good success using the Microliths with epoxy, polyester, and polyurethane resins. I have not done much with the silicones, but I am investigating certain colors suggested by the Dow Corning Corporation. Hopefully, there will be more to report in a succeeding book.

Color pastes of lightfast transparent and opaque pigments are manufactured by such reliable companies as Ferro Corporation, Color Division 4250, East 56 Street Cleveland, Ohio 44105, Crompton and Knowles Corporation, Plastics Color Division, Somerset Valley Industrial Campus, Somerset, New Jersey 08873, and Interchemical Corporation, 150 Wagraw Road, Hawthorn, New Jersey 07506.

You should, of course, make sure by asking the supplier or manufacturer to assure you of the fastness properties of the pigments or dyestuffs which interest you. (The manufacturers mentioned above will not usually sell less than 1 gallon of any of their color pastes.)

DYESTUFFS

I have use dyestuffs manufactured by BASF Corporation, which has branches both in Canada and the U.S., for many years as colorants for thermosetting plastics such as epoxy, polyurethane, and polyester resins. The particular series which I have used is the Neozapon group of colors, a range of organic metal complex dyes which contain no extender of filler. They have good solubility in organic solvents, liquid epoxy, polyester, and urethane resins.

LIGHTFASTNESS OF DYESTUFFS

With polyester resins of the type which we discuss in this book, the following Neozapons give good to excellent lightfastness according to their manufacturer, BASF Corporation. (The BASF Corporation has a scale of 0 to 8, lowest to best, to describe the fastness properties of its pigments and dyestuffs):

NEOZAPON DYE	LIGHTFASTNESS
Neozapon Yellow R	7
Neozapon Red GE	7 - 8
Neozapon Red BE	7 - 8

Aditional information on pigments and dyestuffs can be obtained from BASF Corporation Specialty Colors and Chemicals Department, P.O. Box 289, Paramus, New Jersey 07650.

The lightfastness of the Neozapon Blue FLE is 5 to 6, while the lightfastness of Neozapon Green 3G is 5. For this reason, I prefer the Microlith T pigments for the blue and green transparencies. These blue and green Microliths are based on metallic phthalocyanines. They mix readily with the Neozapons.

BUYING COLORANTS

Basic manufacturers are not geared to sell small quantities of colorants to interested users. They are usually always willing to send data sheets and suggest a retail outlet. Suppliers, such as Resin Coatings Corporation and Polyproducts Corporation in the U.S., and Waldor Enterprises Ltd., Canada, all carry an excellent line of color pastes, sold in small quantities and at a fair price. See Suppliers and Manufacturers section of Appendix for addresses.

Fire and Health Problems

As has been mentioned over and over in this book, there are a few precautions which, if taken when handling any of the epoxy, polyester, silicone, and urethane resins and polymers in their uncured and curing state, will safeguard the user.

PRECAUTIONS

1. *No physical contact, no skin problems.* Wear gloves if necessary. Protective creams are available. Wear goggles while pouring corrosive materials such as hardeners, catalysts, solvents, etc.

2. *Have good ventilation.* Change the air in your working area at least six times per hour. Keep your distance from uncured urethanes since they contain isocyanates which are hazardous when inhaled.

3. *Wash off any spillage on your skin or into your eyes at once with running water.* If chemicals come in contact with your eyes, wash well for 15 minutes, then seek medical attention.

4. *Remove any contaminated clothing at once.*

5. *Work neatly, carefully, and unhurriedly.*

LIST OF REFERENCE WORKS

Here is a list of reference works on the handling, dangers, etc. of these resins:

1. "Recommendations for Handling Epons (epoxy) Resins and Auxiliary Chemicals in Manufacturing Operations," Shell Chemical Corporation Technical Bulletin sc: 57-15, Shell Chemical Corporation, 50 West 50 Street, New York, N.Y. 10019.

2. "Skin Disorders from Epoxy Systems," CIBA Technical Service Notes TSN 89, CIBA Products Company, 556 Morris Avenue, Summit, New Jersey 07901.

3. "The Physiological Properties of Epon (epoxy) Resins," Industrial Hygiene Bulletin sc: 57-87, Shell Chemical Corporation, 50 West 50 Street, New York, N.Y. 10019.

4. "Skin Sensitivity to Epoxy Compounds," CIBA Technical Service Notes TSN 50, CIBA Products Company, 556 Morris Avenue, Summit, New Jersey 07901.

5. "Epoxies—How to Handle Them Safely," the Society of the Plastics Industry, Inc., 250 Park Avenue, New York, N.Y. 10017.

6. "Toxicity of Epoxy Resin Hardener ZZL-0816 (CIBA 956)," 7/28/1966, Union Carbide Corporation statement from Thomas W. Nale, M.D., Medical Director, Union Carbide Corporation, 270 Park Avenue, New York, N.Y. 10017.

7. "Epoxy Resin Systems," reprinted 1964, Hygienic Guide Series, American Industrial Hygiene Association, 25711 Southfield Road, Southfield, Michigan 48075.

8. "Styrene Monomer," (Styrene is usually 30% to 40% of the average polyester resin; styrene is also the volatile part of the polyester resin), reprinted 1968, Hygienic Guide Series, American Industrial Hygiene Association, 25711 Southfield Road, Southfield, Michigan 48075.

9. "Storage and Handling of Styrene-Type Monomers," Dow Chemical Bulletin Form No. 170-280, The Plastics Coatings and Monomers Department, The Dow Chemical Company, Midland, Michigan 48640.

10. "Report on the Non-Toxicity of Versamid Polyamide Resins," Technical Service Department, Chemical Division, General Mills Corporation, Kankakee, Illinois 60901.

11. "Epoxies—How to Handle Them" and "Recommended Procedures for Safe Use of Formulated Epoxy Compounds." These and other bulletins are available from the Society of the Plastics Industry, Inc., 250 Park Avenue, New York, N.Y. 10001.

12. "The Maximum Allowable Safe Concentration of Noxious Gases and Vapors" as listed in the BASF Plastics Manual, shows how many PPM (parts per million) concentration of vapor in air at 77 F. to which a worker may be repeatedly exposed day after day during an eight-hour work period. Just a few products out of several hundred are noted below. Cast your eye on *turpentine*, which is one of the very common solvents used by painters, and compare it with *styrene*, a common ingredient of polyester resins. The last column, Relative Fire Hazards, has been added by the author (a former

Editorial Assistant for N.F.P.A.—National Fire Protection Association).

SUBSTANCE	PPM	RELATIVE FIRE HAZARDS
Acetone	1000	*Extremely* flammable
Ethyl alcohol	1000	Flammable
Formaldehyde	5	Relatively safe in water solutions
Methyl alcohol	200	Very flammable
Styrene monomer (polyester resin ingredient)	100	Flammable
Turpentine	100	Flammable

Most of the vapors of these solvents or reactive diluents, at certain concentrations and at certain temperatures, when mixed with air in confined areas, can be explosive when subjected to sparks of flame. Therefore, be sure to have *adequate ventilation* when working with *any* solvent, reactive diluent, or substance which gives off hazardous vapors. Changing the air 6 times an hour in a studio or plastics workshop appears to make a safe environment for maintaining safe PPM concentrations of styrene, lacquer thinner (often contains MIBK which is safe at 100 PPM), Cellosolve which is safe at 200 PPM, xylene (xylol) and toluene (toluol), both of which are safe at 200 PPM, and other flammable liquids. This safety precaution is one suggested by safety engineers for the Visual Art Center of Westmount, Montreal, Quebec.

13. "Fire and Explosion Hazards with Resins, Plastics and Monomers," Fire Protection Handbook, 13th Edition, National Fire Protection Association, 60 Batterymarch Street, Boston, Massachusetts 02110. (Note especially Chapter IV, Section 7: Process Hazards—Plastics).

14. "Safety in Handling and Processing Urethane Components" is a one-page summary available from Flexible Products Company, manufacturers of Flexipol urethane compounds. Their address is 1225 Industrial Drive, Marietta, Georgia 30061.

Interesting Products

It is impossible for any book to list all of the materials in such a vast field as plastics which might be of interest or use to the artist-craftsman. Therefore an attempt has been made only to present the reader with some inkling of what is available. Such magazines as *Modern Plastics*, published by McGraw-Hill, will give the searcher more complete information on most related subjects in this area. *Modern Plastics Encyclopedia*, which is published in the fall of each year, is a must for the artist-craftsman who wishes to use the plastic materials of the 70's. If you subscribe to *Modern Plastics Magazine*, you will automatically receive the *Encyclopedia*. The first interesting product which we will discuss, and the most exciting because it is a new discovery, is an "odorless" polyester resin.

ODORLESS POLYESTER RESIN HH 571

A new room-temperature curing polyester resin (still in the development stage) has been discovered which is practically odorless. It has less shrinkage than regular clear casting polyester resins such as the Reichhold's 32-032 mentioned frequently in this book. This new polyester resin, when catalyzed with MEK-Px, cures at room temperature (70° F.) more slowly than the 32-032. When cast in clear 1/8" panels, this resin has a light straw color, while sections 1" thick have a light olive color.

The first breakthrough in a 15-year search for an "odorless" polyester resin came in my Longboat Key, Sarasota, Florida laboratory this past May, 1971. This polyester resin formula, which I call HH 571, contains none of the strong "gaslike" smelling styrene which is the reactive diluent for most of the polyester resins now being used. Development quantities of HH 571 may be purchased from the resin suppliers mentioned in Suppliers and Manufacturers section of Appendix.

CHARACTERISTICS OF ODORLESS POLYESTER RESIN HH 571

1. It has very little odor. What odor there is is faint and fruity.

2. It has much less shrinkage than 32-032, and it works very well as a clear casting resin in silicone or mold-released urethane rubber molds.

3. It can be cast in Plexiglas molds at room temperature. Unlike 32-032, higher temperatures do not work, since at this point HH 571 and Plexiglas (methyl methacrylate) appear to bond to one another. Some post-curing of the resin after removal from the mold may be helpful in making the resin harder if desired.

4. Like 32-032, it is not a good air-dry resin. Air-exposed surfaces should be covered if the resin is to be cured at room temperature. Such materials as cellulose acetate, Mylar, or polyethylene sheet or film may be used to cover exposed resin surfaces. A layer of silicone oil also may be used to cover the resin surface until the resin has cured out.

5. It may be colored, thickened, and filled with the same ingredients which are regularly used with the standard clear casting resins.

6. Although HH 571 cures slowly (approximately 24 hours) at room temperature, it is often helpful to post-cure the resin at 100° F. for three to six hours. Of course it may be heat-cured with infrared heat lamps right after the resin is poured.

7. When 50 grams of HH 571 are catalyzed with 3/4% MEK-Px, it will gel in 1/2 hour at 70° F. With 1/4 % MEK-Px, the resin will gel in about two to three hours.

8. For heavy castings, I have found that a coating of HH 571 catalyzed with 1% MEK-Px should first be applied to the mold-released mold. When the polyester resin has gelled or cured, the next pour-in should contain no more MEK-Px than 1/8% to 1/4%—depending upon the thickness of the casting—in order not to get heat build-up.

9. I have successfully tried HH 571 for casting decorative panels (Project 1), rotational casting in cellulose acetate or Mylar molds (Project 5), and cast sculpture in microcrystalline wax, silicone rubber, or urethane rubber molds (Projects 6 and 21).

10. Since HH 571 contains special ingredients which are not presently included in the run-of-the-mill polyester casting resins, it is about 30% more costly than 32-032.

As HH 571 is a new polyester resin system designed for use in the art and craft area, there is a great deal of information yet to be learned about it. I decided that it was worth the calculated risk to present this resin before it has at least had a year of trial use in the art and craft area, however. To me, it would have been tragic not to let an interested reader in on at least one "hot-off-the-griddle" odorless polyester resin system which can be used in a small apartment without resulting in the user's being evicted by the landlord for inflicting noxious vapors on the neighbors. HH 571 and other resins which will copy it most probably will be added as part of the modern materials used by the artist and craftsman. It is necessary to bear in mind that new HH 571 has a character all its own. To use it successfully, as I am learning to do in my laboratory and workshops, requires curiosity, patience, and organization. HH 571 does not *replace* 32-032. It is, however, an excellent supplement.

EPOXY BIRGHTENERS

MDAC Brightener is an organic chemical which, when added in .01% amounts to 502 epoxy resin systems (for example) tends to remove and lighten yellow casts by supplying, in daylight or ultraviolet light, a bright blue-white fluorescence. Check with the manufacturer for the number of hours of stability in sunlight. MDAC Brightener is made by Carlisle Chemical Works Inc., Advance Division, 500 Jersey Avenue, New Brunswick, New Jersey 08903.

EPOXY CURING AGENTS

IPD and *IMD* are two low-viscosity, colorless, curing agents for epoxy resins which have been tried out with success. They are relatively new products and are being evaluated as curing agents or hardeners for Dow Chemical Company's water-clear epoxy resin DER 332. According to technicians at Dow's plant in Texas, these two chemical products, as well as the Ajicure series of N-001, B-001, etc., are most effective as curing agents for water-clear castings made of epoxy resins. Curing agents IPD and IMD, as well as technical literature, are available through Hugo Stinnes Chemical Company, 415 Madison Avenue, New York, N.Y. 10017. There is a nominal charge for samples.

Menthane diamine is a curing agent manufactured by Rohm and Haas Company of Philadelphia. It cures or hardens epoxy resins very slowly (low exotherm). It has low viscosity and is light in color before and after curing. Methane diamine is blended by Resin Coatings Corporation with two other curing agents and sold as *HH 1065 B*. Information and samples can be directly obtained from Resin Coatings Corporation, 14940 N.W. 23 Court, Opa Locka, Florida 33054.

Jeffamine D-230 and *D-400* are low-viscosity colorless curing agents for epoxy resins. I have investigated them and find them most interesting. Technical literature and samples may be obtained from Jefferson Chemical Company, Inc., P.O. Box 53300, Houston, Texas 77052.

EPOXY FILLERS

Cab-o-lite, or *Wollastonite P-4*, is available for use as a filler in epoxy resins. It provides low viscosity at high loadings, high water resistance, and high electrical insulating properties. Chemically, it is a readily available natural calcium silicate used by many industries as an extender in the paint industry. Cab-o-lite is available from Cabot Corporation, Minerals and Chemicals Division, 125 High Street, Boston, Massachusetts 02110.

EPOXY FLEXIBILIZERS

Benzoffex 9-88 and *dibutyl phthalate* are flexibilizers, or plasticizers, which when used in small quantities of 5% to 10% make epoxy and polyester resins more flexible. Available from the resin suppliers listed in Suppliers and Manufacturers section of Appendix.

EPOXY FLOW-OUT AIDS

Beetle Resin 216-8 is often added in small quantities to epoxy resin systems which contain solvents. It gives coatings a better flow-out, or smoothness. This product is manufactured by American Cyanamid Company, Plastics and Resins Division, 30 Rockefeller Plaza, New York, N. Y. 10020.

EPOXY ACCELERATORS

DMP 3-800 LC is a polymercaptain accelerator and flexibilizer for epoxy resins manufactured by Diamond Shamrock Chemical Co., 300 Union Commerce Building, Cleveland, Ohio 44115 (will send technical literature only). Many of the new five-minute adhesives based on resin/hardener systems are formulated around this most interesting product. A curing agent blend of DPM 3-800 LC and hardener DMP-30 is available from Resin Coatings Corporation, 1490 N.W. 25 Court, Opa Locka, Florida 33054 at a very reasonable price, compared with the nationally advertised products available in the hardware and specialty stores. Resin Coatings Corporation calls this blend RC 303. It is mixed in equal proportions with CIBA Araldite epoxy resin 502. It cures in five minutes, and is a very flexible waterproof adhesive.

DILUENTS

Mod-Epox (triphenyl phosphite) is a reactive low-viscosity epoxy resin diluent which the manufacturer claims has the following major properties and advantages when mixed into the epoxy resin system:

1. It is relatively inexpensive in comparison with other reactive diluents.

2. It accelerates epoxy curing with less curing agent.

3. It gives a better bonding strength to the adhesive.

4. It yields equal or improved physical properties.

5. It has low toxicity.

6. It imparts flame retardency.

Mod-Epox is manufactured by Monsanto Chemical Company, Organic Division, 800 North Lindbergh Boulevard, St. Louis, Missouri 63166. I have found this product to be worth investigation. For other advantages, write for Technical Bulletin O/BL-313.

Epoxide 7 is an epoxy reactive diluent of low viscosity. The manufacturer, Proctor & Gamble, 301 East 6 Street, Cincinnati, Ohio 452002, claims this product to have very low toxicity, high wetting properties, and to be virtually nonvolatile. The reactive diluent BGE (butyl glycidyl ether), which is often used to thin down epoxy resins, is not only toxic but, according to Proctor & Gamble, 10.1% of it evaporates in 24 hours while only 0.41% of Epoxide 7 evaporates during this length of time.

ADHESIVES

Tensol Cement 7 is a two-part acrylic monomer/polymer solution which is cured with a peroxide catalyst. It is an excellent adhesive for Plexiglas (Perspex in U. K.), Lucite, etc. In addition, it may be used for embedding small articles such as color transparencies, collages, etc. It is manufactured by ICI America, Inc., 151 South Street, Stamford, Connecticut 06901.

3M Adhesive EC-2296 is a clear, synthetic, rubber-based adhesive which will not dissolve foamed polystyrene such as Styrofoam or foamed polyurethane. It is reasonably priced and is made available in gallon containers by 3M Company, 135 West 50 Street, New York, N.Y. 10020.

RELEASE AGENTS

1711 Release Agent aerosol spray, made by Contour Chemical Company, 4 Draper Street, Woburn, Massachusetts 01801, is excellent.

Conap S-14, according to the manufacturer, is recommended for removing low-temperature cured epoxy compounds and polyurethanes. It is available from Conap, Inc., 184 West Union Street, Allegheny, New York 14706.

Release Agents for all purposes are available from Ram Chemicals, 210 East Alondry Boulevard, Gardenia, California 90247. The Eastern representative is Allied Resin Corporation, Weymouth Industrial Park, East Weymouth, Massachusetts 02169.

Internal Release Agent Int-54, when added to a polyester resin in amounts of 1/4 gram per 100 grams of resin, gives excellent release from glass. This product, which is manufactured by Axel Plastics Research Laboratories, Inc., 14-41 29 Street, Long Island City, New York 11101, may be purchased from Resin Coatings Corporation, 14940 N.W. 25 Court, Opa Locka, Florida 33054.

Internal Release Agent Int-20-E was developed by Axel Plastics Research Laboratories, Inc. and is available from Resin Coatings Corporation, 14940 N. W. 25 Court, Opa Locka, Florida 33054. When added to CIBA Araldite epoxy resin 502 in the following formula, it gives clear solutions which release quickly and well from glass:

CIBA Araldite epoxy resin 502: 90 grams.

Epoxide 7: 10 grams.

HH 1065 B: 25 grams.

Int-20-E: 0.5 grams.

HH 1065 B, a low-viscosity epoxy resin curing agent, is available from Resin Coatings Corporation. *Int-20-E* is manufactured by Axel Plastics Research Laboratories Inc., 41-14 29 Street, Long Island City, New York 11101. This company makes many other release agents as well. Write for their catalog.

Zelec UN, when used in percentages no greater than 1/4% in polyester resins, prevents such resins as Reichhold's 32-032 from adhering to nonporous smooth surfaces such as glass. Zelec UN is a Dupont product. E. I. Dupont de Nemours and Company, Inc., Polychemicals Department, 1007 Market Street, Wilmington, Delaware 19898.

THICKENING AGENTS

Asbestos 244 is an effective low-cost thickening and thixotropic (non-runny-making) agent for epoxy and polyester resins. Often it gives greater transparency than the usual thixotropic agents, such as Cabosil. Asbestos 244 is a product of Union Carbide Corporation, Asbestos Division, 270 Park Avenue, New York, N. Y. 10017.

Resin grade 144 is also recommended by Union Carbide for use in epoxy systems.

PLASTIC DYE RESISTS

Remyzist is a new improved product for "Plastique," which is the modern way to supplement the use of wax in batik. This product is water soluble at room temperature and may be easily applied by brush to almost any fabric, or squeezed on a silkscreen, as a resist in bleaching and dyeing at temperatures above 150° F. After the bleaching or dyeing, the resist is easily washed off in cold water. Remyzist is available from Resin Coatings Corporation, 14940 N.W. 25 Court, Opa Locka, Florida 33054, either as a water solution or as a faster drying alcohol solution.

COLORANTS AND DECORATIVE ADDITIVES

An excellent powdered brass 1102 (approximately 325-mesh sieve size) is available in minimum quantities of 100 lbs., at approximately $1.50 per lb. plus shipping, from New Jersey Zinc Company, 160 Front Street, New York, N. Y. 10038.

Mearlin Silkwhite, A-Pearl, A-Iridescent Red, A-Brilliant Gold, and *A-Pale Gold* are nacreous, or mother-of-pearl-like, pigments consisting of mica flakes coated with titanium dioxide. They are used in resins and plastics in concentrations from 1% to 4% to give the mother-of-pearl effect. I have used them in epoxy and polyester resins with the desired results. These pigments are available from the Mearl Corporation, 41 East 42 Street, New York, N. Y. 10017.

Mille-fiore glass chips are available from Leo Popper and Sons, 143-147 Franklin Street, New York, N. Y. 10013. These multicolored glass canes have been made for hundreds of years by the Italians. They may be glued into or bonded to epoxy resins.

ULTRAVIOLET LIGHT ABSORBERS

Cyanasorbe UV 9 ultraviolet light absorber is added to polyester and polyurethane resins to improve weatherability and increase the lightfastness of dyes which may have been added to these resins. Available from American Cyanamid Company, Intermediates Department, Bound Brook, New Jersey 08805.

Cyanasorbe UV 207 ultraviolet light absorber is claimed to effectively retard the yellowing and embrittlement of amine and amide-cured epoxy coatings. It is my opinion that this product should therefore increase the light-fastness of dyes added to epoxy resin systems. Available from American Cyanamid Company, Intermediates Department, Bound Brook, New Jersey 08805.

Tinuvin 328 ultraviolet light absorber is one of the latest of CIBA-Geigy's Tinuvin products. It has better solubility than Tinuvin P and, according to the manufacturer, it has superior initial and final color when compared with other ultraviolet light absorbers. An information bulletin is available from CIBA-Geigy Chemical Corporation, Industrial Chemicals Division, Ardsley, New York 10502.

CLAYS

Klean Klay 20 modeling clay (non-drying) can be used for sculpting forms. This product, according to Dow Corning Corporation, will not inhibit the curing of silicone rubber mold-making materials such as Silastic E RTV rubber. The product is manufactured by Art Chemical Products, Inc., 1019 Salamonie Avenue, Huntington, Indiana 46750.

Permoplast X-33, manufactured by American Art Clay Company, Inc., 4717 West 16 Street, Indianapolis, Indiana 46222, has, according to Dow Corning Corporation, the same properties as Klean Klay 20.

WAXES

Microcrystalline Impregnating Wax 1290 Y is a yellow engraving wax for casting epoxy and polyester resins. It can also be used for making one-shot molds (see Project 6). It is manufactured by Sun Oil Company, Industrial Products Department, 1608 Walnut Street, Philadelphia, Pennsylvania 19103. A pamphlet entitled "Customer's Guide to Sunoco Quality Wax Products" is available. Resin Coatings Corporation, Polyproducts Corporation, and Waldor Enterprises Limited have comparable products, (see Suppliers and Manufacturers section of Appendix for addresses).

Ceraplast M is employed for precision casting by the lost wax process. It shrinks 0.70% to 0.75% when solidifying at 68° F. from a temperature of 176° F. It is a very hard wax, and is available from BASF Company, 866 Third Avenue, New York, N.Y. 10017.

MOLD-MAKING AND REINFORCING MATERIALS

Cellulose acetate film and *sheet S-704 GG finish,* available in different mil thicknesses and excellent for making vacuum-formed molds, is manufactured by Celanese Plastics Company, 290 Ferry Street, Newark, New Jersey 07105.

Webril non-woven Dynel fabrics, grades E M 470, M 1410, and *M 1450,* are all thin reinforcing materials (varying in thickness from 1 mil to 5.5 mils) for possible use with epoxy and polyester resins. They are manufactured by the Kendall Company, Fiber Products Division, 95 West Street, Walpole, Massachusetts 02081.

Dacron mesh is available as a reinforcing material for plastics and silicone RTV rubbers through Mohawk Fabric Company, Inc., 96 Guy Park Avenue, Amsterdam, New York 12010.

Supergel is a one-minute mold-making material made from a powdered natural product derived from a form of seaweed. When mixed with cold water, the powder is activated. This mold is self-releasing from polyester resins. When carefully handled, it may be reused approximately six times. Supergel is available from Harry J. Bosworth Company, 531 Plymouth Court, Chicago, Illinois 60605.

Conathane TU 75 can be used to make transparent, room-temperature curing, mold-making and coating materials. This intriguing urethane system will have a great many uses for the artist-craftsman. Write to Resin Coatings Company, 14940 N.W. 25 Court, Opa Locka, Florida 33054 for technical data and samples. TU 75 has been well evaluated in our plastics workshops.

Polyform is a new, reasonably priced, modeling plastic that stays soft until heated to 275° to 300° F. for 15 to 30 minutes. After this treatment, the resinous material becomes permanently hard without shrinking, and can then be treated like wood. Among other things, initial tests indicate that this modeling plastic may be a possible mold-making material for models with undercuts which are not very deep. Polyform is manufactured by Polyform Products Inc., 9420 Byron Street, Schiller Park, Illinois 60176.

SELF-RELEASING REDDI-MOLD HH 871

A new self-releasing, easily formed, non-stick modeling clay-like substance which has recently been developed is now available through the resin suppliers mentioned in Suppliers and Manufacturers section of Appendix. Reddi-Mold HH 871, can be used as a mold-making material which can be formed without heat for small relief castings made of epoxy or polyester resins. For this use, Reddi-Mold is molded around an object which has been sprayed with release agent 1711. HH 871 is immediately and carefully removed, lightly sprayed with release agent 1711 and either an epoxy or polyester resin system is poured into this mold. When the resin has cured, it is removed from the Reddi-Mold, which can then be remolded. Since Reddi-Mold is self-releasing, it has many uses, such as gasketing or blocking out certain areas from contact with polyester or epoxy resins.

POLYURETHANES

Isoderm System CPR 1900, 1909, 1914, 1915, and 1917 are all variations of flexible, self-skinning, two-part urethane foams. They are manufactured by the Upjohn Company, CPR Division, 555 Alaska Avenue, Torrence, California 90503.

Artfoam is a designated name of rigid urethane foam blocks or slabs which are being used as a sculpture material which requires no special tools. These are available from Artfoam, 16 Arcadia Road, Old Greenwich, Connecticut 06870.

POLYURETHANE PROTECTIVE FINISHES

Conathane PA-1162, one of many Conap, Inc. polyurethane products, is a single-component polyurethane coating designed as a sealer and finish for concrete floors and wood surfaces. Write for the bulletin on Conathane PA-1162 from Conap, Inc., 184 East Union Street, Allegheny, New York 14706.

Bostic Floor Finish Mark I and *Mark II* are tough, two-part abrasion-resistant polyurethane finishes for the protection of wood, concrete, and composition board. They are manufactured by UPCO, a division of USM Corporation, 140 Federal Street, Cambridge, Massachusetts 02107.

TRANSPARENT PLASTIC SHEETS

Contact brand invisible transparent plastic sheet can be used for lifting or transferring pictures or type printed on clay-coated paper. Apply it to picture or type and rub on firmly. Cold water will remove the clay-coated paper from the transferred ink. This product is manufactured by United Merchants and Manufacturers, Inc., 1407 Broadway, New York, N. Y. 10018.

BUFFING AND POLISHING MATERIALS

Four different buffing compounds—black emery, red rouge, white rouge, and brown tripoly—are available in 3 oz. bars from Sears Roebuck. These work well for machine buffing of plastics.

Buffing wheels for buffing plastics are available from Barker Brothers, Inc., 1666 Summerfield Street, Brooklyn, New York 11227. Write for their catalog.

FOR THE PAINTER

Rhoplex AC-388, according to Rohm and Haas Company, is a new 100% acrylic emulsion polymer medium, similar to, but an improvement upon, the well-established AC-34 which, I have been led to believe, is the base for many of the polymer media available in the art supply stores. Artists eager to save money can buy this product by the 55-gallon drum directly from Rohm and Haas Company, Independence Mall West, Philadelphia, Pennsylvania 19105. It can be purchased by the gallon from certain distributors of Rohm and Haas products. AC-388 and AC-34 have been used by Dennis Jones of Sir George Williams University, Montreal, and by myself with good initial success. Universal colors, such as those which are now readily available in the paint stores, can be used to color the medium. Write to Rohm and Haas for their bulletin available for artists on the use of acrylics in art called

"Acrylic Paints for the Fine Arts," *Resin Review*, 1966, Vol. XVI, No. 3.

Lucite 44, an n-butyl methacrylate polymer which can be made into a 43.0% solution in toluene, has been used for many years as a protective non-yellowing glaze over oil paints by Gabor Peterdi, professor of print-making at Yale University. This product is available through E. I. Dupont de Nemours and Company, Inc., Polychemicals Department, 1007 Market Street, Wilmington, Delaware 19898.

WORKSHOP EQUIPMENT

Gyro-Plastic Mixers were designed especially for blending liquid resins and hardeners. They work well and have been tried by quite a number of my students. They are available through PSH Industries, 3713 Grand Boulevard, Brookfield, Illinois 60513.

Hot air heat guns are available through Master Appliance Corporation, 1745 Flette Avenue, P. O. Box 545, Racine, Wisconsin 53403. These are useful for local heat curing or gelling of resins or silicone RTV rubbers. The price is approximately $55.00.

For degassing such materials as catalyzed and freshly mixed Silastic E RTV rubber or TU 75 urethane rubber, Ace Glass, Inc., 1430 N. W. Boulevard Vineland, New Jersey 08360, makes a two-part Plexiglas globelike chamber which easily hooks up to a vacuum pump. The price of this equipment is about $52.50.

Suppliers and Manufacturers

In this section on resin suppliers, and resin, curing agent, and additive manufacturers, no effort has been made to cover as many companies as possible. In my opinion, this is unnecessary and time consuming for the reader. For complete information on resin manufacturers, etc., consult *Modern Plastics Encyclopedia*, which is available through McGraw-Hill, Inc., New York, as part of the subscription to *Modern Plastics Magazine*.

Companies are mentioned here whose products have been evaluated either by me or by my students. By and large, these are the products which are described in the projects in this book. Implied whenever a particular product is mentioned is the possible use of an equivalent material. No manufacturer has subsidized this book.

RESIN SUPPLIERS IN THE U.S.

A good rule to follow as far as this book is concerned is to contact only one of the three resin suppliers who carry just about everything mentioned. Sometimes they may not have the exact product asked for, but they will have, or will be able to obtain, a comparable substitute.

Resin Coatings Corporation
14940 N.W. 25 Court
Opa Locka, Florida 33054
(305) 685-5751

Polyproducts Corporation
Order Department, Room 25
13810 Nelson Avenue
Detroit, Michigan 48227
(313) 931-1088

RESIN SUPPLIERS IN CANADA

Waldor Enterprises Limited (Division of Ren Plastics, Inc.)

Montreal area:
131 Hymus Blvd.
Montreal 730, Quebec
(514) 695-7914

Toronto area:
2580 Wharton Glen Avenue
Mississauga, Ontario
(416) 277-2303

LIST OF MANUFACTURERS

It is with great hesitation that the following list of manufacturers is presented in this book. The reader is generally *implored not to write for small quantities or for samples* from these manufacturers of basic resins or additives. These companies, however, are happy to send any technical information desired and they may suggest where samples may be obtained. Professional chemists do often obtain evaluation samples. This is one of the reasons why it was possible to write a book such as this.

Ace Glass, Inc. 1430 N.W. Boulevard, Vineland, New Jersey 08360, makes an unbreakable, transparent, two-piece, Plexiglas vacuum chamber and dryer, available in two sizes having inside diameters of either 10" or 6 3/8".

Ajinomoto Company, Inc., 747 Fifth Avenue, New York, N.Y. 10022, makes Ajicure C-001, C-002, B-001, B-002, N-001, and N-002. These are epoxy curing agents which, according to the manufacturer, are relatively nontoxic, give colorless and transparent resins which do not turn brown, and have small cure strain and shrinkage. Furthermore, the Ajinomoto Company adds that Ajicure has excellent adhesive, electrical, mechanical, chemical, and weathering properties. This series of curing agents can cure resins in the presence of water and they do not require exact amounts of material to be used, as in conventional hardeners.

Ashland Chemical Company, a division of Ashland Oil and Refining Company, 8 East Long Street, Box 2219, Columbus, Ohio 43216, makes a series of Aroflint polyester and epoxy systems which, according the manufacturer, have good color and color retention, very little odor, outstanding initial gloss and gloss retention, durability to heat, water, and chemicals, and excellent resistance to wear. Although they are not discussed in this book, I have evaluated some of these products, such as the Aroflint 505 system which is made up of polyester resin 202 and epoxy resin 303. These products must be modified by the artist in order to be usable. They appear to be very interesting as painting materials in instances where solvents can be tolerated and shrinkage is not important. Write to Ashland for their brochure and a distributor of their products.

Canadian Johns-Manville Asbestos Limited, P. O. Box 1500, Asbestos, Quebec, Canada, has several pieces of literature on fiber grades 7 TFL, Plastibest 20, and Plastibest 30. These products are most interesting as fiber reinforcements for polyester and epoxy resins.

Celanese Coatings Company, 443 East Paces Ferry Road, N.E., Atlanta, Georgia 30305, manufactures a line of epoxy resins and hardeners which are generally comparable to CIBA Araldite epoxy resins.

Chemical Products Corporation, King Phillips Road, East Providence, Rhode Island 02914, manufactures Chem-o-sol, which is a clear heat-cured one-part vinyl-like mold-making material. I have evaluated it, and it is most useful for making molds of models which can be exposed to temperatures of 300° F. to 350° F. One big advantage is its lack of moisture sensitivity; also, it does not require degassing before use. Write for catalogs on this product as well as other interesting items.

CIBA-Geigy Products Company, 556 Morris Avenue, Summit, New Jersey 07901, manufactures a complete line of Araldite epoxy resins and curing agents. Although CIBA-Geigy will not sell in less than drum lots, they will be pleased to supply certain pieces of technical literature on epoxies and epoxy curing agents.

Conap, Inc., East Union Street, Allegheny, New York 14706, makes urethane polymers, resins, and elastomers. My students and I have evaluated many of these products with good results. Among those materials tested, the following are of special interest:

TU-75: a two-part urethane rubber mold-making material which is transparent, less flexible than TU-60, easy to use, and not very moisture sensitive. It is an excellent coating material on wood or metal.

CE-1155: a solvent-based polyurethane coating system. Its cured film is hard, tough, and abrasion resistant. It adheres well to clean, dry, oil-free surfaces.

Additional information is available from Conap, Inc.

Diamond Shamrock Chemical Company, Resinous Products Division, 300 Union Commerce Building, Cleveland, Ohio 44115, manufactures the following polymer products of great interest to the artist and craftsman:

Dion 6912: a water-clear all-purpose polyester casting resin which can be used in all of the projects in this book where polyester resins are mentioned.

Nopcofoam HI 112: a high density, 30 lb. per cubic foot, urethane foam, easily made by adding part A to part B, mixing well, and pouring into a mold.

DPM-1002: an elastomeric polymer which can be formulated into a two-part system for making flexible molds.

DPM 3-800-LC: a polymercaptain accelerator and flexibilizer which is added to curing agents such as DION EH-30 (similar to DMP-30) to make curing agent

blends which cure epoxy resins rapidly in five to 30 minutes.

I spent several days in Diamond Shamrock Laboratory in Painsville, Ohio, investigating and confirming observations made over the past several years.

Dow Chemical Company of Midland, Michigan (New York office, 45 Rockefeller Plaza, New York, N.Y. 10020), makes a myriad of polymers, plastics, and resins. Of particular interest in the context of this book are the Dow Chemical epoxy resins. Especially noteworthy is the epoxy resin DER 332, which is water-clear, colorless, and of medium viscosity. There are very few epoxy resins made with such purity. Water-clear colorless curing agents such as the Ajicure series, the Jeffamine series, and IPD and TMD are essential if one is searching for water-clear colorless epoxy resin castings and coatings. Remember that, as far as is known at present, all epoxy resin systems yellow eventually.

Durez Plastic Division, Hooker Electrochemical Company, Walk Road, North Tonawanda, New York 14120, manufacture and supply fire-resistant Hetron polyester resins.

Edmond Scientific Company, 101 East Glouster Pike, Barrington, New Jersey 08807, according to many of my students, has the most intriguing plastic items, which can be used with the resins discussed in this book. Write for their catalog.

Hugo Stinnes Chemical Company, 415 Madison Avenue, New York, N. Y. 10017, handles two very interesting colorless epoxy resin curing agents: IPD and IMD. Good literature is available, as well as samples (available at a packing charge of $5.00). These also have been evaluated with Dow Chemical's DER 332.

Jefferson Chemical Company, Inc., 3336 Richmond Avenue, P.O. Box 533000, Houston, Texas 77052, makes a series of colorless epoxy resin curing agents called Jeffamine Polyoxypropyleneamines. Jeffamine D-230 and D-400 are two which I investigated for use with Dow Chemical's water-clear epoxy resin DER 332. Good bulletins are available for these products.

Koppers Company, Tar and Chemical Division, Pittsburg, Pennsylvania 15219, makes Koplac 108-3 water-clear polyester casting resin, which I have evaluated with success.

Micro-Surface Finishing Products, Inc., P.O. Box 481, Wilton Junction, Iowa 52779, makes Polysand Kit TR-34. I have had excellent results with this sanding kit in polishing and restoring acrylic, epoxy, and polyester surfaces to mirrorlike finishes. Polysand Kit TR-34 contains a series of graded, cushioned, abrasive cloths from 2400 grit to 8000 grit.

Reichhold Chemical Company, RCI Building, White Plains, New York 10602, manufactures Epotuf epoxy resins and hardeners, a complete line of products similar to the epoxies manufactured by the other manufacturers listed in this section. They also manufacture Polylite polyester resins. The Polylites mentioned in this book are 32-032, 32-180, and 32-738. The last mentioned is a rigid, clear, air-drying polymer which cures to a hard, tack-free, glossy surface. I have used it successfully. Write to Reichhold for the many technical bulletins which are available from them.

Rohm and Haas Company, Independence Mall West, Philadelphia, Pennsylvania 19105, manufactures P-444 and P-444 A acrylic polyester resins. These products are considered by many experts to be the most outdoor-stable polyester resins now available. Among the other products manufactured by this company are:
DMP 30 and the slower DMP 10 curing agents for epoxies.
Rhoplex AC-20, AC-33, AC-34, and AC-388, which are all 100% acrylic emulsion polymer extensively used in making up the now well-known polymer mediums used by artists. Technical bulletins are available from Rohm and Haas, but only drums may be purchased directly from them; quarts and gallons may be requested from Resin Coatings Corporation.

Shell Chemical Company, Plastics and Resins Division, 113 West 52 Street, New York, N. Y. 10019, and Shell Oil Company of Canada Limited, Montreal, Quebec, Canada, make Epon epoxy resins and curing agents.

Union Carbide Corporation, 270 Park Avenue, New York, N.Y. 10017, and Union Carbide Limited, Montreal, Quebec, Canada, makes a series of epoxy resins and hardeners, or curing agents, under the Bakelite trademark. Information is available from Union Carbide Corporation.

Upjohn Company, CPR Division, 555 Alaska Avenue, Torrence, California 90503 makes CPR 2117, a two-part system which forms a polyether-based polyurethane rubber for making urethane-rubber molds. It has high tensile and tear strength, low viscosity; a 1" thick casting cures in about 30 minutes at room temperature. With silicone mold-release agents applied to the urethane molds, both epoxy and polyester resins were accurately cast and easily released after cure. Upjohn also makes a flexible two-part urethane foam system as well as many other polyurethane foam products. It is well worth writing for their literature.

Velsicol Chemical Corporation, 341 East Ohio Street, Chicago, Illinois 60611, manufactures Benzoflex 9-88, the flexibilizer which is mentioned time and again in this book in connection with making polyester resin 32-032 less brittle. Technical information is available on this most interesting product.

Vistron Corporation, Silmar Division, 12335 Van Ness Avenue, Hawthorn, California 90250, makes S-40, a water-clear polyester casting resin which appears to give comparable results to those of other water-clear polyester casting resins which I have evaluated.

Glossary

"A" stage. A designation used to describe the beginning reaction in the curing of a thermosetting resin system. The evolving product is not thermosetting; it is soluble in certain solvents, and its three-dimensional molecular network is not yet formed.

Accelerator. A compound, or mixture, which makes a chemical reaction proceed more quickly. In polyester resin systems, cobalt naphthenate hastens the decomposition of the MEK-Px, initiating the polymerization of the polyester-styrene molecules.

Acetate. Shortened term for cellulose acetate, the principal ingredient in one of the tough thermoplastics generally used in the form of sheets or in ribbons of transparent tapes.

Acetate sheet. Shortened term for cellulose acetate sheet, a self-releasing plastic sheet for use with epoxy, polyester, and silicone resins. Polyurethanes do adhere to cellulose acetate sheets or tapes.

Acetone. A very effective organic chemical, used as a solvent for all the uncured thermosetting resins mentioned in this book. It is highly flammable and should be used with adequate ventilation.

Acidic. One of the terms used to describe how a chemical behaves in the presence of water. For example, wine vinegar, which contains a chemical called acetic acid, is acidic.

Acrylic. Designates a thermoplastic, synthetic resin such as Plexiglas (Perspex in U.K.), Lucite, and Acryloid. These are trade names for polymethyl methacrylate. The two most important starting chemicals are called methyl acrylate and methyl methacrylate monomers.

Acrylic latex or polymer. An emulsion or fine dispersion of tiny acrylic resin globules suspended in water and other water-soluble materials. When the water evaporates, the acrylic globules flow into one another and form a film.

Additives. A term used in this book to generally denote any dry and non-oily substance which can be added to any of the liquid resins which have been discussed.

Adhesive. A material which, when placed between two substances, bonds, glues, or adheres one of these substances to the other. The making of a good adhesive involves much chemistry and physics.

Ajicure. The trademark of the Ajinomoto Company, which manufactures the epoxy curing agents C-001, C-002, B-001, B-002, N-001, and N-002.

Alkaline. One of the terms used to describe how a chemical behaves in the presence of water. Baking soda (bicarbonate of soda) is mildly alkaline. It is used to neutralize or react with acidic substances.

Alkyd. A name for the combination of alcohols with an acid. It is often used in the paint industry to describe polyester resins which are modified with such oils as fatty acids and vegetable oils to produce coatings.

Amide curing agent or hardener. A series of curing agents or hardeners for epoxy resins which are also flexibilizers or plasticizers. They are usually less toxic than the amine curing agents.

Amine curing agent or hardener. These curing agents for epoxy resins are based on the presence of nitrogen and usually have an odor similar to that of ammonia. They are generally very caustic and should be washed off immediately with soap and water if they come in contact with the skin. For eye contamination, wash your eyes for 15 minutes in running water and then see a doctor.

Araldite curing agent 840, 965, or General Mills curing agent 140. Polyamide curing agents for epoxy resins; they are considered to be nontoxic. They are also plasticizing or flexibilizing agents.

Araldite. A trademark of the CIBA Company, used to designate their epoxy resins.

Aromatic isocyante. This group of chemicals is part of the urethane resin system. When these materials react with substances called polyols, they produce urethane resins or elastomers (rubbers).

Asbestos 244. This product, manufactured by Union Carbide, is called Calidria resin grade 244 Asbestos. It is a modified asbestos fiber developed for maximum thickening efficiency and thixotropy for certain resins, such as polyester and epoxy.

Asbestos fibers. Plastibest 20, 30, and 7-FT-1 are asbestos fibers manufactured by Canadian Asbestos Company Limited for use as a reinforcement with polyester or epoxy resins. These fibers may be mixed in the resin instead of fiberglass.

Assemblage. The fitting together of a group of items.

"B" stage. The second stage in the curing of a thermosetting resin; at this stage, when the resin comes in contact with certain liquids, it will not completely dissolve, but it will swell. The spatial three-dimensional molecular network is partially formed at this "B" stage.

B-001, B-002, and N-001. A curing agent or hardener for epoxy resins developed by the Ajinomoto Company. It is claimed to be nontoxic and non-yellowing when compared with the usual curing agents for epoxy resins. B-001 also yields colorless products.

Batik. A method of applying wax resist to textiles which are then dyed at temperatures which will not melt the wax.

Beetle resin 216-8. A product often used in the formulation of resinous paint in order to obtain more even coatings.

Benzoflex 9-88. The principal plasticizer or flexibilizing agent used and mentioned in this book. It is manufactured by the Velsicol Corporation and is available from the special suppliers cited in this book.

Bonding. Another word for adhering or gluing.

Bostic floor finish Mark I and II. Polyurethane or urethane coatings which have a high gloss, are very abrasive, and strong. Manufactured by the UPCO division of the USM Corporation. Excellent for wood.

"C" stage. The final stage in curing a thermosetting resin. The three-dimensional network of the molecular polymerization is complete; the polymer will not melt and does not dissolve in the usual lacquer thinner solvents.

Cabosil. A tradename for a special grade of silica sand or silicon dioxide. The product is so finely divided that one gram is supposed to have about 200 square feet of area. Cabosil is used as a thixotropic, or thickening, agent in epoxy, polyester, urethane, and silicone resins.

Canvas stretcher. A set of convenient wood framing pieces which fit together to make a frame for stretching the canvas, silk, or polyvinyl alcohol (PVA) or Mylar film which is used for casting polyester or epoxy resins.

Casting plaster. *See* Plaster of Paris.

Casting resins. Designates such resins as polyester or epoxy which are clear and colorless and are poured into molds which are either self-releasing or to which release agents are added. 32-032 is a polyester casting resin; DER 332 is an epoxy casting resin.

Catalyst. In resins such as polyesters, epoxies, urethanes, and silicones, a catalyst is a material used in small quantities to initiate or speed up the polymerization process. In these reactions, the catalyst is either destroyed or in some way combined with the cured resin system.

Caustic. A term used to describe very alkaline substances such as lye, and epoxy curing agents such as 951 (DETA, manufactured by CIBA). Caustic substances such as these are very dangerous to the eyes. Goggles should be worn when using them. If you do get these substances in your eyes, flush them with running water for 15 minutes and consult a physician.

Cellulose acetate. An acetic acid ester of cellulose which comes from cotton linters. When certain flexibilizers are added, a strong transparent thermoplastic film is produced. Available in various mil thicknesses from 1 mil to 50 mils; easily bonded to itself with acetone.

Centipoise. A convenient term which is used to describe viscosity. Water at room temperature is considered to have a viscosity of 1 centipoise; SAE 10 motor oil is 100 centipoises, and molasses is 100,000 centipoises.

Cero-bend. Tradename for a series of low-melting alloys related to pewter. Some of these alloys melt at temperatures as low as 150° F.

Chemical reaction (plastics). All of the liquid thermosetting resins discussed in this book are converted to solids through the addition of catalysts or curing agents (hardeners) which chemically react to form new polymeric compounds.

Chemical resistance. Chemical resistance should be considered by the artist-craftsman when he is selling to the public. A resin, or plastic, is considered to be chemically resistant to a material such as water, smog, fruit juice, etc., if optical and physical properties (appearance, weight, strength) are unchanged after the plastic has been exposed to these "chemicals" for a reasonable length of time.

Chlorinated rubber paint. A synthetic rubber paint product which contains the chlorine atom. A highly weather-resistant coating.

Chlorinated solvents. A series of nonflammable solvents which, although they do not burn, are relatively toxic when inhaled. Among the most toxic is carbon tetrachloride, and among the least toxic are perchlorethylene, methylene chloride, and ethylene dichloride, which are solution adhesives for acrylic sheets such as Plexiglas, Lucite, etc.

Clay-coated paper. A paper which has been treated with clay in its manufacture. Lifts or transfers of printing inks can be successfully accomplished when they are taken from clay-coated paper. It is easy to recognize this type of paper by wetting your finger and rubbing off the white clay. *Newsweek* and *Time* are printed on such paper.

Cloissoné. According to Webster, this term means, "inlaid between partitions."

Cobalt naphthonate. One of the principal accelerators used in polyester resins to activate the peroxide catalyst to the point where it gives up its nascent, or freshly produced, oxygen. This oxygen initiates the polymeric chain reaction.

Collage. A term which describes the gluing or bonding together of the same or different materials.

Color pastes. Concentrated dispersions of pigments or dyes in a non-drying vehicle. This paste must also be soluble in the resin to be colored.

Compound. A distinct substance formed through the reaction of two or more elements with each other. A mixture is a thoroughly comingled complex of two or more compounds, each of which still retains its own identity.

Curing agent. A term used to describe a chemical compound or mixture which, when added to a thermosetting resin, converts the resin to an infusible non-solvent, soluble plastic. In this book, curing agent and hardener are synonomous and are used in epoxy resin systems.

Curing agent 956. This curing agent for epoxy resins was developed by the Union Carbide Corporation under the name of ZZL 0816 and was promoted by CIBA as CIBA Araldite curing agent 956. I have used this safety hardener for over 10 years with no failures. It is still very important not to let this product get on your hands, since it is possible to become allergic to it.

Dacron fabric. A synthetic resin fiber which is relatively strong and very chemical resistant. It is used as a reinforcing material in such resins as polyesters and silicone rubbers. Mylar sheet is related to Dacron fiber.

DC 200 silicone oils. A series of exotic synthetic oils manufactured by the Dow Corning Corporation. These oils are based upon silicon, a non-metallic element which is similar to carbon, the basic element of the organic compounds studied in organic chemistry. These silicone oils of varying viscosities are excellent mold-releasing substances, barrier creams, and low-temperature lubricants.

DER 332. The numerical designation of Dow epoxy resin which is a pure, water-clear epoxy resin. It is so pure that it is easily crystallized at room temperature. These crystals are dissolved by gently warming the resin until the crystals dissolve.

Dermatitis. A term used in this book to designate skin allergies which can be caused by contact with any of the snythetic resins or polymers discussed in the book. A good rule to remember when handling these resins and curing agents is: no physical contact = no dermatitis. The allergy is usually similar to the reaction to poison ivy.

Dibutylphthalate. One of the main plasticizers or flexibilizers used in the resin and plastic industry.

Although it is not chemically combined with the resin, it does not easily bleed out, or migrate. Araldite epoxy resin 502 contains 17% by weight dibutylphthalate, which makes the resin non-brittle.

DMP-10, DMP-30 (Dion EH 10, Dion EH 30). Many years ago Rohm and Haas developed these two epoxy resin curing agents. They are also used to cure other types of synthetic polymers called polymercaptains and thiokols. Diamond Shamrock Corporation now manufactures the same chemicals under the tradenames Dion EH 10 and Dion EH 30. In both instances, the "10" is a much slower curing agent than the "30."

DPM 3-800 LC. A polymercaptain or organic chemical which contains sulfur. It has the interesting property of acting as an accelerator in the curing or hardening of epoxy resins when it is mixed with a curing agent for epoxies. This product is manufactured by the Diamond Shamrock Corporation.

Dylite. The tradename used by the Koppers Corporation for their expanded polystyrene sheets or blocks. It has a different texture from that of Styrofoam. And for the artist-craftsman it has quite different physical and chemical properties, as well. Dylite makes excellent armatures and also excellent molds for casting materials such as cement and plaster.

EC 2296 M 3M. This product, manufactured by the 3-M Company, was developed as a contact adhesive for Styrofoam or Dylite. It will not dissolve the expanded or foamed polystyrene as will most of the organic solvents such as lacquer thinner, xylene, or acetone. *See also* RC 303.

Elastomer. A rubberlike natural or synthetic product which when physically stretched returns to its original shape and strength.

Embossing. The process which produces a relief from a surface by pushing up the surface or by adding to the surface by adhering other substances.

Emulsion. The suspension of fine particles or globules of one liquid in another. There are two general types of emulsions: in one type, water droplets are dispersed in oils (mayonnaise, for example); in the other type, which are water soluble, substances are dispersed in water (acrylic polymer latexes or mediums, for example).

"Enamel." Used in this book, "enamel" has the meaning of a clear, translucent coating or an opaque, vitreous-like coating (thin or heavy) on such materials as wood, stone, metal, or plastics.

Engraving. The cutting or incising of lines or shapes into materials such as metals, waxes, plastics, etc.

Epicure 87. Epicure 87 is an accelerated curing agent for epoxy resins and is manufactured by the Celanese Corporation. When 100 parts of epoxy resin 502 are mixed with 20 to 25 parts of Epicure 87, the resin/hardener system cures in approximately 20 to 30 minutes. This system is not particularly moisture sensitive.

Epoxide 7. A reactive diluent for epoxy resins. Being a low-viscosity, relatively nontoxic chemical which contains epoxy groups and is not very volatile, it is an ideal thinner for epoxy resins. The classic epoxy reactive diluent, butyl glycidyl ether, is relatively volatile and toxic. Check your epoxy resins to be sure that this latter compound is not present.

Epoxy resin. A class of synthetic polymers in resins. The uncured or liquid resin is called an epoxy resin. Although it may be confusing, the cured epoxy resin, to which has been added the curing agent along with other additives, is still called an epoxy resin.

Epoxy resin 502. This product is manufactured by CIBA and is called by them Araldite 502. This was one of the first epoxy resins which I worked with in 1953. It is a mixture of pure epoxy resin to which 17% dibutyl phthalate is added as a plasticizer or flexibilizer. It is an excellent resin for use, both professionally and nonprofessionally, in the art and craft area.

Epoxy 6004, 6010. These are CIBA liquid epoxy resins which are, for the artist-craftsman's purpose, similar to CIBA epoxy resin 502 but with less flexibility (more brittleness). Roughly 15% more curing agent should be used with these resins. One or the other of these epoxy resins is available from the distributors mentioned in this book.

Epoxy-metal alloy. In this book, the term signifies the intimate union of powdered metals with synthetic resins such as epoxies; polyester or polyurethane can also be used. Often it is possible to mix over 90% metal by weight with an epoxy resin. Once this mixture has cured and has been buffed and polished, the surface of the alloy can be chemically treated as metal.

Ethylene dichloride. A chlorinated solvent available from such plastics distributors as Cadillac Plastic and Chemical Company. The solvent is used as an adhesive for bonding acrylic sheet to acrylic sheet. It works on the principle of dissolving the thermoplastic acrylic polymer. However, the best bonds are made with such adhesives as Tensol 7, made by ICI, and PS 30, distributed by Cadillac Plastic and Chemical Company, (New York office) 1761 Edgar Road, Linden, New Jersey 07036.

Ethylene glycol. Ethylene glycol is used primarily as a permanent antifreeze. However, when mixed with gelatin and water, it helps to make an excellent mold-making material. This material is self-releasing to polyester resins and certain epoxy resin systems containing curing agents which are not particularly moisture sensitive. Such curing agents as Ajicure N-001 and B-001 would be in this category.

Exotherm. A term which denotes a chemical reaction during which heat is given off. Most of the thermosetting resins discussed in this book are cured by the addition of curing agents or catalysts which generate heat when reacting with the resin.

Expanded polystyrene. This term describes two trade names: Styrofoam and Dylite.

Fadeometer. An instrument used to evaulate the lightfastness of dyes and other materials when exposed to sunlight. It is based on the carbon arc, which is the closest man has come to the controlled reproduction of ultraviolet light, the ingredient in sunlight which degrades organic substances. Its primary function is to give some idea of how articles or colors will behave when exposed indoors to sunlight. This and other types of sunlight-like tests cannot be directly related to actual weather tests because of the infinite number of variables in any particular outdoor location. You should always use such light tests in a comparative way, i.e., to check something known against your unknown.

Flexibilizer. *See* Plasticizer.

Gel-coat. A term used in the plastics industry to denote a thin, usually somewhat thixotropic thermosetting resin coating which is directly applied to the "released" mold. This gel-coat is the outside decorative finish of the form in question.

General-purpose polyester resin. This type of polyester is used where translucency or transparency is unimportant with fiberglass or other reinforcement, colors, and additives.

Glass. The use of colored glass in conjunction with the synthetic thermosetting resins is an ever-expanding area in the art and craft field. *Antique* stained glass is handmade in many colors. Its surface is slightly uneven, and it often contains small bubbles of air. The beautiful windows of the catherdral of Chartres are made of antique glass. *Cathedral* stained glass is machine-made and is lackluster when compared with the almost jewel-like quality of antique glass. In Montreal, much antique glass collage is found in public buildings. Here, the glass is bonded either with epoxy resins or silicone translucent adhesive/sealants such as Silastic 140. The technology for this process was developed by the author.

Glygel. A mixture of gelatin, ethylene glycol, water, and other additives. Available as a self-releasing, room-temperature curing, mold-making material. It is obtainable from suppliers of resins listed in this book. Polyester resins and certain epoxy resin/curing agent systems can be successfully cast in such molds.

Gram scale or balance. The various ingredients used in thermosetting, room-temperature curing resins must be accurately measured. The use of a scale which measures grams is most convenient. 453.4 grams is equivalent to 1 lb. or 16 oz. by weight. The recommended scale in this book is the Ohaus Scale. There is a complete chapter on this subject in the Polyester Resins section of this book.

Hardener. This term is used interchangeably with curing agent in this book. It designates a type of substance which, when added in certain specified quantities to such thermosetting resins as epoxy and urethane, converts them from a liquid to a solid. In order to distinguish the different types of solidifying which take place in the polyester resin systems, I have used the term "catalyst" for the organic peroxides which cure or solidify the polyesters.

Heat distortion point. The temperature at which, under the specified conditions set by the American Society of Testing Materials (test D-648), a standard test bar will be deflected. It is easy for any artist-craftsman to set up his own test so that he can compare materials.

Heat gun. The gun described in Project 21. It directs very hot air onto a specified area. A common hair dryer is also considered to be a heat gun.

HH 571. The name of a new polyester resin developed by the author which is practically odorless. It has less shrinkage than 32-032, and when catalyzed with MEK-Px, it cures at room temperature more slowly. It contains none of the "gaslike"-smelling styrene which is the reactive diluent for most of the polyester resins now in use. For complete information on this new resin, see Interesting Products in Appendix of this book.

HH 1065 B. A curing agent developed for a slow cure with very little evolution of heat. The ingredients are menthane diamine (made by the Rohm and Haas Company), ZZ1-0822 (made by Union Carbide Corporation), and curing agent 956 (distributed by CIBA). This curing agent is available through the resin distributors listed in this book.

Infrared heat lamp. Lamps or heaters are most effective as accelerators in the curing of the thermosetting resins. The most reasonable heat source is the industrial 250 watt infrared reflector heat lamp. Do not purchase the red glass bulb; it is more expensive and no more effective.

Inhibitor. Another term for chemicals which are added to another chemical or mixture of chemicals to prevent or retard a chemical reaction.

Inorganic materials. Inorganic materials are substances which do not contain carbon. Generally they do not burn.

Inorganic pigments. Colorants which have been dried out at relatively high temperatures to remove all excess water and organic materials (carbon compounds, for example). Usually these pigments are oxides, sulfides, etc. and are extremely colorfast in sunlight, weather, and heat. Although they are ordinarily not classified as transparent pigments, such companies as BASF have available iron-oxide pigments which are practically transparent.

Intaglio. In graphics, this term signifies the cutting into a plate of metal, wood, or other material in such a way that the incised figure is depressed below the surface of the material.

Internal release agent. A chemical or mixture which is added to a resin or plastic so that the resin or plastic will not adhere to the mold into which it is cast.

Internal Release 54. A product manufactured by Axel Plastics Research Company, which when added in quantities of 0.25% to a polyester resin will prevent that resin from adhering to glass, vitreous surfaces, or polished metal surfaces.

Isocyanate resins. Resins based on the union of chemicals or mixtures which contain, among other things, nitrogen, carbon, and oxygen, and other chemicals or mixtures which are related to alcohol.

Joint, lap. A joint which is made by overlapping one piece of material with another and adhering the materials at this overlap. Much adhesion testing is carried out with lap joint gluing or bonding.

Kiln wash. A convenient coating to brush on top of a kiln shelf so that glass chips can be fused or "jeweled" under heat without sticking to the shelf. Its formula is: 1 part kaolin to 1 part flint (finely ground silica sand) mixed with enough water so that the well-mixed wash can be easily painted on the shelf's surface.

Klean Klay 20. Recommended by Dow Corning as a modeling clay which works well as material from which Silastic RTV rubber molds can be cast.

Lacquer thinner. Usually a mixture of solvents used to thin oil paints and certain resins used as coatings, such as epoxy and urethane resins. The same thinners may be employed to clean brushes. The solvents usually mixed are: xylene, toluene, methyl ethyl ketone or MEK (*not related to MEK-Px*), methyl isobutyl ketone (MIBK), and Cellosolve.

Leather hard. A term which has been borrowed from the potters. When a clay is at a particular dryness, so that it can be cut with a knife or other tool similar to a linoleum-block cutter, the clay is called leather hard. When resins such as epoxy or polyester have not quite reached their final stage or complete cure, they too may be cut with sharp knives, burins, linoleum-block tools, or wood-carving tools.

Lexan. General Electric's trademark for its polycarbonate plastic sheet. This plastic is transparent and practically unbreakable. It appears to have a potential not only for window glazing but also for decorative panels which can be painted with Poly-paint medium.

Light stabilized. A resin is light-stabilized when a chemical has been added which absorbs the ultraviolet light from the sun. These stabilizers generally do not last indefinitely.

Liver of sulfur (K_2S). An inorganic chemical which, when mixed with approximately 97% water, will give a brown to black coloring to metals which contain copper or lead. These metals include sterling silver and bronze. A patina (the chemical coloring of metals) can be given to aluminum with this method by adding about 10% 300-mesh lead powder to the 300-mesh aluminum powder. After the resin binder has cured out naturally, the piece receiving the patina must be buffed to remove the surface resin.

Mearlin Pearlescence. The trade name of a product which, when added to a resin such as an epoxy or polyester, will give a pearl-like appearance to the resultant mixture.

MDAC brightener. The name of one resin-soluble chemical which, when added in small quantities in the presence of sunlight or ultraviolet light, produces a blue fluorescence for a limited amount of time. Like other brighteners, it is temporarily effective in destroying the yellow color in a resin.

MEK. The letters which signify methyl ethyl ketone, an excellent organic solvent or thinner.

MEK-Px. These are the letters which designate methyl ethyl ketone peroxide. This is an organic oxidizing agent which is diluted approximately 40% with a plasticizer and is primarily used to cure, or harden, polyester resins at room temperature. It is considered a hazardous product and should be carefully handled (that is, follow the manufacturer's cautions).

Menthane diamine. A very slow curing agent for epoxy resins. It may be mixed with other curing agents to obtain different properties.

Methylene chloride. Chlorinated solvents such as methylene chloride and ethylene di-chloride dissolve Plexiglas. Therefore, they are used as adhesives for acrylic sheets.

Methyl methacrylate. One of the ingredients used in the manufacture of the acrylic sheets which are sold under such trade names as Lucite, Plexiglas (Perspex in U.K.), etc.

MIBK. An organic solvent, or thinner, which may be used with epoxy resins (to produce thin coatings, for example). The letters stand for methyl isobutyl ketone.

Microballoons. Small, micro-size, hollow spheres made either of phenolic plastics or glass. They are used to fill resin systems such as polyester, epoxy, or urethane, and thus make a mechanical foam which is both light and strong. Such foams are called "syntactic" and they can be easily cut, sawed, or sanded. Resins highly filled with microballoons will float in water. The hollow glass spheres can be obtained from the 3-M Company. The phenolic microballoons are available from the resin distributors listed in Suppliers and Manufacturers section of Appendix.

Microcrystalline Wax 1290 Y. This is the Sun Chemical Company name for its yellow petroleum wax which melts at 178° F.

Mil. This term is commonly used as a measure of one thousandth of an inch. Ordinary paper is about 4 mils thick.

Mille fiore glass chips. These are decorative, candylike glass canes which are used in enameling on silver and copper. They also may be used when "enameling" with epoxy resins. They are available from Leo Popper and Co., 145 Franklin Street, New York, N.Y. 10013.

MirrorGlaze wax. This paste wax produces an excellent release surface. It is easy to apply, and it yields a high polish. Hundreds of people in the author's workshops have had successful results with this product.

Mixture. The result of a thorough blending of two or more compounds, each of which retains its own chemical identity.

Mod-Epox. A reactive epoxy resin diluent. Its manufacturer, Monsanto, claims that it speeds up the curing time, thins down the resin, and is cheaper than the epoxy or its curing agent.

Modern Plastics Magazine and **Encyclopedia.** This magazine, and the encyclopedia which is included with the yearly subscription, is a must for anyone truly interested in the field of resins and plastics. Published by McGraw-Hill.

Mold. Any surface upon which a substance can be poured to eventually make the reverse shape. Negative (female) molds are cavities into which the resin is poured. Positive (male) molds are the opposite.

Molding plaster (casting plaster). *See* Plaster of Paris.

Mold release. Any product which, when applied to the surface of a mold, will cause that surface to become nonadhesive to whatever is poured and hardened upon it.

Mylar. A Dupont trade name for one of its plastic films which is self-releasing for polyester resins.

Neozapon. The trade name for a class of metalized organic dyes which are relatively lightfast and soluble in polyester, epoxy, and polyurethane or urethane resins.

Nonreactive. When a product or chemical does not chemically combine in a system, it is considered to be nonreactive. Generally, organic solvents which are added to paints are nonreactive and evaporate from the paints.

Organasol. The mixture of a vinyl-like liquid, synthetic polymer, and an organic solvent. When the mixture is heated, the solvent evaporates and the polymer is converted into a solid.

Organic materials. Any substance which contains carbon is called organic.

Organic peroxides. This distinction is made since the usual peroxide with which we are familiar is called hydrogen peroxide. Hydrogen peroxide does not contain carbon and is, therefore, inorganic. The peroxides used in curing polyester resins are not soluble, are organic, and are generally more hazardous. They should be handled with care.

Organo-metallic (metal organic compound). This denotes the chemical combination of metal and organic (carbon-containing) meterials in one substance.

Oxidizing agent. The term used to denote substances which readily release oxygen when chemically reacting with certain other materials.

P 444 A. The designation of Rohm and Haas Company's polyester resin, which is extremely resistant to sunlight and weather. Contains not only polyester resin and styrene, but also methyl methacrylate monomer, which gives the product its excellent properties. Sculptors or muralists who want their creations to remain outdoors as transparencies or translucencies would do well to contact this company (listed in Suppliers and Manufacturers section of Appendix) for technical information as well as for information regarding the distributors of P 444 A.

Patina. The chemical coloring of a metal surface is usually referred to as a "patina." Naturally, a patina may be duplicated with paints and other products which will give a similar effect and may still be called a "patina."

Pearlescence. This means having a pearl-like appearance.

Permoplast X 33. One of the non-sulfur modeling clays which Dow Corning recommends for use with such silastic RTV mold-making rubbers as "E." Other modeling clays which might contain sulfur inhibit the curing of this silicone rubber.

Peroxide. *See* MEK-Px.

PHR. These letters signify "parts per hundred resin."

Phthalocyanine or "phthalo" pigments. This class of metallo-organic dyestuff, whose full name contains the word "copper," is among the most resistant to sunlight and weather. There are a series of copper phthalocyanine blues and greens which have different tints of red, green, or blue. Those who are very interested in color should check with such companies as CIBA-Geigy and BASF for their recommendations. Often it might pay to grind your own color in a vehicle which is compatible with the resin. The "phthalo" blues and greens, although they are

pigments, can be extremely transparent when used in resins.

Pigments. These are products which do not dissolve when added to a liquid. They may be very finely ground and evenly dispersed when the proper equipment is available. Pigments may be either organic or inorganic, or a combination of both.

Plaster of Paris. A relatively inexpensive mold-making material. Casting (or molding) plaster is used most often to make molds. Potter's plaster is slightly finer, with a higher degree of absorbency, and is used in ceramic work. Both kinds of plaster are readily available in any art supply store which carries sculpture materials.

Plastic. The term "plastic" describes a vast area of synthetic polymers, many of which are very familiar. The word has a bad connotation in connection with the art and craft area. The use of the word "resin" is preferable in this context. Most of the materials used in this decorative area are called "resins" by the manufacturers.

Plasticizers. This denotes a chemical or mixture, such as Benzoflex 9-88, which when added to a resin gives it added plasticity or flexibility. Also called flexibilizer.

Plastique. A name coined by the author to designate a relatively new method of hot dyeing or hot bleaching of textiles. This method uses a chemical which is liquid at room temperature and insoluble in water above 150°F. When the water cools down again, the resist re-dissolves. The resist is called Lubasin S and may be purchased as such, or as modified product called Remyzist, from the resin suppliers mentioned in Suppliers and Manufacturers section of Appendix.

Plastisol. An organic, vinyl-like liquid which when heated to above 250°F. is converted into a solid polymer.

Plexiglas (Perspex in U.K.), Acryloid, Lucite. Trade names for acrylic products primarily made into sheets.

Plique à jour. A term used in jewelry to denote a transparent enamel section in a metal ornament.

Polycarbonate resin. A relatively new synthetic resin which is cast into transparent sheets. Lexan, which is General Electric's trade name for this product, is extremely strong and unbreakable. It will be used more and more in unbreakable windows. It is interesting to explore its use in decorative panels in conjunction with polyester resins.

Polyester resin, new "odorless." *See* HH 571.

Polyester resin (unsaturated). One of a family of synthetic resins which are readily converted from liquid to solid by the use of organic oxidizing agents such as MEK-Px. Polyester resins contain many different additives, but in their liquid state they are primarily organic polymeric materials dissolved in styrene or other monomers.

Polyethylene. One of the most commonly used thermoplastic products available. Manufactured from ethylene gas, which is one of the byproducts of the petroleum industry.

Polyform. A relatively new modeling material which handles like modeling clay. When it is placed in an oven for 15 minutes at 300°F., it is converted to a relatively hard, rubbery solid which can be cut, sanded, added to with the same material, and painted. Superficial examination makes it appear to be a mixture of a plastisol (a heat-curable, one-part, vinyl-like substance) and materials such as talc, kaolin, etc. Polyform is available through art supply stores. For more information write to: Polyform Products Company, 9416 West Irving Park Road, Shiller Park, Illinois 60176. This product might have some interest as a mold-making material.

Polylite. The trade name for the Reichhold Company's series of polyester resins.

Polymer. "Poly" means many; "meros" means part. Monomer means one part, and when many monomers are joined together they make polymers. The joining together of many straight chains or interconnected straight chains produces thermoplastics. These plastics can be melted at any time and shaped or reshaped under heat with no destruction of the resin. Thermosetting resins are cross-lined, three-dimensional structures. This means that the straight chains of the polymers are connected by crossing from one chain group to another and are thus linked together. Next, if an additional floor of chains and crossings are placed over the first floor and more links are added to join the two floors, this will create a rigid structure which will be very strong but not very flexible. Thermosetting resins can be softened, somewhat reshaped, but not melted.

Polymercaptain. A series of odoriferous organic chemicals and mixtures which contain a chemical grouping called the -SH -, or sulfur-hydrogen, group. DPM 3-800 LC, a polymercaptain, is one of the products which is used in epoxy resin systems to accelerate the curing of the resin.

Polymerization. The chemical combination of many molecules into one solid mass. Often this joining up produces what is called "one giant molecule."

Polyol. In urethane chemistry, polyols are used as one part of the system to make the synthetic polymer. A polyol is an organic chemical which contains what is called an - OH -, or alcohol group or groups.

Poly-paint medium. A name signifying the combination of a polyester resin and other additives to produce a painting vehicle designed expressly for painting on Plexiglas, polystyrene, or cast polyester resin sheet.

Polystyrene sheet. A sheet plastic which is made from styrene. It is easily heat-formed and can be used decoratively with polyester resins or Poly-paint medium.

Polyurethane resin. A family of resins based upon a system of organic chemistry involving the reaction of molecules called isocyanates with polyols.

Polyvinyl acetate. A product which appears on the market as a water emulsion. It is usually mixed with other synthetic polymers and is used as an adhesive or glue.

Polyvinyl alcohol film. A self-releasing, strong, moisture-sensitive film used to cover catalyzed polyester and certain other resins while they are curing. Once the resins are hard, the film is easily removed. It generally comes in 4-mil to 6-mil thicknesses with a mat finish on one side.

Pot life. This term stands for the length of time a catalyzed or activated resin is usable.

Potter's plaster. *See* Plaster of Paris.

PPI. These letters stand for "pounds per square inch."

PPM. These letters stand for "parts per million."

Promoter. Chemicals or mixtures of chemicals which speed up the curing of a resin. In polyester resins, the promoter or accelerator most commonly used is called cobalt naphthonate. It should never be directly mixed with MEK-Px since an explosion will result. It is present in polyester resins in such great dilution that there is absolutely no danger.

PS 30. An adhesive distributed by Cadillac Plastic and Chemical Company. It is used as an adhesive for Plexiglas, etc.

PVC. An abbreviation for Polyvinyl chloride, one of the thermoplastic resins having huge consumer uses (in piping, for example).

Q.S. These letters stand for "quantum sufficit" which means: add just what you think is necessary.

RC 303. An accelerated curing agent manufactured by Resin Coatings Corporation. It is based on DPM 3-800 LC of Diamond Shamrock Corporation. When one part of RC 303 is mixed with one to two parts of CIBA epoxy resin 502, the system cures in about five minutes. This very flexible adhesive will not dissolve Styrofoam or Dylite.

RC 32-180. This polyester resin is modified in such a way that up to 50% by weight of water can be carefully stirred in to make a stable emulsion. This "water in resin" emulsion can then be colored with the standard color pastes and then catalyzed with MEK-Px. The cured, solid water-and-resin mixture that results is stable and paintable. The water, according to the manufacturer, is completely trapped or locked in.

RC 840 or General Mills 140 or CIBA 840. A polyamine curing agent for epoxy resins which is both a flexibilizer and a relatively non-toxic material. It has an additional property in that the hardener/resin proportion, when using this hardener, is not critical. However, the manufacturer's recommendations should be read if you wish to vary from the suggestions in this book.

RC Chem-o-sol. A very low viscosity plasticol (special organic liquid) developed for making transparent molds. When this product is heated to about 350° F., it is converted to a transparent, vinyl-like rubber. Chem-o-sol, or its equivalent, is available from the resin distributors in Suppliers and Manufacturers section of Appendix.

RC DP 116. A 45-second, fast-curing, epoxy resin curing agent. Generally, it has little value to the artist-craftsman because of its speed of cure and sensitivity to materials which contain moisture. It was developed as a low-temperature curing agent and I have used it successfully at below-zero temperatures. At these low temperatures, the system might take as long as an hour to cure.

Reactive diluent. Low-viscosity liquids which thin down epoxy or polyester resins, are allowed to react in the system, and finally become part of the molecular structure when the resin hardens are called reactive diluents. For example, lacquer thinners are solvents which evaporate. The safest and best reactive diluents have a low evaporation rate. Epoxide 7, distributed by CIBA-Geigy, is a safe, reactive epoxy resin diluent. Styrene is a reactive polyester resin diluent. It is not hazardous when used with good ventilation.

Reducing agent. A chemical which, among other things, counteracts an oxidizing agent or can prevent premature oxidation. For example, it is used to stabilize polyester resin, so that the resin will not harden in the container before the peroxide catalyst, MEK-Px, is added.

Release agents. These indicate any chemicals or mixtures which are applied to a hard surface, or mixed into an uncured resin or other liquid, so that there will be no adhesion of cast objects to their molds.

Remyzist. A mixture of ingredients blended together to produce a water-soluble liquid which is easily applied to fabrics. Wet or dry, fabrics may be bleached or dyed at temperatures above 150° F.; Remyzist becomes insoluble and therefore resistant to bleach and dye at such temperatures. Bleaches or dyes can be washed out at room temperature or lower. Since the resist is soluble at these temperatures, it can be removed by agitation or rubbing in the cold water.

Resin. This term is actually interchangeable with the term plastic. This book takes the view that plastics stand for utilitarian objects whereas art and craft forms use resins. The basic manufacturers refer to their epoxies, polyesters, silicones, and urethanes as "resins."

Rhoplex AC 33, 388, 34. Some of the acrylic emulsion polymers or so-called polymer mediums that are manufactured by Rohm and Haas Company.

Rotational casting. A method of casting in which the mold is rotated or turned while the liquid resin is curing.

RTV. These letters stand for room-temperature vulcanizing. This term usually refers to the silicone rubbers or elastomers which cure or turn to rubbers at ambient temperatures.

Saturated polyester resins. In chemistry, saturated means that all available sites for attachment of atoms to other atoms in a molecule are filled up, as when all the seats in a theatre are filled. Generally, we think of the saturated polyesters as fibers. Unsaturated polyesters are the liquid resins discussed in this book.

Sawdust. Much sawdust is manufactured as a filler in the plastics industry. It is also available from companies which manufacture it for the fur-cleaning business and for the polishing of certain materials. Very fine sawdust is called wood flour. Powdered ebony sawdust, which would have to be homemade, is now being used with epoxy resins for black enameling in jewelry.

Self-extinguishing resins. Certain resins in each of the families discussed in this book can be manufactured or made so that they will burn only when a flame is applied to them. When the flame is removed, the resins will extinguish themselves. This is accomplished by chemically building the resin molecules so that they contain such atoms as chlorine or bromine. Additives such as antimony oxide and some phosphorous compounds are also put into resin mixtures to assist in achieving the same fire resistance. All resins which you use should be tested after they have hardened. Light a match and try to burn a sample. Try to use only self-extinguishing resins for murals in public buildings. Check with the manufacturers.

Self-releasing. Certain resins are, or can be made, self-releasing. That is, when these resins are used for molds, the castings will not adhere to them. Silicone resins generally are self-releasing to other than silicones. There are additives that can often be added to resins, such as epoxies, polyesters, and polyurethanes, which will make them more or less self-releasing. The author is doing much research in this area in order to produce cheaper molds.

Sensitizing resins. Since the uncured resins and the curing agents or catalysts mentioned in this book are generally very chemically active, they may, upon contact, have an effect upon the human skin. Resin manufacturers continually caution users: no physical contact with the resin system and you will get no dermatitis. Continual physical contact with these resins may cause you to become sensitized (allergic) so that rashes like those caused by poison oak or poison ivy may result. Once you become sensitized, you cannot work with that resin family. If resin spills on your hands or body, wash with soap, and water; if the resin contacts your eyes, wash them copiously with running water for 15 minutes and go to see a doctor.

Set. Set, cure, harden, "C" stage, etc. are all equivalent terms. They may be used in any of the thermosetting resin systems.

Shrinkage of resins. All the thermosetting resin systems have some decrease in volume when the unfilled resin system is converted from a liquid to a solid. Polyester resins shrink about 7.0%; epoxies shrink about 0.5% after the gel, or "B" stage; silicone rubbers shrink about 0.5% when cured at room temperature. Read the manufacturer's literature carefully if you want to be absolutely sure.

Silastic. This is Dow Corning's trademark for many of its silicone products such as Silastic E and Silastic G, the most tear-resistant of its room-temperature vulcanizing (RTV) rubbers, or elastomers.

Silastic 140 and Silastic 732. These two silicone adhesive sealants are so constituted that when squeezed out of a sealed container, such as a tube, certain inhibiting chemicals evaporate. In the presence of the air's moisture, these silicones cure to a rubberlike solid.

Silastic E and G. These are two of a series of Dow Corning silicone rubber materials which are liquids until cured with special catalysts. Both of these silicone products have very high tensile and tear strengths. Silastic G, according to the manufacturer, is less sensitive to moisture and other sulfur compounds than Silastic E. These particular elastomers (rubbers) are being used for self-releasing molds in such industries as furniture-making.

Silicon. This non-metal is obtained mainly from beach or silica sand. Alcan Metal Powders of Elizabeth, New Jersey, produces 300-mesh silicon powder. This powder, mixed with an epoxy resin system, gives a beautiful gray-black metallic enamel which can be highly polished to a niello-like surface. Niello is an enamel usually used by the craftsmen of India on sterling silver.

Silicone resins. A family of products, based on combinations of atoms of silicon, carbon, hydrogen, oxygen, etc., which can be converted to solids having a myriad of properties that are put to use in greases, heat-stable fluids, release agents, gaskets, insulating varnishes, electrical appliances, etc.

Skin mold. A thin mold made by applying thin layers of mold-making material after each previous layer has hardened. After the first layer, reinforcements such as fiberglass are often added to the additional layers. This is done when the model to be copied is very large or when the mold-making material is very expensive, such as the silicone RTV rubbers. Quite frequently the skin molds are backed with a plaster mother mold. This mother mold is a holding container which prevents the skin mold from distorting when it is being filled.

Solvent. A liquid which dissolves other liquids or solids. Water is a solvent for sugar and alcohol. Lacquer thinners are solvents for epoxy resins and urethane resins. Mineral spirits are solvents for oil paints. Alcohol is a solvent for shellac.

Sprue. An opening which is made in a mold to allow passage of the liquid substance to be cast. When there is a sprue, there must also be a *vent* so that the air can escape while the mold is being filled.

Styrene. The most common reactive diluent for polyester resins. There are others which have less odor, but at the moment the polyester systems are such that they do not cure at room temperature. Such a reactive diluent is diallyl phthalate. It is not dangerous to work with styrene when adequate ventilation is provided; 100 parts per million is considered safe by the health authorities. According to manufacturers, styrene is not considered explosive.

Supergel. An alginate product manufactured by the Harry Boswell Company of Chicago, Illinois for dental supply houses. It is an interesting mold-making material for polyester resins, since it is self-releasing for this resin class. When the powder is mixed with water, a mold can be made which cures to a rubberlike substance in about two minutes. According to its manufacturer, it can be purchased in 100 lb. quantities at a cost of approximately $1.00 to $1.25 per lb.

Synthetic polymer. A man-made substance made of many of the same or similar molecular "building blocks."

Talc. One of the popular, inexpensive fillers for all types of resins and plastics.

Tensile strength. The pull, usually expressed in pounds, required to break or pull apart one square inch of a material.

TETA (triethylene tetramine 951). One of the early curing agents distributed by CIBA for hardening epoxy resins. 10 PHR (parts per hundred resin) can be used with CIBA epoxy resin 502. However, this 951 curing agent is very corrosive, and the vapors are relatively toxic unless used with very adequate ventilation.

Thermoplastic. A term applied to plastics or resins which indicates that they are capable of being melted under heat. Once they are in the liquid state, they can be molded and cooled to return to their solid state. Such plastics as polyethylene, vinyl, and acrylics are classed as thermoplastics.

Thermoset. Materials such as epoxy resins, polyester resins, urethane resins, and silicone resins which, when chemically reacted with curing agents or catalysts at room temperature (sometimes at temperatures as low as near freezing or as high as 350° F.), are converted to solids. These solids are non-melting but often they may be softened, reshaped, or cooled and they will hold the new shape.

Thinner. This term usually refers to solvents added to paints, resins, or other materials. These solvents evaporate over a period of time, depending upon the thickness of the coating, or film. Such solvents can be water, mineral spirits, lacquer thinners, etc.

Thixotropic. This term describes materials which are non-runny when they are not touched. When the material is pushed, it is easily moved and remains exactly in the position or shape in which it was left by contact with the moving object. Such additives as Asbestos 244 and Cabosil (pyrogenic silica sand) when added in small quantities (1% to 4% by weight) to liquid resins make these resins thixotropic.

Tinuvin P, 326, 327, 328. Ultraviolet light absorbers which protect certain resins against ultraviolet, light-induced deterioration. These absorbers also extend the colorfastness of the dyes used to color these resins. Contact CIBA-Geigy Industrial Chemical Corporation, Industrial Chemicals Division, Ardsley, New York 10502, for technical literature and information as to where trial quantities may be obtained.

Titanium dioxide. The most frequently used white metallic oxide pigment available. Blended and ground into certain vehicles, titanium dioxide is the white color paste generally available for coloring plastics and resins.

Translucent. This term refers to a material which will allow some light to be transmitted through it. However, it is not possible to see through a translucent substance (for example, tissue paper is translucent).

TU 75. A two-part urethane compound recommended for making molds. It has been evaluated successfully by the author. Once the cans of material are opened, it is important that they be kept dry and sealed according to the manufacturer's directions. The manufacturer is Conap, Inc. TU 75 is available from resin suppliers mentioned in this book.

Two-part systems. A term applied to the resins discussed in this book. Most of the liquid thermosetting resins which can be made to harden at room temperature or above are composed of part A, the resin, and part B, the curing agent, or catalyst. When the two parts are mixed in the proper proportions, the resin system will harden or cure according to the manufacturer's data.

Urethane. *See* Polyurethane resins.

Vacuum chamber. A container in which such catalyzed, high-viscosity polymers as Silastic RTV rubber E are placed to remove unwanted air entrapped in the mixture. Such vacuum chambers are now made of Plexiglas and are, therefore, unbreakable. The chamber suggested here is manufactured by Ace Glass Company.

Vacuum forming. A method of heating a clamped sheet of plastic, pulling it down into a mold or over a perforated form which is lying upon a porus plate, and externally applying a vacuum which sucks the thermoplastic into the mold or around the form. The vacuum-formed plastic is then cooled and removed from the clamping mechanism.

Vacuum pump. A pump which will suck gas or air from a given area. To be effective in removing air from resins, 29" of vacuum must be obtained in the pump tube.

Vent. A passage made in a mold to allow the air to escape while the mold is being filled through the *sprue*.

Vulcanization. A chemical reaction which takes place primarily in rubbers in the presence of certain curing agents. The liquid rubber polymer, such as silicone, is converted to a solid rubbery material of greater tensile strength and increased elasticity.

Water-clear polyester resins. A designation for clear, colorless polyester resins. Such a resin is Reichhold's clear polyester casting resin 32-032.

Index

A-Brilliant Gold. *See* Additives, decorative.
Accelorators, epoxy, 203-204; polyester, 15-16. *See also* Additives, epoxy.
Acetate. *See* Cellulose acetate.
Acetone, bonding with, 70-71
Adams, Richard, 84, 122; demo. by, 148-149
Additives, decorative, 205; epoxy 93-94; polyester, 24-25
Adhesives, 204; epoxy 129-130, 138-139; polyester, 38; silicone, 166; polyurethane, 186
Air driers. *See* Additives, polyester.
A-Iridescent Red. *See* Additives, decorative.
Airplane cloth, for epoxy-fiberglass sculpture, 193; for polyester resin sculpture, 65
Alfa-methyl styrene. *See* Additives, polyester.
Anderson, Lamont, demo. by, 82-83
A-Pale Gold. *See* Additives, decorative.
A-Pearl. *See* Additives, decorative.
Araldite. *See* Epoxy: curing agents *and* Epoxy resins.
Armatures, acetate sheet, for transparent polyester resin sculpture, 70; expanded polystyrene, for epoxy-fiberglass sculpture, 192-195

B-001. *See* Epoxy: curing agents.
Balance, how to use, 26-29
Batik. *See* "Plastique."
Beasely, Bruce, 114
Bettle resin. See Epoxy: flow-out aids.
Benua, Marjorie P., 22
Benzoflex 9-88. *See* Additives, epoxy, *and* Additives, polyester.
Bleaching, with polyester resin resist, 87
Blin, Claude, 77, 79, 124, 125
Bonding, acetate sheet with acetone, 70-71; ceramicware with epoxy adhesives, 129-130; glass with epoxy adhesives, 138-139; polyester or Plexiglas sheets with polyester adhesives, 39; stained-glass reliefs with epoxy adhesives, 135-142; with acetone/cellulose acetate solution, 71
Bostic Floor Finish. *See* Polyurethane: protective finishes.
Brass 1102. *See* Additives, decorative.
Brighteners, epoxy, 203
Buffing and polishing materials, 203; how to use on epoxy-metal jewelry, 110
Byng, Dennis, 115.

Cab-o-lite. *See* Epoxy: curing agents.
Cabosil. *See* Additives, epoxy, *and* Additives, polyester.
Canvas, relief, painting on with polyester resin medium, 79, 82-83
Casting: an epoxy printing plate, 147-149; decorated polyester resin panels, 31-36; from silicone rubber molds, 169-181; epoxy-metal, 150-155; epoxy-polymercaptain plates, from methyl methacrylate sheets, 147-149; polyester resin, from acetate or Mylar molds, 51-57; polyester resin, from gelatin molds, 47-50; polyester resin, from glass molds, 56-57; polyester resin, from wax molds, 59-64; polyester resin panels for windows or murals, 37-41; polyester resin reliefs, 43-54; rotational, 51-53; still, 53. *See also* Castings.
Castings, clear, 47; filled metal, 47-48; filled non-metal, 48. *See also* Casting.
Catalysts, polyester, 15
Cellulose acetate, and acetone, in a solution for bonding, 71; box, for silicone rubber molds, 172, 174-178; or Mylar molds, for casting polyester resin, 51-57; sheet, for translucent polyester resin sculpture, 70-72. *See also* Mold-making and reinforcing materials.
Cement surfaces, preparing for epoxy resins, 102-103
Ceramic surfaces, unglazed, preparing for epoxy resins, 102-103
Ceramics, and epoxy resins, 129-134; bonding with epoxy adhesives, 130; repairing with epoxy adhesives, 129, 132,133
Ceraplast, 205
CIBA Technical Bulletin 4, quoted, 94
Clays, 205; for negative molds in cast polyester resin reliefs, 43-45; for use with silicone rubber molds, 169. *See also* Additives, epoxy, *and* Additives, polyester.
Clear silicone blocks, 167
Coatings, metallic, for polyester resin reliefs, 44; non-glare polyester resin, 73-75; polyurethane resin, 186, 206; silicone anti-tarnish, 166
Cole, Grover, 100
Coleman, Oliver, demo. by, 68-69
Color plates, 113-129
Colorants, 198-199, 205. *See also* Additives, epoxy *and* Additives, polyester.

Conap S-14. *See* Release agents.
Conathane PA-1162. *See* Polyurethane: protective finishes.
Conathane UF 3. *See* Foams, urethane, *and* Mold-making and reinforcing materials.
Contact brand invisible sheet. *See* Transparent plastic sheets.
Cooper, Jim, demo. by, 158
Curing agents, epoxy, 94-98, 101, 203
Cyanasorbe ultraviolet light absorbers. *See* Ultraviolet light absorbers.

Dacron mesh. *See* Mold-making and reinforcing materials.
Degassing. *See* Dessicator *and* Workshop equipment.
Dessicator, illus. of, 171. *See also* Workshop equipment.
Dibutyl phthalate. *See* Epoxy flexibilizers.
Diluents, reactive, 204. *See also* Additives, epoxy, *and* Additives, polyester.
Dingwall, Myldred, 99
DMP 3-800 LC. *See* Additives, epoxy, *and* Epoxy accelerators.
DP 116. *See* Epoxy: curing agents.
Driers, air. *See* Additives, polyester.
Dryer. *See* Dessicator.
Dyeing, with polyester resin resist, 85-87
Dyes, silicone-soluble, 167
Dyestuffs. *See* Colorants.
Dylite. *See* Expanded polystyrene.

Enameling, with epoxy resins, 105-107
Epoxide 7. *See* Epoxy: diluents.
Epoxy: accelerators, 203-204; additives, 93-94, 203-204; adhesives for bonding stained-glass reliefs, 135-142; adhesives, mixing your own, 139; brighteners, 203; curing agents, 94-98, 101, 203; diluents, 93, 204; fillers, 94, 203; films, transferring color reproductions to, 143-146; flexibilizers, 93, 204; flow-out aids, 203; glazes, 130. *See also* Epoxy resins.
Epoxy painting medium, 156-161; combined with "Plastique," 89-90; on expanded polystyrene ground, 188-191; metalizing, 189
Epoxy resins, 91-111, 129-161; and ceramics, 129-134; casting printing plates from 59-64, 147-149; colorants for, 198-199; enameling with, 105-107; fire and health problems of, 200-201;

introduction to, 93-101; kinds of, 94; microcrystalline wax as an engraving and mold medium for, 59-64; preparing surfaces for, 102-103; waterproofing ceramic pots with, 130. *See also* Epoxy.

Epoxy-fiberglass sculpture, 192-195

Epoxy-metal, casting, 150-155; jewelry, 109-111

Epoxy-polymercaptain resins, casting, 147-149

Expanded polystyrene, armature, for epoxy-fiberglass sculpture, 192-195; for relief murals, 188-191

Fiberglass, and epoxy, for sculpture, 192-195; cloth, for polyester resin sculpture, 65, 70-72; mat, for polyester resin sculpture, 65, 70-72

Fillers, epoxy, 203. *See also* Additives, epoxy.

Fire problems, 200-201

Flame-retardants. *See* Additives, polyester.

Flexibilizers, 203. *See also* Additives, epoxy *and* Additives, polyester.

Flint. *See* Additives, epoxy, *and* Additives, polyester.

Flow-out aids, epoxy, 203

Foams, urethane, 184

Frid, Tage, 99

Gallo, Frank, 92, 94, 100, 113, 120

Garfinkle, Ron, 42

Gelatin molds, for casting polyester resins, 47-50

Gelb, Jan, demo. by, 62-64

Gianakos, Cristos, 17

Glass, and vitreous surfaces, preparing for epoxy resins, 102-103; bonding colored, 135-142; cutting colored, 135, 138, 140-142; "fractured," 37; molds, 31, 37, 56-57

Glass chips, 205. *See also* Additives, epoxy, *and* Additives, polyester.

Glazes, epoxy, 130

Gluing. *See* Bonding.

Glygel, 47-50

Gonzales, Xavier, 42

Gregory, Arch, 58, 60-61

Grog. *See* Additives, epoxy, *and* Additives, polyester.

Guité, Thérèse, 89

Gyro-Plastic Mixers. *See* Workshop equipment.

Hall, Gloria, demo. by, 88

Handbook of Epoxy Resins, 93

Health problems, 200-201

Heat gun, illus. of, 170. *See also* Workshop equipment.

HH 571. *See* New products.

HH 1065 B. *See* Epoxy: curing agents.

Hogenkamp, Clair, 66-67

Hollander, Harry B., jewelry by, 108; sculpture by, 117

Holbrook, Hollis, 116, 127

Hunter, Robert, 185

Hydroquinone. *See* Inhibitors, polyester.

IMD. *See* Epoxy: curing agents.

Inhibitors, polyester, 15

Internal release agents. *See* Additives, polyester, *and* Release agents.

Internal Release 54. *See* Additives, polyester, *and* Release agents.

Internal Release 20-E. *See* Release agents.

IPD. *See* Epoxy: curing agents.

Isoderm system CPR. *See* Polyurethane resins.

Jeffamine. *See* Epoxy: curing agents.

Jewelry, epoxy-metal, 109-111; buffing and polishing, 110

Jones, Allen, 10

Kangas, Gene, 22

Kaolin. *See* Additives, epoxy, *and* Additives, polyester.

Klean Klay 20. *See* Clays.

Lacquer thinner. *See* Additives, epoxy.

Lee, Henry, 93

LePage, Carolyn, 167, 184

Levy, Carol R., 126

Light box, how to build and use, 135

Lightbody, Maya, 14

Love, Arlene, 16, 18, 128

Lucite 44. *See* Plastics for the painter.

Manufacturers and suppliers, 208-210

Masonite, painting on with polyester resins, 79

Massin, Eugene, 121

May, Juanita, demo. by, 45

McCauley, Robert J., 41

McClure, Virginia, demo. by, 56-57

MDAC Brightener. *See* Epoxy: brighteners.

Mearlin. *See* Additives, decorative.

Menihan, John C., 19

Menthane diamine. *See* Epoxy: curing agents.

Merkel, Bernadette, 90

Metal, and epoxy. *See* Epoxy-metal.

Metal powders. *See* Additives, polyester.

Metal surfaces, preparing for epoxy resins, 102-103

Metalizing, epoxy-fiberglass sculpture, 193; epoxy painting medium, 189; epoxy-metal castings, 151

Methyl acrylate. *See* Additives, polyester.

Methyl ethyl ketone peroxide. *See* Additives, epoxy, Additives, polyester, *and* Catalysts, polyester.

Methyl methacrylate. *See* Additives, polyester.

Methyl methacrylate sheets, casting epoxy-polymercaptain plates on, 174-149

MIKB. *See* Additives, epoxy.

Mica. *See* Additives, epoxy, *and* Additives, polyester.

Microcrystalline wax 129 Y. *See* Wax, microcrystalline.

Mille-fiore glass chips. *See* Additives, decorative.

Minisci, Brenda, 17

Mod-Epox. *See* Additives, epoxy, *and* Diluents, reactive.

Modern Plastics, 202

Modern Plastics Encyclopedia, 24, 25, 183, 198, 202

Molds, cast silicone rubber, 171-172; cellulose acetate or Mylar, for polyester resins, 51-57; clay, for polyester resin reliefs, 43-45; clay negative, 43; gelatin, for polyester resins, 47-50; glass, 31, 37, 56-57; glass sheet, for polyester resin panels, 31-36, 37-41; Glygel relief, 47; Multiple-piece silicone rubber, 173; polyurethane resin, 186; preserving silicone rubber, 174; relief, 47; silicone rubber, 164, 169-181; silicone rubber skin, 170; two-piece Glygel, 48

Mold-making and reinforcing materials, 205-206

Morris, Lil, demo. by, 54-55

Morse, Jack, 30, 32

Mouseau, Jean-Paul, 119

Mylar, or cellulose acetate molds for polyester resins, 51-57

Neville, Kris, 93; quoted, 93

New products, 202-207

Non-glare coating, polyester resin, 73-75

Oderless polyester resin. *See* New products.

Ohaus triple beam balance. *See* Balance, how to use.

Opacifiers. *See* Additives, epoxy, *and* Additives, polyester.

Paint, epoxy, 156-161; combined with "Plastique," 89-90

Painter, plastics for the, 206-207. *See also* Paint, epoxy, *and* Paint, polyester.

Paint, polyester, 77-84; and fabric design, 87, combined with "Plastique," 89-90

Painting, with epoxy resins on expanded polystyrene, 188-191; with polyester resins, 77-84

Panels, internally decorated polyester resin, 31-36; painting on with polyester resins, 77-79

Parker, J., 97

Pellan, Alfred, 118

Pelton, Margaret, 86

Permoplast. *See* Clays.

Peroxide. *See* Methyl ethyl ketone peroxide.

Photographs, coating with non-glare polyester resins, 73-75

Pigments. *See* Colorants.

Plafson, Blanche, demo. by, 189-191

Plastics for the painter, 206-207. *See also* Paint, epoxy, *and* Paint, polyester.

Plaster surfaces, preparing for epoxy resins, 102-103

"Plastique" dyeing, 85-88; combined with polyester or epoxy painting mediums, 89-90

Plique à jour, 106, 107, 109, 111, 130

Plywood box, for silicone rubber molds, 172, 179-181

Polishes, silicone, 167

Polishing and buffing materials, 206; how to use them on epoxy-metal jewelry, 110

Polyester: accelerators, 15-16; additives, 24-25; adhesives, 39; catalysts, 15; inhibitors, 15

Polyester casting resins, 16; characteristics of, 16, 20. See also Polyester and Polyester resins.

Polyester painting medium. See Paint, polyester.

Polyester resins, 13-90; cautions when using, 20-21, 200-201; cellulose acetate or Mylar molds for, 51-57; characteristics of, 16, 20; colorants for, 198-199; fire and health problems of, 200-201; gelatin molds for, 47-50; general-purpose, 15, 21; glass molds for, 31, 37, 56-57; in panels, 31-36; in "Plastique" dyeing, 85-88; in reliefs, 43-45; in sculpture, 65-69, 70-72; in three-dimensional windows or murals, 37-41; introduction to, 15-25; microcrystalline wax as an engraving and mold medium for, 59-64; used for non-glare coatings, 73-75

Polyform. See Mold-making and reinforcing materials.

Polymers, for the painter, 206-207; silicone, 165-181. See also Silicone and Silicone polymers.

Polystyrene, expanded, for relief murals, 188-191

Polystyrene sheet, painting on, 79

Polyurethane: adhesives, 186; coatings, 186; molds, 183-184; protective finishes, 206

Polyurethane resins, 183-195, 206-207; and silicones, 163-195; cautions when using, 183-184, 200-201; colorants for, 198-199; fire and health problems of, 200-201; introduction to, 183-187

Precautions, fire and health, when using resins, 200-201

Printing plates, cast epoxy, 59-64, 147-149; cast polyester, 59-64

Prints, coating with non-glare polyester resin, 73-75

Products, new, 202-207

Protective finishes, polyurethane, 206

Pumice. See Additives, epoxy, and Additives, polyester.

RC 125. See Epoxy: curing agents.

RC 303. See Epoxy: curing agents.

Reactive diluents, 204. See also Additives, epoxy, and Additives, polyester.

Reddi-Mold HH 871, 206

Reference works of fire and health precautions, 200-201

Release agent 1771. See Release agents.

Release agents, 204; polyester, 24; silicone, 166

Relief canvas, painting on with polyester resins, 79-83

Reliefs, casting polyester resin, 43-45; stained-glass, bonding with epoxy adhesives, 135-142

Remyzist, for "Plastique" dyeing, 85-88. See also Resists.

Resin grade 144. See Thickening agents.

Resins, epoxy, 91-111, 129-161. See also Epoxy and Epoxy resins.

Resins, polyester, 13-90. See also Polyester and Polyester resins.

Resins, polyurethane, 183-195, 206-207. See also Polyurethane resins.

Resists, 205

Revor, Sister Remy, 88, 123

Rhoplex. See Plastics for the painter.

Rotational casting, 51, 53

Sand. See Additives, epoxy, and Additives, polyester.

Sawdust. See Additives, epoxy, and Additives, polyester.

Scale. See Balance, how to use.

Schluep, Walter, 104

Schnier, Jacques, 21, 127, 182

Sculpture, built-up polyester resin and fiberglass, 65-69; translucent, 70-72

Self-extinguishing fluids, silicone, 166

Silica. See Additives, epoxy, and Additives, polyester.

Silicone: adhesives, 166; anti-tarnish coatings, 166; blocks, 167; colorants, 198-199; dispersions, 166; molds, 166; polishes, 167; release agents, 166; rubber molds, 169-181; self-extinguishing fluids, 166

Silicone polymers, 165-181; and polyurethanes, 163-195; fire and health problems of, 200-201; introduction to, 165-168

Silkwhite. See Additives, decorative.

Simon, Sidney, 21

Singleton, Robert, 187

Sorce, Anthony John, 186

Stained-glass reliefs, bonding with epoxy adhesives, 135-142

"Stained-glass windows," epoxy resin, 130-131, 134

Still casting, 53

Stoetzer, Bob, 107

Stone surfaces, preparing for epoxy resins, 102-103

Styrene. See Additives, polyester.

Styrofoam. See Expanded polystyrene.

Supergel. See Mold-making and reinforcing materials.

Suppliers and manufacturers, 208-210

Surfaces, preparing for epoxy resins, 102-103

Table, for weighing resins, 27; of epoxy resin curing rates, 95; of polyester resin additives, 25; of silicone comparative data, 173; of silicone resin curing rates, 171

Talc. See Additives, epoxy, and Additives, polyester.

Tensol cement, 204

Thickening agents, 204-205. See also Additives, epoxy, and Additives, polyester.

Thixotropic agents. See Additives, epoxy, and Additives, polyester

Three-dimensional polyester resin windows or murals, 37-41

3-M Adhesive EC-2296, 204

Tinuvin 328. See Ultraviolet light absorbers.

Toluene. See Additives, epoxy, and Additives, polyester

Transparent plastic sheets, 206

TU 75. See Mold-making and reinforcing materials.

Turner, James, 99

Ultraviolet light absorbers, 265. See also Additives, polyester.

Urethanes. See Polyurethane resins.

Vinyl. See Additives, polyester.

Waterproofing ceramic pots with epoxy resins, 130

Wax, microcrystalline, 205, as an engraving and mold medium for polyester and epoxy resins, 59-64; as mold for epoxy-metal casting, 151-155; for embossing epoxy resin printing plates, 147

Webril fabrics. See Mold-making and reinforcing materials.

Werthheimer, Esther, demo. by, 177-179

Wheels, buffing, 206

Wollastonite P-4. See Epoxy: curing agents.

Wood surfaces, preparing for epoxy resins, 102-103

Workshop equipment, 207

Xylene. See Additives, epoxy.

Young, Gwynyth, 20

Zelec UN. See Additives, polyester, and Release agents.